National Society
Colonial Daughters
of the
Seventeenth Century, Inc.

Lineage Book

1896  1989

CLEARFIELD

1990 printing made in the United States of America
by C. J. Krehbiel Co., Cincinnati, OH

Library of Congress Catalog Card Number 90-61504

Reprinted for Clearfield Company by
Genealogical Publishing Company
Baltimore, Maryland
2013

ISBN 978-0-8063-5625-9

Made in the United States of America

OBJECTS OF THE SOCIETY

The objects are patriotic, philanthropic, educational and historical, and for the purpose of perpetuating among their descendants the memory of those brave and hardy men who assisted in establishing the Colonies of America and perilled their lives and interests in the various Colonial wars from May 1607 to December 1699, and rendered other distinguished services, laying the foundations upon which the Republic of the United States of America was established; and for the collection and preservation of historic relics and documents, and the placing of tablets to mark places of historic interest relating to that period.

MOTTO

CONSILIO et ANIMIS   (By Wisdom and Courage)

BANNER

The Banner of the Society shall consist of the Cross of St. George on a white field, bearing in the center the seal of the Society, surmounted by a crown and surrounded by the name "Colonial Daughters of the Seventeenth Century – 1607 - 1699" inscribed in gold letters.

INSIGNIA

The foundation of the insignia is a sunburst, in the center of which appears, in continental blue enamel, a spinning wheel with years 1607 and 1699 above and below respectively; surrounding the center piece is a white enamel circle, upon which is the legend "Colonial Daughters of the Seventeenth Century" in letters of gold. Ranging around the outer edge of the circle... and resting on rays, are twelve mayflowers (or hawthorne). These flowers commemorate the original provinces or settlements, namely, Virginia, New York, Connecticut, Massachusetts, New Hampshire, Delaware, Maryland, Rhode Island, New Jersey, the Carolinas and Pennsylvania, and can be replaced with jewels at the discretion of the owner. Surmounting the rays... are the Colonial and National Flags in colored enamel, and between them is a crown encircled by a wreath of hawthorne, being a tribute to James I of England, in acknowledgement of the granting of the Charter.

SYMBOLS OF OUR INSIGNE

The Sunburst symbolizes the dawn of this new Nation.
The Flags are symbolic of Freedom and Service.
The Circle is symbolic of the unbroken links between the Past, the Present, and the Future.
The Hawthornes, resting on the rays, commemorate the original Provinces.
The Crown is tribute to James I of England, acknowledging the granting of the Charter.
The Spinning Wheel is a reminder of the thread that has closely woven the Colonial past to the present.
The Red and White ribbon from which the Insigne is suspended is the symbol of Faith, Courage, and Sacrifice.

BANNER

This volume is affectionately dedicated
to
MARTHA TODD BARKER ROBERTS
(Mrs. Richard Lindsay Roberts)
in grateful appreciation
of her
unfaltering devotion to the
best interests of the Society.

NATIONAL SOCIETY
COLONIAL DAUGHTERS OF THE SEVENTEENTH CENTURY
HONORARY PRESIDENTS GENERAL

HONORARY PRESIDENTS GENERAL

Mrs. Robert Franklin Ives

Mrs. J. Morton Halstead

Mrs. Frank Howland Parcells

Mrs. James Douglas Cockcroft

Mrs. Frederick Gilbert Bauer

Mrs. Charles C. Finehout

Mrs. Harry D. McKeige

Mrs. Hugh L. Russell

Mrs. William Carroll Langston

Mrs. Richard Lindsay Roberts

Mrs. Albert E. Pierce

Mrs. John Kent Finley

Mrs. Richard Edward Lipscomb

Mrs. Frank V. Davis

Mrs. Louis W. Patterson

Mrs. Dan Carmack Gary

Mrs. Donald D. Zimmerman

****

NATIONAL OFFICERS – 1988 - 1991
Pesident General
Mrs. Edward Hungerford
First Vice President General
Mrs. Shirley Ann Pease
Second Vice President General
Mrs. William A. Smith
Chaplain General
Mrs. Ernest L. Cunningham
Recording Secretary General
Mrs. Rudolf John Seifert
Corresponding Secretary General
Mrs. Frank C. Stewart, Jr.
Organizing Secretary General
Miss Georgiana Swanson
Treasurer General
Mrs. T. Stephen Ballance
Registrar General
Mrs. David W. Albertson
Historian General
Mrs. John M. Birmingham

NATIONAL COUNCILLORS

Mrs. Paul A. Adams

Mrs. John Whitfield Clark

Mrs. Michael Phillips

Mrs. John R. Wasilik

IN MEMORIAM

MRS. HUGH L. RUSSELL
(Hallie Call Everett)
HONORARY PRESIDENT GENERAL
Died June 28, 1983

"They rest, still the shuttle moves
That wove their dreams into reality.

Their record stands;
Blazoned forever in the Book of Life."

THURA TRUAX HIRES

PREFACE

The 1989 Lineage Book is the tenth edition published by this society. The first edition was published in 1898. Subsequent editions were published in 1907, 1916, 1923, 1932, 1942, 1946 (50th Anniversary), 1968, and 1979.

The Executive Council voted to print the Lineage Book every ten years. This current edition of the Lineage Book was authorized for the benefit of newer members and Chapters, prospective members, and other researchers of early colonial ancestors. It is an index with both original and supplemental lines and services, names of the living descendant member with the Chapter affiliation.

In order to compile a complete list, a careful search of the original records revealed that several claims did not now meet the requirements of the eligibility listings as they now stand.

The last national number in this volume is 2839.

The Registrar General hereby expresses thanks and support to Mrs. Edward Hungerford, The President General; Chapter Registrars and/or Presidents who furnished requested material; and to the Treasurer General, Mrs. T. Stephen Ballance. Also grateful appreciation for the cooperation given by Mrs. William M. Riddle, Assistant Registrar General, in the compiling of this book.

> Kathryn Estill Albertson
> (Mrs. David W. Albertson)
> Registrar General

May 4, 1989

Compiled from the Records
of the
NATIONAL SOCIETY OF THE COLONIAL
DAUGHTERS OF THE
SEVENTEENTH CENTURY
by
Mrs. David W. Albertson,
Registrar General,
assisted by
Mrs. William M. Riddle,
Assistant Registrar General.

1990

TABLE OF CONTENTS

FOUNDERS CHAPTER

Organized as Colonial Daughters of the Seventeenth Century, May 5, 1896 in Brooklyn, New York; incorporated in State of New York.

Mrs. Harlan Page Halsey,
Founder and Organizing President.
President — Mrs. Robert Louis Roberts,
52 Hicksville Road
Massapequa, NY 11758
Registrar— Mrs. Margaret Emma (Dunton) Tillotson,
167 Kensington Road
Garden City, NY 11530

REGISTER OF MEMBERS

Nat'l No.

1340   Bergelt, Mrs. Edward G. (Janet C. Holzer), Flushing, NY 11358
By right of descent from Edward Wooster

941   Billings, Mrs. George Marshall (Josephine R. Swift), Brooklyn, NY 11217
By right of descent from Daniel Poor

902   Chumasero, Mrs. Robert D., Jr. (Kathryn Josephine Tuthill), Brookfield Center, CT. 06805
By right of descent from Rev. John Youngs

1521   Davies, Mrs. David L., (Marion Eaton Davis), Severna Park, MD 21146
By right of descent from John Hurd

1573   Dunton, Mrs. Robert M., (Elizabeth Ayers), Garden City, NY 11530
By right of descent from Anthony Morris II.

1817   Eberlin, Mrs. Harry W. (Emeline Louise Schumann), Queens Village, NY 11427
By right of descent from Richard Valentine

2711   Filipiak, Mrs.Paul (Gale Marion Seifert), Bay Shore New York 11706
By right of descent from Edward Doty

*849   Greason, Mrs. James Blauvelt, Jr. (Constance Fairchild Read), Weston, MA 12193
By right of descent from Gov. Thomas Weller

1520   Harrill, Mrs. R. Leonard (Joselyn MacFarlane), Upper Montclair, NJ 07043
By right of descent from Francis Cooke

*864   Long, Mrs. Alfred Thomas (Anne Victoria Fields), Sarasota, FL
          34236
          By right of descent from Capt. Matthysen VanKeuren
2474   McCunn, Mrs.Ian (Dorothy Cary Sanford), Canaan, CT 06018.
          By right of descent from John Carey.
**1012   Miner, Mrs. Ross H. (Justine Reynolds Sackett), Hightstown, NY
          08520
          By right of descent from Richard Warren
682   Oenslager, Mrs. Donald Mitchell (Mary Osborne Polak), New
          York, NY 10021
          By right of descent from William Pitken
1124   Pearsall, Mrs. Willard H. (Marilla H. Pratt), Bridgehampton, NY
          11932
          By right of descent from Major Simon Willard
2513   Plett, Miss Norma Vose, Manhasset,NY 11030.
          By right of descent from Richard Vose.
1606   Reed, Mrs. Long- (Susanne Long), Sarasota, FL33577
          By right of descent from Capt. Matthysen Van Keuren
2629   Roberts,Mrs. Robert Louis (Kathleen Joy Doty), Massapequa,NY
          11758.
          By right of descent from Edward Doty.
2711   Seifert,Miss Gale Marion, Hicksville,NY.
          By right of descent from Edward Doty.
2710   Seifert, Mrs. Herbert Otto (Louise Doty),Hicksville,NY.
          By right of descent from Edward Doty.
2116   Smith, Mrs. James (Freda Harmon), Central Islip, NY 11722
          By right of descent from Henry Adams
2619   Starkie,Mrs. Robert A. (Susan Eberlin), Massapequa, NY 11758.
          By right of descent from Richard Valentine.
2135   Tillotson, Mrs. Margaret Emma (Dunton), Garden City, NY 11530
          By right of descent from Anthony Morris II.
*   SUPPLEMENTAL LINES LISTED IN ANCESTOR INDEX
**   LIFE MEMBERS

MISSOURI CHAPTER
Number One

Organized Organized April 10, 1905, St. Louis, Missouri
Mrs. Western Bascome, Organizing President
(declared inactive)
Reorganized April 16, 1964, Mayflower Hotel, Washington, DC
Miss Acena M. Booth, Organizing President
President — Mrs. Charles C. Barnett, Jr., 19 Godwin Lane, Ladue, MO 63124.
Registrar — Mrs. Charles Everett Ragsdale, 7 Pleasant Ct., Kirkwood, MO 63122

REGISTER OF MEMBERS

Nat'lNo.

2544   Adams, Colma Benedict (Mrs. Kenneth H.),Webster Groves,MO 63119.
By right of descent from Lt. Thomas Benedict.

2518   Allen,Margaret Woods (Mrs. Thomas B.),Sikeston,MO 63801.
By right of descent from John Neville.

2300   Barnett, Lanabess Willcockson, (Mrs. Charles C., Jr.)
St. Louis, MO 63124
By right of descent from Willem Gerretse Van Kouwenhoven

2727   Burger, Marilyn Swett(Mrs. Harry), Kirkwood, MO 63122.
By right of descent from Edward C. Digges.

2287   Burk, Mrs. Francis Oratius (Ruth Phebe Powell), Middletown, OH 45042
By right of descent from Major Brian Pendleton

2471   Cavic,Leslie Vander Meulen (Mrs.), Manchester, MO 63021.
By right of descent from Peter Dunbar.

2347   Coombes, Mrs. Burleigh Lee, Jr. (Edith Heget Long), Creve Coeur, MO 63141
By right of descent from Andrew Ford

*2626   Eickmeyer, Lorena Hopkins (Mrs.), Mehlville, MO 63129.
By right of descent from Christopher Hussey.

*1713   Giulvezan, Mrs. Isabel Stebbins (Isabel Christine Stebbins) Affton, MO 63123
By right of descent from John Throckmorton

2280   Hillemeyer, Mrs. John Wright (Mary Ann Berner), Ladue, MO 63124
By right of descent from Hendrick Matthuse Smock/Smack

2212   Johnson ,Gladys Lucille Albright (Mrs. Francis L.), Chesterfield, MO 63017
By right of descent from Deacon John Doane.

2456   Johnston,Pamela Beggs (Mrs. Gilbert E.J.), Affton,MO 63123.
        By right of descent from Phillip Pendleton.
2777   Keefer, Linda Smitten (Mrs. Dan M.), Cape Girardeau, MO 63701.
        By right of descent from John Neville.
1711   King, Berdena Lee (Mrs. Arthur M.), Weatherby Lake ,MO 64152.
        By right of descent from Deacon Samuel Chapin.
2288   Lewis, Mary Katharine Curtius (Mrs. LeRoy R.), Higginsville, MO
        64037.
        By right of descent from Lt. Samuel Maddox.
2540   McReynolds,Louise Robinson (Mrs. Thomas J., III), Webster
        Groves, MO 63119.
        By right of descent from William Brewster.
2535   Malloy, Camille McNeill (Mrs. James E.) , St. Louis, MO 63105.
        By right of descent from Phillip Pendleton.
2493   Mayer, Camilla Paden (Mrs. Robert A.), Town & Country, MO
        63131.
        By right of descent from Captain John Pease.
*2290   Pease, Shirley Ann (Miss), Chesterfield, MO 63005.
        By right of descent from Thomas Rogers.
2396   Peck, Patricia Scott (Lawrence W.), Ladue, MO 63124.
        By right of descent from Valentine Hollingsworth,Sr.
2542   Pollard, Marion Beck (Mrs. Earsel W.), St. Louis, MO 63132.
        By right of descent from Rev. Ralph Wheelock.
•2286   Ragsdale, Mrs. Charles Everett (Nancy Jean Huber), Kirkwood,
        MO 63122
        By right of descent from Thomas Sprigg
2652   Rauch, Linda Pierce (Mrs. Bernard E., Jr.), Sappington, MO
        63128.
        By right of descent from Augustine Warner, Sr.
2336   Sherrer, Mrs. Joseph Diedonne, Jr. (Faye Bryan) Sullivan, MO
        63080
        By right of descent from Gov. Edward C. Digges
2645   Sherman, Lois Joyce (Mrs. Francis F.), Carrollton, MO 64633
        By right of descent from James Chilton.
2575   Tolbert.Bettie Sue Hill (Mrs. Tommy L.), Chesterfield, MO 63017.
        By right of descent from Mareen DuVall.
2337   Walton,Mrs. Josiah Harry (Geraldine Elley Drinkard) Sappington,
        MO 63128
        By right of descent from Gov. Edward Digges
2668   Webster, Harriet (Miss),St. Louis, MO 63143.
        By right of descent from John Alden.

*   SUPPLEMENTAL LINES LISTED IN ANCESTOR INDEX

RHODE ISLAND CHAPTER
Number Two

Organized November 5, 1920, Providence, Rhode Island
Mrs. Arthur M. McCrillis, Organizing President
President — Mrs.Dana W. Jaquith, 19 Peck Ave., Barrington, RI 02806
Registrar — Miss Shirley N.Chace, 258 President Ave.,Providence, RI
02906

REGISTER OF MEMBERS

Nat'l No.

2234   Alden, Miss Priscilla, Barrington, RI 02806
By right of descent from John Alden

2763   Babcock, Mrs. Norman C. (Alice Ranson Noyes) Providence, RI 02906
By right of descent from Nicholas Noyes

1753   Brown, Mrs. Clifford W. (Helen Steere), Providence, RI 02906
By right of descent from Roger Williams

1407   Chace, Mrs. Kip I. (Norma Agatha Barney), Providence, RI 02906
By right of descent from Jacob Barney

2548   Chace, Miss Shirley N. Providence, RI 02906
By right of descent from Jacob Barney, Sr.

2052   Colwell, Mrs. E. Warren (Barbara Frances Steere), Cranston, RI 02874
By right of descent from Roger Williams

2142   Darby, Mrs. Alfred E. (Irene Mae Craft), Rumford, RI 02916
By right of descent from Nathan Lord, Jr.

2159   Eaton, Mrs. Howard K. (Diane C. Dickinson), Swansea, MA 02777
By right of descent from Henry Maddock

2691   Gardner, Miss Catherine, Warwick , RI 02888
By right of descent from Philip Sherman

2058   Greenhalgh, Mrs. John, Jr. (Sarah Shirley Steere), Fairfield, CT 06431
By right of descent from Roger Williams

2160   Haelsen, Mrs. William J. (Eliza Lura Greene), No. Providence, RI 02911
By right of descent from Surgeon John Greene

2053   Hargreaves, Mrs. Jeffrey H. (Leanne Steere Colwell), Clinton, Ct 06413
By right of descent from Roger Williams

2054   Havens, Mrs. Irving H. (Marjorie Louise Steere), Chepachet, RI 02814
By right of descent from Roger Williams

2162   Jaquith, Mrs. Dana W. (Mary Lowell Curtis), Barrington, RI 02806
By right of descent from James Chilton

1565   Malmstead, Miss Helen Josephine, Providence 7, RI 02907
By right of descent from Thomas Angell

2161   O'Kneel, Mrs. George W. (Edith Sawyer Sherman), Providence, RI 02906
By right of descent from Richard Warren

2579   Riley, Mrs. Gerald E., (Frances Ellen Donoway), Cumberland, RI 02864
By right of descent from Henry Kinne(y)

2723   Scanlon, Mrs. William J. (Dorothy E. Parker), Greenville, RI 02828
By right of descent from Francis Peabody

2057   Steere, Mrs. Everett M. (Alcy Mowry Paine), Chepachet, RI 02814
By right of descent from Roger Williams

2056   Steere, Mrs. Robert E. (Mary Sayles Steere), Chepachet, RI 02814
By right of descent from Roger Williams

965   Tucker, Mrs. Stuart H. (Ardelle Chase Drabble), Providence, RI 02906
By right of descent from Robert Fuller

1943   Tuttle, Mrs. Laura Witter Rogers, Riverside, RI 02935
By right of descent from Matthew Cushing

2055   Van Bever, Mrs. Gerald E. (Louisa Maria Steere), Chepachet, RI 02814
By right of descent from Roger Williams

1859   Whitcomb, Mrs. Reginald D. (Virginia Pearce Ray), Riverside, RI 02915
By right of descent from John Howland

1898   White, Mrs. Robert S. (Doris Madeline Horton, East Greenwich, RI 02818
By right of descent from Henry Whitney

2238   Williams, Mrs. Harold P. (Elsie French Bushnell), Cranston, RI 02910
By right of descent from Preserved Abeel

2158   Wilson, Mrs. Richard A. (Marion Bruce Waterman), Providence, RI 02906
By right of descent from Roger Williams

2173   Yeagley, Mrs. William F. (Thelma Elizabeth Darby), Bristol, RI 02809
By right of descent from Nathan Lord, Jr.

*   SUPPLEMENTAL LINES LISTED IN ANCESTOR INDEX

MASSACHUSETTS CHAPTER
Number Three

Organized January 8, 1926, Cambridge, Massachusetts
Mrs. William Atwell Jackson, Organizing President
Declared inactive October 11, 1939

AHWEYNEYO CHAPTER
Number Four

Organized 1934, Penn Yan, New York
Mrs. Ralph T. Norris, Organizing President
Inactive December 1972

JAMESTOWN VIRGINIA CHAPTER
Number Five

Organized April 10, 1934, Richmond, Virginia
Mrs. Philip Wallace Hiden, Organizing President
President — Mrs. Taliaferro C. Dickerson III, Louisa, VA 23093
Registrar — Mrs. Donald F. Fletcher, Jr., Atlantic , VA 23303

REGISTER OF MEMBERS
Nat'l No.

2762 Bryan, Mrs. George H., Newport News, VA 23607
      By right of descent from William Brewster
1487 Bryan, Mrs. James B. (Betty Bingham), Angleton, TX 77515 By
      right of descent from Anthony Fisher
2060 Denton,Mrs. Jeffrey M. Seaford, VA 23692
      By right of descent from Lt. Col.William Randolph
2133 Dickerson, Mrs. Taliaferro C., III, (Sarah Hunt Friend), Louisa,
      VA 23093
      By right of descent from Major Edward Dale
1891 Fletcher, Mrs. Donald F., Jr. (Virginia Carolina Rich-ards), Atlantic,
      VA 23303
      By right of descent from Nicholas Martiau
2576 Fletcher, Miss Susan Madison, Atlantic, VA 23303
      By right of descent from Nicholas Martiau
2695 Graves, Mrs. Henry T., Luray, VA 22835
      By right of descent from Mareen Duvall
1950 Haugh, Mrs. Charles Roland (Elizabeth Ann Oglesby),
      Charlottesville, VA 22902
      By right of descent from Gov. Edward Digges
2454 McCreary, Mrs. Robert W., Herndon, VA 22070
      By right of descent from Richard Borden
1890 McMurran, Mrs. Joseph P. (Suzanne Elizabeth Hiden),
      Barboursville, VA 22923
      By right of descent from Capt. Thomas Graves
2182 McMurran, Miss Suzanne Hiden, Barboursville, VA 22923 By
      right of descent from Capt. Thomas Graves
1419 Morse, Mrs. Frederick Tracy (Mary Genevieve Forbes),
      Charlottesville, VA 22906
      By right of descent from Gov. John Webster
1626 Nunley, Mrs. Richard L. (Julia Watson Graves), Charlottesville,
      VA 22901
      By right of descent from Capt. Thomas Graves
1527 Smith, Mrs. Julian C. (Harriotte Wanamaker), Longwood, FL 32779
      By right of descent from Thomas Angell

RENSSELAERSWYCK CHAPTER
Number Six

Organized October 30, 1936, Albany, New York
Mrs. Frank D. Callan, Organizing President
Re-organized June 4, 1985
Mrs. James V. Fiori, Re-organizing President
President — Mrs. Stuart Hall, North Syracuse, NY.
Registrar — Mrs. Vernon A. Schmitz, 1377 W. Valley Road, Preble, NY
13141.

REGISTER OF MEMBERS

Nat'l No.

2690   Arquit, Mrs. Gordon J. (Nora Harris), Ithaca, NY.
By right of descent from John Harris.

2703   Beard, Mrs. Douglas H. (Marilyn Jones), Endwell, NY.
By right of descent from Robert Park.

2671   Berry, Mrs. James L. (Lois-Ann Fiesinger), No. Syracuse, NY.
By right of descent from John Sturges.

2678   Bohn, Mrs. Harold D. (Myrtle Dunn), Elmira, NY.
By right of descent from Robert Seeley.

2093   Bowen, Mrs. William J., (Mary Lillian Chase) Hempstead, NY
11550
By right of descent from John Gallup III

2686   Chester, Mrs. Reginald F. (Marion Smith),Liverpool, NY.
By right of descent from Stephen Hopkins.

2694   Cook, Mrs. Henry B., Sr. (Ruth Ayers), Binghamton, NY.
By right of descent from Jacques Cossart.

2802   Covell, Mrs. Carleton (Iva Nash), Mechanicville, NY.
By right of descent from Gov. William Bradford.

2774   Cross, Mrs. John H. (Lois Clancy), Syracuse, NY.
By right of descent from Joseph Parsons.

**1278   DuRocher, Mrs. Linus F. (Dora M. Van Vlack), Wappinger Falls,
NY
By right of descent from Hendrick Jockemise Schoonmaker

2679   Eldrett, Mrs. H. Carleton (Shirley Bohn), Elmira,NY.
By right of descent from Robert Seeley.

2774   Farrell, Mrs. John A. (Lios Clancy), Syracuse, NY.
By right of descent from Joseph Parson.

2673   Fiesinger, Mrs. Charles H. (Linda Ann Shurtleff), No. Syracuse, NY.
By right of descent from William Shurtleff.

2184   Fiesinger, Mrs. Edward H. Jr. (Emma Pettis), West Kill NY
By right of descent from John Sturges

2670   Fiesinger, Miss Emma-Jane, Syracuse, NY.
        By right of descent from John Sturges.
2600   Fiori, Mrs. James V. (Gladys Birdsall), Endicott, NY.
        By right of descent from Robert Forman.
2769   Fitzmorris, Mrs. Stanley R. (Ruth Good), Baldwins-ville,NY.
        By right of descent from Johannes Wendell.
1418   Goff, Miss Mary Young, Winchester, KY 40391
        By right of descent from Sir John Clay
2784   Grousset, Mrs. Richard J. (Agnes McClellan), Marietta, NY.
        By right of descent from John Wyeth.
2706   Hall, Mrs. Stuart (Harriett Martin), No. Syracuse, NY.
        By right of descent from Roger Williams.
2725   Hotaling, Mrs. Alton V. (Helen Clifton), Rensselaer, NY.
        By right of descent from Thomas Fuller.
2758   Howard, Mrs. George F. (Alma Boss), DeWitt, NY.
        By right of descent from James Barker, Jr.
2702   Jones,Mrs. David (Beatrice Kane), Erieville, NY.
        By right of descent from Robert Park.
2707   Kelly, Mrs. Francis J. (Wilda Anderson) ,Manlius,NY.
        By right of descent from Francis Hall.
2700   Klausner, Mrs. Karl R. (Doris Jones), Binghamton, NY.
        By right of descent from Nicholas Stilwell.
1495   Love, Mrs. Frank Campbell (Winifred Myers), Syracuse, NY 13203
        By right of descent from Robert Seeley
1551   Nero, Mrs. Allie Francis (Margaret Evangeline Covell), Rome, NY
        13440
        By right of descent from Anthony Hawkins
2641   Phillips,Mrs. Michael (Eloise Kelley) , Skaneateles, NY.
        By right of descent from Lt. William Palmer.
2773   Scheiner, Mrs. Carl J. (Jane Crawford),Baldwinsville, NY.
        By right of descent from Richard Seamer (Seymour).
2708   Schmitz, Mrs. Vernon A. (Marian Kemp), Preble, NY.
        By right of descent from Edward Fuller.
2659   Smith, Mrs. William J. (Esther Miller), Endicott, NY.
        By right of descent from the Hon. Randall Holden.
2635   Warder, Mrs. William O. (Ruth Henderson), Geneva, NY.
        By right of descent from Henry Werthington.
1986   Waters, Mrs. Wayne T. (Marie Chase), Vernon, NY 13476
        By right of descent from John Gallup III
2624   Woodward, Mrs. Gordon H. (Shirley Long), Endicott, NY.
        By right of descent from Louis DuBois.

*   SUPPLEMENTAL LINES LISTED IN ANCESTOR INDEX
**   LIFE MEMBER

CONNECTICUT FARMS CHAPTER
Number Seven

Organized June 8, 1937, Elizabeth, New Jersey
Mrs. John F. McMillan, Organizing President
President — Mrs. Peter J. Metsopulos,105 Roosevelt Blvd., Florham Park,
NJ 07932.
Registrar — Mrs. Cyrus J. Brunini, 232 Pearl Street, Trenton, NJ 08609.

REGISTER OF MEMBERS
Nat'l No.
1900 Andersen, Mrs. Thor B. (Elizabeth Farr O'Hanlon), Elmira, NY
14903
By right of descent from Paulus Van der Beck

171 Blakely, Mrs. Jonathan (Patricia), Cleveland Heights, OH 44118
By right of descent from Richard Treat.

2244 Bowman, Mrs. William M. Jr. (Elizabeth Gaugh Lovell), Toms
River, NJ 08753
By right of descent from Gregory Stone

1020 Browder, Mrs. E. Jefferson (Helen Irene Warren), Hackettstown,
NJ 07840
By right of descent from Jacob Warren

2809 Brown, Miss Eunice Frances, Rutherford, NJ 07070
By right of descent from Robert Harrington.

2405 Brunini, Mrs. Cyrus J. (Nadeene), Trenton, NJ 08609
By right of descent from John Martin, Sr.

2744 Bush, Mrs. Ralph Royal (Dorothy), Fairborn, OH 45324.
By right of descent from Richard Warren.

1446 Cannon, Mrs. John Franklin (Elinor Litchfield Allin), Mesa, AZ
85205
By right of descent from Major John Mason

1103 Cary, Mrs. Edward Knox (Emily Mabel Williams), Tempe, AZ
85205
By right of descent from Jasper Crane II

2331 Cary, Miss Linda A., Queen Creek, AZ 85242
By right of descent from Jasper Crane II.

2755 Christopher, Mrs. Harry Jurgen (Shirley) Warren, NJ 07060
By right of descent from Samuel Drake, Sr.

2684 Colburn, Mrs. Joseph L. (Katherine) Columbus, OH 43229
By right of descent from Edward Howe.

1748 Cornish, Mrs. Albert Campbell (Gertrude Elizabeth Christie),
Princeton, NJ 08540
By right of descent from William Almy

2560   Cunnigham, Mrs. Ernest Lewis (Jean), Denville, NJ 07834-2008
       By right of descent from Thomas Mapes.
2507   Dugan, Mrs. Martin J. (Helen), Little Falls, NJ 07424
       By right of descent from Edward Fuller.
2260   Flanagan, Mrs. John (Virginia Margaret Cheney), Toms River, NJ
       08753
       By right of descent from William Cheney
2320   Golz, Mrs. William M. (Susan Marie Brydon), Mahwah, NJ 07430
       By right of descent from Gov. John Ogden
2797   Hardwick, Mrs. Robert Duncan (Elizabeth), New York, NY 10021
       By right of descent from Paulus Van der Beck.
2761   Hunter, Mrs. William H.,Jr. (Billie), Oklahoma City, OK 73159
       By right of descent from John Goss.
2590   Jakob, Mrs. William A. (Doris), Longwood, FL 32779
       By right of descent from Thomas Mayhew.
2458   Lo Presti, Mrs. Basil G. (Marian) ,Washington Township, NJ
       07675
       By right of descent from Thomas Willett.
2780   Lotz, Mrs. Ronald Allen (Rose), Cloverdale, IN 46120
       By right of descent from John Page.
1132   McCormick, Mrs. Kenneth I. (Dorothy Hunt) Ocean Grove, NJ
       07756
       By right of descent from John Barrell.
2627   Metsopulos, Mrs. Peter J. (Grayce), Florham Park, NJ 07932
       By right of descent from James Taylor I.
2488   Rea, Mrs. Philip L., Jr. (Barbara), Belle Mead, NJ 08502
       By right of descent from Edward Howe.
2792   Romaniak, Mrs. Charles Richard (Laura), Kearny, NJ 07032
       By right of descent from John Burr.
2332   Rose, Mrs. Earl Elroy (Helen Estelle McCarrick) Falls Church, VA
       22043
       By right of descent from Edmund Freeman
2615   Smith, Mrs. Malcolm G. (Virginia), Tranquility, NJ 07879
       By right of descent from Epke Jacobse Banta.
2322   Smith, Mrs. William Alfred (Barbara Jean Carver), Lakewood, NJ
       08701
       By right of descent from Samuel Moore
1401   Sutphen, Mrs. S. Davis (Marion Linton Soverel), Branchville, NJ
       07826
       By right of descent from Jasper Crane II.
2411   Utech, Mrs. John J., Jr. (Nancy), Montclair, NJ 07042-2006
       By right of descent from William Frampton
2490   Utech,Miss Susan, Montclair, NJ 07042-2006
       By right of descent from William Frampton.

2426   Walter, Mrs. Charles F., IV (Marion), Highland Lakes, NJ 07422.
        By right of descent from Robert Titus.

JUNIOR MEMBERS

2781   Cary, Miss Cynthia Marie, Westmont, NJ 08108.
        By right of descent from Jasper Crane II.

*SUPPLEMENTAL LINES LISTED IN ANCESTOR INDEX
**LIFE MEMBER.

BLUE GRASS CHAPTER
Number Eight

Organized February 28, 1940, Lexington, Kentucky
Mrs. Benjamin F. Buckley, Organizing President
President- Mrs. George Phelps Ratliff, Sharpsburg, KY 40374
Registrar - Mrs. James Morrow Richards, Jr., Paris, KY 40361

REGISTER OF MEMBERS

Nat'l No.

2407   Allen, Mrs. Albert Lanham (Julia Hodgkin Winn) Winchester,KY 40391
By right of descent from John Carter

1409   Ardery, Mrs. Fayette (Carolyn Renick Cockrell), Paris, KY 40361
By right of descent from Robert Bruce Polk

2826   Baumgardner, Mrs. Larry K.(Alice Woodford Reynolds) Louisville, KY 40206
By right of descent from George Reade

2311   Bean, Mrs. Ernest Prewitt (Josephine Judy Brown), Mt. Sterling, KY 40353
By right of descent from George Proctor

1770   Buck, Mrs. James Marshall (Patricia Lorene Ward), Hyattsville, MD 20782
By right of descent from Thomas Todd I

2834   Burns, Mrs. Marie Jones (Marie Dudley Jones) North Middletown, KY 40357
By right of descent from Richard Taylor I

2730   Cooper, Mrs. Michael Arthur(Lucy Sims Wilson) Paris, KY 40361
By right of descent from George Reade

1944   Dickerson, Miss Laura, Williamstown, KY 41097
By right of descent from John George

1952   Evans, Mrs. Wilson A. (Ellen Josephine Best), Berea, KY 40403
By right of descent from Burr Harrison

1814   Ewalt, Miss Josephine Hedges, Paris, KY 40361
By right of descent from Henry Filmer

2644   Greene,Mrs. Harold Lewis (Katherine Prewitt) Mt. Stetling, KY 40353
By right of descent from Sir John Clay

2675   Hamilton, Miss Adnee De Mobrey, Lexington, KY 40508
By right of descent from Andrew Monroe

2833   Jones, Mrs. William M.,Jr. (Elizabeth Andrews Jones) North Middletown, KY 40357
By right of descent from Richard Taylor I

2017   Judy, Mrs. Thomas Jefferson (Matilda Renick Ferguson), Paris, KY 40361
By right of descent from David Crawford, I.

2465   Killpatrick, Mrs. Claude Paxton (Alice Miller Pile) Mt. Sterling, KY 40353
By right of descent from Thomas Sprigg

1771   Kincaid, Mrs. Dennis Gill (Todd Brookes Buck) College Park, MD 20874
By right of descent from Thomas Todd I

2728   Kuster, Mrs. Theodore (Mary Elizabeth Reynolds) Paris, KY 40361
By right of descent from George Reade

2757   Lawrence, Mrs. Robert Don (Eleanor Long Ardery) Stockton, CA 95207
By right of descent from Robert Bruce Polk

2379   Layson, Mrs. J. Vimont (Ruth Davidson Womack) Millersburg, KY 40348
By right of descent from Abraham Womack

2597   Layson, Mrs. J. Vimont, Jr. (Patty Page Woodford) Paris, KY 40361
By right of descent from Richard Kenner

1880   Lesueur, Mrs. Alexander Armand (Joan Clay Kavanaugh), Cullowhee, NC 28723
By right of descent from Major Henry Filmer

1488   Lightfoot, Mrs. Lee Gano (Elizabeth Payne Ferguson), Paris, TX 75460
By right of descent from David Crawford II

2374   Morgan, Mrs. Charles Lafayette (Barbara Anne Bean) Winchester, KY 40391
By right of descent from George Proctor

2375   Morgan , Miss Chelsea Anne, Winchester, KY 40391
By right of descent from George Proctor

2376   Morgan, Miss Ellen Proctor, Winchester , KY 40391
By right of descent from George Proctor

*1909   Milburn, Mrs. John T. (Cora Louise Andrews), Ft. Mitchell, KY 41017
By right of descent from Lt. William Andrews

2401   Prewitt, Mrs. Henry Caywood (Margaret Ann Clift) Paris, KY 40361
By right of descent from Lt. Col.William Collier

1269   Privett, Mrs. John Blevins (Harriet Beard Kinnaird), Greensboro,
        AL 36744
        By right of descent from David Wickliffe, Sr.
1923   Roberts, Mrs. Glenn Franklyn (Martha Crouch Reed), Ft. Wright,
        KY 41011
        By right of descent from Capt. Charles Ashton
1323   Roberts, Mrs. Richard Lindsay (Martha Todd Barker), Ft. Thomas,
        KY 41075
        By right of descent from Thomas Todd I
1480   Rogers, Mrs. Fielding Gant (Henrietta Clay Bedford), Paris, KY
        40361
        By right of descent from Major Henry Filmer
1297   Rogers, Mrs. Harvey Allen (Margaret Ferguson), Paris, KY 40361
        By right of descent from David Crawford I
2764   Rogers, Miss Lida Ferguson, Lexington, KY 40511
        By right of descent from David Crawford I
2413   Ratliff, Mrs. George Phelps (Patsy Katherine Prewitt) Sharpsburg,
        KY 40374
        By right of descent from Sir John Clay
2737   Richards, Mrs. James Morrow, Jr. (Jane Carson France) Paris, KY
        40361
        By right of descent from James Baldridge
2632   Smith, Mrs. Rick Dean (Elizabeth Barret Ratliff) Mt. Sterling, KY
        40353
        By right of descent from Sir John Clay
2704   Stephens, Mrs. A. Baldwin (Anne Clay Thomas Baldwin) Lexington,
        KY 40505
        By right of descent from George Reade
2804   Thompson, Mrs. James William F., Jr. (Emily Collins Jones) Paris,
        KY 40361
        By right of descent from Richard Taylor I
1309   Van Zandt, Mrs. Richard K. (Catherine Virginia Kitchen), Hun-
        tington, WV 25701
        By right of descent from Rev. Abraham Pierson
2726   Wilson , Miss Elizabeth Buckner, Paris, KY 40361
        By right of descent from George Reade
2410   Windsor, Mrs. Caroline Van Zandt (Caroline Kitchen Van) Zandt,
        Mt. Sterling, KY 40353
        By right of descent from Rev. Abraham Pierson
*1433   Woodford, Mrs. Buckner (Mary King Koger), Paris, KY 40361
        By right of descent from Richard Kenner
*1456   Wright, Mrs. Chauncey B. (Myra Snyder), Huntington, WV 25701
        By right of descent from Wigard Levering

JUNIOR MEMBERS

2819   Richards, Miss Katherine Carson, Paris ,KY 40361
        By right of descent from James Baldridge
2593   Thompson , Miss Jane Collins, Paris, KY 40361
        By right of descent from David Crawford I
2538   Thompson, Miss Molly Andrews, Paris, Ky 40361
        By right of descent from right of descent from David Crawford I
2537   Thompson, Miss Sarah W., Paris, KY 40361
        By right of descent from David Crawford I
2536   Thompson, Miss Shelby Marie, Paris, KY 40361
        By right of descent from David Crawford I

QUIVIRA CHAPTER
Number Nine

Organized January 27, 1949, Wichita, Kansas
Mrs. Wallace E. Haines, Sr., Organizing President
President — Mrs. Joseph R. Riden, Jr., 8447 Lamar, Overland Park, KS 66207
Registrar — Mrs. Elmer L. Franklin, 2906 North Kansas Ave., Topeka, KS 66617

REGISTER OF MEMBERS

Nat'l. No.

2188 Amos, Mrs. Frederick Clark (Janice Hathaway), Prairie Village, KS 66108
By right of descent from Richard Warren

2225 Brown, Mrs. John H. (Evelyn LaGreta Bute) 3012 East 2nd St., Wichita, KS 67214
By right of descent from James Chilton

2530 Carpenter, Mrs. Albert E. (Thelma Maurice Duvall), Topeka, KS 66606
By right of descent from Mareen Duval (Du Vall)

2520 Carpenter, Mrs. Harry J. (Patricia Ann Eddy), Topeka, KS 66606
By right of descent from Samuel Eddye (Eddy)

1758 Cowger, Miss Pauline May, Salina, KS 67401
By right of descent from John Brown I

1757 Duryea, Mrs. Harold Bliss (Letha Marvel Snow), Overland Park, KS 66204
By right of descent from Nicholas Snow

2171 Engle, Mes d Aurandt (Caroline Kirkham Dayton), Phoenix, AZ 85014
By right of descent from John Dwight

2772 Farney, Mrs. Jacob P. (Shirley Ellen Gibson), Mission Hills, KS 66208
By right of descent from Edward Howe

2328 Finlay, Mrs. Christopher A. (Lydia Ropes Dow), Danvers, MA 01923
By right of descent from Gov. John Endecott

2383 Franklin, Mrs. Elmer L. (Helen Hersh), Topeka, KS 66617
By right of descent from Lt. Robert Feake

2514 Gillin, Mrs. Brallier T. (Marjorie Elizabeth Walters), Glendale, CA 91206
By right of descent from Peter Gunnarson Rambo

2370   Holle, Mrs. Charles G. (Anne Carter Baldwin), Washington, D.C. 20008
        By right of descent from Major Edward Dale

2319   Kline, Mrs. Wilmer G. (Dorthea Mae Slaughter), Garden City, KS 67846
        By right of descent from Maureen Duvall

2227   Kysor, Mrs. Willis E. (Ruth Carey Albright), Junction City, KS 66441
        By right of descent from Deacon John Doane

2751   Lohse, Mrs. Robert R. (Jane Bird), Prairie Village, KS 66208
        By right of descent from William Gerrish

2356   London, Mrs. George A. (Mildred Elaine Haworth), Coffeyville, KS 67337
        By right of descent from Deacon John Doane

2570   Maxwell, Mrs. Eugene K. (Ruth Key Sammon), Selma, AL 36701
        By right of descent from Ensign Wm. Simons

2640   Mitchell, Mrs. Dean W. (Merle Jean Cole), Topeka, KS 66606
        By right of descent from Hugh Cole

2178   Myers, Mrs. John L. (Helen Bibb), Topeka, KS 66604
        By right of descent from David Crawford

1696   Ostenberg, Mrs. Walter M. (Katie Grace Smith), Dodge City, KS 67801
        By right of descent from John Howland

2388   Pamplin, Mrs. Jack C. (Mollie Baker Glass), Falls Church, VA 22046
        By right of descent from Major John Welsh

2177   Parenteau, Mrs. Jerome F. (Lois Marie Scott), Overland Park, KS 66210
        By right of descent from Capt. George Denison

2211   Riden, Mrs. Joseph R., Jr. (Sarah Jane Schmidt), Overland Park, KS 66207
        By right of descent from John Cory

2174   Smith, Miss Lean Ellen, Dodge City, KS 67801
        By right of descent from John Howland

2382   Spencer, Thomas M. III (Rita Carolyn London), Topeka, KS 66614
        By right of descent from Deacon John Doane

2329   Watkins, Mrs. Wm. Homer (Susan Finlay), Dogleville, NY 13329
        By right of descent from Gov. John Endecott

2459   Weisgerber, Miss Virginia Edna, Salina, KS 67401
        By right of descent from Jeremiah Tower, Sr.

*   SUPPLEMENTAL LINES LISTED IN ANCESTOR INDEX.
**   LIFE MEMBER.

FIVE NATIONS CHAPTER
Number Ten

Organized March 30, 1951, Buffalo, New York
Mrs. John W. Heinz, Organizing President
Declared inactive

PENNSYLVANIA CHAPTER
Number Eleven

Organized 25 September 1951, Philadelphia, PA
Mrs. William Carroll Langston, Organizing President
President — Mrs. Alfred Thomas Novello (summer) 405 Millhouse Pond, Wayne, PA 19087 (winter) 505 Shamrock Blvd., Venice, FL 33595
Registrar—Mrs.Arthur Harry Fadenrecht, 128 Mathews Ave., New Britain, Bucks County, PA 18901-5118

REGISTER OF MEMBERS

Nat'l No.
2000   Anderson, Mrs. James M., Jr. (Georgianna Molitor), Glenmoore, PA 19343
By right of descent from Joseph Peck

1816   Baker, Mrs. Donald C. (Rebecca Yeagley) Emigsville, PA 17318
By right of descent from Thomas Brassey

1815   Baker, Mrs. William (Mary Elizabeth Baker) Spring Grove, PA 17362
By right of descent from Thomas Brassey

1920   Balderston, Mrs. Gerald D. (Diana Mary Dutch) Titusville, NJ 08560
By right of descent from Jan Seimens

1107   Baratta, Mrs. John B. (Anne Parker) Atlantic City, NJ 08401
By right of descent from William Parker

1276   Bester, Mrs. William A. C. (Jane Penn Crispin) Sun City, AZ 85351
By right o descent from Thomas Holme

2651   Booi, Mrs. Duane G. (Phyllis Sherman) Chalfont, PA 18914
By right of descent from William Purrier of CT/NY

1926   Bowen, Mrs. Charles W., Sr. (Esther Allen) Dillsburg, PA 17019-0099
By right of descent from Joseph Jenks (Jencks)

2768   Boyd, Mrs. Thomas W. (Joan SwVane) Sewell, NJ 08080
By right of descent from Richard Singletary of MA

2734   Brooks, Mrs. Clifford R. (Joan McVeigh) Norman, OK 73072
By right of descent from Thomas Wynne of PA

2262   Buck, Mrs. Miller Isaiah (Helen Ruth Chandler) Bloomsburg, PA 17815
By right of descent from Edward Beezer of PA

1767   Carousso, Mrs. Georges (Dorothea Hughes) Smithtown, NY 11787
By right of descent from Edmond Freeman

1954   Cox, Mrs. Ralph L. (Jean Cary White) Connellsville, PA 15425
By right of descent from Samuel Allen

1219   Dellinger, Mrs. Nevin W. (Frances Louise Gemmill) York, PA 17403
        By right of descent from Col. Nicholas Greenberry

1304   Denny, Miss Josephine, Waynesburg, PA 15370
        By right of descent from John Woodruff

1300   DeVan, Mrs. William Todd (Charlotte Newman Sheppard) Hanover,
        PA 17331
        By right of descent from Capt. Edmond Scarborough

1417   Dohan, Mrs. David H. W. (Evelene Hinckley Smith) Lima, PA
        19037
        By right of descent from Capt. Thomas Purifoy

1268   Donaghy, Mrs. Edwin Carlton (Ada Howard Delaney) Bryn Mawr,
        PA 19010
        By right of descent from Abraham Op-Den Graef

1921   Dutch, Miss Deborah, Los Angeles, CA 97735
        By right of descent from Jan Seimens

*1744   Edson, Mrs. Charles T. (Charlotte Porter Bayless Scheuren)
        Pennington, NJ 08534
        By right of descent from John Porter

1955   Evans, Mrs. George Webster (Elizabeth Anne Rowland) Hulmeville,
        PA 19047
        By right of descent from Peter Wright

2743   Fadenrecht,Mrs. Arthur Harry (Doris May Briggs) New Britain,
        PA 18901-5118
        By right of descent from Daniel Brainerd of CT

*1252   Finley, Mrs. John Kent (Margaret 5. Gindhart) Haddonfield, NJ
        08033
        By right of descent from Jacob VanDeVer of DE/NJ

1538   Griffiths, Mrs. I. Newton (Dorothy Housenick Miller) East Berlin,
        PA 17316
        By right of descent from John Rhodes

2806   Hardham, Mrs. M. Downes (Marguerite Downes) Hockessin, DE
        19707
        By right of descent from William Harris

1476   Hires, Mrs. Charles Edgar (Mary Warder Bacon) Berwyn, PA 19312
        By right of descent from Samuel Bacon

1919   Hobin, Mrs. David Joseph (Elizabeth Herbert Dutch) Titusville,
        NJ 08560
        By right of descent from Jan Seimens

1953   Hodge, Mrs. John Hires (Mary Elizabeth Gindhart) Devon, PA
        19333
        By right of descent from Jan Seimens

2194   Hollingshead, Mrs. Wickliffe (Mary Cloud Hamilton) Clarksboro,
        NJ 08020
        By right of descent from Major Andrew Moore

*2049   Hungerford, Mrs. Edward (Ann Dukes), Sebastian, FL 32958
        By right of descent from Lewis DeRoachbrune of MD
 1319   King, Mrs. Everett N. (Lena Kathryn Scott) Dunnellon, FL 33263
        By right of descent from Major Thomas Brooke
 1523   Leary, Mrs. James Emerson (Helen Elizabeth Miller) Wascoeville,
        PA 18106
        By right of descent from John Rhoades
 2589   Liggett, Mrs. Robert C. (Frances Hammond) Valley Forge, PA
        19481
        By right of descent from William Harris of MD
 2713   Milbourne, Mrs. C. Gordon (Florie Robertson), Lansdowne, PA
        19050
        By right of descent from John Bolling of VA
 2791   Monk, Mrs. Robert S. (Henrietta Busteed), Brant Beach, NJ 08008
        By right of descent from Lewis DeRochbrune of MD
 2583   Novello, Mrs. Alfred Thomas (Ruth Jean Kirkham), Wayne, PA
        19087/Vencie, FL 33595
        By right of descent from Rev. Robert Owen of PA
 1502   Potts, Mrs. James Webb (Dorothy F. Scott), Dunnellon, FL 32630
        By right of descent from Major Thomas Brooke
 1683   Reitz, Mrs. Thomas Joel (Mary Alice Leary) Bennington, VT 05201
        By right of descent from John Rhoades
 1236   Richards, Mrs. Donald Clark (Helen Costello Painter) Delray
        Beach, FL 33445
        By right of descent from John Coolidge
 2712   Robertson, Miss Margie White, Lansdowne, PA 19050
        By right of descent from John Bolling of VA
*1251   Roelbing, Mrs. Siegfried (Mary M. Gindhart), Trenton, NJ 08618-5099
        By right of descent from Jacob VanDeVer
 1267   Roeder, Mrs. Paul Herbert (Alcine Scott) Philadelphia, PA 19151
        By right of descent from Major Thomas Brooke
 1185   Russell, Mrs. Harold A. (Mildred Louise Huffman) Waynesburg,
        PA 15370
        By right of descent from Solomon Leonard
 1259   Seimes, Mrs. Erwin Frees (Elizabeth Newkirk), Easton, MD 21601
        By right of descent from Capt. Albert Hymanse Roosa
 1807   Skold, Mrs. Robert Eugene (Mary Salome Stauffer), York, PA 17403
        By right of descent from Maureen Duvall
 1403   Spain, Mrs. Frank Edward (Nettie Elizabeth Edwards), Greens-
        boro, AL 36744
        By right of descent from Capt. John Smith of VA
 1239   Strudwick, Mrs. Lewis C. (Phoebe Shelby McNeeley) Baltimore,
        MD 21210
        By right of descent from Humphrey Booth

1412   Taylor, Mrs. Edgar Rives, Jr. (Guin Trau), Pittsburgh, PA 15235
        By right of descent from Peter Folger
*1281   Trau, Mrs. Frank Garland (Imogene Guion), Sherman, TX 75090
        By right of descent from Peter Folger
1247   Vogel, Mrs. Carl Stephens (Emma Coolidge Painter Hoffman),
        Rosemont, PA 19010
        By right of descent from John Coolidge
1589   Whealen, Mrs. John J. (Susan Adams Hires) Berwyn, PA 19312
        By right of descent from Samuel Bacon
1316   Winder, Mrs. William James (Patricia Ann Sheppard) Orlando,
        FL 32804
        By right of descent from Edmund Scarborough
1654   Ziegler, Mrs. Theodore F. (Jane Fontaine Kirk), Philadelphia, PA
        19118
        By right of descent from John Bosman (Bozman)

JUNIOR MEMBERS

1922   Balderston, Miss Bryn Elizabeth, Titusville, NJ 08560 (Jr. #15)
        By right of descent from Jan Seimens
1681   Boden, Miss Kip Kelso, Newark, DE 19711
        By right of descent from John Deane
2767   Booi, Miss Rebecca Ann, Lansdale, PA 19446
        By right of descent from William Purrier of CT/NY
1925   Edson, Miss Page Porter (Scheuren) Pennington, NJ 08534 (Jr. #16)
        By right of descent from John Porter
2682   Hungerford, Miss Dorothy Ann, Van Nuys, CA 91401
        By right of descent from John Gorham of MA

*   SUPPLEMENTAL LINES LISTED IN ANCESTOR INDEX

OKLAHOMA CHAPTER
Number Twelve

Organized June 8, 1955, Oklahoma City, Oklahoma
Mrs. N. Bert Smith, Organizing President
President — Mrs. D. Wayne Lewellen, 5874 E. 21 Pl., Tulsa, OK 74114
Registrar - Mrs. William M. Riddle, 1721 E. 57 Street, Tulsa, OK 74105

REGISTER OF MEMBERS

Nat'l No.

2439   Albertson, Mrs. David W. (Kathryn J. Estill), Tulsa, OK 74145
        By right of descent from William V. Strother

2253   Ashton, Mrs. Robert Lee (Sharron J. Standifer), Norman, OK
        73072
        By right of descent from Zachariah Eddy

1915   Booth, Mrs. John Newton (Glenna Greene), OK City, OK 73107
        By right of descent from William Mullins

2143   Boucher, Mrs. Avery N. (Nellie B. Ashcraft), Tulsa, OK 74135
        By right of descent from Mareen Duvall

2736   Brown, Mrs. Graydon L. (Marquetta Griswold), Ponca City, OK
        74604
        By right of descent from Edward Griswold

2222   Bumpass, Mrs. T. S. (Ruth Allene Young), OK City, OK 73120
        By right of descent from Thomas Rogers

2415   Burdick, Mrs. Joanne Carney, Tulsa, OK 74136
        By right of descent from Capt. Albert Heymanse Roosa

2643   Callier, Mrs. Thomas Paige (Margaret J. Smith), OK City, OK
        73120
        By right of descent from William Heath

1932   Dietrich, Mrs. Ira Jonathan (H. Loreine Collins), Tulsa, OK 74120
        By right of descent from Cornelis Barentsen Slecht

2378   Dunn, Mrs. Frederick E. (Frankie Eileen Morgan), Tulsa, OK
        74063
        By right of descent from James Morgan, Sr.

2680   Edmund, Miss Natalie Anne, Broken Arrow, OK 74012
        By right of descent from William Hunt, Jr.

2667   Ely, Mrs. Paul G. (Sylvia Faye Roye), OK City, OK 73132
        By right of descent from Sion Hill

1956   Evans, Mrs. Bruce L. (Correne N. Griswold), Eufaula, OK 74432
        By right of descent from Edward Griswold

2628   Gilbert, Mrs. Wayne (Doris Poindexter), Wagoner, OK 74467
        By right of descent from George Poindexter

2511   Goodman, Mrs. Mary Frances Nunn, Denver, CO 80203
        By right of descent from William Brewster
2121   Hixon Mrs. Fay Edward (Anna Lee Nunn), OK City, OK 73118
        By right of descent from William Brewster
2709   Hutton, Mrs. Barbara Crew, Bristow, OK 74010
        By right of descent from Dr. Robert Ellyson
2226   Lee, Mrs. Thomas Harvey (Frances F. Terrell), OK City, OK 73120
        By right of descent from Cornelius Dabney
2516   Lewellen, Mrs. D. Wayne (Anne Bracey Edmund), Tulsa, OK 74114
        By right of descent from William Hunt, Jr.
2326   Little, Mrs. Van Allen (Catherine Louise Watson), Del City, OK
        73115
        By right of descent from David Crawford II
2149   Luker, Mrs. E. W.,(Marcelle W. Atwood), OK City, OK 73112
        By right of descent from Nicholas Fountaine
2810   Marshall, Mrs. Willard C. (Inez Esther Holstein), OK City, OK
        73120
        By right of descent from Thomas Garrett I
2224   Ochs, Mrs. Rex W. (Mary Lou Fowler), OK City, OK 73157
        By right of descent from William Brewster
*1472   Patterson, Mrs. Louis Winfield, (Susan Pierce), OK City, OK
        73120
        By right of descent from Capt. Thomas Osborne
2438   Patterson, Mrs. Steven Thomas (Elizabeth Lou Simpson), Pittsford,
        NY 14534
        By right of descent from Capt. John Browning
1857   Pierce, Mrs. Albert R. (Emma Lou Barrow), Huntington Beach, CA
        92647
        By right of descent from Capt. John Lewis
1301   Poe, Mrs. John Hunter (Patty Lee Smith), Tulsa, OK 74114
        By right of descent from Rev. William Williams
2445   Poe, Miss Suzanne Lee, Broken Arrow, OK 74012
        By right of descent from Rev. William Williams
*2400   Riddle, Mrs. William McKinley (Elizabeth Josephine Hetzler),
        Tulsa, OK 74105
        By right of descent from Thomas Miner
*2022   Robinson, Mrs. Mary Louise Davidson, Tulsa, OK 74158
        By right of descent from David Crawford I
2733   Rosey Mrs. William Eugene, Jr. (Patricia Hoover), Muskogee OK
        74401
        By right of descent from William Randolph
2119   Rudy, Mrs. Charles Hilleary (Mary Ann Everett), Sand Springs,
        OK 74063
        By right of descent from Robert Lockwood

2519   Schorn, Mrs Leslie Norman (Catherine Scott), Tulsa OK 74135
By right of descent from Richard Allen

2630   Trolinger, Mrs. Donald C. (Patricia Jane Scruggs), Miami, OK 74354
By right of descent from Richard Scruggs

2416   Wadley, Mrs. Robert L. Sr. (Dian Southworth Milam) , OK City, OK 73112
By right of descent from Simon Hoyt

2241   Watson, Mrs. Lloyd E. (Mary Jo Robinson), Del City, OK 73115
By right of descent from David Crawford II

2268   Woodard, Mrs. Earl Stanley (Dava Dean Sanders), Del City, OK 73115
By right of descent from Lieut. Edmund Greenleaf

1933   Young, Mrs. Arthur L., Jr. (Velma Frances Reaves), Edmond, OK 73034
By right of descent from Edward Bennett

1795   Zellers, Miss Thelma Faye, Guymon, OK 73942
By right of descent from Capt. Thomas Harris

JUNIOR MEMBERS

2666   Patterson, Miss Claudia Gagen (Jr. Member #81), Plano, TX 75023
By right of descent from Dr. Robert Booth

2327   Watson, Miss Martha Ann (Jr. Member #51), Del City, OK 73115
By right of descent from David Crawford II

*   SUPPLEMENTAL LINES LISTED IN ANCESTOR INDEX

ILLINOIS CHAPTER
Number Thirteen

Organized July 10, 1960, Salem, Illinois
Miss Helen May Mcmackin, Organizing President
President — Mrs. James F Cooper, Holly Hill, R.R. 1, Taylorville, IL 62568
Registrar — Miss Edna-Leone Meadows, 4805 W. Main St., Decatur, IL 62522

REGISTER OF MEMBERS

Nat'l No.

2722   Anderson, Mrs. Earl S. (Mary Jane Bruner), Dwight, IL 60420
By right of descent from Thones Kunders

*2264   Armstrong, Mrs. Donald George (Dorothy B. Blagg), Cooksville, IL 61730
By right of descent from William Gaylord

2270   Arnold, Mrs. Leavitt G., (Phyllis Nell Wyckoff), Effingham, IL 62401
By right of descent from Pieter Wyckoff

2584   Ballance, Miss Charlotte Ann, Decatur, IL 62521
By right of descent from Lt. Gen. Thomas Goodrich

2385   Ballance, Mrs. T. Stephen (Juanita Sublette), Decatur, IL 62521
By right of descent from Lt. Gen. Thomas Goodrich

2787   Bauer, Mrs. Robert (Karen Dewey), Greenville, IL 62246
By right of descent from John Gallup, Jr.

2025   Baxter, Mrs. Harry (Gertrude Isabel Marshall), Danville, IL 61832
By right of descent from Harmen Hendricksen Roosekrans

2112   Birk, Mrs. Carl Peter, Sr. (Martha Sue Sublette), Decatur, IL 62521
By right of descent from Lt. Gen. Thomas Goodrich

2441   Birmingham, Mrs. John M. (Mary Lee Monroe), Carefree, AZ 85377
By right of descent from Samuel West

*2291   Bland, Mrs. Elmer Francis, Jr. (Doris Ellen Witter), Fairfield,IL 62837
By right of descent from Gov. Thomas Welles

2399   Bonifacius, Mrs. Arthur W. (Erma D. Veech) Cerro Gordo, IL 61818
By right of descent from James Veitch

2074   Brook, Miss Edith Gertrude, Stronghurst, IL 61480
By right of descent from Johannes Nevius

2406	Buenker, Mrs. Robert (Mildred R. Geheb), Teutopolis, IL 62467 By right of descent from Thomas Wells
2352	Butterfield, Mrs. John (Carolyn Mountjoy), Taylorville, IL 62568 By right of descent from Henry Bagwell
2463	Cooper, Mrs. James F. (Wilda F. Quinn), Taylorville, IL 62568 By right of descent from Mareen DuVall
2213	Cope, Mrs. James (Ruth I. Humphries), Hudson, IL 61748 By right of descent from Samuel Pond
2002	Coslet, Mrs. David F. (Dorothy S. St. John),Altamont, IL 62411 By right of descent from Gov. William Bradford
2814	Cotton, Mrs. Jerry L. (Nancy Jo Colvin), Edmond, OK 73034 By right of descent from Thones Kunders
2345	Culton, Mrs. Willis R. (Margaret L. Swanson) Canton, IL 61520 By right of descent from George Pack
2031	Cunningham, Mrs. W. Scott (Beatrice M. Young), Bismark, IL 61814 By right of descent from John Dodge
2527	Davis, Mrs. Betty Lee Manley, Smyrna, GA 30080 By right of descent from Col. John Waller
*1494	Davis, Mrs. Frank V. (Cornelia H. Casey), Greenville, IL 62246 By right of descent from John Waite
2364	Delahunt, Mrs. Charles R. (Mary L. Kington), Avon, IL 61415 By right of descent from Richard Buffington
1934	Devanny, Mrs. John S. (Mildred E. Smith), Pensacola, FL 32503 By right of descent from John Hughes
2533	DeYoung, Mrs. Roger (Jacquelyn S. Jones), Elgin, IL 60123 By right of descent from Gov. William Bradford
1782	Dittman, Mrs. William H. (Catherine E. Siegmund), Alton, IL 62002 By right of descent from Christian Remich
2210	Feldman, Mrs. Edward C. (Lenore Mae Timberlake), Bartonville, IL By right of descent from Phillip Pendleton
2646	Feller, Mrs. Ivan E. (L. Jane Crain), Cissne, IL 62823 By right of descent from Ralph Houghton
*1745	Finfgeld, Mrs. Clifford (Lois Alma Ryno), Bloomington, IL 61701 By right of descent from George Pack
2659	Flahaven, Mrs. John E. (Mary J. Zeilman), Streator, IL 61364 By right of descent from James Ensign
2134	Flynn, Mrs. Robert T. (Verna Mae Gridley), Sterling. IL 61081 By right of descent from Edward Doty
*2110	Frederick, Mrs. George H. Clark (Nancy M. Gubb), Evanston, IL 60202 By right of descent from Henry Bull

By right of descent from Henry Bull
2620   Fritz, Mrs. Kenneth (Bernice L. Barnes) , Moline, IL 61265
        By right of descent from Maj. Brian Pendelton
2508   Fugate, Mrs. Karen Lisenby, Naperville, IL 60565
        By right of descent from Lt. John Dresser
2209   Gleason, Mrs. Richard J. (Carrie Nell Dyarman), Springfield,IL
        62704
        By right of descent from Capt. John Sprague
2759   Gobezynski, Mrs. Leon (Rebecca M. Sims), Altamont, IL 62411
        By right of descent from Rev. Jonathan Burr
2202   Gravenhorst, Mrs. Theodore S. (Maxine Jaycox), Effingham, IL
        62401
        By right of descent from John Neville
2609   Griswold, Mrs. John C. (Billye Obst), White Hall, IL 62092
        By right of descent from Robert Polk
1910   Hamm, Mrs. James Justin (Ruth Thelma Bitting), Hudson, IL
        61748
        By right of descent from Gov. John Webster
2165   Hannon, Mrs. Harold F. Jr. (Esther May Gilbert), Bloomington, IL
        61701
        By right of descent from Matthias Hughes
2521   Haycraft, Mrs. Marvin (Fontella L. Hinshaw), Heyworth, IL 61745
        By right of descent from John Kendall
2604   Hinshaw, Mrs. Lyle (Joyce E. Schaefer), Bloomington, IL 61701
        By right of descent from Edward Fuller
2776   Jackson , Mrs. Jerald E. (D. Miriam Schory), Decatur, IL 62522
        By right of descent from William Clayton
2669   Jackson, Mrs. William P. (Shirley F. Shields), Champaign, IL
        61820
        By right of descent from Thomas Mears
1561   Johnson, Mrs. Charles M. (Janet M. Overturf), Champaign, IL
        61820
        By right of descent from Joseph Baker
2525   Johnson, Mrs. Hellen M. Manley, Chicago, IL 60643
        By right of descent from Col. John Waller
1764   Killey, Mrs. Ralph A. (Frances A. Brent), Monmouth, IL 61462
        By right of descent from Hugh Brent
2636   Klimas, Mrs. Michael J. (Elizabeth Jane Ballance), Flossmoor, IL
        60422
        By right of descent from Lt. Gen. Thomas Goodrich
2528   Korkosz, Mrs. Elizabeth A. Johnson, El Cajon, CA 92024
        By right of descent from Col. John Waller
1911   Kurz, Mrs. Rudolph F. (Marion I. Everett), Highland, IL 62249

2586   Lawrence, Mrs. Walter Scott (Bernadine M. French), Fairfield, IL
        62837
        By right of descent from John French
2585   Lawrence, Mrs. Wasson W. (Imogene M. French), Fairfield, IL
        62837
        By right of descent from John French
2153   Lucas, Mrs. J. Victor (Jane Gregg), Monmouth, IL 61462
        By right of descent from John Shinn
1957   Ludwig, Mrs. Earle W. (Eleanor L. Finch), Sun City, AZ 85351
        By right of descent from Gov. John Endecott
1780   Luttrell, Mrs. Curtis L. (Mary G. Leaverton), Spring-field, IL
        62704
        By right of descent from Stephen Hopkins
2425   McCartney, Miss Ruth Evelyn, Rock Island, IL 61201
        By right of descent from Thomas Morris
2346   Marquart, Mrs. Wayne (J. Eugenia Ford), Effingham, IL 62401
        By right of descent from Myles Standish
2785   Marty, Mrs. Victor G. (Georganne Spurling), Champaign, IL
        81821
        By right of descent from Nicholas Pyle
1897   Mayer, Mrs. Paul J.(Elizabeth N. Murphy), Webster Grove, MO
        63119
        By right of descent from Thomas Newhall
*2457   Meadows, Miss Edna-Leone, Decatur, IL 62522
        By right of descent from Capt. John Sprague
1935   Meyer, Mrs. Paul G. (Sarah Jane Lorton), Naples, FL 33940
        By right of descent from Nicholas Merriwether II
2130   Michelet, Mrs. Charles J. (Faye I. Fullerton), Wilmette, IL 60091
        By right of descent from Christopher Thomas
2442   Miller, Miss Florence Emeline, Taylorville, IL 62568
        By right of descent from Capt. John Seaman
2783   Miner, Miss Sarah Avice, Decatur, IL 62522
        By right of descent from William Spencer
2424   Morganthaler, Mrs. Michael L. (Clarenda S. Shambaugh), Cerro
        Gordo, IL 61818
        By right of descent from James Veitch
2721   Mosley, Mrs. Arthur E. (Carolyn E. Pond), Decatur, IL 62521
        By right of descent from Samuel Pond
2606   Mudge, Miss Leila Elizabeth, Bloomington, IL 61701
        By right of descent from Micah Mudge
2603   Pettise, Mrs. Thomas W. (Mary H. Jencks), Barrington, IL 60010
        By right of descent from Joseph Jenks
2333   Philp, Mrs. Merritt (Ileeta Walker), Waltonville, IL 62894
        By right of descent from Rev. Joseph Hull

By right of descent from Rev. Joseph Hull
2654   Pigott, Mrs. Lee D. (Ruth S. Rayburn), Decatur, IL 62522
        By right of descent from William Gerrish
1543   Randazzo, Mrs. Marco A. (Louisa W. Casey), Greenville, IL 62246
        By right of descent from John Waite
2571   Richards, Miss Shelia Permell, Watseka, IL 60970
        By right of descent from Wigard Levering
2381   Rittenhouse, Mrs. Floyd M. (Dorothy E. Phillips), Pontiac, IL
        61764
        By right of descent from Edward Northcraft
2448   Robison, Mrs. Charles B. (Katherine L. Parkins), Des Plaines, IL
        60016
        By right of descent from Deacon Samuel Edson
2323   Ross, Miss Dana , Atlanta, GA 30328
        By right of descent from Maj. Lawrence Smith
2023   Savage, Mrs. Clinton H. (Wanda M. Jackson), Beardstown, IL
        62618
        By right of descent from David Crawford
2024   Savage, Mrs. George H. (Pearl L. Jackson), Beardstown, IL 62618
        By right of descent from David Crawford
1877   Saville, Mrs. Edgar S. (Sarah D. White), Monmouth, IL 61462
        By right of descent from Roelof C. Van Houton
2462   Simonson, Mrs. John E. (Margaret K. Huston), Roseville, IL 61473
        By right of descent from Isaac Marston
2509   Sims, Mess Ursell Lavon, Greenup , IL 62428
        By right of descent from Roger Conant
2605   Smith, Mrs. Leland (Alberdine L. Jontry), Galesburg, IL 61401
        By right of descent from William Nickerson
1567   Smith, Mrs. Len Young (Helen S. Tuttle), Winnetka , IL 60093
        By right of descent from Gov. Thomas Mayhew
1582   Smith, Mrs. Wakelee R. (Jane E. Farwell), Hinsdale, IL 60521
        By right of descent from Henry Farwell
2431   Stewardson, Miss Roberta Sue, Brighton, CO 80501
        By right of descent from Lt. Gen. Thomas Goodrich
2685   Summins, Mrs. Mildred Masters, Ottawa, IL 61350
        By right of descent from Thones Kunders
2203   Talbert, Miss Alberta Marie, Fairfield, IL 62837
        By right of descent from Volckert Dirks
2365   Thorp, Mrs. James (Mary E. Cisco), Clinton, IL 62717
        By right of descent from Thomas Halsey
2461   Weisbecker, Mrs. C. Howard (Fern Rosenberger), Mt. Vernon, IL
        62825
        By right of descent from Richard Hall
2808   Wells, Mrs. John K. (Lois Sayre), Decatur, IL 62521

2223   White, Mrs. James E. (H. Priscilla Merrick), Jerseyville, IL 62052
       By right of descent from Gov. Leonard Calvert
2306   Wilkin, Mrs. Glen (Aileen D. Clark), Monticello, IL 61856
       By right of descent from Lt. Richard Stockton
2526   Wollesen, Mrs. James B. (Ruth P. Manley), Chicago, IL 60643
       By right of descent from Col. John Waller
2348   Wood, Mrs. Neil V. (Dorma L. Veech),Cerro Gordo, IL 61618
       By right of descent from James Veitch
*2109 Zimmerman, Mrs. Donald D. (Martha Rosenberger), Harvel,IL
       62538
       By right of descent from Richard Hall

JUNIOR MEMBERS

2554   Birmingham, Miss Georgia Atchison, Carefree, AZ 85377 (Jr. #71)
       By right of descent from Samuel West
2601   Davis, Miss Felicia Louisa Budreck, West Des Moines, IA 50266
       (Jr. #72)
       By right of descent from Capt. Johannes Wendell
2637   Klimas, Miss Katherine Cora, Flossmoor, IL 60422 (Jr. #75)
       By right of descent from Lt. Gen. Thomas Goodrich
2639   Klimas, Miss Rebecca Elizabeth, Flossmoor, IL 60422 (Jr. #77)
       By right of descent from Lt. Gen. Thomas Goodrich
2638   Klimas, Miss Victoria Anna, Flossmoor, IL 60422 (Jr. #76)
       By right of descent from Lt. Gen. Thomas Goodrich
2253   Lyons, Miss Rebekah Ellyn, Fairfield, IL 62837 (Jr. #54)
       By right of descent from Gov. Thomas Welles
2251   O'Daniel, Miss Meghan Allen, Monmouth, IL 61462 (Jr. #45).
       By right of descent from Roelof C. Van Houten

PRAIRIE STATE CHAPTER
Number Fourteen

Organized September 28, 1961, Chicago, Illinois Mrs. George Conrad Gumbart, Organizing President

President — Mrs. Leo Canfield, Jr., 401 West Franklin St., P. O. Box 265, McLean, IL 61754

Registrar — Mrs. Edwin L. Busch, P. O. Box 336, Middletown, IL 62666

REGISTER OF MEMBERS

Nat'l No.

2252   Adams, Mrs. Paul A. (Marian Maxine Ioder), Atlanta, IL 61723
By right of descent from Palmer Tingle (Tingley)

1743   Alvey, Mrs. Homer W. (Mary Elizabeth Irish), Lincoln, IL 62656
By right of descent from James Veitch

1616   Buchanan, Mrs. Walter I. (Lola Lees) Sarasota, FL 33581
By right of descent from Eltweed Pomeroy.

2397   Busch, Mrs. Edwin L. (Rose Alice Glenn), Middletown, IL 62666
By right of descent from Elder John White

2371   Canfield, Mrs. Leo, Jr. (Mary Nell Twomey), McLean, IL 61754
By right of descent from Robert Zane

2372   Gabbard, Mrs. William D. (Sara Jean Vaughn), Fort Wayne, IN 46815
By right of descent from John Loomis

2677   Golden, Mrs. Winifred C. (Winifred Evelyn Coningham), Middletown, IL 62666-0225
By right of descent from John Baldwin

2435   Harkins, Mrs. John D. (Elizabeth Marie O'Bryan), Lincoln, IL 62656
By right of descent from Edmund Beauchamp

2612   Lepehenske, Mrs. Herbert A. (Susan Kay Harkins), Marietta, GA 30062
By right of descent from Edmund Beauchamp

2386   Lessen, Mrs. Larry L. (Susan Vaughn), Springfield, IL 62704
By right of descent from John Loomis

1892   McShane, Mrs. Raymond (Lyndia L. Barber), Joliet, IL 60435
By right of descent from Capt. William Torrey

2315   Mielke, Mrs. Gary Theo. M. (Ruth Austin Woods), Shawnee Mission, KS 66206
By right of descent from Joseph Whiting

2720   Miller, Mrs. E. Randall (Mary Teresa Greenwall), Ekron, KY 40117.
By right of descent from Edmund Beauchamp

2277   Ploog, Mrs. Larry (Deborah Susan Howe), Charlotte, IA 52731
       By right of descent from Dea. Cornelius Waldo
2738   Potter, Mrs. Earl D. (Gwendolyn Chap), Palos Hills, IL 60465
       By right of descent from Joris Jansen Rapalje
2714   Renn, Mrs. Richard L. (Thelma Louise Hall), Louisville, KY 40272
       By right of descent from Edmund Beauchamp
2775   Stone, Miss Marian J., Mason City, IL 62664
       By right of descent from Dea. Simon Stone
2373   Voitlein, Mrs. Stephen P. (Rebecca Sue Gabbard), Fort Wayne, IN
       46835
       By right of descent from John Loomis
2276   Wallen, Mrs. Lloyd F. (Edith Berniece Crownover), Syracuse, NE
       68446
       By right of descent from Wolforte Gerritse Couvenhoven
2316   Woods, Miss Laura, St. Louis, MO 63131
       By right of descent from Joseph Whiting

JUNIOR MEMBERS

2676   Busch, Olivia Nicole Maedgen, Cedar Rapids, IA 52505
       By right of descent from Elder John White
2613   Lepchenske, Jennifer Ann, Marietta, GA 30062
       By right of descent from Edmund Beauchamp
2440   Mielke, Katherine, Shawnee Mission, KS 66206
       By right of descent from Joseph Whiting

*   SUPPLEMENTAL LINES LISTED IN ANCESTOR INDEX
**   LIFE MEMBER

OHIO CHAPTER
Number Fifteen

Organized December 2, 1962, Akron, Ohio
Mrs. Frank 0. McMillen, Organizing President
President — Miss Catherine Elizabeth Macey, 2775 Yellow Creek Road, Akron, OH 44313.
Registrar — Mrs. C. Edward Scott, 707 Austin Ave., S.W., Warren, OH 44485.

REGISTER OF MEMBERS

Nat'l No.
2658　Brinkdopke, Mrs. Henry (Katherine Brewer), Norwood, OH 45212
　　　By right of descent from John Brewer, I
1850　Burlingame, Mrs. William B. (Belva Hall), Cortland, OH 44410
　　　By right of descent from Thomas Hall
2697　Deisz, Mrs. E. F. (Mary Elline Hildebrandt), Cuyahoga Falls, OH 44221
　　　By right of descent from Thomas Eldred
1936　DeMent, Mrs. Norman H. (Jane E. Hall), Defiance, OH 43512
　　　By right of descent from Col. Joseph Bridger
1907　Earle, Miss Elinor Southgate, Akron, OH 44304
　　　By right of descent from Richard Lyman
1906　Earle, Miss Mary Elizabeth, Akron, OH 44304
　　　By right of descent from Christopher Branch
2114　Engle, Miss Virginia Evelyn, Akron, OH 44320
　　　By right of descent from Richard Parrott, Sr.
2648　Foster, Mrs. William David (Judy McCombs), Norton, OH 44203
　　　By right of descent from Albert Heymans Roosa
2279　Fox, Mrs. E. Tunnicliff, Jr. (Julia E. Hildebrandt), Richmond, VA 23226
　　　By right of descent from Thomas Eldred
1577　Frye, Mrs. Bernard C. (Mildred N. Trussell), Akron, OH 44303
　　　By right of descent Cornelius Dabney
1598　Gleason, Mrs. George R. (Edna Ruth Peugh), Akron, OH 44319
　　　By right of descent from Thomas Bradbury
2623　Johnson, Mrs. David Scott (Elizabeth Trefts, M.D.), Henrietta, NJ 14586
　　　By right of descent from Gov. John Webster
2083　Macey, Miss Catherine Elizabeth, Akron, OH 44313
　　　By right of descent from Dr. John Woodson

2081   Macey, Mrs. J. Hugh (Catherine Ebbert), Akron, OH 44313
        By right of descent from Gov. John Webster
2553   Mansfield, Mrs. Donald W. (Marjorie Lee Richard, Defiance, OH
        43512
        By right of descent from Col. John Jackson
1962   Miller, Mrs. Joseph N. (Bessie Ellen Peck), Cuyahoga Falls, OH
        44223
        By right of descent from Deacon William Peck
2228   Monter, Mrs. E. William (Florence Cecelia Stoecklin), Cincinnati,
        OH 45244
        By right of descent from Christopher Robinson
1961   Peck, Miss Mary Elizabeth, Akron, OH 44313
        By right of descent from Deacon William Peck
2543   Plott, Mrs. Charles H. (Audrey Bishop), Warren, OH 44482
        By right of descent from Gov. John Ogden
1960   Ruthenbert, Mrs. Eldora R. (Eldora Peck), Euclid, OH 44123
        By right of descent from Deacon William Peck
2397   Sands, Mrs. Maurice R. (Alice Force Deming), Akron, OH 44305
        By right of descent from Francis Cooke
2546   Scott, Mrs. C. Edward (Hilda Steigman) Warren, OH 44485
        By right of descent from David DesMarets (Demarest)
2273   Scott, Miss Mildred A., Dayton, OH 45409
        By right of descent from James Dashiell, Sr.
2443   Seifert, Mrs. Rudy J. (Marcia Carol Merchant), Brunswick, QH
        44212
        By right of descent from Edward Bennett
2817   Seifert, Miss Mary Francis, Brunswick, OH 44212
        By right of descent from Edward Bennett
1982   Simonds, Mrs. Leroy E. (Anna Katharine Chew), Wilmington, OH
        45177
        By right of descent from Dr. Griffith Owen
2621   Trefts, Mrs. Albert (M. Joan Landenberger), Shaker Hts., OH
        44122
        By right of descent from Cornelius Clasen
2624   Trefts, Miss Deborah Campbell, Sacramento, CA 95819
        By right of descent from Capt. Thomas Munson
2622   Trefts, Miss Dorothy Eleanore, New York, NY 10028
        By right of descent from Gov. Thomas Hinkley
2044   Troop, Mrs. Jean A. (Jean Ann Wyker), Massillon, OH 44646
        By right of descent from Edward Fitzrandolph
2681   Williams, Mrs. Si J. (Velma Groves), Denver, CO 80224
        By right of descent from Hugh Scott
1777   Wyker, Mrs. Clyde Ely (Anna Ruth Galbreath), Massillon, OH
        44645
        By right of descent from Edward Fitzrandolph

NORTH CAROLINA CHAPTER
Number Sixteen

Organized May 13, 1963, Charlotte, North Carolina Mrs. Roy Hester
Crowder, Organizing President
President — Mrs. Laurie McEachern, Rt #1, Box 218, Red Springs, NC 20377
Registrar — Mrs. William A. Sherratt, 604 W. Wilson Creek Drive, New
Bern, NC 20562

REGISTER OF MEMBERS

Nat'l No.

2127   Alexander, Mrs. Ernest Ross (Katherine Imo Barnard) Stoney
Point, N.C. 28678
By right of descent from Thomas Barnard

2090   Alexander, Mrs. James Atwell (Anna Pauline Hill) Stoney Point,
N.C. 28678
By right of descent from Col. John Washington

1988   Barringer, Mrs. Phil Louis (Regina Wilson) Monroe. N.C. 28110
By right of descent from William Arms

1851   Bourne, Mrs. Robert Gordon B.(Mary O'Neal Branch) Raleigh,
N.C. 27607
By right of descent from Hon. Thomas Warren

2189   Bowles, Mrs. George D., Jr. (Sue Ruth Hill) Richmond, Va. 23230
By right of descent from Col. John Mottrom(Matrum)

1852   Burrage, Mrs. Robert L., Jr.(Jacquelin Branch) Concord, N.C.
28025
By right of descent from William Spencer

2040   Byrd, Mrs. Luther N.(June Estelle Stone)Elon College, N.C. 27244
By right of descent from Gov. William Stone

2089   Cook, Mrs. Huestis Pratt, Jr.(Laura Hill Bowles) Richmond, Va.
23226
By right of descent from Lt.Col.Nathaniel Pope

1615   Crowder, Mrs. Roy Hester (Mary Ettawa Wilkinson) Raleigh, N.C.
27606
By right of descent from Lt.Col.Thomas Beale

1610   Crowder, Miss Venia Moye, Raleigh, N.C. 27606
By right of descent from Jeremiah Exum

1867   Davis,Mrs. David (Bonnie Dawn Bourne) Raleigh, N.C. 27607)
By right of descent from Hon.Thomas Warren

1963   Deal, Mrs. Henry C. (Leona Marguerite Davis) Waxhaw, N.C.
28173

By right of descent from William Almy
2010   Douglas,Mrs. James W.(Marian Caroline Millaway) Winston-Salem, N.C. 27104
By right of descent from Robert Bolling
2032   Dunn, Mrs. James Buford (Lillian Evelyn Davis) Delray Beach, FL 33483
By right of descent from Samuel Chew
2042   Eller, Mrs. James Carlton (Doris Cox McMillan) Winston-Salem, N.C. 27106
By right of descent from Thomas Halsey
2281   Franklin, Mrs. Kenneth Cabell C.(Elsie Bolling Turner) Greensboro, N.C. 27408
By right of descent from Nicholas Meriwether
1966   Fullerton, Mrs. Richard Neal (Mary Caroline Sandlin) Advance, N.C. 27006
By right of descent from Robert Bolling
2592   Gillespie, Mrs. Charles H.(Alice Lee Leonard) Richmond, Va. 23226
By right of descent from Samuel Earle I
2339   King, Mrs. Frank Fuller (Frances Elizabeth, McElwee) Statesville, N.C. 28677
By right of descent from John Howland
1946   Lafferty, Mrs. Martin L. (Jacqueline Burrage) Concord N.C. 28025
By right of descent from William Spencer
1947   Laffert , Miss Amy, Concord, N.C. 28025
By right of descent from William Spencer
2340   Leach, Mrs. Hal Thomas (Virginia Ellen Rickert) Burlington, N.C. 27215
By right of descent from Col. John Washington
1990   Lee, Mrs. James Allen II (Regina Elizabeth Barrenger) Monroe, N.C. 28110
By right of descent from Nathaniel Foote
1980   Linney, Mrs. Chauncey Depew (Mittie Hill) Statesville, N.C. 28677
By right of descent from Col. John Washington
1703   Lipscomb, Mrs. Richard Edward (Margaret Elizabeth Smith), Mullins, S.C. 29574
By right of descent from Capt. Nicholas Martiau
1978   McEachern, Mrs. Laurie (Ruth Lenore McCullers) Red Springs, N.C. 28377
By right of descent from Edward Bennett
2241   McLain, Mrs. Harry Phillip (Susan Elizabeth Rickert) Statesville, N.C. 28677

By right of descent from Col. John Washington

1965   Millaway, Mrs. Beverly Kyle, Jr. (Nannie Sue Sandlin) Winston-
Salem, N.C. 27104

By right of descent from Robert Bolling

1991   Mullis, Mrs. David William (Eileen Ernestine Barringer) Goose
Creek, S.C. 29445

By right of descent from Lt. Samuel Smith

1989   Norwood, Mrs. Danny Robinson (Martha Wilson Barringer) Monroe,
N.C. 28110

By right of descent from William Arms

1704   Nye, Mrs. Jackson Lanneau (Ann Marie Tweedie) Mullins, S.C.
29574

By right of descent from Capt. Nicholas Martiau

2237   Palmer, Mrs. Thomas W. (Marianna Alexander) Statesville, N.C.
28677

By right of descent from Major Francis Wright

2157   Parry, Mrs. William Allen (Harriett F.Watts) Brevard, N.C. 28712

By right of descent from Major Francis Dade

1722   Paterno, Mrs. Charles F.,Jr. (Margaret Jacquelyn Nye) Mullins,S.C.
29574

By right of descent from Capt. Nicholas Martiau

2771   Rees, Mrs. James Lester (Franceine White Perry) Greenville, N.C.
27858

By right of descent from Robert Bracewell

2053   Rosier, Mrs. John C. Jr. (Farleigh Hungerford) Lumberton, N.C.
28358

By right of descent from John Gorham

1964   Sandlin, Mrs. George W. (Lula Caroline Ditmore) Winston-Salem,
N. C. 27104

By right of descent from Robert Bolling

1784   Sherratt, Mrs. William Archibald (Evelyn Edward McCullers)New
Bern, N.C. 28562.

By right of descent from Edward Bennett

1938   Sherratt, Miss Martha Kimbra, New Bern,N.C. 28562

By right of descent from Edward Bennett

1705   Smith, Miss Sarah Agnes, Mullins,S.C. 29574

By right of descent from Capt.Nicholas Martiau

1881   Smith, Mrs. Robah Lee(Lois Elizabeth Dodson) Walnut Grove,
N.C. 27052

By right of descent from Gov.William Stone

2106   St.Clair, Mrs. Holland (Annie Sue Holland) Statesville N.C. 28677

By right of descent from Col. John Washington

1994   Stephens, Mrs. Frances Griffin (Frances Griffin) Charlotte,N. C.
28205

By right of descent from Christofer Thomas
2043   Stephenson, Mrs. William Cowles (Elaine McMillan Eller) Roanoke Va. 24015
By right of descent from Thomas Halsey
1848   Taylor, Mrs. Roby Ellis(Alma Vane Denny) Winston-Salem, N.C. 27104
By right of descent from Gov.William Stone
1940   Williams, Mrs. Pickette Laney (Alyce Cornell), Monroe, N. C. 28110
By right of descent from Thomas Dugan
2009   Winstead, Mrs. Benjamin E. Jr. (Peggy Aileen Taylor), Rocky Mount,N.C. 27801
By right of descent from Gov.William Stone
2236   Wren, Mrs. James Robert, Jr. (Frances Jean Stephens), Charlotte, N.C. 28210
By right of descent from Christopher Thomas
1672   Yates, Mrs. Frank Ogburn (Sue Ragland Taylor), Ashboro, N.C. 27203
By right of descent from Gideon Macon

JUNIOR MEMBERS

2330   Ditmore, Diana Eugenia ,Weston, MA 02193
By right of descent from Robert Bolling
2007   Dodson, Martha Claybourne ,Danville, VA 24541
By right of descent from Gov. William Stone
2282   Lee, Elizabeth Allison, Florence, SC 29502
By right of descent from Nathaniel Foote
2660   Morris, Christine Renee, Raleigh, NC 27607
By right of descent from Richard Stockton
2235   Stephens, Jennie Lyn, Charlotte , NC 28210
By right of descent from Christopher Thomas
2656   Wren, Katheleen Frances Anne, Monroe, NC 28054
By right of descent from Christopher Thomas

ARKANSAS CHAPTER
Number Seventeen

Organized June 14, 1963, Fayetteville, AR
Mrs. Arthur Senseny Brown, Organizing President
Inactive

MICHIGAN CHAPTER
Number Eighteen

Organized April 16, 1964, Mayflower Hotel, Washington, D.C.
Mrs. Chester F. Miller, Organizing President
President — Mrs. John A. Collins, P. O. Box 734, Rochester, Michigan 48308
Registrar— Mrs. John F. Weaver, Sr., 305 W. Elm Avenue, Monroe, Michigan
48161

REGISTER OF MEMBERS
Nat'l No.
2051   Altorfer, Mrs. Floyd William (Frances Louise Graves), Fair Haven,
VT 05743
By right of descent from Jonathan Fairebanks I
2665   Barrett, Mrs. Carroll Lewis (Dorothy Lucille Feaster) ,Gladstone,
MO 64118
By right of descent from Griffin Craft (Croft)
2394   Bauer, Mrs. Clarence P. (Isabel Maynard), Saginaw, MI 48602
By right of descent from Cornelis Melyn
2498   Baumhart, Mrs. Donald H. (Laura Jean Crotty), Greensboro, N.C.
27408
By right of descent from Anthony Needham I.
2078   Bienlien, Mrs. William Walter (Lois Ann Babler), Ann Arbor, MI
48106
By right of descent from Gov. Thomas Welles
2807   Bockemuehl, Mrs. Robert T. (Joyce May McGehee), Bloomfield
Hills, MI 48013
By right of descent from Mathew Rodham
2813   Bond, Mrs. Harry (Virginia Ellen Gaulden), Washington, MI
48094
By right of descent from William Spencer
2122   Brewster, Mrs. Robert W. (Ethel Luella Seely), Las Vegas, NV 89103
By right of descent from Giles Hamlin
2123   Brooks, Miss Maralyse Latting, St. Johns, MI 48879
By right of descent from Capt. Edward Richmond
2611   Christie, Mrs. Bruce A. (Margaret Bellows Doud), Ann Arbor, MI
48103
By right of descent from John Tower
2588   Collins, Mrs. John A. (Eva Mae Lomerson), Rochester, MI 48308
By right of descent from Tjerik Claessen DeWitt
2120   Cook, Mrs. Ralph William, Sr. (Arlene Jeanette Feller), Saginaw,
MI 48601
By right of descent from John Lawrence

2216   Davis, Mrs. Franklin Dale (Edith Ann Zorn), Saginaw, MI 48603
         By right of descent from John Fisk
2172   Day, Mrs. John E. (Marian Ardra McDonagh), Saginaw, MI 48603
         By right of descent from Myles Standish
2035   Denton, Mrs. E. Brady, Sr. (Dorothy Ann Sharpe), Saginaw, MI
         48603
         By right of descent from Richard Woodhull
2308   Denton, Mrs. John L. (Mary Jane Reese), Saginaw MI 48603
         By right of descent from Cornelius Corsen
2275   deZeeuw, Mrs. Donald John (Fern Mae Lawhead), Okemos, MI
         48864
         By right of descent from Walter Woodworth
2047   Domson, Mrs. Andrew, Jr. (Lois Yvonne Smith), Saginaw, MI
         48602
         By right of descent from Gov. Thomas Welles
2610   Doud, Mrs. Howard R. (Margaret Bellows), Saginaw, MI 48603
         By right of descent from John Tower
1853   Fenlon, Mrs. Edward H. (Elizabeth Jane Weckbaugh), Petoskey,
         MI 49770
         By right of descent from Jan Cornelissen Van Horne
2207   Fishel, Mrs. Maxine S. (Maxine Emeline Sowle), Saginaw, MI 48602
         By right of descent from John Perrin, Sr.
1719   Francis, Miss Bernice M., Midland, MI 48640
         By right of descent from Thomas Welles
2587   Fysh, Mrs. Walter (Joanna Martina Sackett), Redford, MI 48240
         By right of descent from Richard Sackett
1435   Glover, Mrs. John Wallace (Frances A. Reed), Midland, MI 48640
         By right of descent from Dep. Gov. Francis Willoughby
2302   Grimes, Mrs. William Schuyler (Louise Imogene Root), Alpena,MI
         49707
         By right of descent from John Root
2642   Guzak, Mrs. Joseph Paul (Elizabeth Jean Arnold), Drayton Plains,
         MI 48020
         By right of descent from Thomas Warren
2692   Hallgren, Mrs. George William (Ann Daniels), Bel Air, MD 21014
         By right of descent from Lt. Andrew Newcomb
2423   Hanson, Mrs. Lee D. (Olive Congdon), Birmingham, MI 48009
         By right of descent from Edmund Freeman
1975   Harroun, Mrs. Richard R. (Mary Alice Finney), Tawas City, MI
         48763
         By right of descent from Thomas Hungerford II
1822   Headlee, Mrs. James P. (Johann Audrey Banwell), Rochester,MI
         48063
         By right of descent from John Alden

2242   Henke, Mrs. Orvis L. (E. Marguerite Martin) ,Northville, MI 48167
By right of descent from John Strong

2008   Henry, Mrs. Charles J. (Sandra Kay Kedmocker), Winnetka, IL
60093
By right of descent from John Brockett

2197   Hoopes, Mrs. Rae Stevens (Rae Esther Stevens), Santa Barbara,
CA 93101
By right of descent from Richard Woodhull I

2104   Hunt, Mrs. Maxwell E. (Gloria Dean Bailey), Loudon, TN 37774
By right of descent from Charles Gorsuch

2482   Keller, Mrs. Thomas David (Joan Eileen Butts), Greenbush,MI
48738
By right of descent from Robert Carr

2214   Koerber, Mrs. Ruth E. (Ruth Elaine Zorn), Bay City, MI 48706
By right of descent from John Fisk

2215   Koerber, Mrs. Gene Lewis (Maryon Louise Zorn), Saginaw, Ml
48602
By right of descent from John Fisk

2230   Korte, Mrs. Anthony S. (Dorothy Standish Bassett), Dearborn, MI
48124
By right of descent from Myles Standish

1720   Lang, Mrs. Laurence C. (Janet Rae Glover), Midland, MI 48640
By right of descent from Judge Simon Lynde

2113   LaTarte, Mrs. Robert L. (Mary Elizabeth Crane), Saginaw, MI
48603
By right of descent from Jasper Crane II

2309   Lee, Mrs. Rolland Porter (Doris Evangeline Rosencrantz), East
Tawas, MI 48730
By right of descent from Gov. Thomas Welles

2155   Miller, Mrs. Clarence F. (Meryle Loretta Woodfill), Lehigh Acres,
FL 33936
By right of descent from Thomas Price

2152   O'Keefe, Mrs. Edward T. (Bird-Ellen Gage), Saginaw, MI 48602
By right of descent from Daniel Hovey

2647   Oncley, Mrs. John Lawrence (Lephia Marcia French),Ann Arbor
MI 48104
By right of descent from George Denison

1973   Peters, Mrs. Thomas M. (Jane Caryl Fetters), Troy, MI 48098
By right of descent from John Rogers

2414   Powell, Mrs. Harold F. (Ruth Maxine Burr), Royal Oak, MI 48073
By right of descent from John Winslow

2599   Reardon, Mrs. John J. (Dorothy Winifred Lee), Saginaw, MI 48603
By right of descent from Joseph Peck

2079   Renie, Mrs. Charles J. (Harriet Eleanor Simons), Dimondale, MI 48821
        By right of descent from Henry Peck
2393   Renie, Miss Lenette Charlene, Domondale, MI 48821
        By right of descent from Henry Peck
2243   Serrell, Miss Alice Dorothy, Ft. Pierce, FL 33449
        By right of descent from Nathaniel Dickinson
1948   Smith, Mrs. Carl H. (Caryl Jane Finney), Port Huron, MI 48060
        By right of descent from Samuel Gorton
2303   Sowle, Miss Patricia Ann, Saginaw, MI 48603
        By right of descent from John Perrin, Sr.
2434   Syring Mrs. W. Vernon (Barbara Abigail Barnes), Flint MI 48503
        By right of descent from Col. Matthew Allyn
2779   Warda, Mrs. C. Wernecke (Gretchen Ann Wernecke), Hartford WI 53027
        By right of descent from Matthias St John
1624   Watson Mrs. Joseph Allen, Jr. (Jeanne Elizabeth Miller),Rochester, Ml 48063
        By right of descent from Cornelius Tyson
2137   Weaver, Mrs. John F. Sr. (Elizabeth Jane Case), Monroe, MI 48161
        By right of descent from Capt. Samuel Adams
2778   Wernecke, Mrs. Roland A. (Arloine Jackson), West Bend, WI 53095
        By right of descent from Thomas Betts
2156   Wiltse, Mrs. Dorr Norman (Gladys May Garner), Caro, MI 48723
        By right of descent from Capt. John Johnson
2380   Wurtzel, Mrs. William A. (Thelma Minnie Chamberlin) Saginaw, MI 48603
        By right of descent from Capt. John Johnson

JUNIOR MEMBERS

2102   Wolohan, Miss Mary Elizabeth, Frankenmuth, MI 48734
        By right of descent from Daniel Cole
2100   Wolohan, Miss Noreen Mayy, Frankenmuth, MI 48734
        By right of descent from Daniel Cole
2099   Wolohan, Miss Rosemary Parshall, Frankenmuth, MI 48734
        By right of descent from Daniel Cole
2664   Hunt, Miss Lauren Elyse, Durham, N.C. 27707
        By right of descent from Charles Gorsuch
2666   Hunt, Miss Lindsay Erin, Durham, N.C. 27707
        By right of descent from Charles Gorsuch

CALIFORNIA CHAPTER
Number Nineteen

Organized April 16, 1964, Washington, D.C.
Mrs. Charles A. Christin, Organizing President
Reorganized June 18, 1988, Palo Alto, CA ,
Mrs. George Alexis Hopiak, Organizing President
President — Mrs. George A. Hopiak, 884 No. Calif. Ave., Mountain View, CA
94043.
Registrar — Mrs. Paul von Kempf, 1543 Walnut Dr., Palo Alto, CA. 94301

REGISTER OF MEMBERS

Nat'l No.

2729   Brady, Mrs. Joseph L., (Turalu Reed), Walnut Creek, CA 94598.
By right of descent from Andrew Warde

2746   Cooke, Mrs. John D., (Mariam Bailey), Mountain View, CA 94043
By right of descent from Elizur Holyoke

2748   Degl'Innocenti, Ms. Irene Pardee, Menlo Park, CA 94025
By right of descent from George Pardee

2701   Hopiak, Mrs. George A., (Mariam Parr), Palo Alto, CA 94303
By right of descent from Elizur Holyoke

2745   Kutzcher, Mrs. Detlef Kurt, (Christine Hopiak), Los Gatos, CA
95030
By right of descent from Elizur Holyoke

2735   Lang, Mrs. Robert E., (Samantha Lois Lang), Willows, CA 95988
By right of descent from Edward Stebbins

2728   Lofquist, Mrs. Alden A., Jr., (Frederica Seavey), Knoxville, TN
37922
By right of descent from Henry Sherburne

2751   Lyon, Mrs. William L., (Barbara Steere), Palo Alto, CA 94301
By right of descent from Elizabeth Tilley

2760   Stebbins, Mrs. Albert K., Jr., (Patricia Rule), Palo Alto, CA 94301
By right of descent from Col. George Reade

2747   von Kempf, Mrs. Paul, (Margaret Stratton), Palo Alto, CA 94301
By right of descent from Samuel Wright

ELIZA LUCAS CHAPTER

Number Twenty

Organized April 16, 1964, Mayflower Hotel, Washington, DC
Mrs. Richard Edward Lipscomb, Organizing President
Inactive 1977

TENNESSEE CHAPTER
Number Twenty-One

Organized January 27, 1967, Knoxville, Tennessee
Mrs. James Spencer Bell, Organizing President
President — Miss Grace Elizabeth Gary, P.O. Box 367, Union City, TN 38261-0367
Registrar — Mrs. Arthur A. Thompson, 722 E. Florida Avenue, Union City, TN 38261

REGISTER OF MEMBERS

Nat'l No.

1805   Bell, Mrs. James Spencer, (Kathryn Eldridge Sneed), Memphis, TN 38104
By right of descent from Thomas Owsley

2741   Bell, Miss Katherine S., Memphis, TN 38104
By right of descent from William Richardson

2683   Buckley, Mrs. Thomas Mac, (Shirley Gray), Martin, TN 38327
By right of descent from Joel Bayly/Bailey

2147   Clark, Mrs. William H., (Jane Roberts Carter), Johnson City, TN 37601
By right of descent from Francis Morgan I.

2758   Crain, Miss Tracy Lynette, Spindale, NC 28160
By right of descent from John Clayes/Cloyes

1849   Dienna, Mrs. Jack Breeden (Esther Allene Brown), Conroe, TX 27304
By right of descent from Edward Doty

2559   Evans, Mrs. Sebra, (Roberta Glenn Thurmond), Memphis, TN 38104
By right of descent from John Clayes

*2005   Gary, Mrs. Dan Carmack, (Grace Elizabeth Dietzel), Union City, TN 38261
By right of descent from Isaac Learned

*2006   Gary, Miss Grace Elizabeth, Union City, TN 38261
By right of descent from Isaac Learned

2667   Hayne, Mrs. Robert S., (Margaret McCoy), Memphis, TN 38111
By right of descent from Robert Lindsay

1868   Hillis, Mrs. Russell W., (Florence Elizabeth Elliot), Knoxville, TN 37919
By right of descent from Capt. John Rogers

2551   Latimer, Mrs. Jane Dietzel, Savannah, TN 38372
By right of descent from Isaac Learned

1908   Maxwell, Mrs. Clifford A., (Ruth Barker), Johnson City, TN 37601
        By right of descent from Lt. Col. Walter Chiles

2790   Mclntosh, Mrs. William Jerome, (Vina Hembree), Tucker, GA 30084
        By right of descent from John Phillips

2191   Mettetal, Mrs. Ray W., (Mattie Lowell Wardlaw), Johnson City,
        TN 37601
        By right of descent from Capt. Daniel Gaines

2265   Moore, Mrs. Gedie C., (Camille W. Christmas), Memphis, TN
        38128
        By right of descent from Lawrence Wilkinson

2557   Newby, Mrs. George, (Lucille Ward Moore), Memphis, TN 38128
        By right of descent from Lawrence Wilkinson

2822   Nichols, Miss Sally Carol, Union City, TN 38261
        By right of descent from Edmund Littlefield

2558   Page, Mrs. Lee R., (Elizabeth Christmas Moore), Memphis, TN
        38128
        By right of descent from Lawrence Wilkinson

2085   Perkey, Mrs. Donald R., (Carol King Kelley), Lenoir City, TN
        37771
        By right of descent from Col. John Page

1835   Portwood, Mrs. Ken B.,(Mary Kathleen Russell), Knoxville, TN
        37917
        By right of descent from Robert Adams

2661   Reeser, Mrs. Archibald W., (Marion Virginia Hopkins), Eden, NC
        27288
        By right of descent from Samuel Field

2765   Rouse, Mrs. Robert N., Jr., (Marelle Gertrude Miller), Johnson
        City, TN 37604
        By right of descent from Rev. Pierre Robert

2757   Sharp, Mrs. James R., Jr. (Denise Elaine Mays), Median, TN
        38355
        By right of descent from Simon Gates

2696   Simmons, Mrs. Robert W., (Helen June Pitts), Sharon, TN 38255
        By right of descent from Joseph Bridger

2782   Smith, Miss Crista Linn, Midlothian, VA 23113
        By right of descent from Richard Sears

2012   Steele, Mrs. L. Pat, (Betty Lou Ayers), Fort Smith, AR 72903
        By right of descent from Jeremy Adams

2788   Terry, Mrs. Elbert A., (Celia Hembree Hamlin), Memphis, TN
        38111
        By right of descent from John Phillips

1847   Thompson, Mrs. Arthur A., (Elizabeth Mathes), Union City, TN
        38261
        By right of descent from Thomas Skidmore

2011   Tittsworth, Mrs. Doris T., Jonesboro, AR 72401
By right of descent from Jeremy Adams

2688   Vowell, Mrs. Morris A., (Mary Pursley Kelly), Martin, TN 38237
By right of descent from Thomas Willoughby

2724   Wasilik, Mrs. John R., (Patricia Elayne Sears), Midlothian, VA 23113
By right of descent from Richard Sears

1979   Wiley, Mrs. William L., (Helen Gertrude Russell), Knoxville, TN 37917
By right of descent from Robert Adams

2789   Young, Mrs. L. Ernest, (Maude Hamlin), Knoxville, TN 37914
By right of descent from John Phillips

JUNIOR MEMBERS

2820   Crain, Miss Terri Luanne, Spindale, NC 28160
By right of descent from Jonas Eaton

2839   Dietze, Miss Mary Fitzsimons, Baton Rouge, LA 70809
By right of descent from Jacob Towne

2821   Nichols, Miss Rebecca Ann, Union City, TN 38261
By right of descent from James Trowbridge

*   SUPPLEMENTAL LINES LISTED IN ANCESTOR INDEX

**   LIFE MEMBER

FLORIDA CHAPTER

Number Twenty-Two

Organized September 29, 1975, Ft. Lauderdale, Florida
Mrs. Myrl M. Harrison, Organizing President
President — Mrs. William M. Jones, 7910 S.W. 170 th St., Miami,FL 33157
Registrar—Mrs. Harry H. Lane, P.O. Box 100587, Fort Lauderdale, FL
33310

REGISTER OF MEMBERS

Nat'l No.

2798   Abbey, Mrs. Nathan (Lorena Mae), Holiday, FL 33590
        By right of descent from Charles Chouney
2418   Ager, Mrs. Snowden (Winifred Cameron), Melbourne Beach, FL
        32951
        By right of descent from Harmen Myndertse Van Der Bogart
2499   Alderson, Mrs. Mary Ford, Falls Church, VA 22041
        By right of descent from Thomas Price
2470   Aul, Mrs. Clyde (Betty Jean DeVane), Plant City, FL 33566
        By right of descent from Lt. William Spencer
1591   Barber, Mrs. Robert C. (Leona B.), Ft Lauderdale, FL 33304
        By right of descent from Captain William Torrey
2195   Barkley, Mrs. John W., Jr. (Vera Whitten), Laughlintown PA 15655
        By right of descent from Lt. John Livermore
2565   Barrick, Mrs William H. (Elizabeth Norton), Naples, FL 33940
        By right of descent from John Webster
2455   Bryant, Mrs. Julian E. (Elizabeth Gray), Pompano Beach, FL
        33062
        By right of descent from John Bayly
2472   Campbell, Mrs. James W. (Mary Ellen Jones), Fort Lauderdale,
        FL 33316
        By right of descent from Benjamin Brashears
24 12   Cartier, Mrs R. Walter (Mary Adelaide Linton), Fort Myers Beach,
        FL 33931
        By right of descent from Samuel Griffin
2577   Charles, Mrs. Melvin M. (Ann Cookus), St. Augustine, FL 32084
        By right of descent from John Hatch
2486   Connolly, Mrs. John B. (Doris R. Comey), Boca Raton, FL 33486
        By right of descent from Dr. John Barton
2803   Cmaylo, Mrs. Michael Alexander (Barbara Jean Weaver), Fort
        Lauderdale, FL 33305
        By right of descent from Richard Pace

2800   Dean, Mrs. Robert S., Sr., (Nancy Louise Alderman) Fort Myers, FL 33901
       By right of descent from Robert Wynn

2786   Delk, Mrs. Owington G. (Sarah Frances Channell), Punta Gorda, FL 33950
       By right of descent from Goerge Nosworthy

2495   Donchian, Mrs. Richard D. (Alma C. Gibbs), Pompano Beach, FL 33062
       By right of descent from Richard Warren

1537   Dunmire, Mrs Harold J. (Harlene E. Halsey), Fort Lauderdale, FL 33308
       By right of descent from Thomas Halsey

2201   Dunn, Mrs. Mathon B. (Ellinor A. DeLind, Tierra Verde, FL 33715
       By right of descent from Robert Williams

2487   Erickson, Mrs. Melville A. (Betty Lively), Palm City, FL 34990
       By right of descent from Tobias Saunders

2496   Faw, Mrs. Wylie M. Jr. (Phyllis L. Rickey) Stuart, FL 33494
       By right of descent from Thomas Sayre

2742   Feiring, Mrs. Lester J. (Miriam S. Whalin), Sarasota, FL 34241
       By right of descent from Robert Dutch

2799   Finenco, Mrs. John, Jr.(Clara Nell Newsom), Miami, FL 33143
       By right of descent from James Trowbridge

2805   Frantz, Mrs. Leonard Edwin (Jeanne Gould Dills), North Fort Myers, FL 33903
       By right of descent from Jan Joosten Van Meteren

2614   Gee, Mrs. Herbert C. (Ruth Crew), West Palm Beach, FL 33405
       By right of descent from Nathaniel Merriman

2595   Gluckert, Mrs. Francis A. (Elizabeth Lewis), Satellite Beach, FL 32937
       By right of descent from Nicholas Newlin

2451   Greenleaf, Mrs. John W., Jr. (Dorothy G. Ide), Coral Gables, FL 33146
       By right of descent from Nicholas Ide

2408   Grunwell, Miss Jane Elizabeth, Naples, FL 33940
       By right of descent from James Cudworth

2582   Hirschey, Mrs. Alice Traffarne, Miami, FL 33155
       By right of descent from Thomas Durfee

2389   Hooper, Mrs. Matthew L. (Jessie B. Richmond), Estero, FL 33928
       By right of descent from Giles Driver

2573   Howard, Mrs. Arthur M. (Ruth E. Latchaw), Melbourne, FL 32901
       By right of descent from John Coolidge

1588   Howe, Mrs. Elden L. (Helen D. Bailey) ,Coral Gables, FL 33134
       By right of descent from Elder William Brewster

2500   Huffman, Mrs. Stanley P. (Leona Schubert), Stuart, FL 33497
By right of descent from Henry Farwell

2801   Hutson, Mrs. William Hayes (Pauline Evers Foster), Fort Lauderdale, FL 33304
By right of descent from Charles Gorsuch

2477   Jackson, Mrs. Alison N. (Beaulah Compton), Miami, FL 33056
By right of descent from William DeLa Bowne

2505   Jones, Mrs. William M. (Gayle Fortier), Miami, FL 33157
By right of descent from Louis Juchereau de St. Denis

2812   Kabrich, Mrs. Donald Lee (Marjorie Anne Williams), Floral City, FL 32636
By right of descent from Capt. Thomas Carter

2335   King, Mrs. Sidney S., Jr., (Sarah-Celeste Burnett), Fort Myers Beach, FL 33931
By right of descent from William Farrar

2179   Koski, Mrs. Onni G. (Esther M. Whitten), Satellite Beach, FL 32937
By right of descent from Dr. Grace Sherman Livermore

2432   Lane, Mrs. Harry H. (Imogene T. Hawks), Fort Lauderdale, FL 33310
By right of descent from Eliezer Hawks

2555   Latzer, Mrs. John B. (Martha Frances G. Goss), Delray Beach, FL 33445
By right of descent from George Norton

2633   Lewis, Miss Catherine Bowers, Orlando, FL 32808
By right of descent from John Case

2529   Linskey, Mrs. Edward E., Jr. (Marguerite Dillon), Fort Lauderdale, FL 33308
By right of descent from Samuel Drake

2564   Lonas, Mrs. Leonard L., Jr., (Edna Jo Whisenant) Manassas, VA 22110
By right of descent from Henry Filmer

2811   Love, Miss Marsha Lynn, Delray Beach, FL 33483
By right of descent from Matthew Wallis

2705   McDermott, Mrs. George G. (Martha Louise Latzer), Fort Lauderdale, FL 33308
By right of descent from George Norton

2569   Morrison, Mrs. Richard W. (Geo Laird H. Faw), Fort Lauderdale, FL 33305
By right of descent from Thomas Sayre

2476   Nichols, Mrs. Norton B. (Phyllis Gildersleeve Meakin), Palm Beach, FL 33484
By right of descent from Richard Gildersleeve

2062   Nicholson, Mrs John B. (Nettie A. Gove), Lake Worth, FL 33467
        By right of descent from Edward Gove
1159   Novak, Mrs. Rudolph L. (Isabelle F. Phinney) ,West Borough, MA
        01581
        By right of descent from Dr. Samuel Fuller
2497   Papapetrou, Mrs. Dean, (Nancy Johanna), Cocoa Beach, FL 32932
        By right of descent from Lt. William Spencer
2450   Papenhagen, Mrs. Frank W. (Marion E Defray), Fort Myers, Beach
        FL 33931
        By right of descent from Jacob Theunis DeKay
2718   Park, Mrs. F. D. Ronald, (Helen E. Gates), Delray Beach, FL 33445
        By right of descent from Richard Thayer
2429   Pittman, Mrs. Wilmer T. (Georgie Willey), Portsmouth, VA 23704
        By right of descent from William Thornton
2556   Reusser, Mrs. Patricia Taylor, Studio City, CA 91604
        By right of descent from John Biglo
2428   Rice, Mrs. Clarence M. (Bernice Kinney), Carmi, IL 62821
        By right of descent from Christopher Branch
2200   Slocum, Mrs. Ray E., (Marion Williams), Coral Gables, FL 33133
        By right of descent from Captain John Johnson
2739   Stevenson, Mrs. James T. (Martha Jane Moseley), Winter Haven,
        FL 33880
        By right of descent from David des Marets
2663   Stewart, Mrs Frank C.,Jr.,(Anne G. White), Miami FL 33187
        By right of descent from Colonel Edmund Scarborough
2662   Stewart, Miss Stephanie, Miami FL 33186
        By right of descent from Colonel Edmund Scarborough
2602   Weaver, Mrs. James M., Sr. (Jennie Marguerite Shaw), Fort
        Lauderdale, FL 33304
        By right of descent from Robert Sheppard
2716   Weaver, Miss Mary Alice, Fort Lauderdale, FL 33304
        By right of descent from William Spencer
2715   Weaver, Miss Patricia, Fort Lauderdale, FL 33305
        By right of descent from Samuel Macocke
2427   Wheeler, Mrs. H. Lindsay, Jr. (Janie R. McCaa), Fort Lauderdale,
        FL 33301
        By right of descent from Jabez Whitaker
2460   Whitehurst, Mrs. James L. (Mary N. Quarles), Chapel Hill, NC
        27514
        By right of descent from Colonel William Claiborne
2818   Whitten, Mrs. James Malcolm (Teresa Henderson), Melbourne
        Beach, FL 32951
        By right of descent from Matthew Wallis

2398   Witting, Miss Victoria Leigh, Cherry Hill, NJ 08003
        By right of descent from Edmond Sherman
2672   Yates, Mrs. Harold W., (Jean F. Long), Daytona Beach, FL 32018
        By right of descent from Richard Palgrave

ASSOCIATE MEMBERS

2032   Dunn, Mrs. James B. (Lillian E. Davis), Delray Beach, FL 33444
        By right of descent from Col. Samuel Chew
2049   Hungerford, Mrs. Edward, (Ann Dukes), Sebastian, FL 32958
        By right of descent from Dr. Lewis DeRoachbrune

TEJAS CHAPTER
Number Twenty-Three

Organized April 14, 1977, Mayflower Hotel, Washington, D.C.
Miss Delila M. Baird, Organizing President
President—Miss Josie M. Baird, 909 E.Johnston, Rotan, TX 79546
Registrar—Mrs. Kenneth G. Whisenant, 1297 Lancelot, Abilene, TX 79602

REGISTER OF MEMBERS

Nat'l No.

2717   Allie,Mrs.Richard J.(Linda Elizabeth Brown)Fort Worth,TX 76180
        By right of descent from John Tinker

2650   Augustus ,Mrs. Stanley (Jaunita Sue Pierce),Houston, TX 77069
        By right of descent from Thomas Osborne

*2446   Bachner, Mrs. Thomas E.(Irene Ewing Hoss)Fort Worth,TX 76118
        By right of descent from Henry Thacker

2128   Baird,Miss Josie M.,Rotan, TX 79546
        By right of descent from Col. Ninian Beall

2631   Barnard,Miss Kathleen, Fort Worth, TX 76118
        By right of descent from Henry Thacker

2492   Barnett, Mrs. Carl G.(Margaret Wire), Big Spring,TX 79720
        By right of descent from Major Nathan Gold

2363   Bell,Mrs.Charles Smith, (Jane Woodward), Brownwood,TX 76801
        By right of descent from Col.Thomas Pettus

2367   Blackard,Mrs.Melvin K.(Ophelia Dorward), Snyder,TX 79549
        By right of descent from Anthony Armistead

2293   Canter, Mrs. Dencil Eugene (Lorraine Clemmons), Hempstead,
        TX 77445
        By right of descent from Col. Thomas Pettus

2245   Clark,Mrs.Henry F.(Virginia Preuitt)Snyder,TX 79549
        By right of descent from Joseph Clark

2263   Clark,Mrs.John W.(Joe Heathington)Box 836, Rotan,TX 79546
        By right of descent from Capt. George Dennison

2464   Dawson,Mrs.W.N.(Helen Wilhemina Huling Cobean), Big Spring,
        TX 79720
        By right of descent from Gilbert Updike

2419   Dulaney, Mrs. Gene L. (Mary Arthur Bloomer), Snyder, TX 79549
        By right of descent from Robert Bloomer II

2358   Edwards Frances, Lt . Col . USAF, Ret . Longview, TX 75601
        By right of descent from Thomas Willoughby

2437   Gibson, Mrs. Hubert Lynn(Norma Jean Sparks), Salinas,KS 67401
        By right of descent from John Washington

2756   Gude, Mrs. Elmer W. (Elizabeth Kelsey Warren), San Antonio, TX
        78230
        By right of descent from Lt.Col.Richard Cocke
2634   Harmonson, Mrs. Alva B.(Paulyne Robbins), Keller,TX 76248
        By right of descent from Brian (Bryan) Stott, Sr.
2270   Harris ,Mrs. Alfred P. (Lillian Lore Renfro), Kermit,TX 79745
        By right of descent from Col. Thomas Pettus
2391   Harris, Miss Nanci Dianne; Jr. #59, Odessa, TX 79763
        By right of descent from Col. Thomas Pettus
2390   Harris ,Miss Sandra Susan; Jr. #58, Odessa 79763
        By right of descent from Col. Thomas Pettus
2395   Heathington,Miss Gail Ann; Jr.#60, Rotan,TX 79546
        By right of descent from Capt. George Dennison
2343   Herod, Miss Kelly Lynn; Jr.#53, Fort Worth,TX 76133
        By right of descent from Thomas Walling
2271   Hurt,Mrs. Randolph D.; Jr. (Lorena Ann Hurt)Fort Stockton,TX
        79735
        By right of descent from Col. Thomas Pettus
2732   Jones,Mrs.Felix Henley,Jr.(Lide Summers Black),San Antonio,TX
        78230
        By right of descent from Lt. Col.John Epes
2453   Longbotham, Mrs. Bernard,Jr.(Sadie Estelle Jenkins), Snyder,TX.
        79549
        By right of descent from John Conger(Belconger)
2436   Mclntyre,Miss Christine Sue; Jr.#64, Alice, TX 78332
        By right of descent from Henry Thacker
2249   McIntyre, Mrs. Robert R.(Mary Patrice Whisenant), Alice,Texas
        78332
        By right of descent from Henry Thacker
2368   Moore, Miss Candace Nealie, Brownwood,TX-76801
        By right of descent from James Shelton
2246   Morrow, Mrs. Ruple(Vera Adams), Rotan, TX 79546
        By right of descent from Col. Thomas Graves
2594   Neidemairer,Mrs.Edward John(Louise Pullen), Dallas,TX 75228
        By right of descent from Brian (Bryan) Stott
2294   Nelson, Mrs. Lawrence T.(Ethel Void), Sweetwater ,TX 79556
        By right of descent from Nathaniel Turner
2545   Prince, Mrs. Hiram Thomas(Claudine Southard), Portales,NM
        By right of descent from Col.Thomas Pettus
2314   Russ, Mrs. Rolan G. (Helen Gertrude Vandervort), Hale Center,TX
        79041
        By right of descent from Joris Jansen de Rapalje
2731   Sherman, Mrs. Winthrop C.(Nancy Ruth Collier), Fort Worth,TX
        76133
        By right of descent from John Waller

2402   Sparks, Mrs. Laurence (Jane Sutton) Rotan,TX 79546
        By right of descent from Col.John Washington
2272   Thomas, Mrs. Ernest (Rebecca Lynn Harris), Odessa, TX 79760
        By right of descent from Col. Thomas Pettus
2568   Truitt, Mrs. Robert R. (Dorothy Lynne Butler), Fort Worth,TX
        76112
        By right of descent from Francis Billingsley
2255   Tutt, Mrs. Ferhlin (Connie Aline Hayter), Rotan, TX 79546.
        By right of descent from Christopher Branch
2248   Whisenant, Mrs. Kenneth G. (Mary Sue Scales), Abilene, TX
        79602
        By right of descent from Henry Thacker
2596   Williamson, Mrs. Morris (Connie Estelle Longbotham), Odessa,TX
        79762
        By right of descent from John Conger (Belconger)

TERRITORIAL CHAPTER
Number Twenty-Four

Organized January 6, 1982, Phoenix, AZ
Mrs. J. Montgomery Smith, Organizing President
President — Mrs. Frank J. Windolph, 5838 Camino Esplendora, Tucson, AZ 85718
Registrar — Mrs. Robert I. Bezanson, 749 W. Las Lomitas, Tucson, AZ 85704

REGISTER OF MEMBERS
Nat'l No.
2655 Bezanson, Mrs. Robert I. (Priscilla Hutchins), Tucson, AZ 85704
By right of descent from Joshua Ely
2447 Chmiel, Mrs. Frank S. (Elizabeth B. McKinney), Tucson, AZ 85716
By right of descent from Deacon Samuel Chapin
2823 Concannon, Mrs. James N. (Marian Hagan), Tucson, AZ 85716
By right of descent from Major William Phillips
2625 Crull, Mrs. Ralph L. (Verite L. Greene), Tucson, AZ 85713
By right of descent from Thomas Welles
2481 Finch, Mrs. Stuart M. (Dorothy E. Standish), Green Valley, AZ 85614
By right of descent from Myles Standish
2562 Garrigus, Miss Alice J., Phoenix, AZ 85008
By right of descent from John Root
2170 Glenn, Mrs. Luther A. (Fay E. Black), Sun City, AZ 85351
By right of descent from Burr Harrison
2480 Hardy, Mrs. George A. (Mary A. Taylor), San Benito, TX 78586
By right of descent from Anthony Taylor
*2061 Hubbard, Mrs. Glenn W. (Elizabeth F. Frederick), Tucson, AZ 85704
By right of descent from Major Lawrence Smith
2478 Hunter, Miss Mildred, Phoenix, AZ 85015
By right of descent from William Ball
2796 Peep, Miss Patricia Lynn, Tucson, AZ 85730
By right of descent from Deacon Samuel Chapin
2795 Peep, Miss Susan Renee, Tucson, AZ 85730
By right of descent from Deacon Samuel Chapin
2479 Scheurs, Miss Patricia Anne, Tucson, AZ 85712
By right of descent from Samuel Gorton
2740 Smith, Mrs. Franklin H., (Rose Eleanore Hayes), Tucson, AZ 85745
By right of descent from Leonard Calvert
2563 Swanson, Miss Georgianna M., Phoenix, AZ 85018
By right of descent from Joseph Jewett
2616 Swanson, Mrs. Dewey Raymond (Stella Louise Clearman), Phoenix, AZ 85018
By right of descent from Joseph Jewett
2824 Vath, Mrs. Donald L. (Kerry Ann Concannon), Tucson, AZ 85745
By right of descent from Major William Phillips
2566 Windolph, Mrs. Frank J. (Dixie A. Chrismer), Tucson, AZ 85718
By right of descent from Joshua Pratt

* SUPPLEMENTAL LINES LISTED IN ANCESTOR INDEX

LOUISIANA CHAPTER
Number Twenty-Five

Organized December 15, 1982, Baton Rouge, Louisiana
Mrs. George Carl Hofmeister, Organizing President
President — Mrs. Z. T. Landrum, 208 Clem Drive, Lafayette, LA 70503.
Registrar — Mrs. Lowell A. Elrod, 11136 Glenhaven Dr., Baton Rouge, LA 70815.

REGISTER OF MEMBERS

Nat'l No.

2350   Hofmeister, Mrs. George Carl, Baton Rouge, LA 70815.
By right of descent from Andrew Ward.

2475   Olausen, Mrs. Fredrik G., Baton Rouge, LA 70815—5314.
By right of descent from Humphrey Booth.

2503   Costelloe, Mrs. Robert J., II, Cypress, TX 77429
By right of descent from William Buckman.

2510   Elrod, Mrs. Lowell A., Baton Rouge, LA 70815.
By right of descent from Capt. George Dennison.

2515   Breffeilh, Mrs. George A., Lake Charles, LA 70605.
By right of descent from Samuel Bass.

2522   Saloom, Mrs. Richard G., Lafayette, LA 70502.
By right of descent from Capt. William Lewis

2523   Gremillion, Mrs. Charles M., Falls Church, VA 22041.
By right of descent from Capt. William Lewis

2524   Saloom, Miss Rosalyn Ann, Lafayette, LA 70502.
By right of descent from Capt. William Lewis

2531   Collier, Mrs. H. Grady, Jr., Metairie, LA 70005.
By right of descent from Lawrence Smith.

2539   Zatarain, Mrs. Charles C., III, Metairie, LA 70003.
By right of descent from Lawrence Smith.

2699   Landrum, Mrs. Z. T., Lafayette, LA 70503.
By right of descent from Robert Moulton.

2749   David, Mrs. Salem K., New Orleans, LA 70118.
By right of descent from William Ball.

MEMBERS-AT-LARGE

Nat'l No.
2719   Bailey, Mrs. William, Wesley, AR 72273.
       By right of descent from Richard Smith.
2239   Brannan, Mrs. Charles (Helen Louise McDonald), Fayetteville,
       AR 72701.
       By right of descent from Stephen Hopkins.
2199   Brumfield, Mrs. Roy (Katharine Mudge Prichard), Fayetteville,
       AR 72701.
       By right of descent from William Prichard.
2220   Campbell, Hayden Hucke, Webster Groves, MO 63119.
       By right of descent from Philip Pendleton.
2581   Chaney, Mrs. Lowell, Fayetteville, AR 72703.
       By right of descent from Francis Mauldin.
1675   Ellis, Miss Elizabeth Dupree, Fayetteville, AR 72701.
       By right of descent from Isaac Stearns.
1676   Gray, Mrs. William R. (Ruth Lowary), Portland, OR 97266.
       By right of descent from John Richmond.
2750   Hanna, Mrs. Robert C., Berryville, AR 72616.
       By right of descent from Edward Lloyd.
2124   Leming, Mrs. Howell E. (Lorena Lowe), Fayetteville, AR 72701.
       By right of descent from Thomas Burnham.
2512   Lines, Mrs. Joan F., Fayetteville, AR 72701.
       By right of descent from Phillip Pendleton of VA.
2766   Lucas, Cynthia, c/o Mrs. William Bailey, Wesley, AR 72273.
       By right of descent from John Bailey.
2354   Pietsch, Mrs. Carl E. (Laura Grace Brooks), New Brighton, MN
       55112.
       By right of descent from John Kingsley I.
2359   Rogers, Mrs. Richard (Lucille Alexandra Long), Springdale, AR
       72764.
       By right of descent from Edward Lloyd.
2258   Sharp, Mrs. William, Fayetteville, AR 72701.
       By right of descent from Peter Montague.
1862   Shelton, Mrs. Ellis E. (Ruth Wiggins), Fayetteville, AR 72703.
       By right of descent from Joshua Hoopes.
2014   Shelton, Miss Patty, Little Rock, AR 72205.
       By right of descent from Joshua Hoopes.
2368   Shelton, Miss Rhea Louise, San Francisco, AR 94115.
       By right of descent from Joshua Hoopes.
1981   Thomas, Dr. Elizabeth C., Fayetteville, AR 72701.
       By right of descent from Col. John George.

2572   Williams, Mrs. Earl, Fayetteville, AR 72703.
By right of descent from John Garner.

2204   Williams, Mrs. Eugene J. (Martha W. R. Gross), Fayetteville, AR 72701.
By right of descent from Edwin Conway.

JUNIOR MEMBERS-AT-LARGE

2430   Williams, Mary Julianna, Conway, AR 72032.
By right of descent from Edwin Conway.

INDEX OF ANCESTORS
AND
LIVING DESCENDANT MEMBERS

ABBOTT, GEORGE, 1631-1688/9. Proprietor Andover before 1681.Constable, 1680. Member Serg't. James Osgood's Military Co., 1658-1659.

ABBOTT, GEORGE, 1615-1680. One of the first settlers of Andover, Mass., 1643. In garrison at Andover, 1675.

ABBOTT, DANIEL,—— 1709. Served in King Philip's War, 1675/6. Town Clerk, Providence, R.I., 1677-1681. Deputy, 1694.

ABBOTT, WALTER,—— before 1675. Highway surveyor, Portsmouth, N.H., 1658. Selectman, Portsmouth, 1664.

ABEEL, CHRISTOPHER, 1621-1684. Deacon of the First Reformed Church, Albany, N.Y., 1658. Magistrate, 1658. Commissary,1663,1664.
Denton, Mrs. E. Brady   Michigan

ABEEL, JOHANNES, 1667-1711. Justice, 1689. Councilman, 1688,1690. Alderman, 1691—1692.
Denton, Mrs. E. Brady   Michigan

ABEEL, PRESERVED, 1644-1724. Surveyor, Rehoboth, Mass., 1670. Constable, 1671. Serg't., 1689, 1690. Lieut. in Capt. Gallup's Expedition against Canada, 1690. Narragansett Campaign, 1675.
Williams, Mrs. Harold Pardon   Rhode Island

ABELL, CALEB, 1646-1731. Constable, Norwich, Conn., 1684. Selectman,1682.

ADAMS, ALEXANDER,—— died before 1677. Born in England. Owned property in Boston, 1645. Admitted to church, 1645. Freeman, 1648. A & H.A. Co., 1652, 1st. Sergeant, 1656.

ADAMS, ENS. EDWARD, 1629-1716. Appointed Ensign of Medfield,Mass. Militia, 1681. Rep. Medfield at General Court, 1689-1692.

ADAMS, GEORGE,—— 1696. Born in England. Served in King Philip's War, 1675/6, from Watertown, Mass.

ADAMS, HENRY, 1583-1646. Born in England. Selectman of Braintree, Mass., 1646, and its first Town Clerk.
Smith, Mrs. James   Founders
Weaver, Mrs. John F., Sr.   Michigan

ADAMS, ENS. HENRY, 1663-1747. Ensign, Medfield, Mass., 1681-1699.

ADAMS, JEREMY, 1604-1683. Deputy from Hartford, Conn., 1638. Constable, 1639. Original proprietor of Hartford, Conn.
Steele, Mrs. L. Pat   Member-at-Large
Thompson, Mrs. Arthur A.   Tennessee
Tittsworth, Mrs. Doris T.   Member-at-Large

ADAMS, ROBERT, died after 11 Jan. 1628. Born in Wales. Member of Virginia House of Burgesses from Martin's Hundred, 1623-1624.
Portwood, Mrs. Ken B.   Tennessee
Wiley, Mrs. William Lance   Tennessee

ADAMS, CAPT. SAMUEL, 1617-1689. Born in England, Selectman, 1663-1688. Town Clerk, 1668-1687. Capt. of Foot, Chelmsford, Mass., 1682.
Weaver, Mrs. John F., Sr.   Michigan

ADAMS, LIElJT. THOMAS, —— 1688. Born in England. Chief Serg't of Military Company, Chelmsford, Mass. Ensign, 1678. Lieut., 1682. Selectman, 1658, 1660, 1662, 1664-1672, 1674-1677. Deputy, 1673. King Philip's War, 1675/6. Member Ancient and Honorable Artillery Company, 1644.

ADAMS, WILLIAM, SR., —— 1661. Born in England. Selectman, Ipswich, Mass., 1646.
Greason, Mrs. James B.   Founders

ADAMS, REV. WILLIAM, 1650-1685. Minister at Dedham, Mass., 1672-1685.
Greason, Mrs. James B., Jr.   Founders

ADVERD, (ADFORD), HENRY, circa 1621-1653. Name on Scituate Mass. Company list, 1643.

ALBRO, MAJ. JOHN, 1617-1712. Corporal, Portsmouth, R.I. of the Colonial Militia, 1644, 1661-1666. Lieut., 1675. Capt., 1676. In May 1680, 1681, 1682, Major of the Militia. Commissioner, 1660, 1661. Governor's Assistant, 1671, 1672, 1677-1686. Member of Governor Andros' Council, 1686.

ALCOCK, DR. GEORGE,—— 1640. Deputy from Roxbury, Mass., to General Court of Mass. Bay, 1634-1637.

ALCOCK, DR. JOHN, 1621-1667. School Teacher, Hartford, Conn., 1647. Physician in Boston when he died in 1667.

ALDEN, JOHN, 1599-1687. Passenger on the Mayflower, 1620. Governor's Assistant, 1632, 1633, 1634-1639, 1650-1686. Deputy from Duxbury, Mass. 1641-1649. Treasurer of the Colony, 1656-1659. Member of the Councils of War, 1646, 1653, 1658, 1667.

Alden, Miss (Olive) Priscilla	Rhode Island
Headlee, Mrs. James	Michigan
Weaver, Mrs. John F., Sr.	Michigan
Webster, Miss Harriet	Missouri

ALDEN,PRISCILLA(Mullines), 1602-1685. Died Duxbury, Mass. Mayflower Passenger, 1620

Weaver, Mrs. John F., Sr.	Michigan

ALDRICH, GEORGE—— 1683. One of first settlers of Mendon, Mass., 1663.

Milburn, Mrs. John T.	Blue Grass

ALLEN, BENJAMIN, 1652-1723. Born at Salisbury, Mass, died at Rehoboth, Mass. Served in King Philip's War, 1675.

ALLEN, DANIEL, Episcopal Rector at Yorktown, Virginia, 1665-1670.

ALLEN, GEORGE, 1568-1648. Born in England. Deputy from Sandwich, Mass., 1640-1642.

ALLEN, GIDEON, SR., 1640-1693. Served in King Philip's War, 1675. Died at Milford, Conn.

ALLEN, NEHEMIAH, 1649-1684. Constable, Northampton, Mass., 1672.

ALLEN, RALPH,—— 1698. One of the nine men chosen to govern Rehoboth, Mass., 1644, and named in the first council that year.

ALLEN, RICHARD, —— 1715. Middlesex Co., VA. Foot soldier in the Militia.

Schorn, Mrs. Leslie Norman	Oklahoma

ALLEN, DEA. SAMUEL, 1632-1703. Served in King Philip's War, 1675/6. One of the original landed proprietors of East Bridgewater, Mass. Town Clerk, 1683. Representative to General Court of Mass., Commissioner, 1687. Town Representative to Plymouth, 1689. Deputy 1693. Deacon.
Cox, Mrs. Ralph Lionel						Pennsylvania
Weaver, Mrs. John F., Sr.						Michigan

ALLERTON, ISAAC, 1583-1659. Born in England. Passenger on Mayflower, 1620. Governor's Assistant, 1634. Member of the Representative Body of New Netherlands known as "The Eight Men," 1643.

ALLERTON, MARY (Norris),—— 1621. (Wife of Isaac Allerton) Passenger on the Mayflower 1620.

ALLING, ROGER, —— 1674. New Haven Colony, 1638-1639. Sergeant in first military company, and only selected Treasurer of New Haven Colony until 1669.

ALLIS, CAPT. WILLIAM,—— 1678. Born in England. Lieut. of Troop of Horse, Hampshire Co., Mass., 1672. In command of the Guard at Hatfield, 1677. Magistrate, Hampshire Co. Court, 1676-1678.

ALLYN, MATTHEW, 1605-1670/1. One of the original Proprietors of Hartford, Conn. Representative to the General Court from Windsor, Conn., 1648-1658, excepting 1653. Magistrate of the Colony, 1657-1667. Commissioner for the United Colonies of New England, 1660-1664. Name appears as grantee on Charter by Charles II.
Syring, Mrs. W. Vernon						Michigan

ALLYN, ROBERT, 1608-1683, of Salem, Mass., and Norwich Ct., Constable, 1649. Founder of Norwich Ct., 1656. Secretary at General Court, 1657.

ALMY, WILLIAM, 1601-1676. Born in England. Commissioner from Portsmouth, R.I., 1656, 1657, 1663.
Cornish, Mrs. Albert C.						Conn.Farms
Deal, Mrs. Henry C.						North Carolina

ANDREW, SAMUEL, 1621-1701. Born in England. Constable, Cambridge, Mass., 1666. Selectman, 1681-1693. Town Clerk, 1682-1693. County Treasurer, 1683-1699. Town Treasurer, 1694-1699.

ANDREW, REV. SAMUEL, 1655/6-1737/8. Ordained pastor of church at Milford, Conn., 1685, and served 52 years. One of the founders of Yale College and at one time its acting president.

ANDREW, WILLIAM,—— 1652. Born in England. Constable at Cambridge, Mass., 1635-1640. Selectman, 1635.

ANDREW, HENRY,—— 1653. Born in England. Deputy from Taunton, Mass., 1639, 1643-1649.

ANDREWS, JAMES, before 1635 circa 1684. Born in England, died old Rappahannock Co., Va. Served at Forts on Rappahannock River during Indian attacks, 1675.

ANDREWS, JOSEPH, 1597-1679/80. Born in England. First Town Clerk, Hingham, Mass., 1635, 1636, 1637, 1638. Constable, 1635. Deputy, 1636, 1637, 1638. Surveyor at Duxbury, 1654. Constable, 1664.

ANDREWS, SAMUEL,—— 1693. Oyster Bay and Burlington Co., N.J. One of Proprietors of Oyster Bay, 1665. Surveyor, 1668, 1669. Overseer, 1669. Constable at Oyster Bay, 1676.

ANDREWS, CAPT. THOMAS, 1632-1690. Constable, Hingham, Mass. Selectman, 1670, 1672, 1679, 1685, 1687, 1688. Deputy, 1678. Deputy to Council of Safety, 1689. Captain, King William's War, 1690.

ANDREWS, LIEUT. WILLIAM,—— 1676. Sergeant, New Haven,Conn., 1642. Lieutenant of Artillery, 1648.
Milburn, Mrs. John T.   Blue Grass

ANGELL, JOHN, 1646-1720. Served in King Philip's War, 1675. Deputy, Rhode Island, 1686.

ANGELL, THOMAS, 1618-1694. Born in England. Commissioner from Providence, R.I., 1652-1653. Constable, 1655. Town Clerk,1658-1675.
Malmstead, Miss Helen Josephine   Rhode Island
Smith, Mrs. Julian C.   Jamestown

ANTHONY, CORP. JOHN, 1607-1675. Born in England. Corporal at Portsmouth, R.I., 1644. Deputy from Providence, 1661. From Portsmouth, 1666-1672.

APPLEGATE, THOMAS,—— 1662/3. Patentee, Flushing, Long Island, 1645

APPLETON, SAMUEL, 1586-1670. Deputy from Ipswich, Mass., 1637. Served in Pequot War of 1637. Associate Justice of the Quarter Court, 1637.

ARMISTEAD, ANTHONY, —— ——. Deputy Treasurer Elizabeth City County, VA 1687.
Blackard, Mrs. Melvin K.   Texas

ARMS, WILLIAM, 1654-1731. Served in King Philip's War, 1675/6. Constable, Deerfield, MA.
Barringer, Mrs. Phil Louis   North Carolina
Norwood, Mrs. Danny Robinson   North Carolina

ARNOLD, GOV., BENEDICT, 1615-1678. Born in England. Commissioner from Newport, Warwick, Portsmouth, and Providence, R.I., 1654-1663. Governor's Assistant, 1655, 1660, 1661. President of Providence Plantations, 1657-1660, 1662, 1663. Governor of Rhode Island, 1663-1666, 1669-1672, 1677, 1678.

ARNOLD, BENEDICT, JR., 1641-1727. Deputy, 1686, 1690, 1699. Overseer of Poor, 1687. Assistant, 1690, 1691-1696. Rhode Island.

ARNOLD, CAPT. CALEB., 1644-1719. Deputy from Portsmouth, R.I., 1671-1680. Member of Court Martial during King Philip's War, 1675.

ARNOLD, ELISHA, 1661-1710. Born in Salem, Mass. Deputy, Pawtucket, R.I., 1699.

ARNOLD, JOHN, 1658-1719. Born in England. School Master, Newark, N.J., 1678, at Killingsworth, Conn., 1679, 1680, at Norwich, Conn., 1681—1690, at Mansfleld, Conn., 1690.

ARNOLD, STEPHEN, 1622-1699. Born in England. Deputy, Providence, R.I., 1664, 1665, 1667, 1670, 1672, 1674, 1677, 1684, 1685, 1690. Governor's Assistant, 1672, 1677, 1680, 1690, 1696, 1698.

ARNOLD, WILLIAM, 1587-1676. Born in England. One of the thirteen original proprietors of Providence Plantations, 1640. Commissioner from Pawtucket, 1661.

ASHFORDBY, WILLIAM, baptized 1638-after 1697. Member of First New York Assembly. Sheriff of Ulster Co., N.Y. appointed Oct.1683.

ASHTON, CART. CHARLES, 1621/25-1672. Justice of Peace. Capt. of Militia, Northumberland. Listed as Commissioner, Court held for Northumberland Co., 30 July 1659 and Oct. 1669.
Roberts, Mrs. Glenn Franklyn   Blue Grass

ATEN. ADRIAEN HENDRICKSE,1696. Constable, Flatbush,L.I., 1665.

ATHERTONS, MAJ. GEN. HUMPHREY, 1609-1661. Born in England. Deputy from Dorchester, Mass., 1638, 1639, 1641, 1643-1646, 1648, 1650, 1651, 1653. Governor's Assistant 1654-1661. Commissioner of United Colonies, 1653. Lieutenant, 1643. Captain of Dorchester Co., 1646. Ensign of the Ancient and Honorable Artillery Company of Boston, 1645. Lieutenant, 1646. Captain, 1650, 1658. Major General of Mass. Troops, 1661.

ATTAWAY, CAPT. THOMAS,—— 1709. Commissioner of St. Mary's County, Va., 1694. Captain and Justice.

AVERY, CHRISTOPHER, 1590-1679. Born in England. Selectman of Gloucester, Mass., 1646, 1652, 1654. Constable, 1647. Clerk of the Court, 1652. Served in Pequot War, 1637.
Browder, Mrs. E. Jefferson   CT Farms

AVERY, CAPT. JAMES, SR., 1620-1700. Born in England. Deputy from New London, Conn., 1659-1661, 1664-1665, 1667-1669, 1675-1678, 1680, 1682-1686, 1689, 1690, 1692, 1694, 1695, 1697. Marshal of the Court, 1676, Assistant Military officer of New London Co., 1672. Captain in King Philip's War, 1675, and of the Train Band of New London, 1681.
Browder, Mrs. E. Jefferson   CT Farms

AVERY, CAPT. JAMES, JR., 1646-1728. Born in Gloucester, Mass. Served in King Philip's War, 1675. Sergt., 1683. Lieutenant, 1690. Captain, 1692. Deputy from New London, Conn., 1690-1699.
Browder, Mrs. E. Jefferson   CT Farms

AVERY, CAPT. THOMAS, 1651-1736. Commissioned Capt. of the Train Band, New London Ct., May, 1693. Deputy from New London, 1694. Served in King Philip's War, 1675/6; also in Winthrop's Expedition to Canada, 1690.
Browder, Mrs. E. Jefferson   CT Farms

AVERY, WILLIAM, M.D., 1622-1687. Born in England. Physician at Dedham and Boston. Deputy from Dedham, Mass., 1669. Sergt., 1669. Lieutenant, 1673.

AYER, CORNET PETER, 1633-1699. Cornet of Military Co., Haverhill, Mass., and Deputy, 1680.

AYER, JOHN,—— 1657. Selectman of Haverhill, Mass., 1647.

AYER (S), OBADIAH, 1635/36-1694. Schepen of the town of Woodbridge, N.J. at meeting of the Council of War of New Netherlands held at Fort Willem Hendrick, 24 Aug. 1673.

AYER, THOMAS,—— 1686. Served in King Philip's War, 1676, from Haverhill, Mass.

AYRES, SERGT. JOHN, 1643-1675. Killed near Brookfield, Mass., while serving in King Philip's War.
Browder, Mrs. E. Jefferson   CT Farms

BABCOCK, JAMES, SR., 1612-1679. Born in England. Deputy from Portsmouth, R.I., 1642, 1657-1659.

BABCOCK, CAPT. JAMES, 1633-1736. Captain of Militia before 1690. Town Treasurer. Councilman, 1690, 1693, 1695, of Westerly, R.I.

BABCOCK, JOHN, 1644-1685. Deputy from Westerly, R.I. to General Assembly, 1682, 1684.

BACHILER (BATCHELDER), REV. STEPHEN, 1561-1660. Born in England. First pastor of church, Lynn, Mass., 1632; also of Hampton, N.H., 1638.

BACKER (BAKER), JACOBUS, 1631-after 1669. Shepen, 1656-1669.
Finfgeld, Mrs. Clifford   Illinois

BACON, SAMUEL, 5 July 1627-Nov. 1693. Born in England, died Beacon Neck, N.J. Woodbridge, Mass. Constable, 1678. Magistrate, 1681. Justice, 1688. Member of Provincial Assembly,1685.
Hires, Mrs. Charles Edgar   Pennsylvania
Whealen, Mrs. John J.   Pennsylvania

BAGWELL, HENRY, 1590-1633. "Ancient Planter," Va. Clerk of the first court of Northampton Co., Va., 1637. Member of House of Burgesses, from Accomack, Mar. 1629-1630, and Sept. 1632.
Butterfield, Mrs. John H.   Illinois

BAILEY/BAILY/BAYLY, Joel, B. 1658-d. 1762. Constable of Middletown, PA 1697-'98.
Buckley, Mrs. Thomas Mac   Tennessee

BAILEY, JOHN,—— 1686. Selectman, Freetown, Mass., 1685.

BAILEY, JOHN —— 1690 Served under Gen. Phipps in expedition against Canada in 1690.
Lucas, Mrs. Cynthia Bailey   Member-at-Large

BAILEY, JOHN, JR., circa 1613-1691. Selectman, 1665/6, Newbury, Mass. Constable, 1673. Surveyor of Highways, 1665/6.

BAKER, HENRY,—— after 1698. Member of Provincial Assembly, Bucks Co., Pa., 1685, 1687, 1688, 1690, 1698. Justice of the Peace for Bucks Co., 1689-1698.

BAKER, JOSEPH, circa 1655-1716. Dec., 1686, chosen Constable for Gilead, Chester Co., Pa.
Johnson, Mrs. Charles Morris   Illinois

BAKER, NATHANIEL, 1655-1739. Born in Easthampton, L.I. Trustee of Easthampton, 1693.

BAKER, ENS. THOMAS, 1618-1700. Born in England. Magistrate, Easthampton, L.I., 1651, 1660. Deputy to Hempstead Assembly, 1665. Justice in the Court of Assizes in New York, Southampton and Southold, 1675. Ensign of Troops in Easthampton, 1685.

BALCH, JOHN, 1579-1648. Born in England. One of the four trusty men known as "Old Planters," who founded Salem, Mass., about 1626. Selectman and one of the first thirteen executive rulers of the town.

BALCOM, ALEXANDER, —— 1711. Deputy, Rhode Island, 1683.

BALDRIDGE, JAMES —— ca 16 Jan 1659. Member of first Assembly St. Mary's City , MD 26 Feb 1635.
Richards, Mrs. James Morrow, Jr.   Blue Grass
Richards, Miss Katherine Carson   Blue Grass

BALDWIN, JOHN,—— 1687. Served in Garrison No. 6 at James Pattersons during King Philip's War, 1675/6.
Golden, Mrs. Winifred C.   Prairie State

BALDWIN, JONATHAN, 1649-1739. Selectman, Milford, Conn., 1696-1697.

BALDWIN, JOSEPH,—— 1684. One of the Founders and First Settlers of Milford, Conn., 1639.

BALDWIN, RICHARD, 1622-1665. Settled in Milford, Conn., 1639. Member of New Haven Colony Troop, 1654. Member of Milford General Court, 1662-1664.

BALL, COL. WILLIAM, 1615-1672. Born in England. Colonel, Northumberland Co., Virginia, 1673. Presiding Magistrate and Colonel Commandant, 1680.
David, Mrs. Salem K.   Louisiana
Hunter, Miss Mildred   Territorial

BALLARD, JOSEPH, —— after 1712. Constable of Andover, Mass., 1688.

BALLARD, WILLIAM, 1602-1641. Born in England. Member of Ancient and Honorable Artillery Co., Mass., 1638.

BALLARD, WILLIAM, 1617-1689. Member Ancient and Honorable Artillery Co. of Boston, 1638. Member Military organization, Andover, 1658/9.

BANCROFT, LIEUT. THOMAS, circa 1622-1691. Born in England, settled in Dedham, Mass., before 1648. Chosen Lieut. in Lynn Co., King Philip's War, stationed at Dunstable and Groton, 1675.

BANGS, EDWARD, 1592-1678. Born in England. First Treasurer of Eastham, Mass., 1646-1665. Deputy to Colony Court, 1647, 1650, 1663-1670. Capt. of the Guard against Indians and a member of the Plymouth Military Co., 1643.

BANKS, JOHN, —— 1684. Deputy from Fairfield, Conn., 1651, 1661,1663-1666, 1671, 1673. Deputy from Rye, N.Y., 1671-1672.

BANTA, EPKE JACOBSE, 1619-1686. Born in Holland. Member of the Special Court of Oyer and Terminer at Bergen, N.J., 1679.
Smith, Mrs. Malcolm G.   CT Farms

BARBER, THOMAS, 1614-1662. Served in Pequot War, 1637, from Windsor, Conn.

BARHAM, CHARLES, 1626/7-1666/7, from Kent, England to Surry Co., Va., circa 1654. Vestryman, 1661, Justice, 1668. Sheriff, 1673.

BARKER, DEP. GOV. JAMES, 1623-1702. Commissioner from Newport to General Court of R.I., 1648, 1661, 1663; from Providence, 1655, 1661. Named in Royal Charter of Charles II, 1663. Governor's Assistant 1663-1666, 1671, 1672, 1676-1678. Deputy from Newport to General Assembly of R.I. and Providence Plantations, 1667, 1669-1671, 1674, 1681, 1683-1686. Deputy Governor, 1678, 1679.

BARKER. JAMES JR., 1617 -1702. Ensign 1648,Deputy Governor 1678.
Howard, Mrs. George F.   Renss.

BARNARD, BARTHOLOMEW,—— 1698. Constable, Hartford, Conn., 1655, 1665.

BARNARD, NATHANIEL, 1642-1716. Trustee of Sherburne. Nantucket, 1687.

BARNARD, RICHARD,—— circa 1698. Constable, Chester Co., Pa.,1691, 1694/5.

BARNARD ROBERT,—— 1682. A Founder of Andover, Mass.

BARNARD, THOMAS, circa 1612-1677. Selectman, Amesbury, Mass., 1654.
Alexander, Mrs. Ernest Ross   North Carolina

BARNES, JOHN,—— 1671. Born in England. Served in Pequot War, 1637.

BARNEY, JACOB, SR., 1601-1673. Born in England. Freeman, 1634.
Deputy to General Court, Salem Mass., 1635-1638, 1647, 1653.
Chace, Miss Shirley N.   Rhode Island

BARRELL, JOHN,—— 1658. Ensign of Artillery, 1656. Fourth Sergt., 1651.
First Sergt., 1654. Resided and died at Boston,Mass.
McCormick, Mrs. Kenneth I.   CT. Farms

BARRETT, JONATHAN, before 1659-after 1713. In Garrison in West
Regiment of Middlesex at Great Brook, 1691-1692. One of the 19
Garrisons at Chelmsford, Mass.

BARTHOLOMEW, WILLIAM, 1602-1680. Born in England. Deputy from
Ipswich, Mass., 1635-1641, 1647, 1650. Town Clerk, 1639. County
Treasurer, 1654-1666. Established the first public school in Ipswich,
1650.

BARTHOLOMEW, LIEUT. WILLIAM, 1640-1697. Born in Ipswich, Mass.
Ensign, Hatfield, Mass., 1689. Lieut., 1691. Deputy from Woodstock,
Conn., 1692.

BARTLETT, CHRISTOPHER, JR., 1655-1711. Born in Newbury, Mass.
Served in Narragansett Campaign, King Philip's War, 1675.

BARTLETT, JOSEPH, SR.,—— 1702. Incorporator and one of the first
settlers of Newton, Mass., 1678.

BARTLETT, JOSEPH, JR., 1673-1750. Served in the expedition to Canada,
1690.

BARTLETT, ENSIGN THOMAS, circa 1594-1654. Born in England. Original Proprietor Watertown, Mass. Selectman, 1639, 1644, 1652, 1654. In Pequot War, 1637. Ensign of Watertown Co., 1645-1654.

BARTON, BENJAMIN, 1645-1720. Deputy from Warwick, R.I., 1679, 1681, 1685, 1690-1696. Governor's Assistant, 1674, 1675, 1683, 1684, 1699.

BARTON, DR. JOHN, —12/1694.Salem, MA 1676 -1694. Physician and apothecary chirurgeon.
Connolly, Mrs. John B.   Florida

BARTON, RUFUS,—— 1648. Magistrate at Warwick, R.I., 1647. Member of first Town Council, 1647.

BASS, JOHN, 1622-1716. Born in Roxbury, Mass. Member Colonial Militia at Roxbury, Mass.

BASS, DEACON SAMUEL, 1600-circa 1694. Deputy to Mass. General Court, 1641—1643 and in later years.
Breffeilh, Mrs. George A.   Louisiana

BASSETT, JOSEPH, circa 1635-1712. Constable, Bridgewater, Mass., 1 Jan. 1669. Selectman, Bridgewater, 7 May 1670. Surveyor, Bridgewater, 16 May 1674.

BASSETT, WILLIAM, —— 1667. Deputy from Duxbury and Sandwich, Mass., to Plymouth Colony General Court, 1640, 1642, 1644, 1648. Volunteer in Pequot War, 1637.

BASSETT, CAPT. WILLIAM, 1600-1671/2. Member of the House of Burgesses, Virginia, 1659.

BASSETT, WILLIAM, 1671-1723. Member of House of Burgesses of Va., 1696-1697.

BATCHELLER, JOSEPH,—— 1647. Deputy to General Court from Wenham, Mass., 1643.

BATES, ELDER EDWARD, 1605-1686. Born in England. Deputy from Boston, Mass., 1639-1641; from Weymouth, 1660.

BATES, JAMES,—— —— Hingham, Mass., Selectman, 1637, 1638, 1651. Representative for Hingham, 1641.

BATES, JOHN, 1642-1716. Served in King Philip's War from Chelmsford, Mass.

BATTAILE, JOHN, will prob. 1707/8. Captain of Rangers, Essex Co., Va., 1692. Burgess from Essex Co., Va., 1692, 1693, 1696, 1697.
Ferrenbach, Mrs. David Bradshaw   Missouri

BAYLY/BAILEY, JOEL, 1658-1732. 9 Jan 1697-'98 Constable, Middletown, PA.
Bryant , Mrs. Julian E.   Florida

BEALE, LIEUT. COL. THOMAS, circa 1621-1700. Born in England. Justice of Peace, York Co., Va., 1652, Major in Militia, 1661. Member King's Council, 1662-1699.
Crowder, Mrs. Roy Hester   North Carolina

BEALL, COL. NINIAN, 1625-1717. Born in Scotland. Major, Calvert Co., Maryland, 1690. Commissioner, Maryland Assembly. Sheriff, 1692. Col. Calvert Co. Militia, 1693. Member of House of Burgesses, 1696.
Baird, Miss Josie Mae   Tejas

BEAMSLEY, WILLIAM,—— 1658. Member Ancient and Honorable Artillery Co. of Boston, Mass., 1656.

BEARDSLEY, WILLIAM, 1605-1661. Born in England. Deputy from Stratford, Conn., 1645, 1651-1653

BEARSE, AUSTIN, 1618-169-. Born in England. Member of Barnstable, Mass., Military Co., 1643.

BEAUCHAMP, EDMUND,—— 1691. Clerk for the Eastern Shore, 1666. Clerk of Somerset Co., Md., 1666-1691.
Harkins, Mrs. John D.   Prairie State
Lepchenske, Miss Jennifer Ann   Prairie State
Lepchenske, Mrs. Herbert A.   Prairie State
Miller, Mrs. E. Randall   Prairie State
Renn, Mrs. Richard L.   Prairie State

BECKWITH, MATTHEW 1610-1681. Planter and original land owner near Lyme, CT 1651. One of the first settlers of Hartford, CT in 1642.
Riddle, Mrs. William M.   Oklahoma

BEEKMAN, COL. GERARDUS, M.D., 1653-1723. Physician and Surgeon. Justice of Kings Co., N.Y., 1685. Capt. of Militia at Flatbush, 1681. Major of all the horse and foot in Kings Co., 1689. Member of Colonial Assembly, 1698, 1699.

BEEKMAN, LIEUT. WILHELMUS, 1623-1707. One of the "Nine Men" at New Amsterdam, 1652. Commissioner of Indian affairs under the Dutch, 1658. Vice-Director of Dutch Colony on the South River, 1658-1664. Schout-Fiscaal there, 1661, and at Esopus, 1664-1671. Burgomaster of New Orange, 1674. Lieut. of Burgher Corps at New Amsterdam, 1651, and at New Orange, 1673. President of Schepen's Court, 1657. Alderman, 1678. Mayor of New York, 1685. Member of Council, 1691-1696.

BEERS, CAPT. RICHARD, 1607-1675. Born in England. An Original Proprietor at Watertown, Mass. Deputy to General Court, 1663-1675. Lieut. in Co. Militia, 1663. Captain during King Philip's War.

BEHEATHLAND, CAPT. ROBERT,—— died by 1628. On list of first planters of Jamestown, Va., according to their station.
James, Mrs. Roland M.   Quivira

BELDEN, DANIEL, 1648-1732. Served in King Philip's War, Hatfield and Deerfield, Mass., 1675. On Committee of Fortifications.

BELDEN, JOHN, circa 1631-1677. Trooper under Capt. John Mason, Wethersfield, Conn., 1657, 1658.

BELCHER, GREGORY, Braintree, Mass. To Boston, 1632; Braintree, 1634. Selectman, 1646.

BELL, LIEUT. FRANCIS, 1689/90. Deputy from Stamford,Conn., to New Haven, 1653-1659, 1661-1664. Magistrate, 1652-1663. Commissioned Lieut., Hartford, 11 Oct. 1666.

BELL, CAPT. JONATHAN, 1641-1699. Born in Stamford, Conn. Selectman, 1674. Lieut., 1672. Capt. 1698.

BELL, LIEUT. JONATHAN, 1664 —— Born in Stamford, Conn. Town Clerk, 1689-1699. Lieut. of a Military Co. at Stamford, 1692.

BENEDICT, LIEUT. THOMAS, 1617-1690. Lieut., Town of Jamaica, 1663. Appointed Magistrate, Jamaica, 1663. Delegate to "General Meeting," N.Y., 1665. Appointed Lieut. Foot Co., Jamaica,1665.Town Clerk, Norwalk, 1664, 1674, 1677. Selectman, 1671-1688.Representative for Norwalk in General Assembly, 1670,1675.Deacon in Norwalk Church.
Adams , Mrs. Kenneth H.   Missouri

BENJAMEN, JOHN, 1598-1645. Arr. Boston, 1632. Appointed Constable by General Court, 1633. Freeman, 1632. Proprietor, Cambridge, Mass.

BENNETT, ADRIAEN WILLEMSE, 1637-circa 1698. Constable, New Utrecht, L.I., 1667. Deacon there, 1677. Commissioner from Gowanus, 1687.

BENNETT, WILLIAM ADRIAENSE, —— 1644. Served in the Indian War of 1643 from Gowanus. L.I.

BENNETT, EDWARD,—— 1645/6. Died in Rehoboth. An Original Proprietor and a Founder of Rehoboth, Mass., 1645.

BENNETT, EDWARD, 1578-before 1664. From London, England to Isle of Wight, Va. Received patent 21 Nov. 1621. Burgess, 1628 from "Bennett's Choice." Commissioner of Va. at Court of England, 1629.

McEachern, Mrs. Laurie	North Carolina
Seifert , Miss Mary Francis	Ohio
Seifert, Mrs. Rudy J.	Ohio
Sherratt, Miss Martha Kembra	North Carolina
Sherratt, Mrs. William A.	North Carolina
Young, Mrs. Arthur L.	Oklahoma

BENSON, CAPT. JOHANNES, 1655-1715. Lieut. in Indian War, 1689. Captain, Albany County Militia, 1690.

BENT, JOHN, 1596-1672. Born in England. Selectman, Sudbury, Mass., 1640. Proprietor, Marlborough, Mass.

BENT, CORP. JOHN, 1635-1717. Corporal of Militia, Sudbury, Mass., 1686.

BERGEN, CAPT. MICHAEL HANSEN, 1646-1732. Born in New Amsterdam. Lieut., 1673. Capt., 1688. Justice of Peace, 1698.

BERNARD, COL. WILLIAM, 1598-1665. Born in England. Member of Virginia House of Burgesses, 1644-1648, 1655-1660. Member King's Council. Colonel in militia.

BETTS, CAPT. RICHARD, 1613-1713. Born in England. Deputy from Newtown to Hempstead, L.I., 1665. High Sheriff, 1678. Magistrate, Newton, 1656. Capt., Queens Co., N.Y., Troops,1663

BETTS, SAMUEL, 1660-circa 1734. Representative from Norwalk, Conn., 1694, 1697.

BETTS, THOMAS Bapt. 3. Dec 1615 -d. between 10 May and 4 Dec 1688. Founder Guilford, CT 1639, and Wilton in 1672.

Wernecke, Mrs. Roland A.	Michigan

BEVERLEY, MAJOR ROBERT, 1641-1687. Born in England. Clerk of Va. House of Burgesses, 1670. Justice of Peace, 1673. Member of Council, 1676. Clerk of House, 1685.

BEVIN, JOHN, 1646-1726. Philadelphia, Pa. Justice of Peace, Phila. Co., Pa., 6 Nov. 1685-1689. Member of Assembly, Phila. Co., 1687, 1695, 1699.

BEZER, EDWARD,—— 1688. Member Pa. Assembly, 1687. Justice,Chester Co., Pa. 1687.
Buck, Mrs. Miller Isaiah   Pennsylvania

BIGELOW (BIGLO), JOHN, 1616-1703. Constable, Watertown, Mass., 1663. Selectman, 1665-1671. Pequot War, 1637.
Gary, Mrs. Dan Carmack   Tennessee
Reusser, Mrs. Patricia Taylor   Florida

BIGGS, LIEUT. JOHN, arrived in colonies, 1664-died 1709. Served with Lieut. George Hall, Sir Richard Nicholl's Regiment, N.Y. Ensign, 1670. Lieut., 1687.

BIGSBY (BIXBY), JOSEPH, 1620/1-1700/1. Served in King Philip's War, Narragansett Campaign, 1676. Selectman, Boxford, Mass.,1689, 1693, 1695, 1696, 1697.

BILES, WILLIAM, 1639-1710. Born in England. Member of Provincial Council of Pennsylvania, 1683. Member of Governor's Council, 1683, 1695. Justice, 1689.

BILL, PHILLIP, 1620-1689. Served in King Philip's War, 1675/6. A Narragansett Grantee.

BILLINGS, JOHN, 1637-1704. Selectman, Concord, Mass., 1672.

BILLINGS, NATHANIEL, JR.,—— 1708. Selectman, Concord,Mass., 1689/90. Served in King Philip's War, 1675/6.

BILLINGSLEY, FRANCIS, 1620 -1684.Calvert Co., MD. 1654 Constable. 1683 Commissioner.
Truitt, Mrs. Robert R.   Tejas

BILLIOU, PIERRE, —— 1702. Schout, Staten Island, 1673.

BIRD, THOMAS,—— 1673. Born in England. Bailiff, Dorchester, Mass., 1654. Selectman, 1657.

BIRDSALL, NATHAN, II, 1640-1696. Joined the community at Oyster Bay, L.I. On 9 Jan. 1685, he was one of freeholders to whom residue of Matinecock was conveyed.

BISCOE, NATHANIEL, 1595-1652. Selectman at Watertown, Mass., 1648-1650.

BISHOP, JOHN, 1604-1660. Magistrate, Guilford, Conn., 1639, 1641, 1642. Selectman, 1656.

BISHOP, REV. JOHN,—— 1694. Born in England. Preached in Stamford, Conn., 1644-1694.

BISSELL, JOHN,—— 1677. Deputy from Windsor, Conn. to the General Court 1642 and later member of First Connecticut Cavalry, 1658.

BISSELL, CAPT. JOHN, SR., 1591-1677. Born in England. Assistant Magistrate, 1654. Captain of Windsor Troopers, King Philip's War, 1675-1676; the Bissell house being the garrison. Deputy from Windsor, Conn., to the General Court, Hartford 1648-1664.

BLACHLEY, THOMAS, 1615-1674. Born in England. Deputy, Branford, Conn., 1667—1670.
Greason, Mrs. James B., Jr.   Founders

BLACKLEACH, RICHARD, 1653-1731. Born in Stratford, Conn. Deputy, 1695-1696, 1698-1699. Commissary at Albany, N.Y.,1690.

BLACKMAN (BLAKEMAN), REV. ADAM, circa 1599-1665. First minister at Stratford, 1640.

BLACKWELL, ROBERT,—— 1717. Born in England. Member New York Assembly, 1693-1695.

BLANCHARD, SAMUEL, 1629-1707. Born in England. Selectman Andover, Mass., 1687. Served in King Philip's War, 1675-1676.

BLANSHAN, MATTHYS,—— 1688. Served in militia under Capt.Pawling, 1670, of Hurley, N.Y.
Long, Mrs. Alfred T.   Founders

BLISS, JOHN, 1640-1702. Born in Hartford, Conn. Surveyor, Springfield, Mass., 1669.

BLISS, SERGT. JONATHAN, 1625-1687. Born in England. Sergt. of Militia, Rehoboth, Mass., 1666.

BLISS, THOMAS,—— 1688. Served in King Philip's War, 1675/6 from Saybrook,Conn.

BLOOMER, ROBERT, 1671/3 -1738/9. Constable of Rye, NY.
Dulaney , Mrs. Gene L.   Tejas

BLOOMFIELD, WILLIAM, 1604-1664. Served in Pequot War from Hartford, Conn.

BODINE, JOHN, circa 1620-1694, of Staten Is., N.Y. A Huguenot and Elder of Dutch Reformed Church, 1664.

BOERUM, WILLEM JACOBS, 1617-before 1698. Magistrate of Flatbush, 1657, 1662, 1663.

BOGAERT, TEUNIS GISBERTSON,—— 1687,Nieuw Amsterdam. Delegate to Convention at Flatbush, 1664; Delegate to Convention at Hemstead, 1665.

BOGARDUS, ANNEKE JANS, 1605-1663. Born in Holland. Received a patent from Gov. Van Twiller for 62 acres on Manhattan Island after death of her second husband. Was a first settler of New Amsterdam, New York.

BOGARDUS, REV. EVERARDUS, 1600-1647. Second minister of the Dutch Church in New Amsterdam. Installed, 8 July 1638.

BOLLEN, CAPT. JAMES,—— 1682. Justice of the peace, 1665, 1676, 1677, 1679, 1681. Secretary of the Province of East Jersey, 1668-1670, 1673-1674, 1679.

BOLLING, JOHN , 1676 -1729. Member of House of Burgesses.
Milbourne, Mrs. C. Gordon   Pennsylvania
Robertson, Miss Margie White   Pennsylvania

BOLLING, ROBERT, 1646-1709. Member of House of Burgesses from Charles City County, Va., 1688, 1691, 1699. Justice, 1698. High Sheriff, 1692, 1699
Ditmore, Mrs. Diana Eugenia   North Carolina
Douglas, Mrs. James W.   North Carolina
Fullerton, Mrs. Richard Neal   North Carolina
Millaway, Mrs. Beverly Kyle, Jr.   North Carolina
Sandlin, Mrs. George Washington   North Carolina

BOLTWOOD, ROBERT,—— 1684. A Founder of Hadley, Mass., 1659. Sergt. of Militia after 1659.

BOND, THOMAS, 1654-1704. Watertown, Mass. Soldier in William Turner's Co., King Philip's War, 1675-1676. In garrison at Springfield, 1676.

BOND, CAPT. WILLIAM, 1625-1695. Born in England. Selectman, Town Clerk and Justice of Watertown, Mass. Member Council of Safety, 1689. Speaker at General Court, 1691, 1692, 1693, 1695.Capt. in Watertown Co., 1682.

BONNELL, NATHANIEL, 1648-after 1696. Born in New Haven, Conn. Member Assembly, Newark, N.J. from Elizabeth, 1692-1694.

BOOSY, LIEUT. JAMES,—— 1649. Born in England. Representative from Wethersfield, Conn., 1639-1649.

BOOTH, HUMPHREY—— ——.Virginia. Justice of Rappahannock Co., Va., 1 Dec. 1656.
Strudwick, Mrs. Lewis C.   Pennsylvania
Patterson, Miss Claudia Gagen   Oklahoma

BOOTH, ENS. JOHN,—— 1707. Ensign of Militia in Southold, L.I., before 1689.

BOOTH, SERGT. JOHN, 1653-1728. Served in King Philip's War, 1675. Deputy from Stratford, Conn., 1696.

BOOTH, RICHARD, 1607-1688. Born in England. Selectman, Stratford, Conn., 1669.

BOOTH, DR. ROBERT,—— 1657. Burgess from York Co., Va., 1653. Physician and Clerk at York Co., Va.
Patterson, Mrs. Louis Winfield   Oklahoma

BORDEN, JOHN, 1640-1716. Born in Portsmouth, R.I. Deputy from Portsmouth, R.I., 1670-1680.

BORDEN, RICHARD, 1601-1671. Born in England. Assistant to Governor of R.I., 1653-1654. Treasurer of Colony of R.I., 1650-1655. Commissioner from Portsmouth, R.I., 1654, 1656-1657. Deputy,1667,1671
McCreary, Mrs. Robert W.   Jamestown Virginia

BORDEN, THOMAS,—— 1676. Deputy from Providence, R.I., 1666, 1670, 1672. Governor's Assistant, 1675, 1676.

BORTON, JOHN, 1634-1687. From England. Died in Burlington Co., N.J. Member of New West Jersey Assembly, 1683-1685. A Signer of West Jersey Concession, 3 March 1676.

BOSMAN, JOHN, 1650-1716. Md. Member of Md. Assembly, 1693, 1694, 1695, 1698, 1699. Justice in Council Somerset Co., Md., 1696, 1697, 1698. High Sheriff same Co., 1697. Naval Officer,1698.
Ziegler, Mrs. Theodore F.   Pennsylvania

BOSTWICK, ARTHUR, 1603-after 10 Dec. 1680. One of the first 17 settlers of Stratford, Conn., 1639. Died there.

BOSWORTH, JONATHAN, 1611-1687. Born in England. First settler Rehoboth, Mass., now Attleboro. Constable, 1669.

BOSWORTH, JOSEPH,—— ——.Of Mass. Soldier in King Philip's War. 1675-1676.

BOTSFORD, CORP. HENRY,—— ——.One of first settlers, Milford,Conn., 1639.

BOURNE, THOMAS, 1581-1664. Born in England. Deputy from Marshfield, Mass., 1640, 1642, 1645.

BOUKER, EDMUND,—— 1656. Member Ancient and Honorable Artillery Co., 1646. Born in England, died at Dorchester, Mass.

BOUKER, JOHN, 1651-1721. Served in King Philip's War, 1675,from Marlborough, Mass.

BOUTON, JOHN, 1615-1705. Born in England. Deputy from Norwalk, Conn., 1669-1671
Greason, Mrs. James B., Jr.   Founders

BOWEN, RICHARD,—— 1674/5. Born in Wales. Selectman, Rehoboth, Mass., 1644. Deputy, 1651. Town Clerk, 1654-1658.Deputy to Plymouth General Court from Rehoboth, Mass., 1651.

BOWNE, JOHN, 1627-1695. Born in England. Treasurer, Flushing, L.I., 1665. Member of Assembly, 1691.

BOYCE, CHENEY, 1599-1649. Member Va. House of Burgesses from Shirley Hundred, 1629, 1630, 1632.

BRACEWELL, ROBERT. —— ——. Clergyman. Member House of Burgesses, VA, ca 1651 -1667/8.
Rees, Mrs. James Lester   North Carolina

BRACKETT, CAPT. RICHARD, 1610-1690. Born in England. Member Ancient and Honorable Artillery Co., Boston, 1639 Town Clerk, Braintree, Mass. Many years Third Captain Militia.

BRADBURY, CAPT. THOMAS, 1610/11-1694/5. First Clerk of Writs, 1641. Deputy to General Court, 1651, 1652, 1656, 1657, 1660, 1661, 1666, Salisbury, Mass. Captain of the Militia, 1661.
Gleason, Mrs. George R.   Ohio

BRADFORD, GOV. WILLIAM, 1589-1657. Born in England. Passenger on Mayflower, 1620. Governor, Plymouth Plantation, 1621-1633, 1635, 1637, 1639-1643, 1645-1656. Governor's Assistant 1634, 1636, 1638, 1644. Commissioner of the United Colonies, 1647-1649, 1652, 1656. Member of Councils of War, 1642, 1643, 1653. President of the Councils, 1643, 1653.
Coslet, Mrs. David F.   Illinois.
Covell, Mrs. Carleton   Renss.
DeYoung, Mrs. Roger   Illinois
Greason, Mrs. James Blauvelt, Jr.   Founders

BRADFORD, MAJ. WILLIAM, 1624-1703/4. Born in Plymouth, Mass. Deputy, 1657. Governor's Assistant, 1658-1681. Treasurer of the Colony, 1679-1686, 1689-1692. Commissioner of the United Colonies, 1682-1686. Councilor of the Royal Province of New England, 1686-1689. Ensign, Plymouth Co., 1648. Captain of Troop, 1659. Major, 1685. Member of Council of War, 1657-1658, 1667.
Greason, Mrs. James Blauvelt, Jr.   Founders

BRADLEY, CAPT. STEPHEN, 1642-1702. Born in England. Representative from Guilford, Conn., 1692-1699.
Greason, Mrs. James B., Jr.   Founders

BRADLEY, WILLIAM, —— 1691.Deputy New Haven, CT 1675 and 1676.
Armstrong, Mrs. Donald G.   Illinois

BRADSTREET, HUMPHREY, 1594-1655. Deputy from Ipswich,Mass., 1635.

BRAECKE, DIRCK KLAESSEN,—— 1693. Patentee, Caven Point,N.J. and Stony Point, 1648. Committee to fortify Communipaw, N.J., 1663.

BRAINERD, DANIEL, ca. 1641-1715. Haddam,CT. Deacon 1682.
Fadenrecht, Mrs. Arthur Harry   Pennsylvania

BRANCH, CHRISTOPHER, 1597-1681. Born in England. Member Virginia House of Burgesses, 1639, 1640, 1641. Justice of Peace,Henrico Co., Va., 1656.
Earle, Miss Mary Elizabeth   Ohio
Rice, Mrs. Clarence M.   Florida
Tutt, Mrs. Fehrlin E.   Tejas

BRASHEARS, BRASSEURS, Benjamin, 1590 -1663. Calvert, MD Justice commissioned 21 May 1661.
Campbell, Mrs. James W.   Florida

BRASSEY, THOMAS, —— 1690. Member of Pa. Provincial Assembly, 1682-1683. Justice of First Court of Chester Co., Pa., 1682. Died at Chester.
Baker, Mrs. Don Cruden   Pennsylvania
Baker, Mrs. William Ridgeway   Pennsylvania

BRASWELL, ROBERT, SR., 1612-1668. Came from England to Isle of Wight Co., Va. as Episcopal clergyman, 1653. Member of Virginia House of Burgesses, 1653, from "Bennet's Welcome."

BRATT, ELDER ALBERT ANDRIESSEN, —— 1686. A first settler in Albany Colony of Rensselaerswyck. Elder in Lutheran Church, 1680.

BRECK, EDWARD, 1595-1662. Selectman, Dorchester, Mass., 1642-1646, 1655, 1656.

BRECK, CAPT. JOHN, 1651-1691. Born in Dorchester, Mass. Capt. of Militia, Dorchester, Mass. 1686.

BRENT, DEPT. GOV. GILES, 1606-1671. Born in England. Commander of Kent Fort, Md., 1639-1640. Lieut. Gen. of Militia 1643. Deputy Governor of Md., 1643.

BRENT, HUGH, 1620-1671. Constable of Lancaster Co., Va., 1665.
Killey, Mrs. Ralph A.   Illinois

BRENTON, GOV. WILLIAM, —— 1674. Selectman, 1634-1637. Deputy, 1635-1637. Deputy-Governor of Portsmouth and Newport 1640-1647. Selectman, 1652-1657. President of Newport, R.I. 1660-1662. Commissioner, 1660-1663. Deputy-Governor, 1663- 1666. Governor, 1666-1669. Teaching Elder in Church in MA Colony. Signed Compact preparatory to Settlement of Newport, 1639.

BREWER, JOHN, —— ——.Isle of Wight Co., VA. Served as member of House of Burgess 1629-1630. Governor's Council 1632-1634.
Brinkdopke, Mrs. Henry   Ohio

BREWSTER, JONATHAN, —— 1659. Deputy from Duxbury, Mass.,1639, 1642, 1643, 1644, 1645. Deputy from New London, CT 1650-1658.

BREWSTER, MRS. MARY,—— 1627. Passenger on the Mayflower,1620.

BREWSTER, ELDER WILLIAM, 1566-1644. Born in England. Passenger on the Mayflower, 1620. Chaplain of first Military Co. Plymouth. Chosen Ruling Elder of Plymouth Colony.

Bryan, Mrs. George H.	Jamestown Virginia
Goodman, Mrs. Mary Frances Nunn	Oklahoma
Hixon, Mrs. Fay Edward	Oklahoma
Howe, Mrs. Elden Loring	Florida
Ochs, Mrs. Rex W.	Oklahoma
McReynolds, Mrs. Thomas J. III	Missouri

BRIDGER, COL. JOSEPH, circa 1628-1686. Member of House of Burgesses, 1657-1658, 1663, from Isle of Wight in the Colony of Virginia.

DeMent, Mrs. Norman Hall	Ohio
Simmons, Mrs. Robert W.	Tennessee

BRIDGES, JOSIAH, 1650-1715. Served in King Philip's War, 1675/6 under Major Appleton in the Narragansett Campaign. Surveyor, Boxford, Mass., 1695.

BRIGGS, JOHN, 1609-1690. Born in England. Assistant to the Governor of R.I., 1643. Commissioner for uniting the R.I. towns, 1654. Deputy from Portsmouth, R.I., 1664, 1665, 1666-1668, 1669.

BRIGGS, WILLIAM, 1650-1716. Member of Troop of Horse, Little Compton, R.I., 1667.

BRIGHAM, THOMAS, 1603-1653. Selectman, Cambridge, Mass., 1639, 1640, 1642, 1647. Constable 1639, 1642.

BRIGHTMAN, HENRY, 1640-1728. Served as Deputy at Dartmouth, Mass., 1682, 1685, 1690, 1691. Constable in East Greenwich, R.I..

BRINCKERHOFF, ABRAHAM JORIS, 1632-1714. Born in Holland. Magistrate of Flatlands, L.I., 1673. Deacon, 1672.

BRINCKERHOFF, JORIS DIRCKSEN, 1609-1661. Magistrate of Brooklyn, 1654-1660.

BRINK, HUYBERT LAMBERTSEN, 1659-1696. Served in Capt. Henry Pawling's Co., 1670. Land Director for Petrus Stuyvesant. Witness Signer of Indian Treaty. Witness Capacities Petitioned Esopus, 1680.

BRINSMEAD, (BRINSMADE), JOHN, —— 1673. Deputy from Stratford, Conn. Legislature, Oct. 1671-1672.

BRINTON, WILLIAM, SR.,—— ——.Settled in Chester Co., Pa., 1684.Member of Grand Inquest, 1685.

BROCKELBANK, SAMUEL, 1628-1676. Killed in King Philip's War at Sudbury, Mass., 1676.

BROCKETT, JOHN, 1609-1690. Born in England. Surveyor, 1639. Surgeon, New Haven Colony Troops, 1654. Deputy to General Court of Connecticut, 1671, 1678, 1680, 1682, 1685.
Henry,Mrs. Charles J.   Illinois
Milburn, Mrs. John T.   Blue Grass

BRODHEAD, CAPT. DANIEL,—— 1667. Captain of Grenadiers, who captured New Netherland from the Dutch, 1664. Commanded English forces at Esopus, 1665.

BRONSON (BROWNSON), JOHN,—— 1680. Born in England. Served in Pequot War, 1637. Deputy from Farmington, Conn., 1651. Constable, 1652. One of the original proprietors of Waterbury, Conn., 1674.

BROOKE, GOV. ROBERT,—— 1655. Born in London, England. Arrived Md., 1650. Settled in Charles Co., Md. President Provincial Council, 1652. Acting Governor, 1652-1655.

BROOKE, MAJOR THOMAS, 1632-1676.Born in England. Member Maryland Assembly, 1663, 1665, 1666, 1671, 1674. Deputy to lower House, 1671. Capt. of Militia, 1658-1660. Major, 1661.High Sheriff, 1666, 1668.
King, Mrs. Everett Neville   Pennsylvania
Potts, Mrs. J. Webb   Pennsylvania
Roeder, Mrs. Paul H.   Pennsylvania

BROOKS, THOMAS,—— 1667. Constable, Concord, Mass., 1638. Representative to General Court, 1642-1644, 1650-1654,1659-1662

BROOME, JOHN,—— 1689. Surveyor. Appointed by the Council of Maryland to lay out County Seat in Calvert County. Died while visiting England.

BROWN, REV. CHAD,——-before 1663. First settled pastor of First Baptist Church in Providence, 1642. Signed agreement for a form of government at Providence, 1640.

BROWN, FRANCIS, circa 1610-1668, of New Haven. Signed the Colony Constitution, 1639.

BROWN(E), LIEUT. JAMES, 1623-1710. Born in England. Lieut., Swansea, Mass., Troops in King Philip's War, 1675/6. Assistant,Plymouth Colony, 1665.

BROWN, JOHN, 1584-1662. Born in England. Governor's Assistant Plymouth Colony, 1636, 1638-1655. Commissioner of United Colonies, 1664-1655. Member of Council of War, 1646-1653.
Cowger, Miss Pauline May   Quivira
Davis, Mrs. Frank V.   Illinois

BROWN, JOHN, 1630-circa 1706. Member Town Council of Providence, R.I., 1662-1664. Deputy from Providence, 1663, 1664. Assistant, 1665, 1666
Davis, Mrs. Frank V.   Illinois

BROWNE, JOHN, circa 1621/2 after 1676. Original Proprietor, Newark, N.J. Signer of Fundamental Agreement, 24 June 1667. Townsman, 1674. Sealer of Measurers, 1676, 1679.
Finfgeld, Mrs. Clifford   Illinois

BROWN(E), CAPT. ORIGINAL,—— 1698. Westmoreland Co., Va.Captain in Westmoreland Co. Militia, 1698.

BROWNE, LIEUT. RICHARD, 1629-1687. Born in England. Lieut. of Foot Company, Suffolk Co., N.Y., Militia, 1686.

BROWNELL, THOMAS, 1619-1665. Born in England. Commissioner from Portsmouth, R.I., 1655, 1661—1664.

BROWNELL, WILLIAM, 1648-1715. Freeman, 1677. Surveyor of Little Compton, 1683. Constable, 1684. Rhode Island.

BROWNING, CAPT. JOHN, circa 1588-after 1638. Born in England. Settled in Elizabeth City, Va., 1622. Burgess from Elizabeth City, 1629, 1635
Patterson, Mrs. Steven Thomas   Oklahoma

BROWNING, NATHANIEL, 1618-circa 1670. Born in England. Arrived Boston, 1640, went to Portsmouth, R.I. Freeman, 1654. Served as member of the Council.

BRUEN, OBADIAH, 1606-1680. Deputy from Gloucester, Mass., 1647-1649, 1651. Signed the Fundamental Agreement, Newark,N.J., 1666
Boden, Miss Kip Kelso   Pennsylvania

BUCK, LIEUT. ISAAC,—— ——. Scituate, Mass. Town Clerk. Deputy to Plymouth General Court, 1663, 1664, 1665, Lieut. in King Philip's War, 1676

BUCKMAN, WILLIAM,1650-1716.Bucks Co., PA. Surveyor 1693-'96 and '97.
Costelloe, Mrs. Robert J. II   Louisiana

BUDD, LIEUT. JOHN, 1620-1684. Born in England. Deputy from Southold, L.I., to New Haven, 1657. Resigned as Lieutenant of Military Co., Southold, L.I., 1660. Commissioner from Rye to Hartford, 1663, 1664. Overseer of Southold, 1667. Constable, 1667.

BUDD, LIEUT. JOHN, SR.,—— 1673. Lieutenant, Southold, L.I., before 1654. Deputy to New Haven, 1657. Deputy and Magistrate, Rye, N.Y., then in Conn. 1663-1666.

BUFFINGTON, RICHARD, 1654-1748. Constable,, Chichester, Chester Co., Penn., 1688.
Delahunt, Mrs. Charles R.   Illinois

BULKELEY, REV. GERSHOM, 1636-1716. Born in Concord, Mass. Preached at New London and Wethersfield, Conn. Retired 1677, but practiced as surgeon in several expeditions during King Philip's War, 1675. Representative from Wethersfield, 1679. Justice, 1687.

BULKELEY, REV. PETER, 1583-1658. Born in England. Founder and first minister at Concord, Mass., 1636, and served until death.

BULL, HENRY, circa 1610-1693/4. Deputy to Assembly, 1666. Governor, R.I., 1685, 1686, 1690.
Frederick, Mrs. George Harvey Clark   Illinois

BULLOCK, CAPT. HUGH, circa 1565-1650. York Co., Va. Member Va. House of Burgesses, 1631. Councillor, 1634. Capt. in York Co. Militia, 1634.

BULLOCK RICHARD, 1622-1677. Town Clerk, Rehoboth, Mass., 1659.

BUNNELL (BONNELL), NATHANIEL, circa 1644-circa 1696. Member of Assembly, Newark, N.J., from Elizabethtown, 1692-1694.

BURCHARD, THOMAS, 1597-1684. Deputy from Saybrook, Conn., 1651. Selectman, 1656.

BURDICK, ROBERT,—— 1692. Deputy to General Court from Westerly, R.I., 1680, 1683, 1685.

BURGESS, JOHN,—— 1701. Deputy from Yarmouth, Mass., 1680.

BURGESS, THOMAS, SR., 1603-1685. Born in England. Deputy from Sandwich, Mass., 1642-1668. Member Militia, Plymouth, 1643.

BURGESS, THOMAS, JR.,—— after 1687. Constable, Sandwich, Mass., 1634.

BURGESS, COL. WILLIAM, 1622-1686. Moved from Va. to Anne Arundel Co., Md. Justice, 1655, 1657, 1662, 1674, 1676, 1678-1679. High Sheriff, 1664. Commander of Md. Forces against Indians, 1677. Member of Council, 1682-1686. Burgess, 1668-1682. Deputy Gov., 1684-1686.

BURNHAM, LIEUT. THOMAS, 1623-1694. Deputy from Ipswich to the General Court of Mass. Bay, 1683, 1684, 1685. Sergeant, 1664. Ensign, 1675. Lieut., 1683, in Capt. Samuel Appleton's Co. Soldier in Indian War, 1643. Corporal, 1662. Selectman, 1663.
Leming, Mrs. Howell E.   Member-at-Large

BURNHAM, ENS. THOMAS, JR., 1646-1728. Ensign of Militia, Ipswich, Mass., in King Philip's War, 1675.

BURR, BENJAMIN,—— 1681. Born in England. Served in Pequot War, 1637, from Hartford, Conn.

BURR, DANIEL,—— ——.Commissary from Fairfield, Conn., 1690.

BURR, JEHU, 1600-1672. Born in England. Deputy from Fairfield, Conn., 1641-1645. Commissioner for United Colonies, 1664. Signed deeds for the Indians.

BURR, JOHN, —— ——. Fairfield, CT. Deputy 1666-1668, 1670, 1674, 1685,1686, 1689, and 1690. Sgt. Maj. 1694.
Romaniak, Mrs. Charles Richard   CT Farms

BURR, REV. JONATHAN, 1604-1641. Minister. Dorchester, MA.
Gobesynski, Mrs. Leon   Illinois

BURR, NATHANIEL, 1640-1712. Born in Springfield, Mass. Deputy from Fairfield, Conn., 1692-1695, 1697-1698.

BURR, SIMON,—— 1692. Born in England. Served in King Philip's War, 1675-1676.

BURRAGE, JOHN, circa 1616-1685. Clerk of Market, Charlestown, Mass., 1658-1672. Listed among the first 36 residents of Charlestown, 1637

BURROWS, JOHN, 1642-1716. Born in Stonington, Conn. Patentee, New London, 1663.

BURROWS, ROBERT,—— 1682. Born in England. Of New London, Conn., 1650, where in 1660 he was appointed first ferryman on Mystic River.

BURROWS, WILLIAM,——.One of the first settlers of Providence, R.I. Signed the Agreement, 1640.

BURSLEY, JOHN, 1599-1660. Deputy to General Court, Wymouth, Mass., 1636. Constable, Barnstable, Mass., 1645.
Weaver, Mrs. John F., Sr.   Michigan

BURT, HENRY, 1615-1662. Born in England. First Clerk, Military Co., Springfield, Mass., 1657. Selectman, member first Board, 1644, 1646, 1654.

BURWELL, SERGT. MAJ. LEWIS, 1621-1653. Sergeant Major, Gloucester Co., Va., 1651.

BUSBY, NICHOLAS, 1587-1657. Born in England. Selectman, Watertown, Mass., 1640-1641. Constable, Boston, 1649.

BUSHNELL, FRANCIS,—— 1646. Born in England. Third signer of Covenant at Guilford, Conn., 1639.

BUSHNELL, DEA. FRANCIS, 1609-1681. Deacon of Saybrook, Conn. Church prior to 1681 and until death.

BUSHNELL, LIEUT. WILLIAM,—— 1683. Born in England. Deputy from Saybrook, Conn., 1670. Lieut. of Train Band, 1679. Sergt., 1661.

BUTLER, DEA. RICHARD,—— 1684. Born in England. Selectman, Hartford, Conn., 1649, 1654, 1655. Deputy, 1656, 1665. Clerk Court, 1668.

BUTTERICK (BUTTRICK), SERGT. WILLIAM, 1616-1698. Born in England. Sergeant, Concord, Mass., many years. Petitioned in 1681 to be retired from duty.

BUTTERWORTH, DEA. JOHN, 1630-1708. Deacon at Rehoboth, Mass., 1663. First Board of Selectmen, 1668. Settled at Swansea, Mass. Constable, 1685.

BUTTONS, JOHN, 1594-1681. Born in England. Member Ancient and Honorable Artillery Company, Boston, Mass., 1643.
Greason, Mrs. James B., Jr.   Founders

BYRAM, DR. NICHOLAS,—— 1688. Physician, Bridgewater, Mass. Served in King Philip's War, 1675/6.

BYRD, COL. WILLIAM, 1st., 1652-1704. Born in England. Member Virginia House of Burgesses, 1681. Member General Court, 1683. President of Council. Receiver General Revenue.

CABLE, JOHN,—— 1682. Born in England. During the Dutch and English troubles, 1652, he captured a Dutch vessel.

CADY, CORP. NICHOLAS,—— 1685. Member Watertown, Mass.,Militia, 1653. Constable, Groton, 1685. Corporal, 1673-1675.

CAKEBREAD, THOMAS,—— 1643. Born in England. Member Ancient and Honorable Artillery Co. of Boston, 1637.

CALKINS (CAULKINS), HUGH, 1600-1690. Born in England. Deputy from Gloucester, Mass., to General Court, 1650. From New London, Conn. 1657-1660. Original Prop., Norwich, Conn. Deputy from Norwich 1663-1670. Deacon of Norwich Church.

CALVERT, GOV. LEONARD, 1610-1647. Born in England. First Governor of Maryland, 1634 until death, 1647.
Smith, Mrs. Franklin H.   Territorial
White, Mrs. James Edwin   Illinois

CAMFIELD, MATTHEW, —— 1673. Born in England. Representative from Norwalk, Conn., 1654-1666.

CAMP, NICHOLAS, 1630-1706. Deputy from Milford, Conn., 1670-1672.

CARD, JOSEPH, 1648-1729. Born in Newport, R.I. Member of Assembly, 1671.

CARDER, JOHN, 1648-1700. Deputy for Warwick, R.I., 1678, 1696.

CARDER, RICHARD,—— 1676. One of the original proprietors of Aquidneck, who settled Pocasset (later Portsmouth), 1638. One of the Twelve Purchasers of Warwick, 1642. Commissioner for Warwick, 1659, 1660, 1663. Deputy for Warwick, R.I., to the General Assembly, 1664-1675.

CAREY / CARY, JOHN ,1610-1681. Bridgewater, MA. Constable 1656. Selectman, Town Clerk 1657-1681.
McCunn, Mrs. Ian   Founders

CARLL, THOMAS,—— 1675. Selectman, Hempstead, L.I., 1658,1663.

CARLTON, EDWARD, 1605-1661. Deputy to General Court, Rowley, Mass., 1644-1647. On committee, 1648.
Weaver, Mrs. John F. Sr.   Michigan

CARLTON, JOHN, 1630-1668. Town Clerk, Recorder and Clerk of Writ, Haverhill, Mass., 1664-1668. Selectman, 1668.
Weaver, Mrs. John F. Sr.   Michigan

CARPENTER, EPHRAIM,—— 1697/8. Deputy Constable, Oyster Bay, Mosquito District, L.I., 1681.

CARPENTER, SAMUEL, 1644-1682. A Founder of Attleborough, Mass. 1666.
Fishel, Mrs. Maxine   Michigan

CARPENTER, WILLIAM, 1576-1660. Deputy from Weymouth, Mass.,1640.

CARPENTER, CAPT. WILLIAM, 1605-1659. Born in England. Representative from Weymouth, Mass., 1641, 1643; Rehoboth, 1656.Appointed Capt., 1642.
Baratta, Mrs. John B. L.   Pennsylvania

CARPENTER, WILLIAM, 1631-1703. Town Clerk of Rehoboth, Mass., 1668-1693, excepting one year.

CARPENTER, WILLIAM,—— 1685. Born in England. Elected to General Court, Providence, R.I., 1658, 1663-1665, 1671. Assistant to General Assembly, 1665-1672. Deputy, 1679. Commissioner, 1658-1663.

CARR, GOV. CALEB, 1624-1695. Born in England. Commissioner for Newport, R.I., 1654, 1658-1662. General Treasurer, Colony of R.I., 1661. Deputy from Newport, R.I., 1664, 1665, 1667-1672, 1674, 1678-1690. Assistant to Governor, 1679-1686, 1690, 1691.Governor, 1695.

CARR, GEORGE, 1599-1682. Early settler of Salisbury, Mass. Ordered to lay out road, 1648. Maintained Garrison to protect ferry for transportation of troops, King Philip's War, 1675/6.

CARR, ROBERT, 1614-1681. Newport, R.I. Member of Assembly, 1677. Member King's Commission for R.I., 1664.

CARTER, JOHN, —— 1699. Member House of Burgesses 1649 Upper Norfolk Co., Lancaster Co. 1654. Member Crown Council 1657.
Allen, Mrs. Albert Lanham   Blue Grass
Keller, Mrs. Thomas David   Michigan

CARTER, THEODERICK, 1634-1701/2. Constable, Henrico Co., Va., 1699.

CARTER, CAPT. THOMAS, JR., 1672-1733. Magistrate in Colonial,Va. by appointment 12 June 1699.
Kabrick,Mrs. Donald Lee   Florida

CARTER, CAPT. THOMAS, SR.,—— 1700. Born in England. Captain in Lancaster Co., Va. Militia, 1670, Burgess, 1667.

CARTER, REV. THOMAS, 1610-1684. First Minister of Woburn, Mass.,1641-1642.

CARVER, JOHN, 1637—1679. Constable, Marshfield, Mass., 1661. Surveyor, 1674.

CARY, JOHN,———.Constable at Bridgewater, Mass., 1656. Selectman. Town Clerk, Bridgewater, 1657-1681.

CARY, COL. MILES, 1620-1667. Member House of Burgesses, 1659, 1663. Colonel of Warwick County, Va., 1660. Member of Council,1663-1667

CASE, JOHN, 1616-1703/4. One of First Settlers of Simsbury, Conn., 1669. Appointed constable, 14 Oct. 1669, being first person to hold office in the town. Representative in 1670, and several times thereafter.
Lewis, Miss Catherine Bowers   Florida

CATLETT, COL. JOHN, JR.——— ———.Member of House of Burgesses, Va., 1693, 1696

CATLETT, COL. JOHN, SR.,——— 1670. presiding Justice, Rappahannock Co., Va., 1665. Killed at Port Royal, Va., 1670.
Davis, Mrs. Frank V.   Illinois

CAUDEBEC, JACOB, about 1666-1732. Born in France. One of the seven patentees of the Cuddeback Patent, 14 Oct. 1695. One of the first settlers at Maghakameck, later called Pennpack Flats, Colony of N.Y., 1695. Deed from Indians, 8 June 1696.
Long, Mrs. Alfred T.   Founders

CHAFFEE, NATHANIEL, 1638/42-1721. Born in Nantucket, Mass. Constable at Swansea, Mass., 1670.

CHAFFEE, THOMAS,——— 1678. Born in England. A Founder of Hull (Nantucket), Mass., 1642.

CHALLIS, LIEUT. PHILIP, 1617-1681. Lieut. of Foot Co., Salisbury, Mass., 1658.

CHAMBERLAIN, JACOB, 1658-1721. Of Roxbury, Mass. Soldier in King Philip's War, 1676, at Deerfield and Westfield, Mass.

CHAMBERLAIN, WILLIAM, about 1620-1706. served in King Philip's War., 1675/6.

CHAMPLIN, JEFFERY,——— ———. Member Town Council of Aquidneck, R.I., 1680. Deputy, 1681-1686.

CHAMPLIN, CAPT. JEFFERY,——— ———.Capt., Kings Town, R.I., 1690. Assistant, 1696, 1698, 1699.

CHANDLER, CAPT. THOMAS, 1630-1703. Born in England. Representative to General Court, 1678-1679. Commander of company to defend towns from Dunstable eastward.

CHAPIN, DEA. SAMUEL, 1598-1675. Selectman, Springfield, Mass., 1644-1653. Magistrate, 1652-1654. King Philip's War, 1675.Deputy, 1659.
Chmiel, Mrs. Frank S.   Territorial
King, Mrs. Arthur   Missouri
Peep, Miss Susan Renee   Territorial
Peep, Miss Patricia Lynn   Territorial

CHAPMAN, EDWARD,—— 1675. Killed in King Philip's War, 1675. Resided at Tolland, Conn.

CHAPPELL, GEORGE, 1615-1709. Served in Pequot War, 1637, from New London, Conn.

CHASE, BENJAMIN, 1639-1731. Selectman, Freetown, Mass., 1698, 1699.

CHASE, WILLIAM, 1595-1659. Constable, Yarmouth, Mass., 1639. Drummer in Indian troubles, 1645.

CHASE, WILLIAM, 1622-1685. Born in England. One of first settlers of Yarmouth, Mass. Constable 1639. Drummer in Pequot War, 1637. King Philip's War, 1675.

CHATFIELD, ENS. THOMAS, —— 1687. Planter at Guilford, Conn., 1649. Settled at Easthampton, L.I., before 1659. Constable. Ensign, 1665. Magistrate, Easthampton.

CHAUNCEY, REV. CHARLES, 1592-1692. Born in England. Pastor, Scituate, Mass., 1641. President, Harvard College, 1654.
Abbey, Mrs. Nathan   Florida

CHEESMAN / CHISMAN, EDWARD / EDMUND, ca 1602——. Commissioner of York County, VA 1652.
Crowder, Mrs. Roy Hester   North Carolina

CHENEY, JOHN, 1620-1695. Selectman, Roxbury, Mass., 1661, 1664.

CHENEY, WILLIAM, 1604-1667. Born in England. Member Roxbury, Mass. Militia, 1647. Constable, 1654-1655. Selectman, Roxbury, Mass., 1655-1657, 1661-1664. Town Officer, 1666.
Flanagan, Mrs. John   CT Farms

CHESEBROUGH, NATHANIEL, 1630-1678. Born in England. Served in King Philip's War, 1675. Died at Stonington, Conn.

CHESEBROUGH, WILLIAM, 1594-1667. Born in England. Deputy from Boston, Mass., 1640. Selectman, Stonington, Conn. 1658, 1660-1666. Deputy, 1653, 1655, 1657, 1664.

CHESTER, CAPT. JOHN, 1635-1698. Deputy from Wethersfield, Conn., to the General Court, 1676-1687. Lieut. of Train Band, 1672. Capt, 1677, 1689.

CHEW, COL. SAMUEL, ——1676/7. Member of House of Burgesses, 1659. Sworn Justice of Provincial Court and Court of Chancery, 17 Dec. 1669. Member of Council, 1669, until death. Councillor and Secretary of Province of Maryland. Col. of Provincial Forces, 1675.
Dunn, Mrs. James Butord   North Carolina

CHICKERING, ENS. FRANCIS, 1589-1658. Born in England. Member Ancient and Honorable Artillery Company of Boston, Mass., 1643. Deputy from Dedham, 1644, 1653. Ensign, 1656. Representative, 1657.

CHILD, JEREMIAH, 1645 ——. A Founder of Swansea, Mass., 1669. Selectman, 1682.

CHILES, LT. COL. WALTER, circa 1615-1653. Member of House of Burgesses, representing Charles Co., Va., 1642, 1643, James City Co., 1645, 1646, 1649. Elected Speaker in 1652.
Maxwell, Mrs. Clifford   Tennessee

CHILTON, JAMES, —— 1620. Passenger on Mayflower, 1620. Signer of the Mayflower Compact.
Brown, Mrs. John H.   Quivira
Jaquith, Mrs. Dana W.   Rhode Island
Sherman, Mrs. Francis F.   Missouri

CHILTON, MARY, —— 1679. Passenger on the Mayflower, 1620.

CHITTENDEN, MAJ. WILLIAM, 1593-1660. Born in England. Principal military man, Magistrate and Deputy from Guilford, Conn., 1643. Lieutenant, Artillery, New Haven Colony, 1648.
Greason, Mrs. James B., Jr.   Founders

CHURCH, COL. BENJAMIN, 1639-1718. Deputy from Bristol, R.I., 1682-1684; from Tiverton, 1696. Commissary General in King Philip's War,

1675. Commander of Plymouth Forces, 1676. Major in Command, 1689, 1690, 1692, 1696.

CHURCH, RICHARD, 1610-1667. Born in England. One of the original Proprietors, Hartford, Conn., 1639. A Founder and settler of Hartford.

CHURCH, CAPT. SAMUEL, 1636-1684. Born in England. Called "Captain" in town records of Hadley, Mass. Selectman, 1672.

CHURCHILL, JOSIAH, —— 1687. Born in England. In Pequot War, 1637. Constable at Wethersfield, Conn., 1657, 1670.

CLAIBORNE, COL. WILLIAM, 1587-1676. Born in England. Settled in Henrico Co., Va. Secretary of State, 1625. Member of Council. In command during Indian Wars, 1629, 1644. Deputy Governor, 1653.
Whitehurst, Mrs. James L.   Florida

CLAPP, JOHN, —— ——. Clerk of New York Assembly, 1692.

CLAP (CLAPP), CAPT. ROGER, 1609-1690/1. Capt. of town Militia. Member of Ancient and Honorable Artillery Deputy 1673. Comm. 1665. Deacon and Selectman.
Bachner, Mrs. Thomas Edgar   Tejas

CLAPP, MAJ. SAMUEL, 1641 ——. Major, Mass. Militia. Deputy from Scituate to Plymouth, 1680-1686, 1690-1691. Deputy to General Court of Mass., 1699.

CLARK, CAPT. DANIEL, 1622-1710. One of first settlers, Windsor, Conn. Deputy, 1656-1661. Lieutenant, 1657. Secretary, Colony Conn., 1658-1664, 1665-1666. Magistrate, 1662-1664. Captain, 1664. Served in King Philip's War, 1675.

CLARK, DEA. GEORGE, —— 1690. One of first settlers, Milford, Conn., 1639. Deputy, 1661, 1664.

CIARK(E), HUGH, circa 1613-1693. From England to Watertown and Roxbury, Mass. Member Ancient and Honorable Artillery Co., 1666.

CLARK, JAMES, —— ——. One of first settlers, New Haven, Conn. Signed Fundamental Agreement, 1639.

CLARK, JAMES, JR., —— 1712. Constable, New Haven, Conn., 1680.

CLARK, THOMAS, 1638-1719. Milford, Conn. Deputy to General Court, 1683. Justice of Peace and Commissioner for Milford.

CLARK(E), THOMAS, 1599-1697. Original Proprietor of Harwich, Mass. Came from England to Plymouth, Mass., as Pilot of the "Mayflower," 1620.

CLARKE, SERGT. JOHN, ——— 1673. One of the original proprietors of Hartford, Conn., 1639. Deputy from Milford, Conn., 1649.

CLARKE, JOSEPH, 1618-1694. Commissioner from Newport, R.I., 1648, 1655, 1657—1659, 1668-1672, 1690. Governor's Assistant, 1658, 1659, 1663-1665, 1677—1680. Named in Royal Charter of King Charles II, 1663. Deputy from Newport to General Assembly, 1668, 1672, 1690.
Clark, Mrs. Henry F.   Tejas

CLARKE, LIEUT. WILLIAM, 1609-1690. Born in England. Selectman, Dorchester, Mass., 1646-1653. Deputy, Northampton, 1663-1682. Lieutenant, 1661. Served in King Philip's War, 1675/6.

CLASEN/CLAESEN, CORNELIS/CORNELIUS ——— ca. 1708. Orange Co., NY. Justice 1697.
Trefts, Mrs. Albert   Ohio

CLAY, CHARLES, 1638-1686. Born in Wales, Served in Bacon's Rebellion, Va., 1676.

CLAY, SIR JOHN, 1592- after 1636. Born in Wales. Settled in Charles City, Va. Appears on 1624/5 muster. Capt. of British forces in Va. during seventeenth century wars.
Goff Miss Mary Young   Renns.
Greene, Mrs. Haold Lewis   Blue Grass
Ratliff, Mrs. George Phelps   Blue Grass
Smith, Mrs. Rick Dean   Blue Grass

CLAYES/CLOYES/CLEYES, JOHN, ——— ———. Member of Capt. Mason's Train Band. Member of Grand Jury Falmouth, ME 1664, 1671, and 1672.
Crain, Miss Tracy Lynette   North Carolina
Evans, Mrs. Sebra   Tennessee

CLAYPOOLE, JAMES, 1634-1687. Commission for Registrar General, 1686, Judge of Provincial Court. Member of Governor's Council and Assembly of Pa., 1686-1687.

CLAYPOOLE, NORTON, 1647/1688. Born in England. Settled in Del. 1678. Justice of Peace, Sussex Co., 1683. Member of Assembly of Pa. from Sussex Co., Del., 1686.

CLAYTON, WILLIAM, 1634-1689. Member of First Provincial Council of Pa., 1681. Commissioned by Governor as Justice. Acting Governor of Pa., 1684-1685.
Jackson, Mrs. Jerald E.   Illinois

CLEMENT, ROBERT, 1590-1658. Born in England. Commissioner, 1647. Deputy from Haverhill, Mass., 1647, 1648-1653. Magistrate of the Court of Norfolk Co., Mass., 1648, 1649.
Kurz, Mrs. Rudolph F.   Illinois

CLEVELAND, MOSES, SR., 1624-1702. Born in England. Militia, Woburn, Mass., 1663. Served in King Philip's War, 1675/6. In garrison at Chelmsford, Mass., 1675.

CLEVELAND, MOSES, JR., 1651-1717. Served in King Philip's War from Woburn, Mass., 1675/6.

CLOUD, WILLIAM, before 1630-circa 1702. Constable, Concord, Chester Co., Pa., 1686.

COCKE, LIEUT. COL. RICHARD, 1600-1665. Born in England. Member of House of Burgesses from Weyanoke, Charles City Co., Va., 1632, from Henrico Co., 1644, 1654.
Gude, Mrs. Elmer W.   Tejas

CODDINGTON, GOV. WILLIAM, 1601-1678. Born in England. Magistrate, Boston, Mass., 1630. Assistant to Governor, 1630-1636. Treasurer, 1634-1636. Deputy, 1636. First Judge of R.I. Colony, 1638. Governor, 1640-1647. President of the four united towns of Colony, 1648-1649. Deputy, 1666. Deputy Governor, 1673-1674. Governor, 1674-1676, 1678.

COE, BENJAMIN, —— ——. Town Clerk of Jamaica, L.I., N.Y., Jan. 1676.

COFFIN, JAMES, 1640-1720. Born in England. Judge of Probate, Nantucket, Mass., 1680.

COFFIN, TRISTRAM, 1605-1681. Born in England. Formed Militia Troop, Nantucket, Mass., 1656. First Chief Magistrate, 1671, 1677.

COFFIN, LIEUT. TRISTRAM, JR., 1632-1704. Born in England. Lieutenant, Newbury, Mass., 1683. Deputy, 1695.

COGGESHALL, GOV. JOHN, 1599-1647. Born in England. Selectman, Boston, Mass., 1634. Deputy, 1634. Signed Incorporation Portsmouth,

R.I., 1638. Magistrate, 1639. One of founders, Newport, R.I., 1639. Assistant to Governor, 1640. First Colonial Governor of R.I., called president, Providence Plantations, 1647.

COGGESHALL, JOSHUA, 1623-1688. Born in England. Deputy from Newport, R.I., 1665, 1666-1668, 1670-1672. Assistant to Governor, 1669, 1670, 1672-1676.

COGSWELL, JOHN, 1592-1669. Born in England. Deputy from Ipswich, Mass., 1635-1637.
Weaver, Mrs. John F., Sr.   Michigan

COIT, JOHN, —— 1659. Selectman, Gloucester, Mass., 1648.

COIT, DEA. JOSEPH, —— 1704. Constable, New London, Conn., 1665. Deacon, 1683.

COIT, REV. JOSEPH, 1673-1750. Minister, Norwich, Conn., 1698. First Minister in Plainfield, Conn. 1699.

COLBURN, (COBURN), CORP. EDWARD, 1618-1700. Born in England. Served in King Philip's War, 1675-1676. In command of garrison house until 1692. King Wiliam's War, 1690. Died at Chelmsford, Mass.

COLBY, JOHN, JR., —— ——. Salisbury and Amesbury, Mass. Served in King Philip's War, 1675-1676. In Falls Fight, 1676. Member of Trained Band, 1680.

COLE, DANIEL, —— 1694. Member of Train Band, Yarmouth Co., 1643. Deputy from Eastham, 1652, 1654, 1657, 1661-1674. Selectman for 9 years, from 1667.
Wolohan, Miss Mary Elizabeth   Michigan
Wolohan, Miss Noreen Mary   Michigan
Wolohan, Miss Rosemary Parshall   Michigan

COLE, HUGH, 1627-1699. Selectman, Swansea, 1671-1675. Deputy, 1673, 1675, 1680, 1683, 1686, 1689. Served in Pequot War, 1637.
Mitchell, Mrs. Dean W.   Quivira

COLE, ROBERT, 1591-1655. Born in England. One of thirteen original proprietors and settler of Providence Plantation, 1636. Deputy from Roxbury, Mass., 1632. Justice, Providence, R.I., 1642.

COLE, COL. WILLIAM, 1637/8-1693/4. Virginia. Member of Council, 1689-1691. Member of Virginia House of Burgesses. Founder of The College of William and Mary.

COLLIER, WILLIAM, 1583-1671. Assistant of Plymouth Colony, 1635-1637.

COLLIER, LIEUT. COL. WILLIAM, circa 1640 ——. Born in England. Arrived in York Co., Va. from London, 1670. Went to New Kent Co., Lieut. Colonel, 1675.
Prewitt, Mrs. Henry Caywood   Blue Grass

COLLINS, DEA. EDWARD, 1603-1689. Born in England. Deacon of First Church of Cambridge, Mass., 1638. Clerk of Writs, 1641. Ancient and Honorable Artillery Co., 1641. Representative to General Court from Cambridge, 1654-1670, except 1661.
Cook, Mrs. Ralph William, Sr.   Michigan
Greason, Mrs. James B., Jr.   Founders

COLLINS, HENRY, 1630-1722. Served in King Philip's War, 1675, from Lynn, Mass.

COLTON, QUAR'IERMASTER GEORGE, —— 1669. Deputy from Springfield, Mass., 1669-1671. Appointed Quartermaster, 1668. Ensign, 1681. Lieut., 1688.

COLTON, CAPT. THOMAS, 1651-1728. Selectman, Springfield, Mass., 1687, 1688, 1692, 1694, 1695, 1699. Assessor, 1694, 1696, 1697.

COMSTOCK, CHRISTOPHER, 1625-1702/3. Deputy from Norwalk, Conn., 1686. Sergeant, 1654.

COMSTOCK, WILLIAM, —— 1659. Served in Pequot War, 1637, from Wethersfield, Conn.

CONANT, LOT, 1624-1674. Selectman, Marblehead, Mass., 1662.

CONANT, LOT, JR., 1657-1744, of Mass. Captain in King Philip's War. Took part in attack on Fort Narragansett, 1675.

CONANT, GOV. ROGER, 1592-1679. Governor at Cape Ann and Salem, 1625-1627. Deputy from Salem to General Court, 1634.
Sims, Miss Ursell Lavon   Illinois

CONGER/BELCONGER, JOHN, 1640-1712. Woodbridge, M.J. 1687 Commissioner. 1667 original settler of town. 1688 Town Clerk, 1691 Constable.
Longbotham, Mrs. Bernard, Jr.   Tejas
Williamson, Mrs. Morris   Tejas

CONKLIN, ANANIAS, —— 1659. Selectman, Easthampton, L.I., 1654.

CONKLIN, BENJAMIN, —— 1709. Constable, Easthampton, L.I., 1676, 1681. Commissioner for trials of small causes, 1686. Selectman, 1688. Justice of the Peace, 1694, 1696.

CONKLIN, CAPT. CORNELIUS, 1664-1748. Constable Easthampton, 1691.

CONKLIN, JEREMIAH, 1634-1712. Overseer of Easthampton, L.I., 1633, 1666, 1676, 1680-1686. Selectman, 1674. Commissioner, 1687.

CONWAY, EDWIN, circa 1610-circa 1675. Justice, Northampton Co., Va., 1647 and later. Third Clerk of Northampton Co., Va., 1642-1645.
Williams, Mrs. Eugene Jefferson   Member-at-Large
Williams, Miss Mary Julianna   Member-at-Large

COOK, JOHN, 1631-1691. Born in England. Deputy from Portsmouth, R.I., 1670.

COOK, HENRY, —— 1661. Served in King Philip's War, 1675/6.
Milburn, Mrs. John T.   Blue Grass

COOK, SAMUEL, 1641-1703. Born in Salem, Mass. One of Founders of Wallingsford, Conn. 1669.
Milburn, Mrs. John T.   Blue Grass

COOK, THOMAS, —— 1674. Born in England. Deputy from Portsmouth, R.I., 1664.

COOKE, CAPT. AARON, 1641-1716. Ensign, 1673. Captain Militia, Hadley, Mass., 1678. Deputy 1689, 1691, 1693, 1697.

COOKE, MAJ. AARON, 1610-1690. Born in England. Major, Hartford Troop, 1658. Deputy from Westfield, Mass., 1668. Ensign, 1676. Captain, King Philip's War, 1675-1676.

COOKE, FRANCIS, 1577-1663. Passenger on the Mayflower, 1620. Signer of Mayflower Compact.
Harrill, Mrs. Jacques William   Founders
Miner, Mrs. Ross H.   Founders
Sands, Mrs. Maurice R.   Ohio

COOKE, JOHN, 1610-1695. Passenger on the Mayflower, 1620. Deputy from Plymouth, 1639, 1640, 1642, 1652, 1653, 1654, 1656; from Dartmouth, 1666-1668, 1673-1675, 1678, 1683, 1686. Magistrate, Dartmouth, 1662.

COOKE, LIEUT. JOSEPH, 1610-1673. Lieutenant, Ancient and Honorable Artillery Co., Boston, 1640.

COOKSEY, SAMUEL, —— before 1708/9. Justice and Commissioner, St. Mary's Co., Md., 1694. Naval Officer of the Potomac District, 1695. Gentleman Justice at St. Mary's, 1697.

COOLEY, BENJAMIN, —— 1684. Selectman, Springfield, Mass., 1648, and served for 18 years.

COOLIDGE, JOHN, —— ——. Deputy to Mass. General Court from Watertown, Mass., 1658.
Howard, Mrs. Arthur M.   Florida
Richards, Mrs. Donald Clark   Pennsylvania
Vogel, Mrs. Carl Stephens   Pennsylvania

COOMBS, JOHN, —— living 1642. Treasurer, Plymouth Colony, 1633.

COOPER, JOHN, —— 1689. Deputy and Assistant to Governor, New Haven, Conn., 1676. Member Council of War, 1676.

COOPER, JOHN, JR., 1642 ——. Constable, New Haven, Conn., 1676.

COOPER, LIEUT. THOMAS, 1616-1675. Selectman, Springfield, Mass., 1644-1663. Served in King Philip's War, 1675.

COOPER, THOMAS, JR., —— ——. Constable at Rehoboth, Mass., 1677.
Fishel, Mrs. Maxine   Michigan

CORBIN, HENRY, 1629-1675/7. Justice, 1657. Burgess in Colonial Assembly, 1658-1660. Member of Council of Va., 1663-1675.

COREY, ABRAHAM, —— 1702. Constable, Southold, L.I., 1681.

COREY, WILLIAM, —— 1704. Deputy, Portsmouth, R.I., 1695, 1696.

COREY, CAPT. WILLIAM, —— 1682. Deputy from Portsmouth, R.I., 1678-1680.

CORLISS, GEORGE, 1617-1686. Selectman, Haverhill, Mass., 1648, 1653, 1657, 1670. Constable, 1650.
Weaver, Mrs. John F., Sr.   Michigan

CORNELL, LIEUT. PIETER GUILLIAMSE, —— ——. Lieutenant, Flatbush, L.I., 1686.

CORNELL, RICHARD, 1625-1694. Delegate to First Representative Assembly, under the English, Hepstead, L.I., 1 Mar. 1665, to promulgate the code known as the "Dukes Laws."
Long, Mrs. Alfred T.							Founders

CORNELL, ENS. THOMAS, 1595-1655. Born in England. One of the first settlers in Westchester, N.Y. Constable, 1641. Ensign, 1642. Commissioner, Portsmouth, R.I., 1654-1655, for uniting Towns in Colony Providence.
Long, Mrs. Alfred T.							Founders

CORNELL, WILLIAM GULJANSE, ——— 1702. Magistrate, Flatbush, L.I., 1659-1664.

CORNWALL, WILLIAM, 1634-1677/8. Served in Pequot War from Hartford, Conn. Deputy from Middletown, Conn., 1654, 1664, 1665.
Milburn, Mrs. John T.							Blue Grass

CORSEN, CAPT. CORNELIUS, 1645-1693. Constable, Brooklyn, 1677. Justice of the Peace, Richmond Co., 1684. Captain Militia, Brooklyn, 1685.
Denton, Mrs. John Leet							Michigan

CORTELYOU, JACQUES, ——— 1693. Born in Holland. One of the founders of New Utrecht. Surveyor General of the Colony, 1657. Representative, 1665. Vendue Master, 1672-1685. Justice of the Peace, 1685. Made first map of City of New York.

CORTELYOU, CAPT. JACQUES, circa 1662-1726. Captain of Militia, New Utrecht, 1693.

CORWIN, MATTHIAS, 1590/1600-1658. Born in England. A first settler of both Ipswich and Southold, Mass.

CORY, JOHN, 1618-1685. Appointed Whale Commissioner for the district, 1644. Town Officer.
Riden, Mrs. Joseph Robert, Jr.					Quivira

COSSART, JACQUES, 1639-1685. Manhattan Island (now NY). Founded the village of Bushwick (now Brooklyn, NY). 1666 Treasurer of New Amsterdam (now NY).
Cook, Mrs. Henry B., Sr.						Renss.

CO'lTON, REV. JOHN, 1585-1652. Born in England. Minister of First Church, Boston, Mass., 1633-1652.

COULBOURN, COL. WILLIAM, —— ——. Va. and Md. A founder of Somerset Co., Md. High Sheriff of Co., 1673-1675. Headed Commission for Treaty with Nanticoke Indians.

COURTS, HON. JOHN, before 1620-1697. Born in England. Lord of Maryland Manor. Member of King's Council, 1637.

COWELL, CAPT. EDWARD, —— 1691. Served in King Philip's War as Captain, 1675/6. Died at Boston, Mass.

COWELL, CAPT. JOSEPH, 1640 ——. Served in King Philip's War 1675/6, from Mass.

COWENHOVEN, WILLIAM, 1636 ——. Brooklyn, N.Y. Magistrate, 1661-1662, 1664 in New York.

COX, (COCKE, COXE, COCK), WILLIAM, 1598-before 1656. Burgess, Henrico Co., Va., 1646.

CRAFT/CROFT, GRIFFIN, 1600-1689. 1638 Deputy to the General Court at Boston. 1653 Serg. Craft confirmed as Lt. 1675/6 Craft resigned.
Barrett, Mrs. Carroll Lewis   Missouri

CRANDALL, ELDER JOHN, —— 1676. Commissioner from Newport, R.I., 1658-1659, 1662-1663. Representative, 1670. Deputy from Westerly, R.I., 1670-1671. First Elder of Baptist Society of Westerly, R.I.

CRANE, DEA. AZARIAH, 1647/9-1730. Deacon, 1690. Deputy to Provincial Assembly, 1693/4, 1695. Selectman, Newark, N.J., 1676, 1683, 1694.
La Tarte, Mrs. Robert L.   Michigan

CRANE, HENRY, 1621-1709. Selectman, Milton, Mass., 1679, 1680, 1681.

CRANE, JASPER, 1605-1681. Born in England. Signed the Fundamental Agreement at New Haven, Conn., 1639. Magistrate of New Haven Colony, 1658-1665. Governor's Assistant, Conn., 1665-1667. Deputy from New Haven, 1645, 1647-1649, 1653-1657. Deputy from Newark, N.J., 1675.
La Tarte, Mrs. Robert L.   Michigan

CRANE, JASPER, 2nd., 1651-1712. Member New Jersey Provincial Forces, 1675-1676. Deputy to New Jersey General Assembly from Newark, 1696, 1699. Deputy to Provincial Assembly, 1697-1699. Magistrate, 1696-1699. Townsman, 1681, 1687, 1688, 1693, 1697. Constable, 1690. Surveyor, 1684-1686, 1699.

Cary, Mrs. Edward K.   Ct. Farms
Cary, Miss Linda A.   Ct. Farms
Sutphen, Mrs. S. Davis   Ct. Farms

CRANE, STEPHEN, —— circa 1710. One of the original settlers of
Elizabethtown, 1664/5. Called one of the "Elizabethtown Associates."

CRANSTON, GOV. JOHN, 1625-1679. Commissioner, Deputy and Governor, Rhode Island, 1678-1680.

CRAWFORD, DAVID I, 1625-1710. Born in Scotland. Burgess, Jamestown,
Va., 1692.
Judy, Mrs. Thomas Jefferson   Blue Grass
Myers, Mrs. John L.   Quivira
Robinson, Mrs. Mary Louise   Oklahoma
Rogers, Mrs. Harvey Allen   Blue Grass
Rogers, Miss Lida Ferguson   Blue Grass
Savage, Mrs. Clinton H.   Illinois
Savage, Mrs. George Hubert   Illinois
Thompson, Miss Jane Collins   Blue Grass
Thompson, Miss Molly Andrews   Blue Grass
Thompson, Miss Sarah W.   Blue Grass
Thompson, Miss Shelby Marie   Blue Grass
Wright, Mrs. Chauncey B.   Blue Grass

CRAWFORD, DAVID II, 1662-1762. Born in Va. Vestryman, St. Peter's
Parish, New Kent County, Va., 1687 ——.
Lightfoot, Mrs. Lee Gano   Blue Grass
Little, Mrs. Van Allen   Oklahoma
Watson, Mrs. Lloyd E.   Oklahoma
Watson, Miss Martha Ann   Oklahoma

CREED, WILLIAM, —— 1717. Deputy for Jamaica, L.I., 1687/8. Assessor,
1693. Supervisor, 1696/7.
Long, Mrs. Alfred T.   Founders

CRESSON, CORP. PIERRE, 1609-after 1679. Called Corporal and Member
of the Inferior Court of Justice, Harlem, N.Y., 1660.

CREGIER (KREGIER), CAPT. MARTIN, —— 1713. Capt.-Lieut. of Burgomaster Corps, 1651. Burgomaster, New Amsterdam, 1653. Member of
Governor's Council and its first Captain, 1656. In command of expedition
against the Esopus Indians, 1663. Named in list of Militia Officers, New
Orange (New York), 1673.

CROSBY, GEORGE, SR., circa 1655-Will 1731. Constable for N. Side of Great Wicocomaco, Northumberland Co., Va., 1673.

CROSBY, JOSEPH, 1639-1695. Born in Cambridge, Mass. Selectman, Braintree, 1690. Constable, 1695.

CROSBY, SIMON, 1608-1639. Born in England. Selectman, 1636, 1638-1639. Constable, 1638. Surveyor of Highways, 1637.

CROSBY, REV. THOMAS, 1634/5-1702. Graduated from Harvard as minister, 1653. Minister, Eastham, Mass., 1655-1670.

CROSSMAN, ROBERT, —— 1692. Member Ancient and Honorable Artillery Co., Boston, 1644.

CUDWORTH, JAMES, 1604-1682. 1675 General and Commander-in-Chief Plymouth Colonies in King Philip's War. Deputy and Constable.
Grunwell, Miss Jane Elizabeth   Florida

CULVER, EDWARD, 1600-1685. Born in England. Served in King Philip's War, New London, Conn., 1675-1676.

CURRIER, RICHARD, 1616-1686. Born in England. In Salisbury, Mass., 1641/2. Town Clerk of Amesbury, Mass., 1654, 1658, 1659 and later.

CURTIS, JOHN, 1625-1695/6. Born in England. Justice of the Peace, Burlington County, N.J. Member of Assembly, 1684.

CURTIS, DR. THOMAS, 1598-1681. Born in England. A practical medical man in Wethersfield, Conn., prior to 1657.

CURTIS, WILLIAM, 1592-1672. Born in England. One of first settlers of Roxbury, Mass., 1632.

CURTISS, WILLIAM, 1618-1702, of Stratford and Woodbury, Conn. Represented Stratford, 1667. Captain of Train Band, 1672. A Founder of Woodbury, Conn., 1667. Member of Governor's Council, 1676.

CUSHING, JOHN, 1627-1708. Of Scituate, Mass. Deputy, 1674, 1676, 1679, 1689-1691. Assistant, 1689-1691. Selectman and Representative, Boston, after Plymouth and Mass. Colonies united, 1692.

CUSHING, DEA. MATTHEW, 1589-1660. Born in England. Deacon, First Church Hingham, Mass., before 1660.
Tuttle, Mrs. Laura Rogers   Rhode Island

CUSHMAN, MARY (Allerton), 1616-1696. Born in Holland. Passenger on Mayflower, 1620. Last survivor of the Mayflower Pilgrims.

CUSHMAN, ROBERT, 1577/1625. One of the Recognized Historic Founders of Plymouth Colony, 1620.

CUSHMAN, ELDER THOMAS, 1607/8-1691. Ruling Elder of Plymouth, Mass. Church from 1649 for 42 years.

CUSTIS, MAJOR GENERAL JOHN, 1630-1696. Born in Holland, died Accomac Co., Va. High Sheriff. Surveyor General. Major General. Member of Council of State.

CUTTER, RICHARD, 1621-1693. Born in England. Member Ancient and Honorable Artillery Co., Boston, 1643.

CUTTING, RICHARD, 1621-1695/6. Constable of Watertown, Mass., 1673. Selectman, Watertown, 1693.

DABNEY, CORNELIUS, 1630-1694. Interpreter to Queen of Pamunkey Indians, Va., 1678.
Frye, Mrs. Bernard C.   Ohio
Lee, Mrs. Thomas Harvey   Oklahoma

DADE, MAJ. FRANCIS, 1621-1663. Major in militia, Westmoreland Co., Va.
Parry, Mrs. William Allan   North Carolina

DAGGETT, JOHN, 1626 ——. A first settler of Rehoboth, Mass. North Purchase 1668.

DAGGETT, JOHN, —— 1673. Deputy to Plymouth, Mass. Court, from Rehoboth, Mass., 1648.

DAGGETT, JOSEPH, 1657-1727. Soldier in King Philip's War, Narragansett Expedition, 1676.

DAKIN, THOMAS, 1624-1708. Constable, Concord, Mass., after 1652.

DALE, MAJOR EDWARD, —— 1695. Lancaster Co., Va. Burgess, 1677-1682. Major in Va. Militia, 1680. Justice of Peace, 1669-1684.
Dickerson, Mrs. Taliaferro Crawford   Jamestown Virginia
Holle, Mrs. Charles G.   Quivira

DAMAN, SAMUEL, 1656-1723/4. Born in Reading, Mass. Served in King Philip's War, 1675/6.

DAMON, LT. JOHN, 1620-1708. Born in England. Selectman, Reading, Mass., 1672, 1675, 1681, 1686, Reading Co. Regiment Lieut. prior to King Philip's War.

DANE, REV. FRANCIS, 1616-1697. Born in England. Minister at Andover, Mass., 1649-1697.

DANFORTH, CAPT. JONATHON, 1627-1712. Born in England. Surveyor. Town Clerk. Selectman and Representative, Billerica, Mass. Militia Captain.

DANFORTH, NICHOLAS, 1589-1638. Came from England to Boston in the "Griffin" 1634. Settled in Cambridge, MA. Deputy 1635. Selectman 1635-1636.
Wells, Mrs. John K.   Illinois

DANIEL, ROBERT, —— 1655. Born in England. Constable, Watertown, Mass., 1651.

DANIEL, CAPT. WILLIAM, 1630-1698. Captain in Middlesex Co., Va. Militia, 1689. Justice of Peace, 1686-1690. Vestryman, Christ Church, 1684-1691.

DANNIEL (DANIELS), JOSEPH, 1640-1715. Selectman, Medfield, Mass., 1693-1696.

DASHIELL, JAMES, SR., 1634-1697. Member House of Burgesses, Somerset Co., Md., 1682. Member of Lower House of Assembly of Md., 1681. Commissioner, 1683. Justice several times.
Scott, Miss Mildred Addie   Ohio

DAVENPORT, CHARLES, 1652-1719/20. Served in King Philip's War, from Dorchester, Mass., 1675/6.

DAVENPORT, REV. JOHN, 1597-1670. Pastor, New Haven, Conn., 1638; then First Church, Boston, Mass., 1667.

DAVENPORT, THOMAS, —— 1685. Constable, Dorchester, Mass.

DAVIS, CORNELIUS, 1653 ——. Born in Mass. Served in King Philip's War, 1675/6.

DAVIS, GEORGE, —— 1667. Selectman, Reading, Mass., 1655, 1656, 1658-1660.

DAVIS, JAMES,—— circa 1643. One of First Settlers of Portsmouth, R.I., 1639. Served in Pequot War, 1637.

DAVIS, JAMES, 1585-1679. A First Settler of Haverhill, Mass., 1640. Deputy, 1660.

DAVIS, JOHN, —— ——. Represented Haverhill, Mass., 1660.

DAVIS, THOMAS, 1603-1683. Selectman, Haverhill, Mass., 1646, 1648. Weaver, Mrs. John F., Sr.   Michigan

DAVIS, SERGT. TOBIAS, —— 1690. First Sergeant of the Ancient and Honorable Artillery Co. of Boston, 1668.

DAVISON, NICHOLAS, 1611-1664. Arrived America circa 1630 as Agent for Gov. Craddock. Lived at Charlestown, Mass., 1639. Elected to be Cornett of County Troop.

DAVOL, WILLIAM, —— after 1680. Constable, Rehoboth, Mass., 1649.

DAY, GEORGE, circa 1640-1685. A Founder of Newark, N.J., from Milford, Conn., 1666; signer of Fundamental Agreement.

DAY, JOHN, 1654-1727. Member of Capt. Samuel Moseley's Co., Dedham, Mass., 24 July 1675 and 24 April 1676.

DAY, ROBERT, 1604-1648. One of the Original Proprietors of Hartford, Conn. 1636. Name on Founder's Monument.

DAY, ROBERT, 1605-1683. Selectman, Ipswich, Mass., 1663-1669.

DAYTON, RALPH, 1588-1658. Born in England. Constable, Easthampton, L.I., 1651, 1652.

DAYTON, ROBERT, 1628-1712. Constable, Easthampton, L.I., 1661-1664. Overseer, 1667, 1668. Selectman, 1674.

DEAN, SAMUEL, —— 1703. Selectman of Stamford, Conn., 1680.

DEBART, CHARLES FREDERICK, —— ——. A First Settler, Manakintowne, Va., 1699.

DE BEVOISE, CAREL, —— ——. First Schoolmaster, Brooklyn, L.I., 1660. Secretary to Town Clerk, Court Messenger, 1662-1669.

DE GROOT, WILLIAM PIERTERSGEN, —— ——. Born in Holland. Arrived in America prior to 1654 (date of purchase of land and house). On list of Representative Pioneer Settlers of New Netherland from Haarlem, Holland. Sergt., Ensign., Lt. of 1st Regiment, New Jersey's Middlesex Co. Militia.

DE HART, SIMON AERTESEN, ———— ————. Emigrated to America, 1664. Settled on Long Island. Trustee and Overseer, Brooklyn, 1680-1683.

DEKAY, JACOB THEUNIS, 1630-1691. Warden and Vestryman of Reformed Dutch Church before 1691.
Papenhagen, Mrs. Frank W.   Florida

DEKKER, LIEUT. JAN BROERSEN, ———— after 1682. Member, Military Company, Ulster Co., N.Y., 1660, 1661. Magistrate, Hurley and Marbletown, N.Y., 1673. Lieut., Military Co., Kingston, Hurley and Marbletown, 1673.
Long, Mrs. Alfred T.   Founders 7

DE LA GRANGE, JOHANNES, ———— ————. Emigrated from New Rochelle, France, 1656. A First Settler, New Amsterdam, N.Y., 1660.

DE LA BOWNE ca 1600-1677. Gravesend, LI, later Middletown, NJ. 1648 patentee of Gravesend, LI, Magistrate 1665. Line closed 30 May 1982.
Jackson, Mrs. Alison N.   Florida

DELAMATER, DEA. GLAUDE, 1620-1683. Born in Artois. Magistrate, Harlem, N.Y., four times between 1666 and 1673. Deacon, 1675.

DELAMATER, ISAAC, 1658-1726. Born in Flatbush, L.I. Magistrate, Harlem, N.Y., 1686.

DE LA NOY, CORP. ABRAHAM, 1642-1707. Corporal, Second Burgher Corps, New Amsterdam, 1653.

DEMAREST (DE MAREE), DAVID, 1620-1693. Delegate to Provincial Assembly, New Netherland, 1664. Ruling Magistrate, New Harlem, 1672. Delegate to Landtag Meet in City Hall, 1664.
Scott, Mrs. C. Edward   Ohio

DEMING, SERGT. JOHN., 1615-1705. Deputy, Wethersfield, Conn., 1649-1667. One of Patentees of Connecticut Charter granted by King Charles II, 1662.

DENISON, MAJ. GEN. DANIEL, 1612-1682. Born in England. Capt. of Militia, Ipswich, Mass., 1637. Deputy. Speaker of the House of Representatives, 1649, 1652. Secretary of the Colony, 1653. Major General, 1653. Reserve Commissioner of the United Colonies in 1658, and Commissioner of same, 1654-1662. Assistant, 1664-1682.

DENISON, CAPT. GEORGE, 1620-1694. Born in England. Deputy from Stonington, Conn., 1654, 1656, 1671, 1674, 1675, 1678, 1682-1687,

1689, 1694. Capt. of New London Co. Troops, King Philip's War, 1675/6.

Clark, Mrs. John Whitfield   Tejas
Elrod, Mrs. Lowell A.   Louisiana
Heathington, Miss Gail Ann   Tejas
Oncley, Mrs. John Lawrence   Michigan
Parenteau, Mrs. Jerome Francis   Quivira

DENISON, JOHN, SR., —— 1683. Soldier in King Philip's War, 1675.

DENISON, JOHN B., 1646-1698. Born in Roxbury, Mass. Served in King Philip's War, 1675/6, from Stonington, Conn.

DENISON, WILLIAM, 1571-1653. Born in England. Deputy from Roxbury, Mass., 1634. Member Militia, 1636.

DENISON, CAPT. WILLIAM, 1655-1715. In King Philip's War, 1675/6.

DENNIS, ROBERT, —— 1691. Deputy from Portsmouth, R.I., 1673-1684.

DENTON, REV. RICHARD, 1586-1662. Born in England. Minister at Watertown, Mass., 1634; Stamford, Conn. 1635-1644; Hempstead, L.I., 1644-1659.

DE NYSE, TEUNIS, —— 1685. Came from Holland, 1638. Settled in New Amsterdam, then moved to Brooklyn, L.I. Magistrate, 1658,1661.

DE PEYSTER, JOHANNES, 1620-1685. Schepen of New Amsterdam, 1655-1657, 1658, 1662. Alderman of New York, 1666, 1667, 1669. Burgomaster, New Amsterdam, 1673. Deputy Mayor of New York, 1674.

DE POTTER, CORNELIS, —— before Oct. 1660. Magistrate, Flatlands, L.I., 1654.

DE RAPELJE (RAPALLE), LIEUT. DANIEL JORIS, 1650-1725. Ensign and Lieutenant, 1673. Name on Assessment Roll, Brooklyn, 1675, Census, 1698.

DE RAPELJE, JERONIMUS, 1643 ——. Schepen, Brooklyn, L.I., 1673-1674. Justice, 1689-1690.

DE RAPELJE (RAPALLE), JORIS JANSEN, 1600-1665. Came from France in the "Unity," 1623. Settled in Fort Orange, N.Y. Removed to New Amsterdam, 1626, and Breuckelen, 1653. One of Committee of Twelve, 1641. Magistrate, Brooklyn, N.Y., 1655-1657,1660.

Russ, Mrs. Rolan G.   Tejas

DE REVERE, ELDER ABRAHAM, SR., —— after 1700. First Elder, Tarrytown, N.Y. Dutch Church, 1697.

DE REVERE, ELDER ABRAHAM, JR., —— 1716. Deacon and Elder in Tarrytown Dutch Church. Ordained Elder, 1697.

DEROACHBRUNE, LEWIS, —— Will 5 Dec. 1702. Listed as Physician on document, Maryland, 10 Aug. 1699.
Hungerford, Mrs. Edward   Pennsylvania
Monk, Mrs. Robert S.   Pennsylvania

DESMAREST, DAVID, 1620-1693. Constable, Harlem, 1664. Delegate to Provincial Assembly, New Netherland, 1664. Delegate to Landtag Meet in City Hall, 1664. Overseer, 1667. Ruling Magistrate, New Harlem, 1672.
Stevenson, Mrs. James T.   Florida

DE SILLE, NICASIUS, 1600-1682. Born in Holland. Schout Fiscal of New Netherland, 1656-1664. First Councillor to the Director General, 1653-1664. Commissioner of Boundaries, 1654-1656. Capt.-Lt. of Burgher Corps., 1656.

DE ST. DENIS, LOUIS JUCHEREAU, 1676-1744. Fort Maurepas, MS. 1699 Captain in a colonizing expedition to explore and settle the coast of MS.
Jones, Mrs. William M.   Florida

DEWEY, JOSIAH, SR., 1641-1732. Deacon. Sergt. of guard, Westfield, Mass., 1676.

DE WTT, CORP. PIETER JANSEN, ————. Emigrated from Holland, 1652. Settled in Bushwick, L.I. Magistrate, 1661-1662, 1665. Corporal, 1663.

DE WITT, TJERCK CLAESSEN, —— 1700/01. Magistrate of Ulster Co., N.Y., 1689. Trustee of Kingston, N.Y., 1694/5.
Long, Mrs. Alfred T.   Founders
Collins, Mrs. John A.   Michigan

DEXTER, REV. GREGORY, 1610-1700. Pastor, First Baptist Church, Providence, 1669. President, Providence and Warwick, 1653. Representative, 1650. Went to London and secured charter for Rhode Island.

DEYO, CHRISTIAN,—— Will, 1686/7. Patentee of New Paltz, 1677. (New York)

DEYO, PIERRE, 1649/50 ——. Patentee of New Paltz (New York), 1677.

DICKERMAN, THOMAS, —— 1657. Born in England. Selectman, Dorchester, Mass., 1651.

DICKINSON, NATHANIEL, 1600-1676. Town Clerk, 1645. Deputy to General Court, 1646-1656. War Commission for Wethersfield, 1653, 1654. Town Clerk, Hadley, Mass., 1663. Member Hampshire Troop, 1663.
Serrell, Miss Alice Dorothy   Michigan

DIGGES, GOV. EDWARD, 1621-1676. Born in England, died York County, Va. Governor, 1656-1658. Agent of the Colony to England, Mar. 1658. Governor's Council, 1654, 1670.
Burger, Mrs. Harry   Missouri
Giulvezan, Mrs. Isabel Stebbins   Missouri
Haugh, Mrs. Charles Roland   Jamestown Virginia
Scherrer, Mrs. Joseph Diedonne, Jr.   Missouri
Walton, Mrs. Josiah Harry   Missouri

DILLINGHAM, EDWARD, 1595-1666/7. Surveyor, 1640, 1641, 1653. Deputy to General Court, Plymouth, 1643. On committee to purchase Manomet, 1654.

DILLARD, GEORGE, 1634/5 ——. Received land for military service against Indians in Va., 1660.

DIMMOCK, SHUBAEL, 1644-1732. Ensign, Militia Co., Barnstable Trainband, 1683. Deputy from Barnstable, 1685, 1686, 1689.
Weaver, Mrs. John F., Sr.   Michigan

DIMMOCK, THOMAS, 1604-1658. Selectman, 1635. Founder of Barnstable, 1639. Deputy, Plymouth Colony, Dorchester, Mass., 6 times after 1640, 1641, 1642, 1648, 1649, 1650. Magistrate, 1641, 1644. Lieut., 1643. Council of War, 1642.
Weaver, Mrs. John F., Sr.   Michigan

DIRCKS, VOLCKERT, baptized 1643-about 1696. Member of military, 1663. Magistrate, Boswyck, 1673.
Talbert, Miss Alberta Marie   Illinois

DISBROW, PETER, 1631-1688. Representative from Rye to Court of Conn., 1665.

DOANE, DEA. JOHN, 1590-1685. Born in England. Assistant to Governor, Plymouth, Mass., 1633. Deputy from Plymouth, 1639-1642; from Eastham, 1649-1651, 1653, 1654, 1659. Deacon at both places.
Boden, Miss Kip Kelso duPont   Pennsylvania
Johnson, Mrs. Francis Lee   Quivira

Kysor, Mrs. Willis Earl   Quivira
London, Mrs. George Abraham   Quivira
Spencer, Mrs. Thomas M. III   Quivira

DODGE, JOHN, 1631-1711. Deputy to General Court, 1677, 1680, 1682, 1689-1690. King Philip's War under Capt. Appleton, 1675/6.
Cunningham, Mrs. W. Scott   Illinois

DOGGETT, REV. BENJAMIN, 1637-1681/2. Rector of Christ' Church and St. Mary's White Chapel.

DOGGETT, SAMUEL, 1652-1725. Selectman, Marshfield, Mass., 1684. Constable, 1685.

DOGGETT, THOMAS, 1607-1692. Born in England. Constable, Marshfield, Mass., 1661. Surveyor, 1662. Selectman, 1664/5.

DOLSON, TEUNUS, 1664-1766. Constable of Harlem, 1697.

DOOLITTLE, SERGT. ABRAHAM, 1620-1690. Corp., New Haven, 1657. Member Vigilance Committee, King Philip's War, Wallingford, Conn., 1675. Deputy from New Haven and Wallingford, 1671-1672.
Milburn, Mrs. John T.   Blue Grass

DOTY, EDWARD, 1599-1655. Passenger on Mayflower, 1620.
Dienna, Mrs. Jack Breeden   Tejas
Filipiak, Mrs. Paul   Founders
Flynn, Mrs. Robert T.   Illinois
Roberts, Mrs. Robert Louis   Founders
Seifert, Mrs. Herbert Otto   Founders

DOW, CAPT. HENRY, 1634-1707. From England to N.H. Served in Narragansett Campaign, 1675/6. Capt. in Hampton, N.H. Militia, 1690. Deputy, 1695, 1697, 1699.

DOUGLAS, WILLIAM, I, 1610-1682. Recorder and Moderator, 1667, 1668. Deacon, 1670. Deputy, Hartford, 1672. Sealer and packer, 1673-1674.

DRAKE, CAPT. FRANCIS, 1615-1687. From Essex, England. Justice, Piscataway Co., N.J., 1662. Member of State Assembly. Capt. of Militia, 1675.

DRAKE, JOB, —— 1648. From England to Dorchester, Mass., 1630. Constable, Windsor, Conn., 1652.

DRAKE, JOHN, —— 1659. Born in England. One of the first settlers of Windsor, Conn., 1640.

DRAKE, JOHN, JR., —— 1689. Born in England. A first settler of Windsor, Conn., 1640. Served in King Philip's War, 1675/6.

DRAKE, ENS. JOSEPH, 1661-1731. Constable, Eastchester, N.Y., 1685. Ensign, 1696.

DRAKE, SAMUEL, —— 1686. Deputy to General Assembly at Hartford, Conn., from Eastchester, N.Y., 1662.
Christopher, Mrs. Harry   CT Farms
Linskey, Mrs. Edward E., Jr.   Florida

DRESSER, LIEUT. JOHN, 1640-1723/4. Sergeant, Rowley, Mass., 1686. Lieut. from Rowley, Mass., in Provincial Forces Foot Co., Massachusetts Bay Colony, 1691-1698. Representative, Rowley, 1691.
Fugate, Mrs. Karen Lisenby   Illinois

DREWETT (DROUETT), MORGAN, 1629-1695. One of the first of nine men to form council chosen by Lieut. Gov. Wm. Markham of Penn., 1681.

DRIVER, GILES, 1625/30-1676. 1663 acted as attorney to collect debts. VA.
Hooper, Mrs. Matthew L.   Florida

DRURY, LT. HUGH, —— 1689. Member of Ancient and Honorable Artillery Co., Mass., 1659.

DU BOIS, ELDER LOUIS, 1627-1696. Soldier in Indian uprising, 1663. One of the patentees of Wallkill Grant, 1677. Elder, New Paltz Church, 1683. Indian War, 1670.
Woodward, Mrs. Gordon H.   Renss.

DUDLEY, GOV. THOMAS, 1576-1653. Born in England. Governor, Mass., 1634, 1640, 1645, 1650. Deputy Governor, 1630-1633, 1637-1639, 1646-1649, 1651, 1652. Governor's Assistant in England, 1629; in Mass., 1635, 1636, 1641-1644. Commissioner, United Colonies, 1643, 1647, 1649. Lieut. Col., South Suffolk Regiment, 1636. Sergt. Major General, 1644. A Founder of HarvardCollege.

DUDLEY, WILLIAM, —— 1683. One of the first settlers of Guilford, Conn., 1639. Representative to General Court for Guilford.

DUMBLETON, JOHN, —— 1702. Selectman, Springfield, Mass., 1654-1691.

DUMONT, DEA. WALLERAND, —— ——. 2nd Lieut., New Amsterdam, 1657. Magistrate, Kingston, N.Y., 1669-1671. Deacon, 1673.

DUNBAR, PETER, 1668 ———. Selectman, Hingham, Mass., 1699.
Cavic, Mrs. Leslie V.   Missouri

DUNGAN, THOMAS, 1634-1687. Born in London, England. Settled in E.
Greenwich, R.I. A Patentee, 1677. Rhode Island Assembly,1678-1681.
Williams, Mrs. Pickette Laney   North Carolina

DURFEE, THOMAS, 1643-1712. Portsmouth, RI prior to 1664. Constable
1687, 1688, 1690. 1691-1694 Deputy.
Hirschey, Mrs. Alice Traffarne   Florida

DURY (DURYEE), DEA. JAN, ——— 1698. Deacon, Dutch Church,
Hackensack, N.J., 22 May 1698.

DUTCH, OSMAN, ——— ———. Selectman, Gloucester, Mass., 1650.

DUTCH, ROBERT ca 1663-16 Nov. 1684. Ipswich, MA Bay. Soldier in King
Philip's War.
Feiring, Mrs. Lester J.   Florida

DU TRIEUX, PHILIP, ——— ———. Born in Roubaix, France. Settled in New
Amsterdam. Court Messenger, 1638.

DU VALL, MAREEN, 1630-1694. Born in France. Arrived in America, 1650.
Appointed Commissioner by the General Assembly, 1683. A Patentee,
Anne Arundel Co., Md.
Boucher, Mrs. Avery Neal   Oklahoma
Carpenter, Mrs. Albert E.   Quivira
Cooper, Mrs. James F.   Illinois
Graves, Mrs. Henry T.   Jamestown Virginia
Kline, Mrs. Wilmer Grant   Quivira
Skold, Mrs. Robert E.   Pennsylvania
Tolbert, Mrs. Tommy L.   Missouri

DUYCKING, EVERT, 1621-1702. Born in Holland. In garrison, Fort Hope,
Conn., 1641.

DWIGHT, JOHN, 1605-1660. A Founder of Dedham, Mass., 1635. Member
of First Town Council, 1635. A Founder of Church of Christ, 1638.
Selectman, 1639-1655.
Engle, Mrs. Kline d'Aurandt   Quivira

DYER, DEACON THOMAS, 1612-1670. Born in England. Settled at
Weymouth, Mass. Deputy, General Court, 1646, 1647, 1650, 1653-
1656, 1658, 1660, 1661, 1663, 1665, 1666, 1668, 1674-1676.

DYER, WILLIAM, circa 1612-1677. Rhode Island Commander-in-Chief, 1640-1642. Commissioner, Newport, 1648; Providence, 1655; Warwick, 1661; Newport, 1662.

EAGER, WILLIAM, 1659-1690. Cambridge and Marlborough, Mass. In Capt. Thomas Prentiss' Company, "Middlesex" troopers. Mt. Hope Campaign, and under Lt. Oakes, 1675-1676.

EAMES, ANTHONY, 1595/6-1686. Born in England. Deputy, General Court from Hingham, Mass., 1637, 1638, 1639, 1644. Lieut., Hingham Co., 1638-1645. Deputy, Plymouth General Ct., for Marshfield, 1653, 1658, 1661. Member of Ancient and Honorable Artillery Co.

EARLE, CAPT. RALPH, 1606-1678. Born in England. Treasurer, Portsmouth, R.I., 1649, 1651. Commissioner, from Portsmouth, 1650. Captain of a Troop of Horse after 1667.

EARLE, SAMUEL I., ca 1640-1697. Attorney 24 Sept 1673, of Virginia
Gillespie, Mrs. Charles H.   North Carolina

EARLE, WILLIAM, —— 1715. Deputy, Portsmouth, R.I., 1693.

EASTMAN, ROGER, circa 1611-1694/5. On orginal List of Townsmen, Salisbury, Mass., 1640.

EASTMAN, THOMAS, 1646-1688. Born in Salisbury, Mass. King Philip's War, 1675. Killed by Indians, Haverhill, Mass.

EASTON, GOV. NICHOLAS, 1593-1675. Born in Wales. Under the First Patent, President of Rhode Island, 1650-1652; under Second Charter, Governor, 1672-1674.

EASTON, PETER, 1622-1694. Commissioner, 1660, 1661. Deputy, 1666, 1671, 1677. Assistant to Governor, R.I., 1667. Attorney General, R.I., 1674, 1676. General Treasurer, 1672-1677.

EATON, FRANCIS, —— 1633. Passenger on the Mayflower, 1620.

EATON, JONAS, —— -24 Feb 1674. Selectman, Reading, MA. First settler of Reading, MA 1643.
Crain, Miss Terri Luanne   North Carolina

EATON, GOV. THEOPHILUS, 1591-1658. Born in England. First Governor, New Haven Colony, 1639-1657. Commissioner of the United Colonies, New Haven, 1643-1651, 1653-1657. Governor's Assistant, Colony of Mass. Bay, 1629.

EDDY, ZACHARIAH, 1639-1718. Way-warden and Surveyor of Highways, 1671. Constable, Swansea, Mass., 1683.
Ashton, Mrs. Robert Lee   Oklahoma
Fishel, Mrs. Maxine Emeline   Michigan

EDDYE/EDDY, SAMUEL, Bpt. 15 May 1608-12 Nov. 1687. 1643 member of troop for defense of the colony of MA.
Carpenter, Mrs. Harry J.   Quivira

EDES, JOHN, 1651 ——. Born in England. Soldier in King Philip's War, 1675/6.

EDSON, DEACON SAMUEL, —— ——. Of Bridgewater, MA. Deacon 1664 until death. Representative to Plymouth Court, 1676. Member of Council of War 1666.
Robison, Mrs. Charles B.   Illinois

EDWON, DEACON SAMUEL,—— ——. Of Bridgewater, Mass. Deacon, 1664, until death. Representative to Plymouth Court, 1676. Member of Council of War, 1666.

ELDRED, SERGT. SAMUEL, 1620-1697. Born in England. Member of Ancient and Honorable Artillery Co. of Boston, 1641. Constable, Wickford, R.I., 1670. King Philip's War, 1675/6.

ELDRED (ELDRIDGE), THOMAS, 1648-1726. Constable, Kings Town, R.I., 1686. Lieut., 1692.
Deisz, Mrs. E.F.   Ohio
Fox, Mrs. E. Tunnicliff, Jr.   Ohio

ELIOT, REV. JOHN, 1664-1690. Born in England. Died in Roxbury, Mass. Ordained first minister, Roxbury, Mass., 1632. Translated Bible into the Indian tongne. Established church for Indians, Natick, Mass. Preached to Indians in their language, Cambridge. Translated some of the Psalms into Indian metre, 1651. The Bay Psalm Book translated by John Eliot and others, printed 1640. Known as "The Apostle to the Indians."

ELIOT, REV. JOSEPH, 1638-1694. A "Teacher," Northampton, Mass., 1662-1664, to assist Rev. Eleazer Mather. Ordained, Guilford, Conn. 1665, preaching there for about thirty years until his death.

ELIOT, COL. PHILIP, 1602-1657. Deputy from Roxbury, Mass. to General Court of Mass. Bay, 1654-1657. Col. of Militia, Roxbury; Member of Ancient and Honorable Artillery Co., Boston, 1638.

ELLINGWOOD, RALPH, JR., 1657-1740. Member of Capt. Gardner's Swamp fight, 1675.

ELLIS, LIEUT. JOHN, circa 1619-1677. At Sandwich, Mass., 1643. Appointed by Court to be Lieut. of Militia, 1651.

ELLIS, THOMAS, ―― 1688. Registrar General of Pa. at time of death, 1688.

ELTON, JOHN, ―― 1670. One of the earliest settlers of Middletown and Branford, Conn. At Southold, L.I., 1640.

ELY, JOSHUA, 1647-1702. Born in England. Constable for "The Falls of the Delaware," 1685. Justice, Burlington Co., West Jersey, 1699.
Bezanson, Mrs. Priscilla, H.   Territorial

ELY, NATHANIEL, 1605-1675. Born in England. Constable, Hartford and Windsor, Conn., 1639. Selectman, 1643. Assisted making first settlement, Norwalk, Conn. Constable, 1649. Selectman, 1656. Deputy, 1657. Removed to Springfield, Mass., 1659. Selectman, Springfield, Mass., for several years from 1661.

ELY, WILLIAM, 1647-1717. Deputy, Lyme, 1689, 1695-1697, to Connecticut General Assembly.

ELLYOT, LIEUT. COL. ANTHONY, ―― circa 1666. Born in England. Arrived in Va. before 1645. Lieut. Colonel, Va. Militia; Burgess, Elizabeth City, Va., 1647.

ELLYSON, ROBERT, ―― before 1671. Sergt.-at-Arms, Virginia House of Burgesses, 1660-1663. Rank of Captain. Sheriff, St. Mary's, Md.; Lawyer and physician in York and James City Cos.,Va.
Hutton, Mrs. Barbara Crew   Oklahoma

EMERSON, REV. JOHN, 1625-1700. Ordained first minister, Gloucester, Mass., 6 Oct. 1663, and preached there until his death.

EMERSON, MICHAEL, ―― 1709. Constable, Haverhill, Mass., 1659.

EMERSON, ROBERT, ―― 1694. Born in England. Constable, Haverhill, Mass., 1679. Selectman, Rowley, 1671, 1676, 1678, 1687.

EMERY, JOHN, JR., about 1628-Will, 1695. Selectman, Newbury, Mass., 1670-1673.

EMERY, JOHN, SR., 1598-1683. Selectman, Newbury, Mass., 1661.

EMLEY, WILLIAM, 1648-1704. Representative, West Jersey, 1682. Member of Governor's Council, 1684.

ENDECOTT, GOV. JOHN, 1588-1665. Deputy Governor, then Governor several terms, Mass. Bay Colony, 1628-1665; except between 1650-1654.
Finlay, Mrs. Christopher A.   Quivira
Ludwig, Mrs. Earl W.   Illinois
Watkins, Mrs. William Homer   Quivira

EPES, LT. COL. JOHN, 1626-1679/80. Justice and member of Co. Militia, Charles City Co. VA.
Jones, Mrs. Felix Henley, Jr.   Tejas

ENSIGN, JAMES, ——— ———. Among first settlers of Hartford, CT.
Flahaven, Mrs. John E.   Illinois

EVERDEN, ANTHONY, —— 1687. Deputy from Providence, R.I., 1667. Member of Town Council, 1667.

EWEN, CAPT. RICHARD, ——— ———. Justice, Maryland, 1654-1657. Captain, 1655. Speaker, Upper House, 1657-1659.

EXUM, JEREMIAH, —— 1720. Settled in Isle of Wight Co., Va., by 1681. Justice, Surry Co., Va., 1681. Justice, Isle of Wight Co., Va., 1693-1694.
Crowder, Mrs. Roy Hester   North Carolina
Crowder, Miss Venia Moye   North Carolina

FAIRBANKS, CAPT. GEORGE, —— 1682/3. Born in England. Signed Dedham Covenant, 1636. Member Ancient and Honorable Artillery Co., of Boston, 1644. A first settler, Sherburne, Mass., 1674. Selectman, 1678-1682. Incorporator town, 1662.

FAIRBANKS, JONATHAN, I, before 1600-1668. A Founder of Dedham, Mass., 1636.
Mrs. Floyd William Alterfer   Michigan

FAIRBANKS, DR. JONATHAN, 1662-1699. Born in Dedham, Mass. Selectman, Sherburne, Mass., 1685-1699. Clerk, 1699.

FAIRCHILD, THOMAS, —— 1670. Born in England. Appointed to press men for service in Narragansett expedition, Stratford, Conn., 1654. Representative, 1654-1669.
Greason, Mrs. James B., Jr.   Founders

FAIRFIELD, ENS. WALTER, 1631-1723. Born in England. King Philip's War, 1675/6.

FALES, JAMES, —— 1708. Surveyor, Walpole, Mass., 1670. One of Town's first settlers.

FALKINBURGH, HENRY JACOBS, 1655-1725. Born in Holstein. Interpreter between Indians and English; between Dutch and Swedes. One of the Founders, Little Egg Harbor, N.J.

FARLEY, GEORGE, 1615-1693. King Philip's War, 1675/6. Owned house for Garrison at Billerica, Mass.

FARNSWORTH, THOMAS, —— ——. Constable, Chesterfield Township, N.J., 1689.

FARRAR, WILLIAM, 1593/5-1637. Commissioner for Upper part of Va., 1628. Member of Council, 1623-1633.
King, Mrs. Sidney Scott, Jr.   Florida
Tutt, Mrs. Fehrlin E.   Tejas

FARROW, JOHN, 1639-1716. Constable, Hingham, Mass., 1672.

FARWELL, HENRY, 1605-1670. Took Oath of Allegiance, Freeman of Mass. Bay Colony, 14 Mar. 1638/9. Deacon, Chelmsford.
Smith, Mrs. Wakelee Rawson   Illinois
Huffman, Mrs. Stanley P.   Florida

FAXON, THOMAS, 1601-1680. Born in England. Deputy, Braintree,Mass., 1669-1672.

FAY, JOHN, 1648-1690. King Philip's War, 1675. Constable, Marlborough, Mass., 1688.

FEAKE, HENRY, circa 1590-Will, 1657. Deputy, Sandwich, Mass.,1643-1644.

FEAKE, LIEUT. ROBERT, 1610-1660. From England in fleet with Governor Winthrop, 1630. Settled in Watertown, Mass. Freeman, 1631. Lieutenant, 1632. Selectman, 1637, 1639, 1640. Deputy, 1634-1636. Justice, 1636. Removed to Greenwich, Conn., 1639; in Flushing, L.I., 1650.

FELT (FELCH), GEORGE, 1601-1693. A First settler of North Yarmouth (Casco Bay, Maine), 1643.

FELT, GEORGE, JR., 1639/40-1675. Killed in King Philip's War, Portland, Maine, 1675.

FENN, BENJAMIN, before 1640-1672. Representative, Milford, Conn., 1653. Assistant, Milford, 1654. Proprietor, New Haven Colony. Magistrate, New Haven, 1660. Commissioner, New Haven, 1661-1663.

FENNER, CAPT. ARTHUR, 1622-1703. Born in England. Commissioner, Providence, R.I., to General Court, 1653, 1655, 1660, 1662-1663. Assistant to Governor, R.I., 1657, 1665-1668, 1672-1676, 1679-1686, 1690. Deputy, 1664, 1670, 1672, 1678-1679, 1692-1699. Captain before 1670. King Philip's War, 1675/6.

FENNER, CAPT. JOHN, —— 1709. Born in England. Town Sergeant, Providence, R.I., 1657.

FENNER, MAJ. THOMAS, 1652-1718. Born, Providence Plantation, R.I. King Philip's War, 1676. Deputy, 1698.

FENNO, JOHN, 1629-1708. King Philip's War, 1675.

FERRIS, JEFFREY, 1610-1666. A First Settler of Watertown, Mass., 1635; of Stamford, Conn., 1641.

FERRIS, JOHN, —— 1715. Patentee, Westchester, N.Y. Named in Patent, 1667.

FIELD, JOHN, —— 1686. A Signer of the first written Compact of Town of Providence, R.I., 1637. Deputy, 1676.

FIELD, CAPT. PETER, 1647-1707. Born in Virginia. Member of Va. House of Burgesses; Captain in Militia, Henrico Co., Va., 1693.

FIELD, ROBERT, 1605-1673. In Newport and Portsmouth, R.I., 1638; Providence, 1640. Member, Court of Elections. Special Commissioner to take measures to defend the Colony against the Dutch. In Flushing, L.I., 1645. Deputy, 1653.

FIELD, ROBERT, JR., 1636-1701. Constable, Newtown, L.I., 1697. Overseer, 1672, 1674, 1675, 1678, 1680.

FIELD, SAMUEL, 1651-1696. Soldier in Turner's Falls Fight 19 May 1676. King Philip's War, killed by Indians 1697.
Reeser, Mrs. Archibald W.   North Carolina

FIELD, THOMAS, —— 1717. Deputy, Rhode Island, 1667, 1670, 1683, 1685, 1692, 1695. Town Council, 1681, 1683. Assistant 1673, 1674. Town Treasurer, 1674, 1680, 1688.

FILKIN, CAPT. HENRY, 1651-1713. Born in England. Justice of the Peace, 1693. Member of Assembly from Kings Co., N.Y., 1693-1696. Captain, 1697.

FILMER, MAJOR HENRY, —— 1673. Born in England. Member of Virginia House of Burgesses from James City and Charles City Counties, Va., 1642/3.

Ewalt, Miss Josephine Hedges	Blue Grass
Lesueur, Mrs. Alexander Armand	Blue Grass
Lonas, Mrs. Leonard L., Jr.	Florida
Rogers, Mrs. Fielding Gant	Blue Grass

FINNEY, JEREMIAH, 1662-1748. Born in Barnstable, Mass. A First Settler, Bristol, R.I., 1681.

FINNEY, JOHN, —— ——. Born in England. A First Settler, Bristol, R.I., 1681.

FISH, JOHN, 1608 ——. Of Stonington, Conn. King Philip's War, 1675. Schoolmaster, 1679.

FISH, CAPT. SAMUEL, 1656-1733. Of Groton, Conn. Selectman. Served in King Philip's War, 1675.

FISH, THOMAS, —— 1687. Constable, Portsmouth, R.I., 1665-1670. Selectman, 1674.

FISHER, ANTHONY, 1591-1670/1. Born in England. Member Ancient and Honorable Artillery Co. of Boston, Mass., 1649. Deputy, Dedham, 1649. County Commissioner, 1660.

Bryan, Mrs. James B.	Jamestown Virginia

FISHER, CAPT. DANIEL, 1620-1683. Born In England. Settled at Dedham, Mass. Selectman, 1650. Town Clerk, Speaker of House of Deputies, 1680, 1681, 1682. Captain of Artillery Company, 1673.

FISK, JOHN, 1619-1684. Served in King Philip's War, Watertown, Mass., 1675/6.

Davis, Mrs. Franklin Dale	Michigan
Koerber, Mrs. Gene Lewis	Michigan
Koerber, Mrs. Ruth E.	Michigan

FISKE, WILLIAM, 1613-1654. Born in England. Town Clerk, Wenham, Mass., 1643-1654. Deputy, 1646, 1649-1652.

FISKE, LIEUT. WILLIAM, 1642/3-1728. Born Wenham, Mass. Ensign, Wenham, Mass., 1683. Lieutenant, 1686. Deacon, Congregational Church, 1679.

FITCH, DEP. GOV. THOMAS, 1612-1704. Clerk of Norwalk Train Band, 1655. Deputy-Governor of Connecticut.

FITCH, CAPT. THOMAS, 1630-1690. Captain in King Philip's War, 1675.

FITZ RANDOLPH, EDWARD, 1614-1675. A Settler of Barnstable, Mass., 1643; also Piscataway, N.J. Took Dutch Oath at Piscataway, 1673.
Troop, Mrs. Horace W., Jr.   Ohio
Wyker,Mrs.Clyde Ely   Ohio

FLAGG, LIEUT. GERSHOM, 1641-1690. Killed in Indian fight at Lee, N.H.,1690.

FLAGG, LIEUT. THOMAS, 1615-1698. Born in England. Selectman, Newbury, Mass., 1671-1678. Lieutenant and Town Officer, Watertown, Mass., 1681

FLEETE, HENRY, circa 1600-before 1660. Born in England. Died in Lancaster Co., Va. Member Va. House of Burgesses, Lancaster Co., 1652. Justice, 1653, 1655. Lieut. Colonel of Militia, 1656.

FLETCHER, DEA. JOHN, —— 1662. Deacon, Milford, Conn., 1662.
Greason, Mrs. James B., Jr.   Founders

FLETCHER, ROBERT, 1592-1677. Born in England. Constable, Concord, Mass., 1637—1639.

FLETCHER, SAMUEL, 1657-1744. Born in Concord, Mass. Served in King Philip's War, 1675/6.

FLINT (FLYNT), REV. HENRY, 1613-1668. Born in Matlock, Derbyshire, England. Minister at Braintree, 1640-1668.
Davis, Mrs. Frank V.   Illinois

FLINT, THOMAS, 1603-1653. Deputy to Mass. General Court, 1638-1641. Assistant to Governor, 1642-1651.

FLINT, WILLIAM, 1603-1673. Surveyor, Lynn, Mass., 1658.

FOLGER, PETER, 1619-1690. Indian and English Interpreter, 1659. Missionary to Indians, 1663. Clerk of the Courts, Nantucket, R.I., 1673.
Taylor, Mrs. Edgar B.   Pennyslvania
Trau, Mrs. Frank Garland   Pennsylvania

FOLIOTT, REV. EDWARD, 1610-1690. Minister of York, Marston and Hampton Parishes, Va., before 1690.

FOLSOM, DEA. JOHN, 1641-1715. One of the Founders of Hampton, N.H.; Deputy to General Court, 1688-1695.

FOOTE, NATHANIEL, 1593-1644. Born in England. Deputy from Wethersfield, Conn., 1641-1642, 1644. Delegate to General Court, 1644. Magistrate, Conn. Colony. One of the Patentees in the Charter of Wethersfield.
Lee, Miss Elizabeth Allison   North Carolina
Lee, Mrs. James Allen   North Carolina

FOOTE, QUARTERMASTER NATHANIEL, 1647-1703. Quartermaster at Falls Fight, King Philip's War, Wethersfield, Conn., 1675/6.

FORD, ANDREW, 1620-before 1692/3. Chosen Warden, Weymouth, Mass., 12 Nov. 1662, for the ensuing year.
Coombes, Mrs. Burleigh Lee, Jr.   Missouri

FORD, THOMAS, —— 1676. Born in England. Deputy from Windsor, Conn., 1637, 1638-1640.
Bachner, Mrs. Thomas Edgar   Tejas

FORMAN, ROBERT, 1605-1671. Born in England. One of the incorporators of Flushing, L.I., 1645. Magistrate, Hempstead, 1658; also Oyster Bay, 1664.
Fiori, Mrs. James V.   Renss.

FOSTER, HOPESTILL, —— ——. Of Dorchester, Mass. Ancient and Honorable Artillery Co., 1642. Ensign in Train Band, 1644-1662. Selectman, 1646. Deputy, 1659-1676.

FOSTER (FFOSTER), JOHN, 1618-1687/8. Served in King Philip's War under Capt. William Turner, 7 Apr. 1676.

FOULKE, THOMAS, 1624-1714. Born in England. Commissioner for establishing the Quakers in New Jersey, 1677.

FOUNTAINE, NICHOLAS, 1640-1708. In expedition against the Nanticoke Indians, Somerset Co., Md., 1678.
Luker, Mrs. E.W.   Oklahoma

FOWKE, COL. GERARD, —— ——. Of Virginia. Born in England. Colonel and County Lieut., Westmoreland Co., Va., 1660. Burgess for Westmoreland Co., 1663. Burgess for Charles Co., Md., 1665.

FOWLER, HENRY, SR., —— 1687. Deputy from Providence, R.I. to General Assembly in Newport, 1671.

FOWLER, HENRY, JR., circa 1657-1733. Justice of Peace, Eastchester, N.Y., 1699.

FOWLER, WILLIAM, —— 1660. Born in England. Magistrate, New Haven Colony, 1643, 1644, 1646, 1653, 1654. Deputy from Milford, Conn., 1657.

FOWLER, CAPT. WILLIAM, —— 1683. Lieut. of Militia, Milford, Conn., 1666. Capt., 1676. Deputy, 1670-1677, 1679, 1680. Member of Council of War, 1673.

FOXWELL, RICHARD, —— 1668. Private, Barnstable, Mass., Militia, 1643.

FRAME, THOMAS, —— ——. Member of Train Band, Amesbury, Mass., 1680. School Master, 1693.

FRAMPTON, WILLIAM, CA 1650-1686 PA. Justice of Peace 1685. Member of Governor's Council 1685-1686.
Utech, Mrs. John J., Jr.   CT Farms
Utech, Miss Susan   CT Farms

FRARY, JOHN, —— 1695. Selectman, Medfield, Mass., 1651, 1653, 1654, 1661.

FRARY, SAMPSON, 1642-1704. Born in Medfield, Mass. Selectman, Deerfield, Mass., 1691.

FREEMAN, EDMUND, 1590-1682. Governor's Assistant, Plymouth Colony, Mass., 1640-1645. Deputy from Sandwich to General Court of Plymouth, 1646. Member of Councils of War, 1642, 1647.
Carousso, Mrs. Georges   Pennsylvania
Hanson, Mrs. Lee D.   Michigan
Rose, Mrs. Earl   CT Farms

FREER, DEACON HUGO, —— ——. Of France and New Paltz, N.Y. Patentee of New Paltz, 1677. Deacon, 1683.

FRENCH, JOHN, 1612-1692. Clerk of the Training Band, prior to 1690.
Lawrence, Mrs. Walter Scott   Illinois
Lawrence, Mrs. Wasson W.   Illinois

FRENCH, THOMAS, 1639-1699. Of New Jersey. One of the Signers of Agreements and Concessions, 3 Mar. 1676-1677.

FRENCH, CAPT. WILLIAM, 1603-1681. Born in England. Member Ancient and Honorable Artillery Co., Boston, Mass., 1638. Sergeant, 1643, 1646. Lieutenant, 1647. Ensign, 1650. Captain, 1681. Representative, Billerica, Mass., 1663-1664.

FRETWELL, PETER, 1659-1718/19. Justice of the Peace, Burlington Co., N.J., 1695, 1696, 1697, 1699. Treasurer, Province West, N.J., 1694, 1699.

FRINK, SERGT. JOHN, —— 1718. Served in King Philip's War, Stonington, Conn., 1675/6.

FRISBIE, EDWARD, 1620-1690. Born Va. Colony. One of the Signers of the "New Plantation," Branford, Conn., 1644. "Church Covenant of Branford," 1667.
Armstrong, Mrs. Donald George   Illinois

FRY, THOMAS, 1666-1748. Born in Newport, R.I. Deputy from East Greenwich, R.I., 1696.

FRY, GEN. SERGT. THOMAS, 1632-1704. General Sergt., Newport, R.I., 1676, 1677, 1678, 1681, 1690, 1691.

FRYE, JOHN, 1603-1695. One of the first settlers of Andover, Mass., 1644. Selectman, 1670.

FRYE, DEA. JOHN, 1600-1693. Born in England. Representative from Andover, Mass., 1692.

FULLER, EDWARD, 1575-1621. Passenger on Mayflower, 1620. Twenty-first Signer of the Mayflower Compact.
Dugan, Mrs. Martin J.   CT Farms
Hinshaw, Mrs. Lyle   Illinois
Schmitz, Mrs. Vernon A.   Renss.

FULLER, JOSEPH, 1658-1731. Born in Ipswich, Mass. Sergt., Militia, King Philip's War, 1675/6.

FULLER, DR. MATTHEW, circa 1603-1678. Born in England. An early Surgeon, Barnstable, Mass. Member of Council of War. Lieut., Capt., Barnstable Co. by 1668.

FULLER, ROBERT, 1604-1706. Advanced money toward the support of King Philip's War, 1675.
Tucker, Mrs. Stuart H.   Rhode Island

FULLER, DR. SAMUEL, 1580-1633. Passenger on Mayflower, 1620. A Signer of the Mayflower Compact. Physician.
Novak, Mrs. Rudolph Leonard   Florida

FULLER, LIEUT. THOMAS, 1618-1698. Sergeant, 1656. Lieut., 1685. Selectman, Woburn, Mass., 1663, 1664, 1685. Deputy, 1664.
Hotaling, Mrs. Alton V.   Renss.

GAGER, JOHN, —— 1703. Constable, Norwich, Conn. 1674-1688.

GAGER, WILLIAM, —— 1630. Deacon, First Church, Charlestown, Mass., before 1630.

GAINES, CAPT. DANIEL, after 1632-1682. Captain in Virginia Militia, 1680.
Mettetal, Mrs. Ray W.   Tennessee

GALLUP, BENADAM, 1655-1727. Born in Stonington, Conn. Served in King Philip's War, 1675-1676. Town Attorney, 1667.

GALLUP, CAPT. JOHN, SR., 1590-1650. Born in England. In fight with Pequot Indians off Block Island, 1636. Called the first naval engagement in New England waters.

GALLUP, JOHN, JR., 1616-1675/6. Born in England. Served in Pequot War, 1637. Captain in King Philip's War, 1675. Indian Interpreter. Representative to General Court, 1665-1667.
Bauer, Mrs. Robert   Illinois

GALLUP, JOHN, 3rd, 1646-1735. Born in Boston, Mass. Served in King Philip's War, from Stonington, Conn., 1675. Representative to General Court, Stonington, Conn., 1685.
Bowen, Mrs. William J.   Renss.
Waters, Mrs. Wayne T.   Renss.

GARDINER, DAVID, 1636-1689. Deputy from towns on eastern end of Long Island to Hartford, Conn., 1689. Second Lord of the Manor of Gardiner's Island.

GARDINER, ENSIGN GEORGE, —— circa 1677. Of Rhode Island. Constable and Senior Sergeant, 1642. Ensign, 1644. Commissioner, 1662.

GARDINER, LIEUT. LION, 1599-1663. Lieutenant of Troops, Conn. 1636-1639. In command during Pequot War, at Fort Saybrook, 1637. First Lord of the Manor of Gardiner's Island.

GARDINER, WILLIAM, circa 1651-1711. Born in R.I. Constable, 1688.

GARDNER, RICHARD, —— 1688. Chief Magistrate, Nantucket, 1673-1675.

GARDNER (GARDINER), THOMAS, 1592-1674. Born in England. Overseer, Cape Ann Colony under the auspices of the Dorchester Company. Representative, 1637. Member Town Council, Salem, many years. Deputy, Salem, Mass., 1636, 1637. Selectman, 1642-1645, 1650, 1655, 1656. Chief Magistrate, Nantucket, 1673.

GARNER, JOHN, 1633-1703. Constable of Cherry Point Neck, Northumberland, Co., Va., 5 May 1665.
Williams, Mrs. Earl   Member-at-Large

GARRETT, THOMAS I., ca 1622/33-1710. Constable and Juryman from 1683-1694, of PA.
Marshall, Mrs. Willard C.   Oklahoma

GASSAWAY, COL. NICHOLAS, 1630-1691. Born in Maryland. Capt., Major, Colonel, Md. Militia 1678-1691. Justice, Anne Arundel Co., Md., 1680, 1682, 1684, 1685, 1689, 1691.

GATES, SIMON. —— ——. Soldier in King Philip's War.
Sharp, Mrs. James R., Jr.   Tennessee

GAY, JOHN, —— 1688. Signed the Dedham Covenant, 1636. Original Proprietor. Member of Assembly, 1636-1654. (Mass.)

GAY, SAMUEL, 1639-1718. Selectman, Dedham, Mass., 1698.

GAYLORD, WILLIAM, 1585-1673. Came from England in the "Mary and John," 1630. Deacon, Dorchester, Mass., 1630. Selectman, Representative, Windsor, Conn., forty-one semi-annual sessions, 1639-1664.
Armstrong, Mrs. Donald George   Illinois

GEORGE, COL. JOHN, 1604-1678. Major, Lt. Col., Col., Isle of Wight Co., Va. Burgess, 1647, 1648, 1652. Councillor, 1652.
Dickerson, Miss Laura   Blue Grass
Thomas, Dr. Elizabeth   Member-at-Large
Lohse, Mrs. Robert R.   Quivira
Pigott, Mrs. Lee D.   Illinois

GERRITSEN, LUBBERT, —— 1673. Born in Holland. Magistrate, Harlem, N.Y., 1672.

GIBBONS, CAPT. AMBROSE, —— 1656. Associate Governor, New Hampshire, 1640. Captain, 1642.

GIDDINGS, GEORGE, —— 1676. Selectman, Ipswich, Mass., 1661, 1675.

GIFFORD, WILLIAM, —— 1687. Born in England. One of the first settlers, Monmouth, N.J., 1667.

GILBERT, CAPT. HENRY, 1661/2-1740. In command of men sent to build Fort Gilbert, West Brookfield, Mass., 1688.

GILBERT, JONATHAN, 1618-1682/3. Born in England. Interpreter, Indian Wars, 1653-1657. Member troop of cavalry, 1657-1658.

GILBERT, THOMAS, circa 1624-1662. Selectman, Springfield, Mass., 1656, 1659/60.

GILBERT, THOMAS, JR., 1658/9-1698. One of men to scout and fortify against the Indians, North Brookfield, Mass., 1688.

GILDERSLEEVE, RICHARD, circa 1601-1681. One of Earliest Elders of Church, Hempstead, L.I., N.Y. Dutch Magistrate, 1643-1664. Magistrate, Hempstead, L.I. 1652-1663.
Corder, Miss Lois B.   Founders
Nichols, Mrs. Norton B.   Florida

GILMAN, JOHN, 1624-1708. Lieut., 1669. Member of Council, N.H., 1680. Speaker of Assembly, 1692/3. Member of Assembly, 1697.

GIST, CHRISTOPHER, —— ——. Colonist, Baltimore County, Md., before 1682. Justice, Baltimore Co., commissioned 4 Sept. 1689.

GILL, THOMAS, 1616-1704/5. Selectman, Hingham, Mass., 1645, 1676, 1684, 1690. Constable, 1668.

GLADDING, JOHN, 1640-1726. Born in England. First settler, Bristol, R.I., 1681.

GLOVER, HENRY, 1612-1689. Commissioner of Fortifications, 1644. Treasurer, 1665. Deputy, New Haven Colony, Conn., 1675.

GLOVER, JOHN, 1600-1653. Born in England. One of the Founders of Colony of Mass. Bay. Deputy, Dorchester, Mass., 1637-1644, 1647-1651. Assistant to Governor, 1652-1653.

GLOVER, JOHN, 1648-1679. Constable, New Haven, Conn., 1676.

GLOVER, NATHANIEL, 1631-1657. Born in Dorchester, Mass. Selectman, Dorchester, Mass., 1655-1657.

GODDARD, WILLIAM, 1627-1691. Born in England. Selectman, Watertown, Mass., 1668, 1669. King Philip's War, 1675/6.

GOLD, MAJ. NATHAN, —— 1694. Assistant to Governor, Conn., 1656-1657, 1659, 1667-1668, 1687, 1689-1694. Judge, Fairfield, 1687. Lieutenant, Fairfield Troops, 1657. Captain, 1669. Major, 1673. Chief Military Officer, 1672.
Barnett, Mrs. Carl G.   Tejas

GOLDSMITH, JOHN, —— 1703. Overseer, Southold, L.I., 1696.

GOOCH, LIEUT. COL. HENRY, —— ——. Lieut. Col., York Co., Va. Militia, in service as officer in Bacon's Rebellion, 1676.

GOOCH, REV. JOHN, 1625-1683/4. Jamestown, VA. Pastor of James City Parish 1676-1677.

GOODENOW, CAPT. EDMUND, 1604-1688. Representative to General Court from Sudbury, Mass., 1645-1650, 1656-1675, 1679-1680. Capt., King Philip's War, 1675-1676.

GOODENOW, THOMAS, 1608-1663. Selectman, Marlborough, Mass., 1661, 1662, 1664.

GOODHUE, DEA. WILLIAM, 1612-1699/1700. Deacon, First church at Ipswich, Mass., 1658. Representative to Colonial Legislature, 1666. Selectman, Ipswich.

GOODRICH, THOMAS, 1614-1679. Born in England. Justice, Rappahannock Co., Va., 1664-1666. Lieut. General in command of northern Va. troops, Bacon's Rebellion, 1675-1676.
Ballance, Miss Charlotte Ann   Illinois
Ballance, Mrs. T. Stehpen   Illinois
Birk, Mrs. Carl Peter, Sr.   Illinois
Klimas, Miss Katherine Cora   Illinois
Klimas, Mrs. Michael J.   Illinois
Klimas, Miss Rebecca Elizabeth   Illinois
Klimas, Miss Victoria Anna   Illinois
Stewardson, Miss Roberta Sue   Illinois

GOODWIN, MAJOR JAMES, 1618-1678. Born in England. Member of Va. House of Burgesses from York County, 1658. Justice, 1657-1662.
Crowder, Mrs. Roy Hester   North Carolina

GOODYEAR, DEP. GOV. STEPHEN, —— 1658. First Dep. Governor, New Haven, Conn., Colony, 1641-1657. Commissioner, United Colonies, 1643.

GOOKIN, MAJ. GEN. DANIEL, 1612-1687. Born in England. Captain, Cambridge, Mass., 1648. Representative, 1649-1651. Speaker, 1651. Assistant, 1652-1686. Chief Commissioner, 1654-1655. Superintendent of the Indians, 1656-1687. Major-General, 1681.
Davis, Mrs. Frank V.   Illinois

GORDON, ALEXANDER, 1630/31-1697. King William's War, Exeter, N.H., 1690, 1695-1696.

GORE, JOHN, 1st, —— 1657. Born in England. Member Ancient and Honorable Artillery Co. of Boston, Mass., 1638 and its' clerk, 1655.

GORHAM, CAPT. JOHN, 1621-1676. Born in England. King Philip's War, 1675-1676. Deputy, from Yarmouth, Mass., 1653.
Hungerford, Miss Dorothy Ann   Pennsylvania
Rozier, Mrs. John C., Jr.   North Carolina

GORSUCH, CHARLES, 1642-1720. Commissioner from Baltimore County, Md. to Maryland Assembly, 10 Nov. 1683.
Hunt, Mrs. Maxwell E.   Michigan
Hutson, Mrs. William Hayes   Florida

GORTON, JOHN, —— 1714. Of Warwick, R.I. Served in King Philip's War, 1675-1676.

GORTON, SAMUEL, 1592-1677. One of the founders of Warwick (Shawomet), R.I., 1642. Fought in Pequot Wars. Commissioner to England, 1644. General Assistant, 1649-1652. President of Providence and Warwick, R.I., 1651. Commissioner from Warwick, 1651, 1652, 1655-1660, 1662, 1663. Deputy, 1664-1667, 1670.
Frederick, Mrs. George H. C.   Illinois
Scheurs, Miss Patricia Anne   Territorial
Smith, Mrs. Carl H.   Michigan

GOSMER (GOSMORE), JOHN, 1574-1661. Born in England. Magistrate, Southampton, L.I., 1651. Deputy, 1651, 1655.

GOSS, JOHN ca 1640-by 1694. Captain. Member of Board of trade. Minister of Southwarke Parrish.
Hunter, Mrs. William H., Jr.   CT Farms

GOULD, CAPT. JOHN, 1635-1709/10. Selectman, Topsfield, Mass., 1663, 1686, 1689 and many other years. Ensign 1671. Lieut., 1686. Captain, 1693.

GOULD, ZACCHEUS, 1589-1668. Original settler, Topsfield, Mass., 1650. First house he built was used for garrison to defend the inhabitants from the Indians.

GOULDING (GOLDEN), WILLIAM, —— after 1686. Granted patent, Monmouth Co., N.J., 1665. Became permanent settler, Middleton, N.J., 1667.

GOVE, EDWARD, 1637-1691. Assemblyman for N.H., 1680, from Hampton, 1682. Lieut. in Militia.
Nicholson, Mrs. John B.   Florida

GRANT, JOHN, 1642-1684. Born in Windsor, Conn. King Philip's War from Windsor, Conn., 1676.

GRANT, DEA. MATTHEW, 1601-1681. Came from England. Settled in Dorchester, Mass., 1630; then to Windsor, Conn. Deacon of the first church and Recorder, 1652-1677.

GRAVES, ISAAC, —— 1677. Born in England. Sergeant, Colonial Militia. Clerk of Writs, Hatfield, Mass. Selectman, 1670. Killed in Indian attack on Hatfield, 19 Sept. 1677.

GRAVES, CAPT. THOMAS, circa 1580-1635/6. Born in England. Arrived in Va., 1608. Represented Smyth's Hundred, first House of Burgesses, 1619, the earliest English deliberative body in America. Represented Accomack Co., 1630, 1632. Subscriber and officer, Va. Company.
McMurran, Mrs. Joseph P.   Jamestown Virginia
McMurran, Miss Susanne Hiden   Jamestown Virginia
Morrow, Mrs. Ruple   Tejas
Nunley, Mrs. Richard L.   Jamestown Virginia

GRAVES, REAR ADMIRAL THOMAS, 1605-1653. Born in England. Commissioned for bravery on the high seas. Commanded first vessel ever built in Boston, Mass., for foreign trade, 1642.
Weaver, Mrs. John F., Sr.   Michigan

GRAY, JACOB, —— 1712. Born in Fairfield, Conn. Constable, 1685.
Greason, Mrs. James B., Jr.   Founders

GRAY, WILLIAM, 1650-1723. Sergt. under Capt. Gorham, Narragansett Campaign, King Philip's War, 1675/6.

GREELEY, ANDREW, 1617-1697. Selectman, Salisbury, Mass., 1652, 1658, 1663. Constable, 1653.

GREEN, LIEUT. HENRY, 1638-1717. Born in England. Lieutenant, King Philip's War, 1675. Representative from Malden, Mass., 1689-1694.

GREEN, JOHN, 1610-1674. Born in England. Representative from Stamford, Conn., 1669-1671, 1673-1674.

GREEN, MARSHAL GEN. JOHN, 1636-1690/1. Marshal General, Cambridge, Mass., Colony, 1680-1681.

GREEN, THOMAS, 1606-1667. Selectman, Malden, Mass., 1652, 1658, 1659.

GREENBERRY, COL. NICHOLAS, 1627-1697. Born in England. Member of Maryland Council, 1692. Lt. Governor and Acting Governor of Md., 1693. Chancellor, 1693-1694. Colonel of Anne Arundel Co., Md., 1694.
Dellinger, Mrs. Nevin W.   Pennsylvania

GREENE, BENJAMIN, circa 1665-1719. Deputy to General Assembly of Rhode Island, 1698.

GREENE, JAMES, 1626-1698. Commissioner, Warwick, R.I., 1660-1663. Governor's Assistant, 1660-1661, 1670-1671. Town Clerk, 1661.

GREENE, DR. JOHN, circa 1590/3-1659. Came to Boston, Mass. from England in the "James," 1635. Settled in Warwick, R.I., 1636. Member of Councils, 1647, 1649. Representative, 1648. Magistrate, 1649. Commissioner, four times, 1650-1657. First professional medical man in Providence Plantation.
Haelsen, Mrs. William H.   Rhode Island

GREENE, MAJ. JOHN, 1620-1708. Born in England. Commissioner from Warwick, R.I., 1652-1663. General Recorder, 1652-1654. General Solicitor, 1655. Attorney General, 1657-1660. Governor's Assistant, 1660-1673, 1678, 1680-1690. Deputy Governor, 1690-1699. Major for the Main, 1683-1686, 1690, 1691, 1696.

GREENE, THOMAS, 1628-1685. Born in England. Settled in Warwick, R.I. Commissioner, 1662. Deputy, 1667-1684. Assistant, 1678-1685.

GREENE, THOMAS, JR., 1662-1698/9. Deputy, R.I., 1698.

GREENE, GOV. THOMAS, —— 1650. Appointed Governor of Maryland, 9 June 1647, 1648, 1649.

GREENHILL, SAMUEL, ————. Died in Hartford, Conn. A First Settler, and Original Proprietor, Hartford, 1636.

GREENLEAF, LIEUT. EDMUND, 1573-1671. Born in England. Ensign, Newbury, Mass., 1639. Lieutenant, 1642.
Woodard, Mrs. Earl Stanley   Oklahoma

GREGORY, JACHIN, —— 1697/8. Born in Norwalk, Conn. Deputy, 1695.

GREGORY, JOHN, 1615-1689. Deputy from Norwalk, Conn., 1665, 1679-1681. Selectman, 1669.
Robinson, Mrs. Mary Davidson   Oklahoma

GREGSON, THOMAS, —— 1646. Judge, New Haven Town, 1640-1643. Assistant, New Haven Colony, 1643, 1646. Commissioner to United Colonies, 1643. Colonial Agent to Parliament, 1644.

GRENAWAY (GREENWAY), JOHN, —— ——. First Settler, Dorchester, Mass. Chosen with twenty other men to "arrange the affairs of the Plantation," 1637.

GRIFFEN, EDWARD, 1602 ——. Born in England. Interpreter between Indians and English, 1661. Overseer, Flushing, L.I., 1680.

GRIFFEN, JOHN, 1655-1742. Constable, Flushing, L.I., 1681.

GRIFFIN, SAMUEL, 1625-1703. High Sheriff Rappahannock Co. VA 1670. Member House of Burgesses 1678. Presiding Justice Northumberland Co. Lt. Col. Co. Militia.
Cartier, Mrs. R. Walter   Florida

GRIFFING, LIEUT. JASPER, 1648-1718. Lieut., Suffolk Co., N.Y., Troops, 1693.

GRIMSLEY, THOMAS, 1661-1744. Constable, (Old Rappahannock Co., Va.) Richmond Co., Va., 1692.

GRISWOLD, EDWARD, 1607-1691. Born in England. Deputy from Windsor, Conn., to General Court, 1650, 1658, 1662, 1663.
Brown, Mrs. Graydon L.   Oklahoma
Evans, Mrs. Bruce Lively   Oklahoma

GRISWOLD, LIEUT. FRANCIS, 1632-1671. Born in England. Deputy from Saybrook and Norwich, Conn., 1664-1671. Lieutenant, 1665-1666.

GRISWOLD, LIEUT. MATTHEW, 1620-1698. Deputy from Lyme, Conn., 1654, 1667, 1668, 1685. Lieut., 1677.

GROSVENOR, JOHN, 1641-1691. Of Roxbury, Mass. Town Constable.

GROVES, PHILIP, —— 1675. Assistant to Governor, Stratford, Conn., 1654-1656. Ruling Elder in church, Stratford, Conn.

GRUBB, JOHN, JR., 1652-1708. Member Colonial Assembly of Pa. for New Castle Co., 1692, 1698. Justice of Peace, New Castle Co., Pa., 1693.

GULLIVER, CAPT. JONATHAN, 1659-1737. Of Milton, Mass. Captain of Milton Militia.

GUTHRIE, ROBERT, —— 1692. Town Clerk and Assistant Warden, Block Island, 1676.

HAINES, DEACON SAMUEL, 1611-1686. Born in England. Arrived New England, 1635. An organizer, and Deacon, North Church, Portsmouth, N.H., 1671. Selectman, 1663.

HALE, DEACON ROBERT, —— 1659. Deacon, Charlestown, Mass. Church, 1633. Member Ancient and Honorable Artillery Co., 1644. Ensign, Selectman, 11 years.

HALE, SERGT. THOMAS, 1606-1682. Born in England. Sergeant, Newbury, Mass., 1652-1657. Selectman, Haverhill, 1646. Constable, 1649.

HALL, BENJAMIN, 1650-1730. Deputy from Portsmouth, R.I., 1699.

HALL, FRANCIS, circa 1608-1689. Original Signer of New Haven Covenant, 1639. Constable, Stratford, Conn., 1669. Deputy for Stratford, 1661, 1676, 1677, 1678, 1679, 1680, 1685. Deputy to General Court, Hartford, 1676.
Finfgeld, Mrs. Clifford   Illinois
Kelly, Mrs. Francis J.   Renss.

HALL, DR. ISAAC, circa 1629-1714. "Chirurgeon" to Army before Oct. 1690. Also served, 1697.
Finfgeld, Mrs. Clifford   Illinois

HALL, JOHN, 1605-1676. Born in England. Served in Pequot War, 1637.

HALL, RICHARD, —— 1688. Elected to Provincial Assembly from Calvert Co., Md., 12 Dec. 1665. Commissioner, 1683.
Weisbecker, Mrs. . Howard   Illinois
Zimmerman, Mrs. Donald D.   Illinois

HALL, THOMAS 1649-1711. Town clerk in Wallingford, CT from 1670. Founder of Wallingford, CT.
Burlingame, Mrs. William B.   Ohio

HALL, WILLIAM, 1613-1675/6. Born in England. Commissioner from Portsmouth, R.I., 1654-1663. Deputy, 1665-1668. Town Council, 1672.

HALLETT, SAMUEL, 1657-1724. Assessor, Newton, L.I., 1692.
Long, Mrs. Alfred T.   Founders

HALLETT, WILLIAM, SR., 1616-1705. Came from England to New London, Conn., 1648. Joined in making settlement at Greenwich. Owner Hallet's Cove, now Astoria, L.I. Patentee, Newtown. Magistrate, 1654. Sheriff, 1656. Deputy, 1664. Commissioner.
Long, Mrs. Alfred T.   Founders

HALLETT, CAPT. WILLIAM, 1648-1729. Of Newtown, L.I. Captain. Justice of the Peace. Commissioner, 1688-1689. Capt of Foot Co.

HALLOCK, PETER, 1600-1688/9. Born in England. One of the thirteen original settlers of Southold, L.I., 1640.

HALSEY, THOMAS, 1591/2-1679. Born in England. One of original patentees and founders Southampton, L .I., 1640. Signed the original grant and the agreement with the Indians. Magistrate. Adjutant to Military Company and served in Indian Wars. Deputy to Hartford, Conn., 1664.
Dunmire, Mrs. Harold James   Blue Grass
Eller, Mrs. James Carlton   North Carolina
Stephenson, Mrs. William Cowles   North Carolina
Thorp, Mrs. James   Illinois

HALSEY, THOMAS, JR.,1627-1697. Born in England. Deputy to New Haven Colony, 1664. Served in Indian Wars.

HALSTEAD, JONAS, —— after 1682. Born in England. Constable, Oyster Bay, L.I., 1666. Overseer of Jamaica, L.I., 1675.

HAMBLETON, WILLIAM, 1636-1677. Justice of the Peace and Judge of County Court, Talbot Co., Md., 1670.

HAMLIN, GILES, 1643-1712. Deputy to General Court, 1666-1668, 1673. Member of committee to establish and commission military officers, secure provisions, horses for service. Assistant, 1685, 1687, 1689. Justice of Peace, 1687.
Brewster, Mrs. Robert W.   Michigan

HAMLIN, (HAMBLIN), JAMES, —— 1690. Born in England. Constable, Barnstable, Mass., 1639-1643.

HAMMOND, BENJAMIN, 1621-1703. Constable, Yarmouth, Mass., 1652. Constable town of Sandwich, 1675.

HAMMOND, LIEUT. JOHN, 1624-1709. Born in England. Selectman, Watertown, Mass., 1664, 1667, 1692, 1698. Lieutenant, King Philip's War, 1675-1676. In garrison at Wrentham.

HAMMOND, MAJOR JOHN, 1643-1707. Born in Isle of Wight. Justice, Anne Arundel Co., Md., 1685. On Council, 1692. Delegate to General Assembly, 1693. Member of House of Burgesses, 1694. Major, Troop of Horse. Justice of Provincial Court, 1698.

HAMMOND, NATHANIEL, 1643-1691. Selectman, Newton, Mass., prior to 1691.

HAMMOND, THOMAS, 1587-1675. One of the first settlers of Hingham, Mass., 1636.

HAMMOND, 'WILLIAM, 1575-1662. Born in England. Selectman, Watertown, Mass., 1648.

HANCOCK, REV. JOHN, 1671-1752. Preached in Lexington, Mass. Ordained 2 Nov. 1698.

HARDENBERGH, GERRIT JANSE, 1639-1696. Commissioned, 1690 to sail against the French as Commander of the sloop "Royal Albany."

HARLAN, GEORGE, 1650-1714. Was made one of the Provincial Governors of the "Three Lower Counties" (now Delaware), 1695.

HARRINGTON, ROBERT 1616-17 May 1707. Selectman, Watertown, MA 1679-1700.
Brown, Miss Eunice Frances   CT Farms

HARRIS, CAPT. DANIEL, —— 1701. Deputy from Middletown, Conn., 1678, 1684, 1687, 1689.

HARRIS, JOHN, 1607-1674/5. Among founders of Rowley, MA ca. 1643. Selectman 1677.
Arquit, Mrs. Gordon J.   Renss.

HARRIS, THOMAS, 1615-1687. Born in England. A soldier who went against Indians, 1643, and given land in Ipswich, Mass., for his services.

HARRIS, CAPT. THOMAS, 1586-1658. Born in England. Settled in Henrico Co., Va., 1611. Capt. in Indian War, 1622. Founder of Manakin. Member Va. House of Burgesses, 1623, 1624, 1639, 1647.
Zellers, Miss Thelma   Oklahoma

HARRIS, LIEUT. THOMAS, SR., 1600-1686. Born in England. Signed First Compact, Providence, R.I., 1637. Commissioner, 1652-1657, 1661-1663. Lieut., 1654. Deputy, 1664, 1666, 1667, 1670, 1672, 1673. Member of Town Council, 1664, 1665, 1666, 1669. Assistant, 1666, 1667, 1668, 1669, 1671-1675.

HARRIS, THOMAS, JR., 1641-1711. Born in Providence, R.I. Deputy from Providence, 1671, 1679, 1682, 1685, 1691, 1694, 1697. Member Town Council, 1684-1686.

HARRIS, WILLIAM, 1609-1682. Born in England. Commissioner from Providence, R.I., 1660, 1662, 1663. Deputy, 1665, 1666, 1672, 1673. Governor's Assistant, 1666, 1667, 1668, 1673-1676. General Solicitor, 1671.
Hardham, Mrs. M. Downes   Pennsylvania
Hungerford, Mrs. Edward   Pennsylvania
Ligget, Mrs. Robert C.   Pennsylvania

HARRISON, BENJAMIN, —— circa 1645. Born in England. Member of Colonial Council of Va., 1628. Clerk of Colonial Council, 1633-1634. Member of Va. House of Burgesses, 1642.

HARRISON, BURR, 1637-1706. Born in England. Member Virginia House of Burgesses from Stafford Co., 1679. Justice of Peace, 1670. Sent by House of Burgesses on Embassy to Piscataway Indians, 1699.
Evans, Mrs. Wilson B.   Blue Grass
Glenn, Mrs. Luther A., Sr.   Quivira

HARRISON, ISIAH, 1666-1740. Born in England. A First Settler of Oyster Bay, L.I., N.Y.
Livenick, Mrs. Corwin   Prairie State

HARRISON, ISAAC, —— 1676. Killed while fighting in King Philip's War, Hadley, Mass., 1675/6.

HARRISON, JAMES, 1630-Will 1712. Justice at Rappahannock Co., Va., at Court held for Rappahannock Co., 3 Sept. 1690.

HART, STEPHEN, 1608-1682/3. Deputy from Farmington, Conn., 1647-1655, 1660. Served in Pequot War.
Milburn, Mrs. John T.   Blue Grass

HART, THOMAS, 1607-1673/4. Selectman, Ipswich, Mass., 1663.

HART, THOMAS, 1643-1726. Deputy to General Court, Conn., 1690. Capt. of Train Band, Farmington, Conn., 1693.
Milburn, Mrs. John T.   Blue Grass

HART, LIEUT. THOMAS, 1640-1717. Lieut. of Foot Co., King Philip's War, from Ispwich, Mass., 1675. Representativc, 1693, 1694.

HARTWELL, SAMUEL, 1645-1725. Born in Concord, Mass. Served in King Philip's War, 1675/6.

HARTWELL, QUARTERMASTER WILLIAM, 1613/14-1689/90. Born in England. Quartermaster, Concord, Mass., 1673. King Philip's War, 1675/6.

HARVEY, THOMAS, 1652-1716. Member of Train Band, Amesbury, Mass., 1680. Deputy to General Court, 1690-1691.

HARWOOD, CAPT. THOMAS, —— 1652. Born in England. Burgess from Mulberry Is., Warwick Co., Va., 1629-1649. Speaker of the House, 1648-1649.

HASBROUCK, MAJ. ABRAHAM, —— 1717. Member of New York Assembly, 1698, 1699. Lieutenant of Foot, 1685. Captain, 1689. Major of Ulster Co., N.Y., Troops.

HASEY, LIEUT. WILLIAM, 1619-1689. Born in England. Member Ancient and Honorable Artillery Co. of Boston, Mass., 1652. Served in King Philip's War, 1675.

HASKELL, CAPT. WILLIAM, 1617-1693. Born in England. Capt. of Train Band, 1681. Selectman, Gloucester, Mass., 1688. Deacon of First Church.

HASTINGS, JOHN, 1654-1717/18. Born in England. In King Philip's War, from Watertown, Mass., 1675.

HASTINGS, DEA. JOHN, —— 1657. Deacon in church, Cambridge, Mass., 1656. Freeman, Braintree, 1645.

HASTINGS, THOMAS, 1605-1685. Born in England. Selectman, Mass. Bay Colony, Watertown, Mass., 1638-1643. Representative, 1638-1673. Town Clerk, 1676-1677, 1680.

HATCH, JOHN 1614-1681. Justice 1654. Sheriff 1646-48. Justice 1658-1660 MA.
Charles, Mrs. Melvin M.   Florida

HATCH, LIEUT. WILLIAM, circa 1598-1651. Born in England. Lieut. of Train Band, Scituate, Mass., 1643. First Ruling Elder of the Second Church, Scituate, 1643.

HATCHER, WILLIAM, 1614-1680. Born in Careby, England. Member of Virginia House of Burgesses, from Henrico Co., 1644-1659. Took part in Bacon's Rebellion, 1676.

HATHAWAY, JOHN, 1613-1696/7. Born in England. Settled in Taunton, Mass. Occupied numerous positions of trust and honor. Representative 1680-1684, 1691.

HATHAWAY, JOHN, —— 1729/30. Selectman, Freetown, Mass., 1687, 1688, 1698, 1699.

HAVEN, SERGT. RICHARD, 1620-1703. Born in England. Sergt. from Lynn, Mass., in King Philip's War, 1675/6.
Davis, Mrs. Frank V.   Illinois

HAVENS, WILLIAM, —— 1683. One of 29 settlers, who formed government of Portsmouth, R.I., 1638/39.

HAVILAND, WILLIAM, —— 1667. Freeman, Newport, R.I., 1653. Commissioner, 1655. Deputy, 1656.

HAWKINS, ANTHONY, —— 1673/4, of Windsor and Farmington, Conn. Patentee, Conn., 1662. Deputy, 1665-1667. Governor's Assistant, 1668-1670.
Milburn, Mrs. John T.   Blue Grass
Nero, Mrs. Allie Francis   Renss.

HAWKINS, WILLIAM, —— 1699. Signed an agreement for a form of government at Providence, 1640.

HAWKS, ELIEZER, 1655-1727. 1676 King Philip's War. One of first settlers and Selectman from Deerfield, MA.
Lane, Mrs. Harry H.   Florida

HAWLEY, JOSEPH, 1603-1690. Town Clerk, Stratford, Conn., 1650-1666. Treasurer, 1663. Deputy, 1665-1687. Commissioner, 1682-1690.

HAWLEY, THOMAS, —— 1676. Killed in King Philip's War, 1676.

HAYNES, DEA. JOHN, 1621-1697. Deacon of First Church of Sudbury, Mass., from 1666 until death. Petitioned General Court for establishment of Quissigamond, 1664.

HAYNES, LIEUT. JOSIAH, 1623-1698. Sergt., Sudbury, Mass., 1664. Selectman, 1666. Served in King Philip's War, 1675/6. Lieutenant.

HAYNES, WALTER, 1583-1665. Born in England. Of Watertown and Sudbury, Mass. Builder of Haynes Garrison House at Sudbury. Member Ancient and Honorable Artillery Co., 1639. Representative, 1641.

HAYWARD, GEORGE, 1604-1671. Born in England. One of first settlers of Concord, Mass., 1637, and Overseer for the South Quarter.

HAYWARD, JOSEPH, 1643-1714. Born in Concord, Mass. Served in King Philip's War, 1675/6.

HAYWARD, SAMUEL, 1646-1713. Selectman, Mendon, Mass., 1692.

HAYWARD, WILLIAM, —— 1717. A First Settler of Swansea, Mass., 1669.

HAZARD, ROBERT, 1635-1710. Recruiting Master, Ordinance Officer in King Philip's War, 1675/6. Deputy from Portsmouth, R.I., 1664, 1665.

HAZARD, THOMAS, 1610-1680. Born in England. Founder of Newport, R.I., 1639. Member of Governor's Council, R.I., 1654. Magistrate, 1652-1655.

HAZELTINE, DAVID, circa 1644-1717. Born in Bradford, MA. Overseer, Bradford, Mass., 1668-1669. Town Clerk, Bradford, Mass., 1690.

HAZELTINE, ROBERT, —— 1674. One of the first three settlers of Rowley, Mass. Selectman, 1668-1669.
Weaver, Mrs. John R., Sr.   Michigan

HAZEN, EDWARD, —— 1683. Selectman, Rowley, Mass., 1650, 1651, 1654, 1660, 1661, 1665, 1666, 1668. Judge, 1666.

HAZEN, LIEUT. THOMAS, 1657-1735. Born in Rowley, Mass. Served in King Philip's War, at Bloody Brook and Narragansett, 1675.

HEARD, ELIZABETH HULL, 1628-1706. Maintained a frontier garrison during Indian Wars, Dover, N.H., 1689.
Zimmerman, Mrs. Donald D.   Illinois

HEARD, JOHN, circa 1628-1688. Member of Court for Providence of Maine held at Saco, 25 June 1640. Selectman, Old Kittery, Maine, 1648 and years proceeding.
Zimmerman, Mrs. Donald D.   Illinois

HEATH, WILLIAM, 1610/20-1687. Commissioner of government giving patented lands in Surry Co., VA in Josefly Swamp 1663.
Callier, Mrs. Thomas Paige   Oklahoma

HEATON, ROBERT, —— ——. Born in England. Arrived America, 1667. Served as one of William Penn's Soldiers, Bucks Co., Pa., before 1688.

HEDGE, SAMUEL, circa 1650-1714. Born in England. Surveyor General, Fenwick's Colony, 1678. Signer of West Jersey Concessions

HEDGE, CAPT. WILLIAM, —— 1670. Captain, Yarmouth, Mass., Militia, 1659.

HEDGES, STEPHEN, 1635-1734. Constable, Easthampton, L.I., 1663. Trustee, 1687-1689.

HEDGES, WILLIAM, —— 1674. Born in England. Constable, Easthampton, L.I., 1663.

HEGEMAN, ADRIAEN, —— 1672. Came from Holland, 1650. Settled in Flatbush, L.I. Magistrate, 1654-1658, 1660, 1663. Secretary, Flatbush, Flatlands, 1659-1661. Schout Fiscal, five Dutch Towns, 1661. Secretary, Flatbush, Flatlands, Brooklyn, New Utrecht, 1662-1665. Secretary, Flatbush, 1671.

HEGEMAN, JOSEPH, —— circa 1725. Cornet of Horse, Kings County, 1690. Overseer, Micwout, L.I., 1680.

HELM, CAPT. ISRAEL, 1618-1701. Representative to General Assembly of
· Province of West Jersey, 1685-1686. Justice of Court, 1664, 1676, 1685. Member Governor's Council, 1667-1673.

HERITAGE, RICHARD, —— 1702. From Warwickshire, England. First of this name in West Jersey. Settler and Proprietor of Gloucester, laid out in 1686.

HERRING, THOMAS, —— 1684. Born in England. Signed Dedham, Mass. Covenant, 1636. Proprietor and first settler. Served in King Philip's War, 1676.

HEYWOOD, JOHN, 1612-1701. Born in England. A Founder of Concord, Mass. Constable, Concord, Mass., 1676.

HICKS, JOHN,—— 1672. Of Hempstead, L.I. Member Provincial Congress, New Amsterdam, 1653. Deputy, 1666.

HICKS, CAPT. THOMAS, 1642-1717. Capt. Queens Co., N.Y. Troops, 1686. Called Colonel, 1693. Judge of Court of Common Pleas, Queens Co., N.Y., 1691-1699.

HIDE, SAMUEL, 1637-1677. Original Settler of Norwich, Conn., 1660.

HIDE, WILLIAM, 1637-1682. Original Settler of Norwich, Conn., 1660.

HIGGINS, ENS. JONATHAN, 1637——. Born in Eastham, Mass. Ensign, 1675.

HIGGINS, RICHARD, —— 1677. Deputy from Plymouth, Mass., 1647. Member of Council of War, 1653.

HIGGINSON, REV. FRANCIS, 1587-1630. Came to Salem, Mass., from England in the "Talbot," 1629, with a company of merchants who obtained a charter from Charles I., whereby they were incorporated the "Governor's Company of Massachusetts Bay Colony." First Clergyman of the Colony.

HIGGINSON, CAPT. ROBERT, —— 1649. Commander of Forts, Middle Plantation, Va., 1644-1646.

HIGHLEY, CAPT. JOHN, 1649-1714. Deputy from Sims-Bury, Conn., 1689. Lieutenant, 1690. Captain, 1698.

HILDRETH, LIEUT. RICHARD, 1605-1692/3. Selectman, Cambridge, Mass., 1645. One of the Trustees, Chelmsford, Mass., 1656. Lieut. Military Co., Chelmsford, Mass., 1682-1693.

HILL, JOHN, —— circa 1664. Born in England. Resided Dorchester, Mass. Member of Ancient and Honorable Artillery Co., 1647.

HILL, JONATHAN, 1646 ——. Selectman, Billerica, Mass., 1698.

HILL, RALPH, —— 1663. Selectman, Woburn, Mass., 1649.

HILL, SION, 1654-1703. 1687 member of Foot Militia of VA.
Ely, Mrs. Paul G.   Oklahoma

HILL, WILLIAM, —— 1649. Born in England. Selectman, Dorchester, Mass., 1636. Deputy, Windsor, Conn., 1639-1644.

HILL, WILLIAM, JR., —— 1684. Born in England. Town Clerk, Fairfield, Conn., 1648, 1650 and other years.

HILLS, CAPT. JOSEPH, 1602-1688. Selectman, Malden, Mass., 1644. Deputy, 1646. Speaker of the House of Deputies, 1647. Captain of the Train Band. Deputy, Malden, 1664.
Davis, Mrs. Frank V.   Illinois

HILLS, JOSEPH, —— ——. Settled in Glastonbury, Conn., circa 1640.

HILLS, SERGT. SAMUEL, 1652-1732. Sergt., King Philip's War, 1675.

HINCKLEY, GOV. THOMAS, 1618-1706. Deputy from Barnstable, Mass., 1646, 1648, 1649, 1653, 1654, 1655, 1659. Governor's Assistant, 1658-1679. Deputy Governor, 1680. Commissioner of the United Colonies, 1673-1684, 1686, 1689-1691. Councillor of the Royal Province of New England, 1686-1689. Governor of Plymouth Colony, 1681-1686, 1689-1691.
Trefts, Miss Dorothy Eleanore   Ohio

HINMAN, SERGT. EDWARD, —— ——. Served in Indian Campaign, 1644.

HIRONS, SIMON, 1645-1706. Justice of the County Court of St. Jones (Kent), Del., 1680.

HITCHCOK, LT. JOHN, 1642-1712. Served in King Philip's War, 1675. Representative to Mass. General Court, 1699.

HITCHCOK, CAPT. LUKE,—— 1659. Born in England. Captain, Crown Point, 1645. Selectman, Wethersfield, Conn., 1653, 1656.
Greason, Mrs. James B., Jr.   Founders

HOAGLAND (See Hooglandt).

HOBART, EDMUND, 1574-1646. Came from England, 1633, settled in Charlestown, Mass. Constable, 1634. Representative from Hingham, Mass., 1639, 1642. Commissioner, 1637, 1639, 1641.

HOBART, REV. JOSHUA, 1628-1717/18. Ordained pastor of church in Southhold, L.I., 1674-1699.

HOBART, REV. PETER, 1604-1679. Born in England. First Minister at Hingham, Mass. Preached forty-three years.

HODGES, CAPT. HENRY, 1652-1717. Born in Taunton, Mass. Member, Third Squadron, 1682. Selectman, 1687. Member Town Council, 1689-1690. Ensign, 1690, Commissioned Captain.

HODGES, WILLIAM, 1629-1654. Born in England. Name appears on list of Males able to bear arms, at Taunton, Mass., 1643. Freeman, 1649. Constable, 1651.

HODGKINS, WILLIAM, 1622-1693. Served in King Philip's War, Ipswich, Mass., 1675.

HOLBROOK, CAPT. JOHN, 1617-1699. Born in England. Capt. in King Philip's War, 1675/6. Selectman, Weymouth, Mass., 1645-1646, 1651-1654.

HOLBROOK, THOMAS, SR., 1594-1674. Born in England; died at Weymouth, Mass. A First Settler of Sherbourne, Mass., incorporated May 1674.

HOLCOMB, JOSHUA, 1640-1690. Deputy from Simsbury, Conn., 1670-1690.

HOLCOMB, THOMAS, 1601-1657. Born in England. Member of Militia, Windsor, Conn., 1649. Deputy, 1639, 1649.

HOLDEN, CAPT. RANDALL, 1612-1692. Born in England. Marshall and Corporal, Portsmouth, R.I., 1636. Assistant to Governor, 1647, 1653-1664. Captain, 1664. Justice, 1687-1688.
Smith, Mrs. William J.   Renss.

HOLGRAVE, JOHN, 1580-1670. Born in England. Deputy from Salem, Mass., 1634-1635. Assistant from Gloucester, Mass., 1647.

HOLLINGSWORTH, VALENTINE, 1632-1711. Born in England. Member of First Pa. Assembly, 1682-1683; of Assemblies, from New Castle, Co., Pa., 1687, 1688, 1689, 1695.
Peck, Patricia Scott   Missouri

HOLLIS, JOHN, —— 1700. Served in King Philip's War, Mass., 1675/6.

HOLLISTER, LIEUT. JOHN, 1612-1665. Born in England. Deputy, Mass., 1644; Conn., 1645-1656. Lieut., Hartford Militia. Served in King Philip's War, 1675/6.
Greason, Mrs. James B., Jr.   Founders

HOLLISTER, LIEUT. JOHN, 1642-1711. Born in Wethersfield, Conn. Lieutenant, 1676.

HOLMES, JOHN, 1635 ——. Selectman, Bedford, N.Y., 1693, 1694, 1697-1699.

HOLMES, JOHN, JR., 1670 ——. Selectman, Bedford, N.Y., 1693, 1694.

HOLMES, CAPT. JONATHAN, 1633/4-1713. Born in England. Member Assembly, N.J., 1670-1672. Captain, 1673. Deputy, 1689-1699. Speaker, Member Governor's Council, R.I.

HOLMES, JOSHUA, —— 1694. Died at Westerly, R.I. Served in King Philip's War, 1675.

HOLMES, NATHANIEL, 1639-1711. Born in Roxbury, Mass. Representative, 1689.

HOLMES, REV. OBADIAH, 1606-7-1682. Pastor, First Baptist Church, Newport, R.I., 1652. Commissioner, 1656-1658. Member Council. Representative, 1656. Served in King Philip's War.

HOLMES, OBADIAH, —— ——. High Sherif, Monmouth Co., N. J., 1699.

HOLMES, ROBERT, —— 1697. Served in King Philip's War, 1675. Resided at Stonington, Conn.

HOLMES, THOMAS, —— ——. Member of Governor's Council, 1683. Surveyor and City Planner for William Penn, 18 April 1682, 1684.
Bester, Mrs. William A. C.	Pennsylvania

HOLTON, DEA. WILLIAM, 1611-1691. Original proprietor in Hartford, Conn., 1636. Deacon of church, Northampton, Mass., 1663. Deputy, 1664-1671. Member of first Board of Magistrates.

HOLYOKE, EDWARD, —— 1660. Deputy from Lynn, Mass., 1639-1648. Member Quarterly Court, 1639, 1643, 1647.

HOLYOKE, ELIZER, 1616-1675/6. MA. Commissioned Ensign 1653 and Capt. 1667. Deputy for Springfield 1652-59.
Cooke, Mrs. John D.	California
Hopiak, Mrs. George A.	California
Kutzcher, Mrs. Detlef Kurt	California

HOOGLANDT, LIEUT. CHRISTOPHER, 1634-1684. Schepen, 1664. Named in list of Militia Officers for New York, 1673. Alderman, 1669, 1678. Assistant in Court of Admiralty, 1678.

HOOKER, REV. THOMAS, 1586-1647. Born in England. Fled to Holland to avoid persecution. Came to Boston, Mass. Established church in Cambridge, 1633. He and congregation moved to Hartford, Conn., 1636.

HOOPES, JOSHUA, —— 1724. Member of Provincial Assembly, Bucks Co., Pa., serving intermittenly from 1686 to 1699.
Shelton, Mrs. Ellis E.   Member-at-Large
Shelton, Miss Patricia Elaine   Member-at-Large
Shelton, Miss Rhea Louise   Member-at-Large

HOPKINS, CONSTANCE, 1607/8-1677. Passenger on the Mayflower, 1620.

HOPKINS, MRS. ELIZABETH, —— 1659. Passenger on the Mayflower, 1620.

HOPKINS, GYLES, —— 1688/90. Passenger on the Mayflower, 1620. Volunteer in Pequot War, 1637. Surveyor of Highways, Yarmouth, Mass., 1642, 1643. Surveyor of Highways, Eastham, Mass., 1650, 1662, 1671.

HOPKINS, STEPHEN, —— 1644. Passenger on the Mayflower, 1620. In the "First Encounter," 18 Dec. 1620. Assistant, 1633-1637. Member of the Council of War for the Colony, 1642-1644. Volunteer in Pequot War, 1637.
Brannan, Mrs. Charles F.   Member-at-Large
Chester, Mrs. Reginald F.   Renss.
London, Mrs. George Abraham   Quivira
Luttrell, Mrs. Curtis Loren   Illinois

HOPKINS, THOMAS, 1616-1684. Born in England. Commissioner from Scituate, R.I., 1652, 1659, 1660. Deputy, 1665-1667, 1672. Member of Town Council, 1667, 1672.

HORSFORD, JOHN, —— 1683. Born in England. Member of the first body of Connecticut Colony Cavalry formed by Major John Mason, 1658.

HORTON, BARNABAS, 1600-1680. Born in England. Deputy from Southold, L.I., to New Haven, Conn., 1654-1661. Deputy from Hartford, Conn., 1663-1664. Magistrate, 1664-1680.

HORTON, CALEB, 1640-1702. Supervisor, Southold, L.I., 1697.

HORTON, CAPT. JONATHAN, 1648 ——. Born in Southold, L.I. Captain, First Foot Company, 1670. Served in garrison to protect frontier from Indians, 1689-1690.

HOSKINS, JOHN, —— 1648. Delegate to Conn. General Court from Windsor, Conn., 1637.

HOSKINS, WILLIAM, —— 1695. First Town Clerk, Middleboro, Mass., 1669-1693.

HOSMER, JAMES, 1605-1685. Born in England. Selectman, Concord, Mass., 1660.

HOSMER, JAMES, JR., 1637-1676. Born in England. Killed at Sudbury, Mass., during King Philip's War.

HOSMER, STEPHEN, 1642-1714. Born in Concord, Mass. Selectman, Concord, 1689, 1690. Served in King Philip's War, 1675/6.

HOSMER, DEA. STEPHEN, 1654-1693. Selectman, Hartford, Conn., 1673, 1676, 1677, 1689. Deacon of the First Church, 1686.

HOSMER, THOMAS, 1603-1687. Selectman, 1643, 1647. An original proprietor of Hartford, Conn., 1636. Constable, 1639, 1663. Deputy, 1641-1645. Removed to Northampton, Mass.

HOUCHIN, JEREMY, —— 1670. Member Ancient and Honorable Artillery Co. of Boston, Mass., 1641. Representative, eight years from Hingham. One year from Salisbury.

HOUGHTON, SIR RALPH, 1623-1704/5. Town Clerk of Lancaster, Mass., 1656-1682. Deputy, 1675-1689. Founder of Lancaster.
Feller, Mrs. Ivan E.   Illinois

HOVEY, DANIEL, 1618-1692. Of Ipswich, Mass. Selectman, 1659. Surveyor of Highways, 1648-1649. Constable, 1658. Also served in defense of the Colony.
O'Keefe, Mrs. Edward T.   Michigan

HOWE, ABRAHAM, 1637-1695. Served in King Philip's War, from Marlborough, Mass., 1675.

HOWE, ELDER EDWARD, —— 1644. Born in England. Deputy from Watertown, Mass., 1634-1639, 1642, 1643. Selectman, 1637, 1639, 1641-1643. Ruling Elder.
Colburn, Mrs. Joseph L.   CT Farms
Farney, Mrs. Jacob   Quivira
Rea, Mrs. Philip L., Jr.   CT Farms

HOWE, JAMES, 1598-1702, of Roxbury and Ipswich, Mass. A Denison subscriber, 1648. Highway Commissioner, Constable, 1646.

HOWE, JOHN, 1607-1680. Born in England. Selectman, Sudbury, Mass., 1642; Marlboro, 1656, 1661-1664.

HOWE, JOSIAH, 1650-1711. Listed Oct. 1675, to defend the town of Marlborough, Mass., in King Philip's War. On List of Proprietors of Ockoocangansett Plantation.

HOWE, SAMUEL, 1642-1713. Served in King Philip's War in Capt. Nathan Davenport's Co., and was officer in Militia, 1675-1676. Born and died at Sudbury, Mass.

HOWE, THOMAS, 1656-1733. Born at Sudbury, Mass. Died at Marlborough, Mass. Soldier in King Philip's War, 1675.

HOWES, THOMAS, circa 1590-1665. Born in England. Deputy from Yarmouth, Mass. to General Court at Plymouth, 1652, 1653, 1658, 1662. Member of Council of War, 1658.

HOWELL, EDWARD, 1584-1654. Born in England. Arrived Boston, Mass., 1639/40. A Founder of Southampton, L.I. Assistant Governor of Conn., 1647-1653.

HOWLAND, JOHN, 1592-1673. Passenger on "Mayflower," 1620. Thirteenth Signer of the Mayflower Compact. Assistant to Governor, 1633-1635. Deputy, 1641-1670. Selectman, 1666.
King, Mrs. Frank Fuller   North Carolina
Ostenberg, Mrs. Walter Milton   Quivira
Smith, Miss Lean Ellen   Quivira
Whitcomb, Mrs. Reginald D.   Rhode Island

HOWLAND, HENRY, —— 1671. Constable, Duxbury, Mass., 1635.

HOWLAND, LIEUT. JOHN, 1627 ——. Born in Plymouth, Mass. Moved to Marshfield, then to Barnstable, 1658. Freeman, 1658. Held many town offices. Ensign, Lieutenant. Served in King Philip's War, 1675.

HOWLET, SERGT. THOMAS, 1599-1678. Born in England. Deputy from Ipswich, Mass., 1635. Ensign, 1636. Deputy from Topsfleld, 1665.

HOXIE, JOSEPH, 1667-1727. Selectman, Sandwich, Mass., 1691.

HOXIE, LODOWICK, —— after 1681. Soldier from Sandwich, Mass., to muster at Yarmouth, 1660. Assessor, 1671.

HOYT, SERGT. JOHN, 1610-1696. Born in England. Sergeant, Salisbury, Mass., 1658.

HOYT, MOSES, —— after 1712. Patentee of Eastchester, N.Y., 1666. Deputy-Constable, 1683. Town Commissioner, 1686.

HOYT, SIMON, 1590-1657. One of the Founders of Charlestown, Mass., 1629/30. Member of Militia, Windsor, Conn., before 1640.
Wadley, Mrs. Robert L., Sr.   Oklahoma

HUBBARD, GEORGE, 1594-1683. Born in England. Deputy from Wethersfleld, Conn., 1639. Magistrate, 1652-1666. Member Assembly at Union, Hartford, and New Haven, 1666-1667.

HUBBARD, SAMUEL, 1610-1688/1692. Chosen second General Solicitor of Rhode Island, 1664.

HUCKINS, COM. GEN. THOMAS, 1617-1679. Born in England. Came to Boston, Mass., circa 1630. Ensign, Ancient and Honorable Artillery Company, 1639. Moved to Barnstable. Constable, 1646. Selectman, eight times, 1668-1678. Deputy, 8 times, 1669-1678. Council of War, 1671. Commissary General, 1675. Town Council, 1676.

HUDSON, JOHN, —— ——. Treasurer, New Haven, Conn., 1681-1683. Constable, 1670.

HUGHES, JOHN, —— ——. Scottish minister.
Devanny, Mrs. John Stormont   Illinois

HUGHES, MATTHIAS, 1639-1703. Military Officer, Anne Arundel Co., Md., 1694-1697.
Hannon, Mrs. Harold F., Jr.   Illinois

HULL, GEORGE, —— 1659. Born in England. Assistant Magistrate, Windsor, Conn., 1651-1654. Governor's Assistant, 1654. Deputy, 1634-1635, from Fairfield, Conn., 1656.

HULL, DR. JOHN, 1640-1711. Surgeon, King Philip's War, 1676. Selectman, Derby Conn., 1677, 1680, 1683, 1687.

HULL, REV. JOSEPH, 1595-1665. Born in England. Deputy from Hingham, Mass., 1636, 1637. Magistrate, 1638. A Founder of Barnstable. Deputy, 1639. Served in Narragansett War, 1645. Minister of Gospel.
Philp, Mrs. Merritt   Illinois
Weaver, Mrs. John F., Sr.   Michigan
Zimmerman, Mrs. Donald D.   Illinois

HULL, LIEUT. JOSIAH, 1616-1675. Born in England. Representative from Killingworth, Conn., 1659, 1660, 1662, 1665, 1667, 1674.

HULL, RICHARD, 1599-1662. One of first settlers New Haven, Conn. Signed Fundamental Agreement, 1639.

HUMFREY (HUMPHREY), SERGT./MAJOR GENERAL JOHN,—— 1661. Deputy-Gov., Colony of Mass. Bay, 1629. Gov. Assistant, 1634-1641. Sergt.-Major General, 1641. Named in First Patent of Conn., circa 1631. A Founder of Harvard College. Member of Ancient and Honorable Artillery Co., of Boston, 1640.

HUNGERFORD, THOMAS, II, 1648-1714. Selectman, East Haddam, Conn., 1687.
Harroun, Mrs. Richard R.   Michigan

HUNNEWELL, CAPT. RICHARD, —— 1703. Soldier in King Philip's War, 1675/6. Ensign, 1680. Lieut., 1689. Noted Indian fighter, Scarborough, Me., prior to 1700.

HUNT, EPHRAIM, 1610-22 Feb. 1686/7. Chosen Sergt., Weymouth, Mass., 8 Oct.1662.

HUNT, JOHN, —— 1711. Constable, Westchester, N.Y., 1682.

HUNT, DEA. JONATHAN, 1637-1691. Selectman, Northampton, Mass., 1675, and later. Deacon, 1680. Representative, 1690.

HUNT, SAMUEL, 1633-1675/6. In Falls Fight, King Philip's War, 1675/6.

HUNT, SAMUEL, 1657-1742. In Falls Fight, King Philip's War, 1675/6. House used as garrison, near Wamesit.

HUNT, THOMAS, 1640-1694. Overseer, Westchester, 1682.

HUNT, WILLIAM, circa 1605-1676. King Philip's War, Marlborough, Mass., 1675/6.

HUNT, WILLIAM, JR., ca 1670-ca 1714. Settled in Charles City, VA. Doctor of Physick (Physician), Kesmons Warehouse, VA before 1695.
Edmund, Miss Natalie Anne   Oklahoma
Lewellen, Mrs. D. Wayne   Oklahoma

HUNTINGTON, CHRISTOPHER, 1627-1691. Born in England. Came to Mass., 1633. Aided in founding town of Norwick, Conn. Town Clerk, 1678. Served on Committee, "to make provision for maintaining the reverend Ministers," 1686.

HUNTINGTON, DEA. SIMON, 1629-1706. Deacon, Norwich, Conn., 1661-1696. Delegate, Norwich, Conn., 1674, 1685. Townsman, Norwich, Conn., 1690-1696.

HUNTINGTON, WILLIAM B., before 1625-1689. Born in England. Arrived Boston, 1633. Settled at Roxbury, Mass. A First Settler of Salisbury, Received land, 1640. A Founder of Amesbury.

HUNTTING, ELDER JOHN, 1597-1689. Founder and Elder of Dedham, Mass., 1638-1639.

HUNTTING, REV. NATHANIEL, 1675-1753. Second Pastor in Easthampton, L.I., installed 1699.

HURD, JOHN, 1613-1681. Born in England. Deputy from Windsor, Conn. to General Court, 1649.
Davies, Mrs. David L.   Founders

HUSSEY, CAPT. CHRISTOPHER, 1599-1688. Came from England about 1630. One of original settlers of Hampton, N.H. Selectman, 1636. Deputy, 1637, 1639. Justice of the Peace and Town Clerk, 1639. Lieutenant and Captain, 1650. One of the purchasers of Nantucket, Mass., 1659.
Eickmeyer, Mrs. Lorena Hopkins   Missouri
Trau, Mrs. Frank Garland   Pennsylvania

HUSSEY, MARY, —— ——. Original grantee, settler and founder of Hampton, MA Bay.
Eickmeyer, Mrs. Lorena Hopkins   Missouri

HUSSEY, STEPHEN, 1632-1718. One of the Trustees of Sherburne, Nantucket, 1687.

HUTCHINS, JOHN, 1604-1674. Constable of Haverhill, Mass., before 1664.

HUTCHINSON, CAPT. EDWARD, 1613-1675. Deputy from Boston, 1658. Ensign of Military Company, Boston, 1645. Lieutenant of Ancient and Honorable Artillery Co., 1654, and its Captain, 1667. Captain of the Three County Troops, 1659-1674. In King Philip's War, 1675.

HUTCHINSON, WILLIAM, 1586-1642. Deputy from Boston to General Court of Mass. Bay, 1635-1636. A Founder of Charter Colony of Portsmouth, R.I., 1638.

HYATT, THOMAS, 1641-1695. Served in King Philip's War from Conn., 1675-1676.

HYDE, DEACON SAMUEL, 1610-1689. Born in England. Second Settler of Cambridge, Mass. Village Deacon of Cambridge Village Church. Constable, 1653.

HYDE, WILLIAM, —— 1681. Born in England. One of the original proprietors of Hartford, Conn. Also of Norwich, Conn. Elected frequently Selectman, Norwich.

IDE, NICHOLAS, 1620-1690. One of the First Settlers of Attleborough, Mass., 1666. Served in the Narragansett Campaign under Major Bradford, 1675/6.
Fishel, Mrs. Maxine Emeline   Michigan
Greenleaf, Mrs. John W., Jr.   Florida

INMAN,EDWARD, —— 1706. Commissioner in R.I., 1658. Deputy.

ISHAM, CAPT. HENRY, 1628-1675. Born in England. Justice, 1657. Captain of Henrico Co., Virginia Militia and High Sheriff, 1669-1670.

IVES, JOHN, SR., baptized 1644-1681/2. Born New Haven. A Signer of the Wallingsford Agreement, 1669. A Founder of Wallingsford, Conn.
Milburn, Mrs. John T.   Blue Grass

IVES, WILLIAM, 1607-1648. A Founder of the Quinipac Colony, Conn.
Milburn, Mrs. John T.   Blue Grass

JACKSON, EDWARD, 1599-1681. Born in England. Deputy from Cambridge, Mass., 1637-1654, 1656, 1665-1668, 1675-1678. Selectman, 1665-1682.

JACKSON, HENRY, —— 1686. Born in England. Surveyor. Laid out boundary lines between Stratford and Norwalk, Conn., 1664.

JACKSON, COL. JOHN, 1645-1725. Patentee, Hempstead, L.I. Commissioner, 1683. Judge, 1685. High Sheriff, 1691-1695. Member Assembly, 1693. Deputy, twenty-three years. Colonel, 1699.
Long, Mrs. Alfred T.   Founders
Mansfield, Mrs. Donald W.   Ohio

JACKSON, JOHN, 1602-1675. Of Cambridge, Mass. Served in King Philip's War, 1675.

JACKSON, JOHN, —— 1689. One of the first Proprietors of Eastchester, N.Y., 1665 and named in its Patent of 1666.

JACKSON, ROBERT, —— 1684. Born in England. Settled in Stamford, Conn. Moved to Hempstead, L.I., 1640. Magistrate many years. Deputy, 1665. Constable and Overseer, many years from 1666. Schepen, 1673.
Long, Mrs. Alfred T.   Founders

JACKSON, WILLIAM, —— 1688. Overseer, Rowley, Mass., 1656, 1660-1661.

JACOB, NICHOLAS, 1608-1657. Born in England. Settled in Watertown, Mass., 1633. Moved to Hingham, 1635. Freeman, same year. Selectman, 1637. Representative, 1648, 1649.

JACOBS (JACOB), CAPT. JOHN, 1630-1693. Came from England, 1633. Settled in Hingham, Mass. Commanded Company during King Philip's War. Selectman at various times, 1662-1689. Member Ancient and Honorable Artillery Co.

JAGGER, JEREMIAH, —— 1658. Moved from Watertown, Mass., to Wethersfield, Conn. Served in Pequot War, 1637.

JAGGER, JOHN, —— 1698. Granted twenty acres of land, 1671. Constable of the East Riding of L.I., 1677.

JANES, ABEL, circa 1644-1718. Among the men of Northampton, Mass. who were engaged in battle at Turner's Falls, 19 May 1676.

JANES, REV. WILLIAM, 1610-1690. Born in England. An early settler of New Haven, Conn., 1637. A member of General Court, New Haven, 1648. Teacher. Minister, Northampton, Mass., 1656; Northfield, Mass., 1670.
Trau, Mrs. Frank Garland   Pennsylvania

JAQUE (JAQUITH), ABRAHAM, 1644-1679. Served in King Philip's War, 1675/6.

JAQUES, HENRY, 1618-1687. Born in England. Chosen to act for Prudential affairs, Newbury, Mass., 1663, 1664. Selectman, 1675-1676, 1678-1679.

JAQUETTE, GOV. JEAN PAUL, 1615/20-1684. Second Dutch Governor of Delaware, 1655. Appointed Vice Director and Chief Magistrate, 1655.

JEFTS, HENRY, SR., 1604-1700. One of the incorporators of Billerica, Mass., 1654. Surveyor, 1659-1660, 1661.

JENINGS, GOV. SAMUEL, 1640-1709. Born in England. Deputy Governor, West Jersey, 1680. Governor, 1683.

JENKS (JENCKS), JOSEPH, 1632-1717. One of the Founders of Pawtucket, R.I., 1671. Deputy, 1679, 1680, 1681. Assistant, 1680-1698. Chosen with 5 others to write congratulations to William and Mary on their assession, 1690. Chosen by Assembly to run the eastern line of the Colony, 1695.
Bowen, Mrs. Charles W., Sr.   Pennsylvania
Pettise, Mrs. Thomas W.   Illinois

JENNISON, ENS. SAMUEL, 1645-1701. Born in Watertown, Mass. Commissioned as Ensign.

JESSUP, EDWARD, —— 1666. Magistrate, Newton, L.I., 1659-1662; Westchester, N.Y. 1663-1664.

JEWETT, JOSEPH, 1609-1660. Deputy to General Court from Rowley, Mass., 1651-1654, 1660. A Founder of Rowley, 1639.
Swanson, Mrs. Dewey   Territorial
Swanson, Miss Georgiana   Territorial
Weaver, Mrs. John F.   Michigan

JEWETT, MAXMILIAN, circa 1607-1684. Born in England. Deputy to General court from Rowley, Mass., 1642-1648. Deacon of church 45 years. Selectman. Moderator of town meetings.

JOHANNES, MYNNE, —— 1693. Constable, Flatbush, L.I., 1676, 1677, 1679. High Sheriff, Orange County, N.Y., 1685, 1686.

JOHNSON, CAPT. ISAAC, 1615-1675. Born in England. Settled in Roxbury, Mass., 1630. Freeman, 1635. Member Ancient and Honorable Artillery Co., 1645. Captain, 1653. Representative, 1671. Killed in Narragansett Fort fight.

JOHNSON, CAPT. JOHN, 1593-1659. Born in England. Settled in Roxbury, Mass., 1630. Freeman, 1631. Representative, 1634-1648. Member Ancient and Honorable Artillery Co., 1638. Held title "Surveyor General of all ye Armies," Roxbury, Mass.
Slocum, Mrs. Ray Emerson   Florida
Wiltse, Mrs. Dorr Norman   Michigan

JOHNSON, SOLOMON, —— 1687. An original proprietor at Sudbury, Mass., 1639; also at Marlborough, Mass., 1660. Selectman, 1661-1665. Constable, 1663-1664.

JOHNSON, WILLIAM, 1653-1727. Constable, Andover, Mass., 1691.

JONES, (JOHNES), EDWARD, —— 1657. Constable, Charlestown, Mass., 1638-1641.

JONES, HUGH, circa 1635-1688. Surveyor of Highways, Salem, Mass., 1669-1670, 1671-1672, 1682-1683.

JONES, JOHN, —— ——. Died in Framingham, Mass. Served in King Williams' War, 1690.

JONES, REV. JOHN, 1593-1665. Born in England. Ordained at Concord, Mass., 1637. Minister, Fairfield, Conn., 1664-1665.

JONES, ROLAND, 1640-1688. First Rector of Bruton Parish, Williamsburg, Va., 1674-1688.

JONES, CAPT. WILLIAM, 1609/10-1669. Justice of Northampton Co., Va. Member Va. House of Burgesses, 1652, 1658.

JONES, LIEUT. GOV. WILLIAM, 1624-1706. Came from England to New Haven, Conn., 1660. Magistrate, New Haven Colony, 1662. Lieut. Governor, 1662. Dep. Governor, 1664. Magistrate, 1665. Assistant, Colony, Connecticut, 1655-1691. Lieut. Governor 1691-1698.

JOOSTEN, BARENT, —— ——. Emigrated from Emberland, 1652. Magistrate, Brooklyn, 1663-1664. Constable, New Utrecht, 1683, 1686, 1687.

JORDAN, JAMES, —— 1655. Died in Dedham, Mass. Name on original list when lands granted in Dedham, Mass., 6 Dec. 1642.

JORDAN, THOMAS, 1600 ——. Soldier, 1623, under Sir George Yeardley in Va. Burgess to Va. Assembly, 1629, 1631-1632. Commissioner, 1637.

JOSLYN (JOSL1N), THOMAS, 1591/2-1660/1. Born in England. Proprietor and Grantee, Hingham, Mass. Subscriber to town covenant, 1637. Selectman, 1645. A signer of Civil Compact of Lancaster, Mass.
Trau, Mrs. Frank Garland   Pennsylvania

JOY, JACOB, —— ——. Soldier in Narragansett Campaign, King Philip's War, 1675-1676.

JOY, JOSEPH, SR., 1645-1697. Born in Boston, Mass. Constable, Hingham, Mass., 1673.

JOY, JOSEPH, 1668-1716. Born in Hingham, Mass. Constable, Hingham, 1697.

JOY, THOMAS, 1611-1678. Born in England. Settled at Boston, Mass., 1629/30. Member of Ancient and Honorable Artillery Co., 1658. Died at Hingham, Mass.

JUDD, DEACON THOMAS, circa 1608-1688. A First Proprietor, Settler. Deputy to General Court from Farmington, Mass., to Hartford, Conn., 1647-1651, 1657-1659, 1661-1663, 1666, 1668, 1670, 1677-1679. Second Deacon, Farmington.

JUDSON, CAPT. JAMES, 1650-1721. Born in Stratford, Conn. Served in King Philip's War. Lieutenant, 1690. Deputy, twelve years from 1691. Captain, 1698.
Greason, Mrs. James B., Jr. Founders

JUDSON, LIEUT. JOSEPH, 1616-1690. Came from England with his father, Wm. Judson, 1634. Resided in Concord, Mass. Removed to Stratford, Conn., 1638. Lieutenant, 1672. In King Philip's War, 1675-1676. Deputy, 1684-1686.
Greason, Mrs. James B., Jr. Founders

KEEP, JOHN, circa 1640-1676, of Longmeadow, Mass. Selectman, Springfield, Mass., 1673, 1674, 1675. Slain by Indians in King Philip's War.

KELLOGG, DANIEL, 1630-1688. Deputy from Norwalk, Conn., 1670, 1679, 1680, 1683.

KELLOGG, LIEUT. JOSEPH, 1626-1707. Born in England. Appointed Ensign of Foot Co. of Hadley, Mass., 9 May 1678. Lieut., 7 Oct. 1678. In King Philip's War, 18 May 1676, at Falls Fight. Selectman, 1665, 1674, 1677, 1679, 1681, 1685, 1692.

KELSEY, WILLIAM, 1600-1680. One of the original Proprietors of Hartford, 1636. Selectman, Hartford, 1659, 1661. Original Proprietor of Killingsworth, 1664. Deputy from there to General Court at Hartford, 1671.

KENDALL, JOHN, 1642-1732. Soldier in King Philip's War.
Haycraft, Mrs. Marvin Illinois

KENDRICK, GEORGE, 1607-1688. Born in England. Volunteer soldier in Pequot War, 1637. Deputy from Scituate, Mass., 1642-1644.

KENDRICK, JOHN, 1602-1686. Born in England. Constable, Newton, Mass., 1671.

KENNER, RICHARD, 1625-1692. Born in England. Member of Virginia House of Burgesses, 1688, 1691, 1692.
Layson, Mrs. J. Vimont, Jr.   Blue Grass
Woodford, Mrs. Buckner   Blue Grass

KENNON, DR. RICHARD, 1650-1696. Born in England. Justice of Henrico Co., Va., 1678. Burgess for Henrico Co., 1685-1686.

KENT, SERGT. JOHN, 1641-1717/8. Born in Newbury, Mass. Selectman, Newbury, Mass., 1684/5. Named as Sergeant on all records.

KENT, ENS. JOSEPH, JR., 1665-1734/5. Deputy from Swansea, Mass., 1697.

KENT, RICHARD, —— 1654. Commissioner, Newbury, Mass., 1650. Town Officer, appointed 23 May 1650.

KERLEY, CAPT. HENRY, 1632-1713. Born in England. Representative to General Court for Marlborough, Mass., 1693. Lieut. in Lancaster Co., 1675. Capt. in Marlborough Co., 1693. Served in King Philip's War. A Founder of Lancaster, 1653.

KERLEY, WILLIAM, SR., —— 1670. Born in England. A Founder of Lancaster, Mass., 1653. Selectman, 1657-1659.

KERMER, ISAAC, 1671-after 1726. Member of Ulster Co., N.Y. Militia, under Major Peter Schuyler, 1692.
Long, Mrs. Alfred T.   Founders

KETCHAM, LIEUT. JOHN, —— 1697. Constable, Setauket, L.I., 1662. Commissioner, 1664. Deputy from Huntington, L.I., 1665. Lieut. before 1666.

KETCHAM, SAMUEL, 1651-after 1697. Constable, Huntington, L.I., 1687.

KIERSTEDE, DR. HANS, —— 1666. Came from Germany to New Amsterdam, 1638. Surgeon. Forces at Fort Orange, 1645. Official Surgeon of West India Co., 1638.

KILBOURN, JOHN, 1624-1703. Boundary Line Committee at Hatford and Wethersfield, Conn. Representative to General Court. Constable. Selectman, 1657-1681.

KILLAM, AUSTIN, 1595-1667. Constable, Wenham, Mass., 1649.

KIMBALL, BENJAMIN, 1637-1695. Overseer of Bradford, Mass., 1668. Soldier under Capt. Appleton, 1683-1684. Known as Cornet Kimball, Salisbury, Mass.
Weaver, Mrs. John F., Sr.   Michigan

KIMBALL, JOHN, 1631-1698. Selectman of Boxford, Mass., 1691.

KIMBALL, RICHARD, 1595-1674/5. Born in England. One of the seven men appointed to govern Ipswich, Mass., 1645. Surveyor, Watertown, Mass., 1635; Ipswich, Mass., 1653.
Weaver, Mrs. John F., Sr.   Michigan

KIMBALL, RICHARD, II, circa 1623-1676. Born in England. Settled at Wenham, Mass. Selectman, 1658 and later. Committeeman to build new Meeting House, 1660.

KIMBALL, THOMAS, 1633-1676. Constable, Merrimack (later Rowley), Mass., 1668/9. Selectman.
Weaver, Mrs. John F., Sr.   Michigan

KIMBERLY, NATHANIEL, ————. Constable, New Haven, Conn., 1683.
Greason, Mrs. James B., Jr.   Founders

KIMBERLY, THOMAS, —— 1671/2. Born in England. Marshal, New Haven Colony, 1653-1661. Deputy, 1653. Selectman, 1663, 1664. Constable, 1665.
Greason, Mrs. James B., Jr.   Founders

KING, CLEMENT, —— 1708. Constable, Marshfield, Mass., 1655. Member of Train Band, Providence, R.I., 1686.

KING, MAJOR ROBERT, 1636-1680. Major in Colonial Virginia Militia. Justice before 1674.
Woodford, Mrs. Buckner   Blue Grass

KINGE (KING), WILLIAM, circa 1595-1650/1. One of the Founders of Salem, Mass., 1635/6. Had original Land Grant. Died in Salem, Mass.
Woodford, Mrs. Buckner   Blue Grass

KINGSBURY, LIEUT. JOSEPH, 1656/7-1741. Selectman, Haverhill, Mass., 1697-1698, 1699.

KINGSLAND, ISAAC, 1648-1698. Councilman under Gov. Laurie of N.J., 1684, 1685, 1686; under Gov. Hamilton, 1692, 1698; under Gov. Lord Niel-Campbell, 1686-1687. Capt. of a Foot Co., 1686. Lord High Sheriff of Essex, Bergen Co., N.J., 1682-1683.
Richardson, Mrs. James A.   North Carolina

KINGSLEY, JOHN, I, —— buried 6 Jan. 1678. One of the Seven Signers of the church covenant, Dorchester, Mass., 23 June 1636. A Founder of Second Church of Dorchester. Ordained Elder before 1653.
Pietsch, Mrs. Carl E.   Member-at-Large

KINGSLEY, STEPHEN, —— 1673. Representative from Dorchester, Mass., 1650. Ruling Elder, 1653. Representative from Milton, Mass., 1666.

KINNE(Y), HENRY, 1623-1712. MA. Soldier ca. 1654, served under Maj. Sedgwick 1673, capture of Ft. Narragansett. Served in King Philip's War.
Riley, Mrs. Gerald E.   Rhode Island

KIRBY, JOHN, 1623-1677. Born in England. Member Military Co., Plymouth, Mass., 1643.
Greason, Mrs. James B., Jr.   Founders

KIRTLAND, NATHANIEL, 1616-1686. Selectman, Lynn, Mass.

KNAPP, JOSHUA, 1634-1684. One of two who bargained with Indians to purchase Bedford Parish from them, 1680. Member of committee to establish boundary line between Greenwich and Rye.

KNIGHT, JOHN, —— 1670. Selectman, Newbury, Mass., 1638.

KNIGHT, JOHN, 1622-1678. Surveyor and Attorney, Newbury, Mass., 1677.

KNIGHT, JOSEPH, 1652 ——. Surveyor, Newbury, Mass., 1690.

KNIGHT, DEA. RICHARD, 1603-1683. Born in England. Selectman, Newbury, Mass., 1636. Deacon.

KNOWLES, ALEXANDER, —— 1663. Assistant to Governor, 1654, 1658. Commissioner, 1656. (Conn.)

KNOWLTON, JOHN, 1633-1684. Of Ipswich, Mass. Died at Wrentham, Mass. Served in Narragansett Expedition, King Philip's War, 1675.

KUNDERS, THOMAS (THONES), 1648-1729. Founder of Germantown, Pa., 1683.
Anderson, Mrs. Earl S.   Illinois
Cotton, Mrs. Jerry L.   Illinois
Summins, Mrs. Mildred Masters   Illinois

KUYPER, CLAES JANSEN, circa 1617-1688. Elected Schepen for Ahasimus, (now Jersey City) in Bergen Court, 1674. Surveyor of highways in Bergen Co. by Act of the General Assembly, New Jersey, 1682.

LADD, DANIEL, —— 1693. Selectman, Haverhill, Mass., 1668. Soldier in King Philip's War, 1675/6.
Weaver, Mrs. John F., Sr.   Michigan

LADD, SAMUEL, 1649-1697/8. Soldier in King Philip's War, 1676.
Weaver, Mrs. John F., Sr.   Michigan

LANDON, DANIEL, —— ——. Served in King Philip's War, from Boston, 1675.

LANE, CAPT. JOHN, Of Malden Mass. Selectman, 1676, 1679, 1681. Representative for Billerica, Mass., 1676, 1679.

LANGHORNE, REV. THOMAS, —— 1710. Born in England. Minister, Bucks Co., Penn., 1684.

LANSING, GERRET, —— 1679. Patentee, New Albany, N.Y., 1667, 1668, 1670, 1676.

LAPHAM, JOHN, 1635-1710. Born in England. Deputy from Newport, 1673. Constable, 1675. King Philip's War, 1675.

LARKIN, EDWARD, —— 1652. Member of Ancient and Honorable Artillery Co. of Boston, Mass., 1644.

LARKIN, JOHN, —— ——. Member of Assembly from Anne Arundel County, Maryland, 1683-1692.

LATHAM, CARY, —— 1685. Born in England. Settled in Cambridge, Mass., then to New London, Conn., 1645. Constable, 1645. Selectman, 16 years. Deputy to General Court from New London, Conn., 1664-1670.
Trau, Mrs. Frank Garland   Pennsylvania

LAURANCE, DEA. RICHARD, —— 1691. Founder of Branford, Conn., 1644. Founder of Newark, N.J., 1666. Townsman, 1667. Deacon of the First Church, 1670, 1671. Member of Commission to debate with Governor concerning a Patent, 1674-1675.

LAW, RICHARD, 1587 ——. Born in England. Deputy from Stamford, Conn., 1641—1664. Assistant to Governor, 1647.

LAWRENCE, ENOCH, 1648/9-1744. Born in Watertown, Mass. Served in King Philip's and King William's Wars. Was in garrison at Groton, Mass., 1691-1692.
Cook, Mrs. Ralph William, Sr.				Michigan

LAWRENCE, GEORGE, 1637-1708/9. Constable, Watertown, Mass., 1691. Selectman, 1695.

LAWRENCE, JOHN, 1609-1667. Born in England. Selectman, Groton, Mass., 1664-1665. Surveyor of Highways, Groton, Mass.
Cook, Mrs. Ralph William, Sr.				Michigan

LAWRENCE, NATHANIEL, 1630-1724. A Representative to Mass. General Court, 1692-1693.

LAWRENCE, ROBERT, ————. Justice and Commissioner, Isle of Wight Co., Va., 1659-1660.

LAWRENCE, CAPT. WILLIAM, 1623-1680. Magistrate, Flushing, L.I., 1655, 1658, 1661, 1662. Capt. Burgher Corps., New Netherland, 1655, and commanded Flushing Troops, 1673.

LAWRENCE, WILLIAM, —— before 22 May 1704. Deputy-Constable and Overseer, 1669. Town Constable, Monmouth, N.J., 1671.

LAWSON, JOHN, —— 1658. born in England. Commissioner of Maryland, 1654-1657.

LAWSON, ROWLAND, SR., —— 1661. Justice of Lancaster County, Va., 1652-1656.

LAWSON, CAPT. ROWLAND, JR., —— 1706. Captain of Rangers, Lancaster Co., Va., 1679.

LAWTON, GEORGE, —— 1693. Deputy from Portsmouth, R.I., to General Assembly, 1665, 1672, 1675, 1676, 1679, 1680. Member of Council of War, 1671. Assistant to Governor, 1680-1686, 1689, 1690. Commissioner from Portsmouth to General Court of Rhode Island, 1648.

LAY, ROBERT, 1617-1689. Born in England. Deputy from Saybrook, Conn., 1666, 1678.

LAYLAND (See LELAND).

LEAR, CAPT. JOHN, —— 1696. Member of Governor's Council, 1683. Member of Virginia House of Burgesses, 1666. Captain in military establishment of Colony of Va.

LEARNED, ISAAC, baptized 1630-1657. Selectman, Chelmsford Mass., 1654. Commissioner and Deacon, 1656.

Gary, Mrs. Dan Carmack   Tennessee
Gary, Miss Grace Elizabeth   Tennessee
Latimer, Mrs. Jane Dietzel   Tennessee

LEARNED, ISAAC, 1655-1737. Member of Capt. Nathaniel Davenport's Co. and was wounded in Narragansett Fight, 19 Dec. 1675.

LEARNED, WILLIAM, circa 1590-1646. On First Board of Selectmen, 1644-1645. Constable, Woburn, Mass., 1644-1645.

Gary, Miss Grace Elizabeth   Tennessee

LE CHAIRE, FRANCOIS,—— after 1670. On Muster Roll of Capt. Pawling's Militia of Hurley, N.Y., 5 Apr. 1670.

Long, Mrs. Alfred T.   Founders

LE CHAIRE, JAN, 1665-after 1717. Trustee of the Freeholders of Kingston, N.Y., 1695-1699.

Long, Mrs. Alfred T.   Founders

LEE, RICHARD, 1613-1664. Secretary of State, Va., 1649-1652. Burgess, York Co., Va., 1647.

LEE, RICHARD, II, 1646-1714. Member of Governor's Council, 1673.

LEE, ROBERT,—— ——. Came to Plymouth, Mass., 1636. Freeman, 1637. Served in Militia, 1643.

LEEDS, DANIEL, circa 1652-1720. First Surveyor-General of West Jersey, 1681. Member of General Assembly, 1682.

LEEK, EBENEZER, 1647-1726. Born in New Haven, Conn. Constable, Easthampton, L.I., 1699.

LEEK, CORP. PHILIP, 1611-1676. Born in England. Corporal, New Haven, Conn., 1638-1649. Collector for Yale College, 1646.

LEETE, GOV. WILLIAM, 1613-1683. Came from England to New Haven, Conn. in company Rev. Wm. Whitfield. One of signers of the "Plantation Covenant," 1639. Clerk of the Plantation, 1639. Dep. Governor, New Haven Colony, 1658-1661. Governor, 1661-1665. Dep. Governor of Connecticut, 1665-1676. Governor, 1676-1683.

LELAND, DEA. HOPESTILL, 1653-1729. Of Dorchester, Mass. Moved to Sherburne, 1678. Deacon, Orthodox Church. Selectman, 1689-1699.

LEONARD, CAPT. JAMES, SR., 1620/21-1691. Defended his Garrison House in King Philip's War, Taunton, Mass., 1675.
Love, Miss Marsha Lynn   Florida

LEONARD, JOHN, —— 1676. Killed in King Philip's War in Springfield, Mass., 1676.

LEONARD, JOSIAH, 1658-1689. Soldier in Fall's Fight, King Philip's War 19 May 1676.
Cook, Mrs. Ralph W., Sr.   Michigan

LEONARD, SOLOMON, 1610-1675. Original Proprietor of Bridgewater and member of Colony Company of Plymouth, Mass.
Russell, Mrs. Harold A.   Pennsylvania

LEONARD, JUDGE THOMAS, 1640-1713. Deputy from Taunton to Plymouth Colony, 1680-1686, 1689, 1690. Deputy to the General Court of Mass., 1692-1696, 1698, 1699. Judge of the Superior Court of Common Pleas, Bristol County, 1692-1699. Captain, 1690.

L'ESTRANG, DANIEL, 1661-1706/7. Born in France. Justice of the Peace, New Rochelle, N.Y., 1694.

LEVERING, WIGARD, circa 1648-1745. Born in Germany. A Founder of Roxborough, Pa., 1691/2.
Wright, Mrs. Chauncey B.   Blue Grass
Richards, Miss Shelia Permell   Illinois

LEWIS, DAVID, circa 1670 ——. Soldier in Capt. Staats Co., 1689-1690.

LEWIS, JOHN, —— 1657. First settler, Malden, Mass., 1633.

LEWIS, THOMAS, 1633-1709. Born in England. One of the first settlers of Bristol, R.I., 1681.

LEWIS, CAPT. JOHN, circa 1640-1726. Captain of New Kent Co., Va. Militia, 1680.
Pierce, Mrs. Albert Reynolds   Oklahoma

LEWIS, CAPT. WILLIAM, 1620-1690. Arrived from England, 1632. In Hartford, Conn., 1636, settled in Farmington. Sergeant, 1649; Lieutenant, 1651; Captain, 1654. Served in King Philip's War, 1675-1676. Deputy to General Court, 1689-1690.
Gremillion, Mrs. Charles M.   Louisiana
Saloom, Mrs. Richard G.   Louisiana
Saloom, Miss Rosalyn Ann   Louisiana

LEYDECKER, CAPT. RYCKE, —— before 1666. Magistrate, Bushwick, N.Y., 1662, 1663, 1665. Capt. of Militia, 1663.

LIGON, COL. THOMAS, 1586-1675/6. Surveyor, Henrico Co., Va., 1655-1656. Justice of Peace, Henrico Co., Va., 1657. Lieut. Col. of Charles City Co., Va. Militia. Member of House of Burgesses.

LILLINGTON, MAJ. ALEX, 1643-1697. Of North Carolina. Appointed Associate Justice, 1679. Deputy Governor, 1693.

LINCOLN, BENJAMIN, 1643-1700. Selectman, Hingham, Mass.

LINDALL, DEA. HENRY,—— 1660. Born in England. Deputy from New Haven, Conn., 1651-1660. Deacon of First church, 1659.

LINDSAY, ROBERT, ca 1641-after 1701. Clerk of Fairfield Parish, Cherry Point, Northumberland Co. VA, 1681-1682.
Hayne, Mrs. Robert S.   Tennessee

LINGAN, GEORGE, —— 1705. Commissioner, Calvert Co., Md., 1681, 1684-1689. Member of House of Burgesses, 1688.

LINNELL, ROBERT,—— 1663. Born in England. Member of Barnstable, Mass., Military Co., 1643.

LIPPINCOTT, RICHARD, —— 1683. Deputy from Shrewsbury, N.J., to General Assembly of East Jersey, 1669-1677. Overseer, Shrewsbury, 1670.

LITTLEFIELD, EDMUND, 1592-1661, of MA Bay. Selectman 1654 and 1657.
Nichols, Miss Sally Carol   Tennessee

LITTLEFIELD, FRANCIS, 1619-1712. Came from England to Boston, Mass., 1637. Resident, Dover, Me. Deputy, 1648. Moved to Wells, 1650. Deputy, 1665. Resident, York. Deputy, 1668, 1676.

LIVERMORE, GRACE SHERMAN, 1615-1690. Physician. Was among members of Fundamental Agreement, New Haven Colony, 1642. Attended General Court, 1647.
Koski, Mrs. Onni G.   Florida

LIVERMORE, JOHN, II, 1638-1719. Lieutenant and Ensign, King Philip's War, 1675. Selectman, 1692. Other Town offices before 1695.
Barkley, Mrs. John W., Jr.   Florida

LLEWELLYN, JOHN, 1652-1698. Of St. Mary's Co., Md. Secretary to Lieutenant General, 1677. Clerk of the Council, 1677-1678. Justice of St. Mary's Co., 1692.

| Blakeley, Mrs. John Kirby | Jamestown Virginia |
| Sommers, Mrs. George, Jr. | Jamestown Virginia |

LLOYD, EDWARD,—— 1696. Deputy Governor, Anne Arundel Co., Md., 1650. Member of council, 1657-1660.

| Hanna, Mrs. Robert C. | Member-at-Large |
| Rogers, Mrs. Richard de Roulhac | Member-at-Large |

LOCKWOOD, LIEUT. JONATHAN, 1634-1688. Lieut. of Colonial Forces of Conn., 1657.

LOCKWOOD, SERGT. ROBERT, baptized 1600-1658. Sergeant, Fairfield, Conn., 1657.

| Rudy, Mrs. Charles H. | Oklahoma |

LOGAN, JAMES, —— ——. Arrived in Pa., as Secretary to William Penn, 1699.

LOMBARD, ENS. BERNARD, 1608-1664. Ensign, Military Co., Barnstable, Mass., 1653.

LONG, DEA. ROBERT, 1621-1690. Born in England. Selectman, Newbury, Mass., 1674, 1675, 1683, 1684.

LONG, ROBERT, 1639-1693. Member Ancient and Honorable Artillery Co., Charlestown, Mass., 1639.

LOOMIS, DEA. JOHN, 1622-1688. Deacon of church, Windsor, Conn. Deputy to General Court, 1666, 1667, 1675-1687.

Gabbard, Mrs. William D.	Prairie State
Lessen, Mrs. Larry L.	Prairie State
Voitlein, Mrs. Stephen P.	Prairie State

LOOMIS, JOSEPH, 1590-1658. Born in England. Deputy from Windsor, Conn., 1643-1644.

LOOMIS, NATHANIEL, circa 1626-1688. Born in England. Member of Windsor, Conn. Troop of Horse, King Philip's War, 1675.

LORD, NATHAN, JR., 1656-1733. Constable, 1692-1693. Highway Surveyor, Kittery, Me., 1694, 1695, 1696, 1697.

| Darby, Mrs. Alfred Ellery | Rhode Island |
| Yeagley, Mrs. William F. | Rhode Island |

LORD, DR. THOMAS, 1580-before 2 Aug. 1676. One of the original proprietors of Hartford, Conn., 1636. Given first medical license in New England, 1652.

LOTHROP, BARNABAS, 1636-1715. Born in England. Representative from Barnstable, Mass., 1674-1679. Assistant to Governor, 1681-1686. Councilor under Governor Andros, 1686-1689. Chief Justice, many years from 1692.

LOTHROP, REV. JOHN, 1584-1653. First minister at Scituate, Mass., 1634-1639. Minister, Barnstable, Mass., 1639-1653.
Milburn, Mrs. John T.   Blue Grass

LOTHROP, SAMUEL, 1620-1700. Member Barnstable, Mass., Military Co., 1643. In expedition against Ninigret, 1654.

LOTT, ENGLEBERT, 1654-1728. Born in Flatbush, L.I. Sheriff, Brooklyn, 1698.

LOTT, PETER, —— 1693. From Holland, 1652, and settled in Flatbush, L.I. Magistrate, 1656-1673. One of the Patentees in grant by Governor Thomas Dongan, 1685.

LOUW, PIETER CORNELLIS, —— 1707/8. In Foot Co. under Capt. Matyson, Kingston, N.Y., 1686/7.
Long, Mrs. Alfred T.   Founders

LOVEJOY, JOHN, —— 1690. Served in King Philip's War, from Andover, Mass., 1675-1676.

LOWELL, JOHN, —— 1647. Town Clerk, Newbury, Mass., 1642. Magistrate, 1645.

LOWELL, PERCIVAL, —— ——. Of Newberry, Mass. One of Original Proprietors of Newberry, 1642.

LUBBERTSON, FREDERICK, 1609-1679. Born in Holland. One of twelve men representing Breukelen at Convention, Nieuw Amsterdam, 1641. Magistrate, 1653-1655, 1664-1673. Small Burgess, 1657. Member of Convention to arrange with Dutch Towns for a system of defense, 1663.

LUCAS, THOMAS, SR., —— Will prob. 1673. Justice, 1657. Burgess, 1657-1658. Rappahannock Co. Va.
Davis, Mrs. Frank V.   Illinois

LUDLOW, DEP. GOV. ROGER, 1590-1665. Born in England. Assistant to Governor of Mass., 1630-1634. Deputy Governor, Conn. Colony, three terms, 1639-1648. Magistrate, 1640-1653. Commissioner United Colonies, 1651-1653. Served in Pequot War.

LULL, THOMAS, 1637-1719. Constable, Ipswich, Mass., 1683.

LUMPKIN, WILLIAM, —— Will prob. 29 Oct. 1671. One of Proprietors, Yarmouth, Mass., 7 Jan. 1638/9. Constable, 1639-1640. Deputy to Colony Court and held many public offices.

LUPTON, THOMAS, —— ——. Member of the General Court, New Haven, Conn., 1644.
Milburn, Mrs. John T.   Blue Grass

LUTHER, REV. SAMUEL, —— 1717. Of Rehoboth, Mass., 1662. Deputy, Swanzey, 1677-1679. Ordained Minister, 1685.

LYMAN, RICHARD, 1580-1640/1. Came from England in the "Lion," 1631. Settled in Roxbury, Mass. Removed to Charlestown, and later with his family joined the party of one hundred which settled Windsor and Hartford, Conn. His name is inscribed on "Founders' Monument," Hartford, Conn.
Earle, Miss Eleanor Southgate   Ohio

LYMAN, RICHARD, JR., 1618-1662. Selectman, Northampton, Mass., 1658, 1659, 1660. Commissioner for holding court, Springfield, 1659.

LYNDE, SAMUEL, 1658-1721. Member of Ancient and Honorable Artillery Co., 1691.

LYNDE, SIMON, 1624-1687. Of Boston, Mass. Clerk of Ancient and Honorable Artillery Company, 1661.
Lang, Mrs. Lawrence C.   Michigan

LYON, HENRY, —— 1703. One of the founders of Milford, Conn., 1639; and Newark, N.J., and signer of Fundamental Agreement, 1667. Member of General Assembly, N.J., 1675. Justice of the Peace, 1681. Judge of small causes, and member of the Governor's Council. Commissioner, 1682, 1684.

LYON, RICHARD, —— 1678. Commissioner from Fairfield, Conn., 1669.

LYON, WILLIAM, 1620-1692. Born in England. Died in Roxbury, Mass. Member of ancient and Honorable Artillery Co., from Roxbury, 1645.

MABIE, PIETER CASPARZEN, ―― ――. In New Amsterdam 1647. On Excise Committee, 1654. Corporal, 4th Co., New Amsterdam, 1653.

MACKALL, JAMES, ―― ――. Constable, Marshfield, Mass., 1690.

MACOCKE (MAYCOCK), CAPT. SAMUEL, ca. 1599-1622. Member of Governor's Council, VA 1617-1618. Minister 1617.
Weaver, Miss Patricia   Florida

MACON, GIDEON, 1637-1702. Arrived from France in Charles City and York Cos., Va., circa 1660. A Huguenot, Indian interpreter for Gov. Berkeley, Burgess from New Kent Co., Va. Died, James City Co., Va.
Yates, Mrs. F. Ogburn   North Carolina

MACY, THOMAS, 1608-1682. Chief Magistrate, Nantucket, Mass., 1675.

MADDOCK, HENRY,―― 1706. Member of Assembly for Chester County, Penn., 1684.
Eaton, Mrs. Howard K.   Rhode Island

MADDOX, SAMUEL,―― 1684. Lieut., St. Mary's Co., Md., 1675, 1678.
Lewis, Mrs. LeRoy Ramey   Missouri

MAKEPEACE, THOMAS, 1592-1667. Member of Ancient and Honorable Artillery Co. of Boston, 1638.

MAN, RICHARD, 1652 ――. Born in Scituate, Mass. Served in King Philip's War from Conn., 1675.

MANJE (MANNING), JAN, ―― 1643. Served in Dutch and English War against Indians, 1643. Died at Stamford, Conn.

MANSFIELD, ANDREW, 1621-1683. Town Clerk, Lynn, Mass., 1660. Selectman, 1678. Deputy to General Court, 1680-1683.

MANSFIELD, ROBERT, ―― 1666. Constable, Lynn, Mass., 1646, 1647.

MAPES, THOMAS, 1628-1687. Born in England. Justice of the Peace, Southold, L.I., many years until his death. Constable, 1667.
Cunningham, Mrs. Ernest Lewis   CT Farms

MARCELLISSEN, PETER,―― 1691. Born in Amsterdam. Schepen, Bergen, N.J., 1673.

MARCH, HUGH, SR., 1619-1693. Selectman, Newbury, Mass., 1662, 1668.

MARKS, JOSEPH, —— ——. Served in Albany, N.Y., against French, 1689. Taken prisoner to Canada.

MARSH, ALEXANDER, —— ——. Of Braintree and Boston, Mass. Selectman of Braintree, 1682. Representative, 1692.

MARSH, SAMUEL, 1626-1683. Member of New Haven Militia, 1646.
Finfgeld, Mrs. Clifford   Illinois

MARSHALL, JOHN, 1645-1702. Born in Boston. Overseer and Master of Garrison, Billerica, Mass., 1675.

MARSHFIELD, SAMUEL, 1630-1692. Selectman, Springfield, Mass., 1663. Constable, 1659/60. Deputy, 1680, 1683-1684.

MARSTON, ISAAC, 1647/8-after 1714. Hampton, N.H. 1681 Selectman.
Simonson, Mrs. John E.   Illinois

MARTIAU, CAPT. NICHOLAS, 1592-1657. Born in France. Arrived in Va., 1620. Captain during Indian massacre, 1622. Member House of Burgesses from York Co., 1623, from Isle of Kent, 1632. A Justice of York Co., Va., 1633-1657.
Crowder, Mrs. Roy Hester   North Carolina
Fletcher, Mrs. Donald F., Jr.   Jamestown Virginia
Fletcher, Miss Susan Madison   Jamestown Virginia
Lipscomb, Mrs. Richard Edward   North Carolina
Nye, Mrs. Jackson Lanneau   North Carolina
Paterno, Mrs. Charles F., Jr.   North Carolina
Smith, Miss Agnes   North Carolina

MARTIN, GEORGE, —— 1686. Surveyor, Amesbury, Mass., 1664.

MARTIN, JOHN, circa 1616-1666. Member of House of Burgesses, Va., 1652-1653.
Brunini, Mrs. Cyrus J.   CT Farms

MARTIN, JOHN, 1650-1693. Served in King Philip's War, under Captain Cutter, Mass., 1675-1676.

MARVIN, MATTHEW, 1600-1680. Surveyor-Hartford, 1639, 1647. Deputy from Norwalk, 1654. Named on monument in Hartford.
Greason, Mrs. James B., Jr.   Founders

MARVIN, LIEUT. REINOLD, 1631-1676. Represented Lyme in General Court, 1670, 1672-1676. Sergt. for Saybrook and Lyme, 1661.

MASON, QUARTERMASTER DANIEL, 1652-1736/7. Commissioned Quartermaster, New London Troop, 16 Oct. 1673. Deputy, 1683. Schoolmaster of Norwich.

MASON, CAPT. HUGH, 1605-1678. Born in England. Town Clerk, Watertown, Mass. Selectman. Deputy, ten times, between 1644-1677. Lieutenant, 1649. Captain, 1652. Commander Volunteers against the Manhattoes, 1664.

MASON, MAJ.-GEN. JOHN, 1600-1672. From England, circa 1630. Capt. in Pequot War, 1637. First called Major, 1654. War Committee for Saybrook, 1653-1654. Major, Conn. Colony Troop, 1658. Deputy, Windsor, to Conn. Legislature, 1637, 1638, 1639, 1641. Assistant, Conn. Colony, 1642-1659. Deputy Gov. of Conn. Colony, 1660-1665. Patentee, Royal Charter, 1662. Commissioner, to United Colonies, 1654-1657, 1660-1661. Commissioner to treat with N.H. Colony, 1663. Commissioner for Mass. and R.I. boundaries, 1664.
Cannon, Mrs. John Franklin   Conn. Farms

MASON, SAMPSON, —— 1676. One of first settlers Rehoboth, Mass., 1666.

MASON, NOAH, 1651-1699. Born at Dorchester, Mass. Died at Rehoboth, Mass. Served in Narragansett Campaign, King Philip's War, 1675.

MASTERS, JOHN, —— 1639. Born in England. Selectman, Watertown, Mass. Joined Governor Withrop on prospecting expedition, 1631.

MATHER, REV. ELEAZER, 1637-1669. ordained, 1661, and was First Minister in Northampton, Mass.

MATHER, REV. RICHARD, 1596-1669. Came from England to Boston, Mass., 1635. Pastor of Church, Dorchester. Assisted "The Apostle" Eliot in translation of the Bible into the Indian language; and with others published "The Bay Psalm," the first book printed in the British-American Colonies, 1640.

MATTHEWS, CAPT. PETER, circa 1650-Will prob. 1719. Commanded company of men on expedition against Mohawk Indians, 1692/3. Aide to Gov. Fletcher, 1692; also Gov. Belmont, later.
Denton, Mrs. E. Brady   Michigan

MATHEWSON, JAMES, —— 1682. Deputy, Rhode Island, 1680.

MATTROM (MATRUM), COL. JOHN, before 1619-before 1655/6. Member House of Burgesses, Va., 1645, 1652. Capt., also Col. in Militia.
Bowles, Mrs. George D., Jr.   North Carolina

MAULDIN, FRANCIS, —— 1734. Justice-Commissioner of MD.
Chaney, Mrs. Lowell   Member-at-Large

MAXSON, JOHN, 1639-1720. Deputy from Westerly, R.I., 1670, 1686, 1690.

MAXSON, RICHARD, —— ——. Proprietor, Portsmouth, R.I., 1638. Signed Portsmouth Compact, 30 Apr. 1639.

MAY, JOHN, 1663-1730. Selectman; Deacon, Roxbury, Mass.

MAYHEW, GOV. THOMAS, 1593-1682. Came from England, 1633. Settled in Watertown, Mass. Freeman, 1634. Deputy, 1636-1644. Selectman, 1637-1643. Colonial Governor, Martha's Vineyard, and Nantucket, 1671, 1681, under grant from William, Earl of Stirling.
Jakob, Mrs. William A.   CT Farms
Smith, Mrs. Len Young   Illinois

MAYNARD, JOHN, —— ——. Soldier in King Philip's War, from Marlborough, Mass., 1675.

MEAD, JOHN, 1634-1699. Deputy from Greenwich, Conn., to Hartford, 1679, 1680, 1686.

MEARS, THOMAS, —— ——. Providence, MD before 1674. Commissioner 1650-1658. Judge of Provincial Court 1655. Burgess from Lower Norfolk Co., VA. 1644-1648.
Jackson, Mrs. William P.   Illinois

MEIGS, JOHN, 1612-1672. Came from England to Weymouth, Mass., 1634. Removed to New Haven, Conn. Constable of Guilford in defiance of the New Haven jurisdiction. Clerk of New Haven Train Band, 1648. Judge of Guilford Town, 1663.
Greason, Mrs. James B., Jr.   Founders

MELYN, CORNELIS, 1602 ——. One of the eight men to govern New Amsterdam, 1643. Patron of Staten Island, 1642, 1659.
Bauer, Mrs. Clarence P.   Michigan

MERRIWETHER, NICHOLAS, 1631-1678. Clerk of Governors Council of the Virginia Colony, 1654. Clerk of County Court, Surry Co., Va., 1652. One of the commissioners to raise supplies for General Nathaniel Bacon's expedition against the Indians, 1677.
Franklin, Mrs. Kenneth Cabell Clay   North Carolina

MERIWETHER, NICHOLAS, II, 1667-1744. Vestryman, St. Peter's Parish, 1658-1698; also of St. Paul's Parish, New Kent Co. Va.
Meyer, Mrs. Paul G.   Illinois

MERRICK, THOMAS, 1620-1704. Born in England. Constable, Springfield, Mass., 1683.

MERRICK, THOMAS, JR., 1663/4-1743. Born in Springfield, Mass. Surveyor Highways, 1693-1694.

MERRILL, JOHN, 1635-1712. Townsman, Hartford, Conn., 1684, 1694.

MERRILL, NATHANIEL, 1601-1655. Original Proprietor, and Charter Member of Newbury, Mass., 1638.
Weaver, Mrs. John F., Sr.   Michigan

MERRIMAN, NATHANIEL, circa 1614-1693/4. Served in Pequot War; Sergt. New Haven Artillery Co., prior to 1664. Ensign, New Haven Train Band, May 1664; Sergt. of same, July 1665.
Gee, Mrs. Herbert C.   Florida
Milburn, Mrs. John T.   Blue Grass

MERSELISE, PIETER, —— 1681. Schepen of Bergen, N.J., 1673. Magistrate, 1673.

MERRYMAN, CAPT. CHARLES, 1649-1725. Born in Virginia. Captain, Provincial Militia, Baltimore, Md., 1696.

METCALF, MICHAEL, 1586-1664. Born in England. Selectman, Dedham, Mass., 1641.

MEYER, JAN DIRCKSZEN, —— ——. Born in Holland. Member of the 4th Co., Burgher Corps, New Amsterdam, 1653.

MIDDAGH, JAN AERTSEN, —— 1709. Constable, Brooklyn, N.Y. 1679.

MILLER, LIEUT. JEREMIAH, 1655-1723. Commissioner, Easthampton, L.I., 1687. Trustee, 1692.

MILLER, JOHN, —— 1664. Born in England. Settled in Lynn, Mass. A Founder of Easthampton, L.I. Original Proprietor of what is now Elizabethtown, N.J., 1664.
Finfgeld, Mrs. Clifford   Illinois

MILLER, THOMAS, —— 1675. Killed by Indians in burning of Springfield, Mass., King Philip's War, 5 Oct. 1675.

MILLER, WILLIAM, circa 1640-1711. Overseer, Easthampton, L.I., 2 Apr. 1682.
Finfgeld, Mrs. Clifford   Illinois

MINOR, EPHRAIM, 1642-1724. Represented Stonington, Conn., 1677, 1681. Selectman, 1675, 1676, 1678-1694. Served in King Philip's War, 1675/6.

MINOR, THOMAS, 1608-1690. Represented Stonington, Conn., 1665, 1670, 1672, 1677, 1679, 1680, 1689. Town Clerk, 1660-1662, 1669-1674. Selectman, 1658-1661, 1663, 1664, 1666-1671.
Riddle, Mrs. William McKinley   Oklahoma

MINOT, GEORGE, 1592-1671. Born in England. Representative from Dorchester, Mass. Ruling Elder for 30 years.

MITCHELL, EXPERIENCE, 1609-1689. Member of Militia, Duxbury, Mass., 1643.

MITCHELL, MATTHEW, 1590-1645. Came from England with Rev. Richard Mather. Settled in Charlestown, Mass. Removed to Concord, thence to Springfield. Signer of the celebrated "Compact" at Springfield. Deputy from Wethersfield, Conn., 1636. Served in garrison at Saybrook Fort, under Lion Gardiner, in the Pequot War. Associate Judge of Plantation Court.

MITCHELSON, EDWARD, 1604-1681. Marshal General, Cambridge, Mass., Colony, 1637.

MIX, THOMAS, —— 1691. Soldier, King Philip's War. Resided at New Haven, Conn.

MOLENAAR, DEA. JOOST ADRIANS, —— 1683. Born in Holland. Alderman, Kingston, N.Y., 1672-1678. Deacon.

MOLLINEUX, THOMAS, —— ——. One of eight men to govern Westchester, N.Y., 1665. Overseer, 1678.

MONKCLOTHLAN, (CHLAFLIN), ROBERT, —— before 1690. Born in Scotland. Soldier in expedition against Indians, 1688.

MONFORT (MONFOORT), DEA. PIETER, 1605-1661. Came from Holland to Brooklyn, N.Y., 1625. Magistrate, 1658. Deacon, Dutch Church, 1661.

MONROE, MAJ. ANDREW,—— 1668. Born in Scotland. Member of Maryland Assembly, 1642. Commissioner of Virginia, 1660.
Hamilton, Miss Adnee de Mobrey   Blue Grass

MOODY, WILLIAM, 1606-1682. Born in England. Selectman, Newbury, Mass., 1637, 1642.

MONTAGUE, PETER, 1603-1659. Member Va. House of Burgesses from Nansemond and Lancaster Cos., 1652-1658.
Sharp, Mrs. William　　　　　　　　　　Member-at-Large

MONTAGUE, RICHARD, 1614-1681. Born in England. Selectman, Hadley, Mass., 1671, 1677. Town Clerk, 1681.

MOORE, MAJOR ANDREW,—— 1668. Member Maryland Assembly 1642. Commissioner to VA 1660.
Hollingshead, Mrs. Wickliffe　　　　　　　　Pennsylvania

MOORE, GOLDEN, —— 1698. Original Proprietor, Billerica, Mass., 1658. In garrison at Thomas Pattin's during King Philip's War, Billerica, Mass., 8 Aug. 1675.

MOORE, DEA. JOHN, 1622-1677. Born in England. Deputy from Windsor, Conn., 1665, 1667. Served in King Philip's War, 1675. Deacon, 1651.

MOORE, REV. JOHN, —— 1657. Deputy and Commissioner, Southampton, L.I., 1644.

MOORE, HON. JOHN, 1656-1732. From England to Philadelphia, Pa., then to Carolinas, and returned to Philadelphia. Security of the Carolinas. Member of Governor's Grand Council. Registrar General of Pa., 1693. Crown Advocate, 1695.

MOORE, RICHARD, —— circa 1654. Attorney (barrister), St. Mary's Co., Maryland, until his death, 1654.

MOORE, SAMUEL, 1630-1688. Constable, 1669. Town Clerk, 1669-1688. Deputy to General Assembly, 1668. Assistant to Surveyor General, 1670. Woodbridge, Patentee, 1667. Provost Marshall, 1672-1673. Province Treasurer, East Jersey, 1675, 1678. High Sheriff, Middlesex Co., N.H., 1683.
Smith, Mrs. William Alfred　　　　　　　　Conn. Farms

MOORE, THOMAS, 1615-1691. Deputy from Southold, to New Haven, 1658. Constable, 1658. Overseer, 1683. Magistrate, 1685.

MORGAN, FRANCIS, I, circa 1600-1656/7. Member of House of Burgesses from York Co., Va., 1647, 1652, 1653.
Clark, Mrs. William Harrison　　　　　　　Tennessee

MORGAN, JAMES, SR., 1607-1685. Served in Pequot War, 1637. Deputy for New London to the General Court at Hartford, nine times between 1657 and 1670 inclusive.
Dunn, Mrs. Frederick E.   Oklahoma

MORGAN, CAPT. JAMES, 1644-1711. Deputy for New London to Conn. General Court, 1689, 1691, 1692, 1695, 1699. Capt. of Dragoons, New London, 1690. Advisor of the Pequot Indians in New London, 1694.

MORGAN, CAPT. JOHN, 1645-1712. Born in Roxbury, Mass. Indian Commissioner and Deputy, Groton, Conn., 1690-1694. Lieutenant and Captain, 1693.

MORGAN, CAPT. MILES, 1615-1699. Captain, King Philip's War, 1675. Built block house which he defended against the Indians, Springfield, Mass., 1675. Selectman, Springfield, 1655, 1657, 1660, 1662, 1668.

MORRILL, ABRAHAM, 1586-1662. Member of Ancient and Honorable Artillery Co., of Boston, Mass., 1638.

MORRILL, ISAAC, 1588-1662. Born in England, died at Roxbury, Mass. Member of Ancient and Honorable Artillery Co., 1638.

MORRIS, ANTHONY, II, 1654-1721. Settled in Pa. Justice of Supreme Court of Pa., 1694. Representative from Philadelphia to Assembly, 1698, 1699.
Dunton, Mrs. Robert M.   Founders
Tillotson, Mrs. C. Roger   Founders

MORRIS, LIEUT. EDWARD, 1630-1689. Born in England. Deputy from Roxbury, Mass., 1678-1684. First Military Officer of Woodstock, Conn.

MORRIS, LEWIS, circa 1655-1694/5. Sheriff, Monmouth City, 1682-1683. Ensign, Shrewsbury Co. of militia, 1682-1683. Justice of the Court of Common Right, Monmouth Co., 1692-1695.
Acton, Mrs. Ralph   Ohio

MORRIS, THOMAS, —— 1673. Early Settler of New Haven, Conn., 1638. Signer of the Plantation Covenant at New Haven, 1639.
McCartney, Miss Ruth Evelyn   Illinois
Milburn, Mrs. John T.   Blue Grass

MORRIS, REV. THOMAS, —— ——. Living in Middlesex Co., Va., 1702. Rector at Christ Church, Middlesex Co, 1663.

MORSE, ANTHONY, circa 1607-1686. Born in England. Arrived Newbury, Mass., on ship "James," 1635. Freeman, 1636. Lieutenant in Newbury Militia.

MORSE, DANIEL, 1613-1690. Born in England. Signed Dedham, Mass. Covenant and member first Assembly, 1636-1637. Selectman, Medfield, 1674-1688. Commissioner to negotiate sale of land with Indians, 1680.

MORSE, ROBERT, circa 1630 ——. One of the first settlers of Elizabeth, N.J., 1665.

MORSE, SAMUEL, 1587-1654. Born in England. Selectman, Watertown, Mass., 1636. Signed Covenant, Dedham, 1636. One of first settlers there.

MOSHER, HUGH, 1633-1709/13. Born in Mass. Ensign, serving during trials of Indians engaged by King Philip, 1672.

MOSS, CORP. JOHN, 1604-1707. Corporal, New Haven, Conn. Train Band, 1642. Deputy from Wallingford, Conn., 1667-1686. Judge, 1672-1677. Deputy to New Haven Legislature, 1664.
Milburn, Mrs. John T.   Blue Grass

MOTT, ADAM, 1596-1661. Born in England. Clerk of the Militia, Portsmouth, R.I., 1642.

MOTT, ADAM, JR., 1623-1673. Born in England. Deputy from Portsmouth, R.I., 1673.

MOULTON, JOHN, 1599-1649. Born in England. Deputy to Boston Court from Hampton, N.H., 1639.

MOULTON, ROBERT, —— ca. 1665. Representative of Charleston of the first Court in 1634, executive rulers of Salem.
Landrum, Mrs. Z. T.   Louisiana

MOULTON, WILLIAM, 1617-1664. Selectman, 1649.

MOWRY, ROGER M., —— 1666. Born in England. Commissioner from Providence, R.I., 1658.

MUDGE, JOHN, 1654-1733. Soldier under Capt. Joseph Sill, from Mass., in King Philip's War, 1675.

MUDGE, MICAH, 1650-1724. MA. Surveyor, appointed 18 Mar 1686, 1697 moved to Lebanon, CT and served as surveyor and assisted in layout of town of Lebanon.
Mudge, Miss Leila Elizabeth   Illinois

MULFORD, JOHN, 1606-1686. Born in England. Selectman, Easthampton, L.I., many years from 1651. Magistrate, 1660. Justice, 1674.

MULFORD, THOMAS, 1650-1732. Trustee of Easthampton, L.I., 1680, 1681, 1687, 1692.

MULFORD, WILLIAM, 1620-1687. Constable, Easthampton, L.I., 1657. Townsman, 1664.

MULLINES, ALICE (MRS.), —— 1621. Passenger on "Mayflower," 1620.
Weaver, Mrs. John F., Sr.   Michigan

MULLINES, WILLIAM, 1575-1621. Passenger on the "Mayflower," 1620. Signer of the Compact.
Booth, Mrs. John Newton   Oklahoma
Weaver, Mrs. John F., Sr.   Michigan

MUMFORD, THOMAS, —— 1692. Constable, Portsmouth, R.I., 1670, 1683-1686.

MUNSON, SAMUEL, baptized 1643-1692. Ensign, Wallingford Train Band, 1675.
Armstrong, Mrs. Donald George   Illinois

MUNSON, THOMAS, circa 1612-1685. Pequot War, 1637. Captain of New Haven Troops, 1675. Representative to Assembly, 1666-1682.
Armstrong, Mrs. Donald George   Illinois
Trefts, Miss Deborah Campbell   Ohio

NAGEL, SERGT. JAN, —— 1657. Military service, New Amsterdam, five years. Sergeant, 1652.

NAGEL, JURIAEN, 1653-1732. Served in Militia, New Amsterdam, 1689-1690.

NASH, LIEUT. JAMES, —— ——. Of Weymouth, Mass. Settled in Mass. Bay Colony, 1645. Representative for Weymouth, 1655, 1662,1667.

NASH, THOMAS, —— 1658. Born in England. Signed Fundamental Agreement, New Haven, Conn., 1639.

NASH, LIEUT. TIMOTHY, 1626-1699. Born in England. Lieut. from Hadley, Mass., 1678. Deputy, 1690, 1691, 1695.

NASON, RICHARD, —— Will adm., 1696. Born in Kittery, Maine. Ensign, Kittery, Me., 1653.

NEEDHAM, LIEUT. ANTHONY, 1627-after 1678. Served in King Philip's War, under Capt. Manning, Ipswich, Mass., 1675-1676.
Baumhart, Mrs. Donald H.   North Carolina

NEEDLES, JOHN, —— ——. Commissioner and Justice, Talbot County, Md., 1697—1698.

NELSON, JOHN, —— 1713. Overseer, Mamaroneck, N.Y., 1697. Constable, 1699.

NELSON, CAPT. PHILIP, 1648 ——. Born at Rowley, Mass. Capt. in Sir William Phip's Expedition to Quebec, 1690.

NEVILLE, JOHN, circa 1618-1664. Member of Assembly of Maryland, 1662, 1664.
Allen, Mrs. Thomas B.   Missouri
Gravenhorst, Mrs. Theodore S.   Illinois
Keefer, Mrs. Dan M.   Missouri

NEVIUS, JOHANNES, baptized 1627-1672. Schepen, New Amsterdam, 16541655. Secretary, Burgomaster's Court, 1658.
Brook, Miss Edith Gertrude   Illinois

NEWBERRY, CAPT. BENJAMIN, 1634-1689. Born in Dorchester, Mass. Deputy, Windsor, to Conn. Legislature, 1656, 1662, 1665. Commissioner for Mass. and R.I. boundaries, Oct. 1664. First called Capt., 1662. Commanded Military Department of the Colony. Capt., King Philip's War, 1675-1676. Assistant to Governor, 1685.
Bachner, Mrs. Thomas Edgar   Tejas

NEWBERRY, THOMAS, —— 1635/6. Selectman, Dorchester, Mass., 1634. Deputy to Mass. General Court, 1634, 1635.

NEWCOMB, LIEUT. ANDREW, 1640-1708. Born in Boston, Mass. Constable, Edgartown, Martha's Vineyard, 1681. Townsman, 1693. Overseer, 1693. Lieutenant, 1691. Commander of Fortifications, 1691.
Hallgren, Mrs. George William   Michigan

NEWDIGATE (NEWGATE), JOHN, 1580-1665. Constable, Boston, 1635. Representative, 1638. Deputy, Town Officer.

NEWHALL, THOMAS, —— 1674. A Founder-grantee on list of 1638, Lynn, Mass. Member of Train Band, Lynn, Mass., released 1649.
Davis, Mrs. Frank V.　　　　　　　　　　　　　　　　Illinois
Mayer, Mrs. Paul Joseph　　　　　　　　　　　　　　Illinois

NEWLIN, NICHOLAS, 1630-1699, of Concord, Pa. Member of the Provincial Council, 1685-1687. Justice of the Peace and Court, 1684-1691.
Gluckert, Mrs. Francis A.　　　　　　　　　　　　　Florida

NEWMAN, GOV. FRANCIS, —— 1660. Born in England. Deputy from New Haven Colony, 1645-1649. Magistrate, 1653-1657. Secretary of the Colony, 1646-1649, 1653-1657. Governor, New Haven Colony, 1658-1660.

NEWMAN, DEA. SAMUEL, 1625-1710/11. Born in England. Representative from Rehoboth, Mass., 1696, 1697, 1698.

NEWMAN, REV. SAMUEL, 1602-1663. Born in England. First minister of first church, Weymouth, Mass., 1638-1643. Ordained in Rehoboth, 1644.

NEWTON, JOHN, —— 1697. Born in England. Justice of the Peace, Westmoreland Co., Va.

NEWTON, RICHARD, —— 1701. Served in King Philip's War from Marlborough,Mass., 1675.

NEWTON, CAPT. SAMUEL, —— ——. Deputy from Milford, Conn., 1690, 1694, 1696, 1699. Militia service in Indian War.

NICHOLS, CALEB, —— 1690. Born in England. Selectman, Stratford, Conn., 1661.

NICHOLS, SERGT. FRANCIS, —— 1650. Sergeant, Stratford, Conn., 1639.

NICHOLS, ISAAC, —— 1695. Deputy from Stratford, Conn., 1662-1665.

NICHOLS, THOMAS, —— after 1708. Served in King Philip's War, 1675/6. Deputy, East Greenwich, R.I., 1679, 1685, 1686, 1690, 1698.

NICHOLSON, CHRISTOPHER, 1638-1688. Born in Marblehead, Mass. Minister and Burgess in North Carolina.

NICHOLSON, SAMUEL,—— circa 1690. Named in First Patent of Fenwick's Colony, N.J., 1675. First Justice of the Peace, West Jersey, 1676. Signed Agreements and Concessions of West Jersey, 1676-1677.

NICHOLSON, WILLIAM, —— ——. Served in Middlesex County, Va., Militia, 1687.

NICKERSON, WILLIAM, 1603/4-1689/90. Deputy from Yarmouth to the Court at Plymouth, 1655. One of the ratemakers chosen by citzens of Eastham, Mass., 1671, 1672, 1673-1676.
Smith, Mrs. Leland   Illinois

NICOLL, MATTHIAS, —— 1687. Secretary of Province, 1664. Member of New York City Council, 1667-1680. Mayor of New York, 1672. Speaker of First Assembly, New York, 1683. Judge of Court of Admiralty, 1686.

NOBLE, JOHN, 1662-1714. Born in Springfield, Mass. Constable, Westfield, 1696.

NOBLE, THOMAS, 1632-1704. Born in England. Constable, Westfield, Mass., 1674.

NORTHCRAFT, EDWARD —— ——. Land patent granted 4 July 1677, Anne Arundel Co., MD. Incomplete.
Rittenhouse, Mrs. Floyd M.   Illinois

NORTHRUP, JOSEPH, —— 1669. Born in England. A Founder of Milford, Conn. and Member of Town Council.

NORTHRUP, STEPHEN, —— 1687. Born in England. Town Sergeant, Providence, R.I., 1660.

NORTON, GEORGE, —— 1659. Selectman, Gloucester, Mass., 1642/3. Representative, 1642, 1643, 1644.
Latzer, Mrs. John B.   Florida
McDermott, Mrs. George G.   Florida

NORTON, HENRY, 1618-1659. Provost Marshal of the Georges Colony, 1645. Recorder of the City of Georgeana, 1646/7. Selectman, 1650. Marshal, when Mass. took over the Government, 1653.

NORTON, NICHOLAS, 1610-1690. Constable, Weymouth, Mass.,1646.

NORTON, ENS. THOMAS,—— 1648. Born in England. Ensign, Guilford, Conn., Pequot War, 1637.
Greason, Mrs. James B., Jr.   Founders

NOSWORTHY, GEORGE, —— ca 1702. VA. Lt. Colonel and Commander-in-Chief.
Delk, Mr. Owington G.   Florida

NOYES, REV. JAMES, SR., 1608-1656. Born in England. Minister, Medford, Mass.; Watertown, Mass.; Newbury, Mass., 1635-1656.

NOYES, REV. JAMES, JR., 1640-1719. Minister, Stonington, Conn., 1674. Chaplain and physician to Colonial troops in Indian Wars.

NOYES, DEA. NICHOLAS, 1616-1701. Deacon, 1633, 1634. Deputy from Newbury, Mass., 1660, 1679, 1680, 1681.
Babcock, Mrs. Norman C.   Rhode Island

NOYES, PETER, 1593-1657. Born in England. Deputy from Sudbury, Mass., 1640, 1641, 1650.

NUTHALL, JOHN, 1620-1667. VA. Signed submission to Parliament in VA. 1651 Justice. 1663/4 Commissioner of St. Mary's Co. MD.
Ragsdale, Mrs. Charles L.   Missouri

ODELL, WILLIAM,—— 1676. One of the first settlers of Rye, N.Y.

OGDEN, DAVID, 1643-1692. Took oath of allegiance to Dutch Government, 1673. His wife was the first white person to land in New Jersey. Townsman, Elizabeth Towne, 1679-1680.

OGDEN, GOV. JOHN, 1609-1682. Founder of Elizabeth Towne and Newarke, N.J. County Collector, 1631. Magistrate, Colony of Conn., 1656-1658. Member Upper House, 1660-1661. Member King's Council, Province of New Jersey, 1668. Schout and Acting Governor of the English Colony, East Jersey, 1673.
Golz, Mrs. William M.   Conn. Farms
Plott, Mrs. Charles H.   Ohio

OGLE, JOHN, 1649-1734. Member of Col. Nicoll's military expedition, 1664.

OLCOTT, THOMAS,—— ——Original Proprietor and Settler, Hartford, Conn., 1635. Served in Pequot War, 1637.

OLDS, DR. ROBERT, 1645-1728. One of the Proprietors of Suffield. First man to have title of doctor given him. Representative from Suffield to General Court, Boston, 1694.

OLIVER, JOHN, 1616-1646. Seventh signer, Ancient and Honorable Artillery Co., 1637. Member General Court, 1637, 1638. Jr. Sgt., 1638; Sr. Sgt., 1639. Surveyor, Treasurer, kept Towne books. Selectman, 1641-1645. Graduate of Harvard, 1645. Minister at Romney Marsh for two years before his death.

OLIVER, THOMAS, 1567-before 1657. Ruling Elder, First Church,Boston, Mass. Town Officer.

OLMSTED, JAMES, 1580-1640. Constable, Newton (now Cambridge), 1634. Original Proprietor of Hartford, Conn.

OLMSTEAD, CAPT. JAMES,—— 1731. Born in Hartford, Conn. Town Clerk of Norwalk, Conn., 1678-1699. Deputy, 1691-1693, 1699. Lieut., 1680. Captain, 1691.

OLMSTEAD, LIEUT. JOHN, 1649-1704/5. Baptized, Hartford, Conn. Appointed Lieut. for Norwalk, 1691.

OLMSTEAD, CAPT. NICHOLAS, 1612-1684. Served in Pequot War, 1637. Deputy to the General Court, 1672, 1673. Corporal, Hartford Troop, 1658. Captain, 1675.

OLMSTEAD, CAPT. RICHARD, 1612-1686. Born in England. Deputy from Norwalk, Conn., 1653, 1660-1679. Lieut., 1659. Muster Master for Fairfield County, 1673. Commissioner, 1668-1677. King Philip's War, 1675/6. Captain, 1680.

OLNEY, EPENETUS, 1634-1698. Deputy for Providence, R.I., 1666-1688.

OLNEY, THOMAS, 1600-1682. Born in England. One of the 13 original Proprietors of Providence, R.I. Treasurer, 1638-1669. Assistant, 1649, 1653-1656, 1664-1667. Commissioner, 1656-1663. Deputy, 1665, 1667, 1670-1671. Member Town Council, 1665-1666, 1669-1671, 1674, 1677, 1681. Judge, 1655.

OPDEN GRAEFF, ABRAHAM, —— ——. Of Germantown, Pa. Burgess for Germantown, 1682. Member of Pa. Assembly, 1689, 1690, 1692.
Donaghy, Mrs. Edwin Carlton   Pennsylvania

OPDYCK, JOHANNES 1651-1728/9. Born New York, died Hopewell, NJ residing Gravesend and Newtown. Interpreter for the English and Dutch, on Newtown census of 1675.
Riddle, Mrs. William McKinley   Oklahoma

OPDYCK, Louris Jansen, before 1620 Holland, died after 1659 Gravesend, NY. 1655 Autumn-Soldier in the Second Indian War.
Riddle, Mrs. William McKinley   Oklahoma

ORDWAY, JAMES, 1618/20-1687. Soldier of Newbury, Mass., 1688 Freeholder, Selectman, 1681-1682.

OSBORN, DAVID, —— before 10 Nov. 1679. One of first settlers of East–chester, N.Y., 1664.

OSBORN, CORP. JERMIAH, —— 1676. Corporal, New Haven, Conn., 1667. Deputy, 1672 and after.

OSBORN, CAPT. RICHARD, 1612-1686. Born in England. Served in Pequot War, 1637. Signed the Fundamental Agreement at New Haven, Conn., 1639.

OSBORNE, CAPT. THOMAS, —— Will, 1660. Arrived from England, 1619. Died in Henrico Co., Va. Member of Virginia House of Burgesses, 1629-1633.
Augustus, Mrs. Stanley   Tejas
Patterson, Mrs. Louis W.   Oklahoma

OSGOOD, CAPT. JOHN, 1595-1651. Born in England. First Deputy from Andover, Mass., 1651. Captain, 1666.

OSGOOD, CAPT. JOHN, 1630-1693. Sergeant of Militia, Andover, Mass., 1658, 1661. Lieutenant, 1666-1675, 1677-1680. Captain, 1682. Select-man, 1689-1690.

OUGE (OUG), (WIDOW) FRANCES, —— circa 1636. Came from England. An Original Settler and Proprietor of Watertown, Mass.

OWEN, GRIFFITH, circa 1661-1763. Settled at Hilltown Township, Pa. Member of Provincial Council of Pa., 1683-1699.
Simonds, Mrs. LeRoy Edward   Ohio

OWEN, REV. ROBERT, 1674-1714. Licensed for service in Maryland 12 Aug 1699.
Novello, Mrs. Alfred Thomas   Pennsylvania

OWSLEY (OUSLEY), CAPT. THOMAS, 1663-1700. Born in England. Mem-ber, Virginia House of Burgesses from Stafford Co., 1693-1696. Captain of Stafford militia. Justice of the Peace, Clerk of House, 1692. Sheriff, 1695-1696.
Bell, Mrs. James Spencer   Tennessee

OXENBRIDGE, REV. JOHN, 1608-1674. Minister at First church, Boston, Mass., 1670-1674.

PACE, RICHARD, ca 1585-1627. First settlers of Jamestown, VA
Cmaylo, Mrs. Michael Alexander   Florida

PACK, GEORGE, 1634-1704. A Founder of Elizabethtown, N.J.,1664. One of original Associates.
Culton, Mrs. Willis Henry Ray   Illinois
Finfgeld, Mrs. Clifford   Illinois

PACKARD, SAMUEL,—— 1684. Died at Bridgewater, Mass. Served in King Philip's War, 1675/6.

PAGE, COL. JOHN, 1627-1691/2. Member of Virginia House of Burgesses, York Co., 1655-1657. Colonel of militia, 1680-1685.
Lotz, Mrs. Ronald Allen   CT Farms
Perkey, Mrs. Donald Ray   Tennessee

PAGE, ROBERT, 1604-1679. Member of N. H. General Assembly,1657. Selectman of Hampton, N.H., 1647-1670. Deacon of Church, 1660-1679.

PAINE, STEPHEN,—— 1679. Settler of Hingham, Mass., 1641.

PAINE, THOMAS, 1586-1650. Deputy from Yarmouth, Mass., to the Plymouth Colony, 1639.

PALGRAVE, RICHARD, ca 1585-1651. Served as a physician in Charlestown, MA Bay. Chyrugeon.
Yates, Mrs. Harold W.   Florida

PALMEAR, DEACON GERSHAM 1644-1719. Deacon at Stonington, CT 9 Dec 1696. Served in King Philip'sd War 1676.
Parenteau, Mrs. Jerome Francis   Quivira

PALMER, HENRY, circa 1600-after 1662. Surveyor, Wethersfield, Conn.,1662.

PALMER, JOONAH,—— 1709. Constable, Rehoboth, Mass., 1680.
Fishel, Mrs. Maxine   Michigan

PALMER, MOSES, 1640-1690. Born in Charlestown, Mass. Selectman, Stonington, Conn., 1690.

PALMER, NEHEMIAH, 1637-1717. Born in Charlestown, Mass. Deputy from Stonington, Conn., 1668, 1676, 1685, 1686, 1689-1691,1699.

PALMER, WALTER, 1585-1661. Born in England. Deputy from Rehoboth, Mass., to Plymouth, Mass., 1645.
Parenteau, Mrs. Jerome Francis   Quivira
Riddle, Mrs. William McKinley   Oklahoma

PALMER, LT. WILLIAM, 1610/15-1660. Ensign 1638, Serg. 1639. Lt. 1642 in MA.
Phillips, Mrs. Michael   Renss.

PALSGRAVE, DR. RICHARD, —— 1656. First doctor in Charlestown, Mass., 1631.

PARDEE, GEORGE, 1624-1700. Teacher at Hopkins Grammar School, Ct. 1663-1667.
Degl' Innocenti, Ms. Irene Pardee   California

PARK, ROBERT, 1580-1664/5. CT. Deputy 1641, 1642. Selectman 1658.
Beard, Mrs. Douglas H.   Renss.
Jones, Mrs. David   Renss.

PARKE, ROBERT, 1580-1665. From England, to Salem, Mass., 1630. Thence to Boston. Settled at Wethersfield, Conn., 1639. Freeman, 1640. Deputy, 1641-1642, 1646-1647, 1652. Removed to New London, thence to Mystic. Selectman, New London, 1651. Selectman, Stonington, Conn., 1658.

PARKE, DEA. THOMAS, —— 1709. Came from England to America 1630. Settled in Preston, Conn. Deacon First church, 1698. Deputy, 1652. Served in King Philip's War.

PARKE, THOMAS, circa 1628/1690. Constable, Cambridge, Mass.,1665.

PARKE, DEA. WILLIAM, circa 1604/1685. From England, 1630. Settled in Roxbury, Mass. Freeman, 1630. Selectman, several times. Deputy, thirty-three years, 1635-1679. Member Ancient and Honorable Artillery Co., 1638. Deacon, First Church. One of endorsers Free School. Surveyor-General, Arms and Ammunition for the Colony, 1660.
Parenteau, Mrs. Jerome Francis   Quivira

PARKER, SERGT. GEORGE, 1611-1656. Born in England. Sergeant, Portsmouth, R.I., 1643-1644. General Sergeant, 1655-1656.

PARKER, CAPT. JAMES, 1617-1701. Lieut. of Groton Military Co., 7 May 1673. Capt., 15 Oct. 1673, marched with Maj. Simon Willard to Brookfield, 1675. Deputy, 1683. Commanded garrison, Groton, Mass.

PARKER, ENS. NATHANIEL, 1651-1737. Born in Reading, Mass. Selectman, Reading, 1695, 1697. Called "Ensign" on town records.

PARKER, DEA. THOMAS, 1609-1683. Born in England. Selectman, Reading, Mass., 1661, 1665-1667, 1668. Deacon of the First Church.

PARKHURST, GEORGE, 1617-1698. Born in England. Appointed to inspect the inhabitants regarding their fidelity, Watertown, Mass., 1677-1678.

PARKHUR5T, JOSEPH, SR., 1629-1709. Born in England. Died at Chelmsford, Mass. A member of the Garrison, Chelmsford, Mass., 1691-1692.

PARMENTER, DEA. JOHN, 1588-1671. Born in England. One of the first settlers, Sudbury, Mass., 1639. Selectman, 1639.

PARMENTIER (PALMENTIER), LIEUT. MICHIEL, —— —— Magistrate, Brooklyn, N.Y., 1679, 1681. Lieut. of Foot, Kings County, N.Y., 1689.

PARMENTIER (PALMENTIER), PETER, —— 1701. Overseer, Brooklyn, N.Y., 1671.

PARRISH, EDWARD, 1600/4-1680. Surveyor General, Province, Md., West River, Anne Arundel Co., 1640.

PARROTT, RICHARD, SR., —— 1686. Vestryman, Christ Church, Middlesex Co., Va. Commissioner, 1656. High Sheriff, 1657. Senior Justice, 1673.
Engle, Miss Virginia Evelyn   Ohio

PARSONS, GEOFFRY, baptized 1627-1689. Selectman, Gloucester,Mass., 1657-1689.

PARSONS, HUGH, 1613-1684. Born in England. Member Troop of Horse, Portsmouth, R.I., 1667. Constable, 1662, 1668, 1676. Deputy, 1678.

PARSONS, JOSEPH, ca 1617-1683. MA Bay. Surveyor Springfield 1646, Assessor 1652. Cornet,Hampshire militia ca 1672-78.
Farrell, Mrs. John A.   Renss.

PARSONS, SAMUEL, SR., —— —— One of the Founders of Easthampton, L.I., 1649/50.

PARSONS, SAMUEL, JR., 1630-1714. Constable, Easthampton, L.I., 1684, 1695. Trustee, 1693.

PARTRIDGE, GEORGE, —— 1696. One of first settlers of Duxbury, Mass., 1636. One of original proprietors of Bridgewater, Mass., 1645. Constable.
Weaver, Mrs. John F., Sr.   Michigan

PARTRIDGE, REV. RALPH,1658. Minister at Duxbury, Mass., 1637-1658.

PARTRIDGE, COL. SAMUEL, 1645-1740. Conn. and Mass. Representative, 1685-1686. Colonel of Regiment, Judge of Probate, member of King's Council.

PASTORIUS, FRANCES DANIEL, 1651-1719. A Founder of Germantown, Pa., 1683. Justice of Peace, 1687. Member of Assembly, 1687-1691.

PATE, MAJOR THOMAS, 1640-1710. Of Gloucester Co., Va. Burgess, 1684. Major in Gloucester Co. militia. Justice, 1686.
Crowder, Mrs. Roy Hester   North Carolina

PATTEN, NATHANIEL, 1643-1745. Served in King Philip's War from Cambridge, Mass., 1675.

PAWLING, CAPT. HENRY, —— 1695. Born in England. Member of Governor's Council, 1670. High Sheriff, Ulster Co., N.Y., 1684. Capt. of militia, 1674-1688.

PAYSON, DEA. JOHN, 1643 ——. Deacon, First Church, Roxbury,Mass., 1674. In King Philip's War, 1675/6. Constable, Dorchester, 1680, 1681.

PEABODY, FRANCIS 1612/14-1697-8. Grand Juryman 1649, Hampton, Norfolk, Co., MA.
Scanlon, Mrs. Wiliam J.   Rhode Island

PEAKE, CHRISTOPHER, —— 1666. Member Roxbury, Mass., Military Co., 1647.

PEARCE, GILES, 1651-1698. Born in Portsmouth, R.I. Deputy from East Greenwich, R.I., 1690.

PEARSALL, NICHOLAS, —— —— Constable, Flushing, L.I., 1664.

PEARSON, DEA. JOHN, —— 1693. Deacon, Rowley, Mass., 1686. Deputy, 1678 and other years.

PEASE, CAPT. JOHN, 1630-1689. Member of Ancient and Honorable Artillery Co., Salem, Mass., 1661. First Selectman, Enfield, Conn., 1688.
Mayer, Mrs. Robert A.   Missouri
Pease, Miss Shirley Ann   Missouri

PEASE, CAPT. JOHN, 1654-1734. Constable, Enfield, Conn., 1683. Capt. of Militia, 1683. Selectman, 1688.

PECK HENRY, —— Will 1651. One of the Founders of New Haven, Conn.
Signed Fundamental Agreement, 4 June 1639.
Renie, Mrs. Charles J.   Michigan

PECK, JOSEPH, 1587-1663. Came to America, 1638. Representative,
Hingham, Mass., 1640-1642. Selectman, Justice of the Peace.
Reardon, Mrs. John J.   Michigan

PECK, CAPT. NICHOLAS, 1630-1710. Born in England. Deputy from
Seekonk to Plymouth, 1669, 1677, 1687, 1689, 1690. Called Ensign,
Lieutenant and Captain in records.

PECK, DEA. PAUL, 1608-1695. Member Plymouth Co. Militia, 1643-1645.
Surveyor of highways, 1658, 1665. Deacon, Congregational Church, 1691.
Milburn, Mrs. John T.   Blue Grass

PECK, DEA. WILLIAM, 1601-1694. Born in England. One of founders of
New Haven Colony, 1638. Deputy from New Haven, Conn., 1640-1648.
Deacon, New Haven, 1659 until death 4 Oct. 1694.
Milburn, Mrs. John T.   Blue Grass
Miller, Mrs. Joseph N.   Ohio
Peck, Miss Mary Elizabeth   Ohio
Ruthenbert, Mrs. Eldora R.   Ohio

PECKHAM, JOHN, circa 1645-circa 1712. Served in King Philip's War, from
Rhode Island, 1675-1676.

PELL, SIR JOHN, 1643-1702. Born in England. Second Lord of the Manor
of Pelham, N.Y., 1687. First Judge of Court of Common Pleas,
Westchester Co., N.Y., 1688. Member of First Provincial Assembly,
1691-1695. Capt. of Troop of Horse, 1684. Mayor, 1692.

PENDLETON, MAJ. BRIAN, 1599-1680. Born in England. Deputy from
Watertown, Mass., 1635. Settled in Sudbury. Selectman, 1638, 1639.
Member Ancient and Honorable Artillery Co., 1646. Deputy at Ports-
mouth, N.H., five years. Commissioned to receive submission of Me. to
Mass., 1652. Major and Deputy Governor, Province of Me. Served in
Early Colonial Wars.
Burk, Mrs. Francis Oratius   Missouri
Fritz, Mrs. Kenneth   Illinois
Pease, Miss Shirley Ann   Missouri

PENDLETON, CAPT. JAMES, 1626-1709.   Capt. in King Philip's War,
1675/76. Deputy to General Court, Westerly, R.I., 1662-1663.
Pease, Miss Shirley Ann   Missouri

PENDLETON, PHILLIP, 1650-1721. Born in Norwich, England. Died in King and Queen Co., Va. Deputy Clerk, Rappahannock Co., Va., 1679.

Campbell, Dr. Hayden Hucke	Member-at-Large
Feldman, Mrs. Edward C.	Illinois
Johnston, Mrs. Gilbert E.	Missouri
Lines, Mrs. Joan F.	Member-at-Large
Malloy, Mrs. James E.	Missouri
Robinson, Mrs. Mary Davidson	Oklahoma

PENGRY (PINGREE), AARON, 1652-1714. Served in King Philip's War from Ipswich, Mass., 1675.

PENGRY (PINGREE), DEA. MOSES, 1610-1695. Representative, Ipswich, Mass., 1665. Served in King Philip's War, 1675.

PENNELL, ROBERT, 1640-1728/9. Settled in Middletown, Chester Co., Pa., 1686. Constable, Middletown, 1687.

PENNOYER, ROBERT, 1614-1680. From England, to Boston, Mass. Moved to Gravesend, L.I., 1642. Received a patent of land from Gov. Kieft and was a first settler of Brooklyn, 1645. Removed to Stamford, Conn., 1648.
Miner, Mrs. Ross H.   Founders

PERKINS, SERGT. JACOB, 1624-1699. Sergeant of Military Co., Ipswich, Mass., 1664.

PERKINS, SERGT. JOHN, 1590-1654. Born in England. Sergeant of Allied English and friendly Indians, Ipswich, Mass., 1631. Deputy from Ipswich, Mass., 1636.

PERKINS, DEA. THOMAS, 1616-1686. Selectman, Topsfield, Mass., 1675/6 and other years. Deacon of the first Church there.

PERKINS, REV. WILLIAM, 1607-1682. Lieut., 1642. Capt., 1644. Deputy, 1644. Member Ancient and Honorable Artillery Co. of Boston, Mass., 1644. Minister, Gloucester, Mass., 1650, 1655.

PERRY, EDWARD, circa 1632-1695. Surveryor, 1657, 1668, 1674. Recorder, R.I., 1674.

PERRY, EZRA, —— 1690. Born in England. Constable, Sandwich, Mass., 1679. Appointed to settle claims with the Indians, 1671.

PERRIN, JOHN, SR., 1614-1674. Born in England. Arrived at Boston, Mass., 1635. A Founder of Rehoboth, Mass., 1643. Signer of the Seeconk Compact, 1643.

Fishel, Mrs. Maxine Emeline	Michigan
Sowle, Miss Patricia Ann	Michigan

PETERS, ANDREW, 1634/1713. Born in England. In King Philip's War, Andover, Mass., 1675-1676. Town Treasurer, 1697-1698.

PETERS, WILLIAM, 1672-1696. Born in Andover, Mass. Member of Garrison, 1696.

PETTEE, WILLIAM, 1595-1667. Selectman, Weymouth, Mass., 1643-1666.

PETTINGELL, RICHARD, circa 1620-after 1695. Magistrate's Assistant, Salem, Mass., 1644.

PETTIT, NATHANIEL, 1630-1714/15. Born in England. One of the first settlers of Newtown, L.I., 1655.

PETTIT, THOMAS, SR., 1610——. Born in England. Marshal of Newtown, L.I., 1657.

PETTUS, COL. THOMAS, circa 1610-after 1662. Clerk of the Vestry of Lower church, New Kent Co., Va., 1635-1646. One of His Majesty's Council of State, 1641-1660.

Bell, Mrs. Charles Smith	Tejas
Canter, Mrs. Dencil Eugene	Tejas
Harris, Mrs. Alfred P.	Tejas
Harris, Miss Nanci Dianne	Tejas
Harris, Miss Sandra Susan	Tejas
Hurt, Mrs. Randolph D., Jr.	Tejas
Prince, Mrs. Hiram Thomas	Tejas
Thomas, Mrs. Ernest	Tejas

PEYTON, MAJOR ROBERT, 1640-1694. Born in England. Major of Militia, Gloucester Co., Va., 1680.

PHELPS, GEORGE, 1605/1687. Born in England. One of ten men chosen to order the affairs of the colony of Dorchester, Mass., 28 Oct. 1634. Deputy, Windsor, Conn., 1646-1647.

PHELPS, DEA. NATHANIEL, circa 1627-1702. One of the First Settlers of Northampton, Mass., and one of the first Deacons of the Church, 1656.

PHELPS, WILLIAM, 1599-1672. Born in England. One of a commission of seven persons appointed by the Mass. Co., to govern the new Colony of Conn. at time of emigration to Windsor and Hartford, 1635. Magistrate, several years, from 1639. Deputy, 1651.

PHILLIPS, REV. GEORGE, 1593-1644. First minister at Watertown, Mass.

PHILLIPS, REV. GEORGE, 1664-1739. Graduate of Harvard, 1686. Minister, Setauket, L.I., 1697-1699.

PHILLIPS, JOHN, 1620-1655. 1 Jan 1652 appointed Clerk and Sheriff of Lancaster Co., VA.
Gerry, Mrs. Elbert A.   Tennessee
McIntosh, Mrs. William Jerome   Tennessee
Young, Mrs. L. Ernest   Tennessee

PHILLIPS, DEA. NICHOLAS, circa 1611-1672. Deacon, Weymouth, Mass.

PHILLIPS, REV. SAMUEL, 1625-1696. Graduate of Harvard, 1650. Minister, Rowley, Mass., 1651 until death.

PHILLIPS, MAJOR WILLIAM, 1610-1683. MA. Appointed Major in 1665.
Concannon, Mrs. James N.   Territorial
Vath,Mrs. Donald L.   Territorial

PICKARD, JOHN, 1622-1697. Deputy from Rowley, Mass., 1661, 1695.

PICKERING, LIEUT. JOHN, 1637-1694. Born in England. Died at Salem, Mass. Served in Essex Regiment, King Philip's War, 1676.

PIERCE, ANTHONY, 1609-1678. Born in England. Selectman, Watertown, Mass., 1677.

PIERCE, JOHN, 1588-1661. Born in England. Deputy from Watertown, Mass., 1638, 1639.

PIERCE, JOSEPH, 1647-1713. Born in Watertown, Mass. Served in King Philip's War, 1675/6.

PIERCE, CAPT. MICHAEL, 1615-1676. Died at Central Falls, R.I. Killed in battle called "Pierce's Fight," King Philip's War, March, 1676.

PIERCE, THOMAS, 1583-1666. Born in England. Appointed Commissioner, Charlestown, Mass., 1642. Selectman, Woburn, Mass., 1660.

PIERSON, REV. ABRAHAM, circa 1608-1678. Ordained at Boston Mass., 1640. Minister, Southampton, L.I., 1640-1647; Branford, Conn., 1647-1666; Newark, N.J., 1666-1678.
Van Zandt, Mrs. Richard Karl   Blue Grass
Windsor, Mrs. Caroline Van Zandt   Blue Grass

PIERSON, REV. ABRAHAM, JR., 1645-1706/7. Graduate of Harvard, 1668. Assistant Minister, Newark, N.J., 1671; and later Minister. Minister, Killingworth, Conn., 1692. First President, Yale College.

PIERSON, HENRY, —— 1680/1. One of the Founders of Southampton, L.I., N.Y. Town Clerk, 1650-1680.

PIETERSEN, DEA. LIEFFIES, 1660-1748. Born in Holland. Deacon Reformed Church, Flatbush, L.I., 1680. Constable, 1692.

PIETERSZEN, PIETER, —— —— Served as soldier at Esopus, N.Y., 1660.

PIKE, JAMES, SR., —— 1699. Born in England. Moved from Charlestown, Mass. to Reading, Mass., 1647. A first settler of Reading, Mass.

PINCKNEY, CAPT. PHILIP, —— 1688/9. Named in the first patent of Eastchester, N.Y., 1666. Deputy, 1680. Commissioner (called Captain) to treat with the Indians, 1681.

PINGREE (See PENGRY).

PINNEY, HUMPHREY, —— 1683. One of the first settlers of Windsor, Conn., 1635.

PITKIN, WILLIAM, 1635-1694. Born in England. Appointed by General Assembly, Hartford, Conn., as Prosecutor for the Colony, 1662. Attorney General, 1664. Represented Hartford in Colonial Assemblies, 1675-1690.
Oenslager, Mrs. Donald M.   Founders

PITT, ROBERT, —— ——. Born in England. Settled in Accomac Co., Va., circa 1672. Member of Commission of Trade, Accomac Co., 1699.

PLATS, JONATHAN, —— 1680. Selectman, Rowley, Mass., 1668, 1671.

PLATT, JOHN, before 1647—after 1686. Member of Lower House of General Court of Conn., 1680-1686.

PLATT, DEA. RICHARD, 1603-1684. One of the founders of Milford, Conn. Deacon, Milford, Conn., 1669.

POINDEXTER, GEORGE, 23 Dec 1627-1692. Williamsburg, VA. 1679 Vestryman, Bruton Parish Church. 1681 Vestryman, St. Peter's Parish.
Gilbert, Mrs. Wayne   Oklahoma

POLHEMUS, REV. JOHANNES THEODORUS, 1598-1676. Minister of the Dutch Churches of Kings Co., N.Y., 1654.
Corder, Miss Lois B.   Founders

POLK, ROBERT BRUCE, 1640-1703/4. Born in Ireland. Line closed.
Ardery, Mrs. Fayette, Jr.   Blue Grass
Griswold, Mrs. John C.   Illinois
Lawrence, Mrs. Robert Don   Blue Grass

POLLY, JOHN, 1618-1689. Born in England. Served in King Philip's War from Roxbury, Mass., 1675.
Fishel, Mrs. Maxine   Michigan

POMEROY, ELTWEED, 1585-1673. Born in England. Died at Northampton, Mass. First Selectman, Dorchester, Mass., 1633. Constable, 1634.
Buchanan, Mrs. Walter I.   Prairie State
Cook, Mrs. Ralph William, Sr.   Michigan

POMEROY, JOSEPH, 1652-1734/39. Born in Windsor, Conn. Soldier in King William's War, 1688-1698.

POMEROY, JOSEPH, 1672-1712. Born in Northampton, Mass. Corporal in the Northampton Cb. in King William's War, Deerfield, Mass., 1696.
Cook, Mrs. Ralph William Sr.   Michigan

POMEROY, DEA. MEDAD, 1638-1716. Baptized Windsor, Conn. Selectman, Northampton, Mass., 27 years from 1669. Deputy, 1677-1692. Clerk of Writs from 1678. Commissioner, 1684. Town Clerk, 1692. Treasurer, 1695. County Treasurer, 1698, 1699. Associate Justice, Hampshire Co. King Philip's War, "Turner's Falls Fight," 1676.
Cook, Mrs. Ralph W., Sr.   Michigan

POND, DANIEL, 1627-1698. Born in England. Settled at Dedham, Mass. Selectman, Dedham, Mass., 1660.

POND, SAMUEL, II, 1648-1718. At Branford, Conn., 1667. Deputy to General Court, 1678, 1682, 1683, 1687, Lieut., 1695.
Cope, Mrs. James Charles   Illinois
Mosley, Mrs. Arthur E.   Illinois

POOR, DANIEL, —— 1690. Surveyor, Andover, Mass., 1673. Selectman, 1673, 1675, 1677, 1683, 1684, 1686, 1687.
Billings, Mrs. George M.   Founders

POOR, JOHN, 1615-1684. Selectman, Newbury, Mass., 1666-1669.

POPE, LIEUT. COL. NATHANIEL, circa 1610-1660. Born in England. Arrived St. Mary's Hundred, Md., 1637. Member of Maryland Assembly, 1641-1642. Lieut. Col. of Westmoreland Co., Va. Troop, 1655.
Cook, Mrs. Huestis Pratt, Jr.   North Carolina

PORTER, JOHN, 1600-1648. Born in England. Constable, Windsor, Conn., 1639, 1643. Deputy, 1646, 1647.
Greason, Mrs. James B., Jr.   Founders

PORTER, JOHN, —— 1674. A Founder of historic Charter Colony of Portsmouth, R.I., 1638. One of the eighteen original Proprietors of Aquidneck, who settled Pocasset, named in the Royal Charter of Charles II, 1663. Assistant, 1640-1644, 1650, 1664. Commissioner, 1658-1661.

PORTER, JOHN, 1596-1676. Settled at Hingham, Mass. and Salem,1641. Deputy from Hingham, 1644.
Edson, Mrs. Charles T.   CT Farms
Edson, Miss Page Porter   Pennsylvania

PORTER, SAMUEL, —— 1689. Member of the Ancient and Honorable Artillery Co. of Boston, 1640. Cared for wounded soldiers, King Philip's War, Hadley, Mass., 1675.

PORTER, SAMUEL, 1660-1722. Townsman, Hadley, Mass., 1691, 1697. Sheriff, Hampshire Co., Mass., 1695, 1696.

POST, LIEUT. ABRAHAM, 1640/1-1713/14. Ensign, Train Band, Saybrook, Conn., 1667. Deputy, 1670. Lieut., Saybrook Fort, 1680.

POST, JOHN, 1628-1711. Selectman, Norwich, Conn., 1674.

POST, LIEUT. RICHARD, —— 1689. Came from England to Lynn, Mass. Lieutenant, Southampton, L.I., 1640. Constable, 1651.

POST, STEPHEN, —— 1659. Born in England. One of the first settlers of Hartford, 1636. Constable, Hartford, Conn., 1642.

POTTER, NATHANIEL, —— circa 1644. From England to Portsmouth, R.I. A Founder of Aquidneck Island, 1639. A Signer of Rhode Island Compact, 1638.

POTTER, ROBERT, —— 1655. Born in England. Commissioner from Warwick, R.I., 1651.

POWELL, THOMAS, 1641-1721. Recorder, Huntington, L.I., 1683. Constable, 1667-1682. Overseer, 1671-1681. Commissioner, 1684-1686.

POWELL, CAPT. WILLIAM, —— 1623. Capt. of Guards, Lt. Governor and Commander at Jamestown, Va. member of Virginia House of Burgesses, 1619.

POWER, NICHOLAS, —— 1675. Killed in Great Swamp Battle, King Philip's War, Narragansett, R.I.

POWER, NICHOLAS, —— 1734. Commissioner of Providence, R.I., 1650-1656.

PRATT, JOHN, 1620-1655. Representative from Hartford, Conn., 1639, and several terms after. Constable, 1644.

PRATT, JOHN, JR., 1638-1689. Born in Hartford, Conn. Chosen to order the affairs of the Town, 1653-1665. Constable, 1660, 1669, 1678,1682.

PRATT, JOSEPH, 1637-1720. Died at Weymouth, Mass. Soldier in King Philip's War, 1675.

PRATT, JOSHUA, —— 1659. Surveyor to layout village of Plymouth, MA. Constable.
Windolph, Mrs. Frank J.   Territorial

PRATT, MATTHEW, —— 1672. Born in England. Selectman, Weymouth, Mass., 1648.

PRATT, PHINEAS, 1593-1680. Born in England. Representative from Charlestown, Mass., 1662.

PRATT, LIEUT. WILLIAM, 1622-1678. Deputy from Saybrook, Conn., 1666-1677. Lieutenant, Train Band, 1661.
Greason, Mrs. James B., Jr.   Founders

PRENCE, GOV. THOMAS, 1600-1673. Born in England. Died in Plymouth, Mass. Fought against Pequot Indians, 1637. Governor, 1634-1638, 1657-1673. Member of Council of War. Commissioner for United Colonies, 1645.

PRENTICE, CAPT. JOHN, 1631-1691. Born in England. Town Attorney, New London, Conn., 1667. Deputy, 1668. Capt. of several ships.

PRENTICE, CAPT. JOHN, JR., 1652-1715. Born in England. Captain of Forts, New London, Conn., 1692-1695.

PRESCOTT, JOHN, 1605-1681. Born in England. Died in Lancaster, Mass. A Founder of Lancaster, Mass., 1653. Owner and defender of Garrison, 1675-1676.

PRICE, JOHN, 1584-1628/38. Member of Virginia House of Burgesses, 1625.

PRICE, THOMAS, 1610-1701. Member of the Council, St. Mary's, Md., 1694.
Alderson, Mrs. Mary Ford   Florida
Miller, Mrs. Clarence F.   Michigan
PRICHARD, WILLIAM —— 1675. Constable 1662. Committee to direct affairs 1667. Sergt. in militia 1672. Clerk of Writs 1675, King Phillip's War 1675.
Brumfield, Mrs. Roy   Member-at-Large

PRIEST, DEGORY, circa 1580-1621. Of London, England. Passenger on the Mayflower, 1620. A signer of Mayflower Compact.

PRINCE, JOHN, —— 1703. Born in England. Constable, Hingham,Mass., 1674.

PROBASKO, ELDER CHRISTOFFEL, 1649-after 1724. Elder, Flatbush Church, 1678, 1690. Magistrate, 1678, 1686. Justice of the Peace, 1693.

PROCTOR, GEORGE, —— circa 1678. Soldier in Bacon's Rebellion 1676/7. One of three signers of Surry Grievances, 1676. Repaired prison and listed prisoners, Surry Co., Va., 1676/7.
Bean, Mrs. Ernest Prewitt   Blue Grass
Morgan, Mrs. Charles Lafayette   Blue Grass
Morgan, Miss Chelsea Anne   Blue Grass
Morgan, Miss Ellen Proctor   Blue Grass

PROCTOR, ROBERT, —— 1697. Constable, 1660. Original Proprietor of Chelmsford. Signer of Petition to General Court. Commanded West End Garrison in the West Regiment of Middlesex, 16 March 1691/2. Served in King Philip's War, 1675.

PROVOOST, BENJAMIN, 1646-1720. Trustee of Kingston, 1688-1689. Signed Kingston Patent, 1687.
Long, Mrs. Alfred T.   Founders

PROVOOST, SERGT. DAVID, 1608-1656. From Holland to New Amsterdam, circa 1624. Commander of Fort Good Hope, 1642-1647. One of "Nine Men," 1652. Sergeant, Blue Flag Co., 1653. First separate schout of Brueckelen, 1655. Schout and Secretary of Amersfoort and Midwout until his death.
Long, Mrs. Alfred T.   Founders

PROVOOST, DAVID, 1642-1721. Born in New York. Assessor, 1694-1698. Alderman, 1698-1699. Member of General Assembly, 1699.

PUREFOY, CAPT. THOMAS, circa 1578-1652/5. Born in England. Died Elizabeth City Co., Va. Commissioner of Elizabeth City Co. Member of King's Council, 1631—1652. Member Va. House of Burgesses, 1629-1630.
Dohan, Mrs. David H. W.   Pennsylvania

PUREFOY, THOMAS, JR., —— ——. Justice, Elizabeth City Co., Va., 1674.

PURRIER, WILLIAM, 1599-1676. Deputy from Southold, L.I. to New Haven, Conn., 1653, 1656, 1661.
Booi, Mrs. Duane, G.   Pennsylvania
Booi, Miss Rebecca Ann   Pennsylvania

PUTNAM, JOHN, 1579-1662. An Original settler of Salem Village, Mass., 1640/1.

PUTNAM, LIEUT. NATHANIEL, 1619-1700. Born in England. Constable, Salem, Mass., 1656. Deputy, 1690-1691. Lieutenant, 1688.

PUTNAM, LIEUT. THOMAS, 1614/15-1686. Selectman, Lynn, Mass., 1643. Lieut. of First Troop of Horse, Essex Co., Salem Village, 1672. Constable and Town Clerk. Deacon, 1680.
Burdette, Mrs. Clinton Maxfield   Ohio

PUTNAM, SERGT. THOMAS, 1652-1699. In Narragansett Campaign, Salem, Mass. 1675

PYLE, NICHOLAS, ca 1666-ca 1717. Served in PA Provincial Assembly.
Marty, Mrs. Victor G.   Illinois

PYNCHEON, WILLIAM, circa 1590-1662. Born in England. Magistrate, Springfield, Mass., 1636.

QUIMBY, JOHN, 1620——. Born in England. Representative, Westchester, N.Y., 1663.

QUIMBY, JOSIAH, 1663-1728. Constable, Westchester, N.Y., 1688.

QUIMBY, WILLIAM, —— circa 1710. One of the seventeen men to found and settle Stratford, Conn., 1639.

QUINCY, JUDGE EDMUND, 1681-1738. Born in Braintree, Mass. Member Council of War. Colonel, Suffolk Regiment, 1699.

QUINCY, LIEUT. COL. EDMUND, 1627-1698. Born in England. Settled in Braintree, Mass. Representative, 1670, 1673, 1675, 1679. Member Committee of Safety, 1689. Lieut.-Col., Suffolk Regiment, 1698.
Davis, Mrs. Frank V.   Illinois

RAMBO, PETER GUNNARSON/GUNNARSSON, 1605-1698. Warden 1676. Justice of the Peace 1676-77. Member of Governor's Council 1676.
Gillin, Mrs. Brallier T.   Quivira

RANDOLPH, LT. COL. WILLIAM, 1651-1711. Came from England to Henrico Co., Va., 1669. Clerk of Henrico Co., Va., 1673. Captain of Militia, 1680. Member House of Burgesses, Va., 1685, several terms. Speaker, 1698. Lieutenant Colonel, 1699. Attorney General. Member of Council.
Denton, Mrs. Jeffrey Michael   Jamestown Virginia
Rowsey, Mrs. William Eugene, Jr.   Oklahoma

RAPALJE, JORIS JANSEN, —— circa 1665. One of twelve men representing the New Netherlands, 1641. Magistrate of Breuckelen (Brooklyn), 1655, 1656, 1657, 1660, 1662.
Potter, Mrs. Earl D.   Prairie State

RATHBONE, JOHN —— 1702. Deputy for New Kingston, R.I., 1681, 1683, 1684.

RAWSON, EDWARD, 1615-1693. Came from England to Mass. Deputy to General Court, 1638-1639, 1642-1644. Commissioner of Boston, 1658. Secretary of Mass. Bay Colony, 1650-1686.

RAY, SIMON, 1638-1736/7. Justice, Quarterly Sessions, R.I., 1687, 1688.

RAYMOND, DEA. JOSHUA, —— 1676. Cornet of Capt. Palmer's Co. of Troopers, New London Co., Conn., 1672. Deacon, New London, circa 1649.

RAYMOND, CAPT. WILLIAM, 1637-1709. Served in King Philip's War, 1675. Lieutenant Commander of Beverly and Wenham, Mass. Troops. Commander (as Captain) in expedition against Canada, 1690. Deputy from Beverly to General Court, 1685-1686.

RAYNER, REV. JOHN, —— ——. Of Plymouth, Mass. Minister at Plymouth, 1625 and for eighteen years; thereafter at Dover, N.H.

READ, JOHN, 1598-1685. Member of Ancient and Honorable Artillery Co. of Boston, 1644.

READAWAY, JAMES, —— 1684. Born in England. A First Settler in Attleborough, Mass., 1666.

READE (REED), ESTRAS, —— 1680. Born in England. Settled in Mass. Representative, Wendham, 1649, 1651. Trustee, Chelmsford, 1654. Returned to Boston, 1661.

READE, COL. GEORGE, 1600-1671. Came to Va. from England, 1637. Secretary to the Colony, 1637. Acting Governor, 1638. Burgess, 1649, 1656. Member King's Council, 1657-1671. Colonel.
Baumgardner, Mrs. Larry K.   Blue Grass
Cooper, Mrs. Michael Arthur   Blue Grass
Crowder, Mrs. Roy Hester   North Carolina
Kuster, Mrs. Theodore   Blue Grass
Stebbins, Mrs. Albert K., Jr.   California
Stephens, Mrs. A. Baldwin   Blue Grass
Wilson, Miss Elizabeth Buckner   Blue Grass

READE, WILLIAM, 1605 ——. Deputy to Mass. General Court, 1636-1638.

READING, COL. JOHN, —— 1717. Born in England. Member of Assembly, Burlington, N.J., 1685. Clerk of the County, 1688. Member of First Council of Proprietors of West Jersey.

REED, JOHN, 1640-1721. Born in Weymouth, Mass. Served in King Philip's War, 1675.

REEVE, JAMES, —— 1698. Overseer, Southold, L.I., 1681, 1694. Supervisor, 1691.

REEVE, JAMES, 1672-1732. Selectman, Southold, L.I., 1699.

REEVES, HENRY, SR., —— ——. Constable, Old Rappahanock Co., Va., 1684.

REMICK, CHRISTIAN, 1631-1710. Selectman, Treasurer, Proprietor of Kittery, Maine. A signer of the submission to Mass., 1652.
Dittmann, Mrs. William Henry, II   Illinois

REMSEN, JAN, 1648-1696. Magistrate, Flatbush, L.I., 1682.

RYERSEN, MARTEN, —— ——. Magistrate, Brooklyn, N.Y., 1679.

REYNOLDS, JAMES, —— 1700. In North Kingston, R.I., 1665. Took Oath of Allegiance, 1671. Constable, 1671. Overseer of Poor, 1687. Conservator of the Peace, 1690.

REYNOLDS, JOHN, 1612-1660. Born in England. One of the Proprietors and first settlers of Watertown, Mass., 1642.

REYNOLDS, JOHN, JR., circa 1639-1701. Justice of the Peace, Greenwich, Conn., 1687. King's Commissioner, 1690-1697.

REYNOLDS, JONATHAN, 1636-1673. Born at Wethersfield, Conn. Deputy to General Court, Hartford, 1667.

REYNOLDS, LIEUT. NATHANIEL, 1627-1708. Member Ancient and Honorable Artillery Co. of Mass., 1658-1681. Lieutenant in King Philip's War, 1675.

REYNOLDS, ROBERT, —— Will 1659. At Boston, Mass., 1632. Fought in Pequot War, 1637.
Miner, Mrs. Ross H.   Founders

REYNOLDS, WILLIAM, circa 1650-circa 1700. Born in England. Constable, Rappahannock Co., Va., 1685-1686.

RHOADS, JOHN, 1639-1701. Of Chester Co., Pa. Member of Provincial Courts of Pa., 1683.
Griffiths, Mrs. I. Newton   Pennsylvania
Leary, Mrs. James Emerson   Pennsylvania
Reitz, Mrs. Thomas Joel   Pennsylvania

RHODES, ZACHARIAH, 1603-1665. Commissioner, Providence, R.I., 1658-1663. Town Treasurer, 1665.

RICE, DAVID, 1659-1723. One of the founders of Framingham, Mass., 1699.

RICE, DEA. EDMUND, 1594-1663. Born in England. Deputy from Sudbury, Mass., 1640, 1643, 1648, 1652-1654. Magistrate, 1641.

RICE, CORP. HENRY, 1616-1710/11. Served in King Philip's War, from Sudbury, Mass., 1676.

RICE, JOSEPH, 1637/8-1706/14. Born in England. Deputy to General Court for Sudbury and Marlborough, Mass., 1673. Served in King Philip's War, 1675.

RICE, THOMAS, —— 1681. Owner of Garrison House, Marlborough, Mass., King Philip's War, 1675.

RICHARDS, EDWARD, 1610-1684. Born in England. Selectman, Dedham, 1645.

RICHARDS, THOMAS, 1590-1650. Born in England. Member of the Court of Selectman, Dorchester, 1633. Selectman, Weymouth, Mass., 1643. Member Ancient and Honorable Artillery Co., Boston, Mass., 1648.
Greason, Mrs. James B., Jr.   Founders

RICHARDSON, AMOS, before 1617/8-1683. Attorney at law. Representative to General Court, from Stonington, Conn. 1676, 1677.

RICHARDSON, EZEKIEL, 1602-1647. Born in England. Deputy, 1635. Selectman, Woburn, Mass., 1644-1647.

RICHARDSON, CAPT. JOSIAH, 1635-1695. Born in Charlestown, Mass. Captain, King William's War, 1689-1695.

RICHARDSON, SAMUEL, —— ——. Of Pa. Member of Governor's Council, 1688-1695. Member of Assembly, 1692, 1694, 1696. Justice of the Peace and Courts, 1692, 1697.

RICHARDSON, THOMAS, baptized 1608-1651. One of the Commissioners chosen by the Church, Charlestown, Mass., 1640; to commence settlement of Woburn, Mass. and to form a church there. Woburn established, 1642. Town Officer.

RICHARDSON, THOMAS, 1645-1720/1. A Soldier in Company of Samuel Gallup's land expedition to Canada by way of Albany, N.Y., 1690.

RICHARDSON, WILLIAM, —— 1697. Justice, Anne Arundel Co. MD. Member of Assembly 1677-1683.
Bell, Miss Katherine S.   Tennessee

RICHMOND, CAPT. EDWARD, 1632-1696. Lieutenant, King Philip's War, Providence, R.I., 1675. Captain, 1690. Deputy to Assembly from Newport, 1678-1679; Little Compton, 1686. Attorney General, R.I., 1677-1680.
Brooks, Miss Maralyse Latting   Michigan

RICHMOND, JOHN, 1594-1664. Born in England. Died in Taunton, Mass. Commissioner, Newport, R.I., 1656.
Gray, Mrs. William R.   Member-at-Large

RIDDICK, CAPT. JAMES, —— after 1723. Member of militia, Isle of Wight, Co., Va., 1687.

RIDGELY, COL. HENRY, —— ——. Of Va. Justice in Va., 1679. Captain in militia, 1689. Burgess, 1692. Lt. Col., 1694. Col., 1696.

RIGGS, SERGT. EDWARD, circa 1614-1668. Sergt. in Pequot War, Roxbury, Mass., 1637. Original Proprietor of Newark, N.J. and Signer of Fundamental Agreement, 1667.
Finfgeld, Mrs. Clifford   Illinois

RIGGS, JOSEPH, circa 1646-1689. Original Proprietor, Newark, N.J., 1666/67. Townsman, 1682, 1683; Fenceviewer, 1682. Surveyor and Layer-Out of Highways, 1685.
Finfgeld, Mrs. Clifford   Illinois

ROBBINS, JOHN, —— 1660. Townsman (Selectman), 1652. Member of General Court, 1653, 1656, 1657, 1659.

ROBBINS, LIEUT. JOSHUA, 1651/2-1738. Ensign; confirmed Lieut. of Train Band, Wethersfield, Conn., 12 May 1698.

ROBBINS, NICHOLAS, —— 1650/1. First settler in Cambridge, Mass., 1636.

ROBERT, REV. PIERRE, 1625-1717. Born in St. Imier, Switzerland. Died in South Carolina. Minister at French Santee, S.C., 1686.
Rouse, Mrs. Robert N., Jr.   Tennessee

ROBERTS, HUGH, 1650-1702. Born in Wales. Society of Friends Pa., 1683. Provincial Council, 1692.

ROBERTS, GOV. THOMAS, —— 1674. Born in England. President of the Court, Dover, N.H., 1639. Governor, 1640, and until Dover was put under Jurisdiction Mass. Member Ancient and Honorable Artillery Co., 1644.

ROBESON, ANDREW, JR., 1654-1720. Member of Governor's Council of Providence, of N.J., 1697. Chief Justice of the Providence of Pa., 1693-1699.

ROBINSON, CHRISTOPHER, 1645-1693. Member of the Council and House of Burgesses, 1691. Secretary of State, Va., 1692.
Monter, Mrs. Edward William   Ohio

ROBINSON, GEORGE, —— 1699. Of Rehoboth, Mass. Member of Rehoboth North Purchase Comm., 1668.

ROBINSON, ISAAC, —— ——. Of Massachusetts. Deputy from Barnstable, Mass. to General Court at Plymouth, Mass.,1645-1651.
Krum, Mrs. Richard C.   Renss.

ROCKWELL, DEA. WILLIAM, —— 1640. Settled in Dorchester Mass., 1630. Deacon in church founded at New Hospital, Plymouth. One of first three Selectmen, Dorchester, Mass.

RODHAM, MATHEW,ca 1620-1672/75. Kent Island, MD. Vestry of Chicacone Parish-March 1672. Jury of Inquest 10 Feb 1662. Juror 20 May 1653. Justice 26 May 1656.
Bockemuehl, Mrs. Robert T.   Michigan

ROE, JOHN, 1631-1714. Elected Constable and Trustee, Brookhaven, L.I., 10 Jan. 1688.

ROGERS, JAMES, 1615-1687. Born in England. Served in Pequot War, 1637. Representative from Saybrook, Conn., 1661, 1668. Representative from New London, seven times, 1662-1673.
Peters, Mrs. Thomas M.   Michigan

ROGERS, JOHN, SR., circa 1611-1685. In Garrison during King Philip's War, at Rev. Samuel Whiting's House, 1675/6.

ROGERS, JOHN, JR., 1641-1695. King Philip's War, Garrison in Rev. Samuel Whiting's house, 1675/6. Killed by Indians, Billerica, Mass.

ROGERS, JOHN, 1611-1692. Deputy from Duxbury, Mass., 1657. Constable, 1666, 1681, 1683.

ROGERS, JOHN, circa 1632-1717. Selectman, Marshfield, Mass., 1692.

ROGERS, CAPT. JOHN, 1620-1680. Vestryman, Chicacone Parish, Va. Justice of Northumberland Co., Va., 1655.
Hillis, Mrs. Russell W.   Tennessee

ROGERS, REV. JOHN, 1630-1684. Born in England. Graduate of Harvard, 1649. Filth President of Harvard College, chosen 1676, declined, elected 1682 and installed 1683.

ROGERS, JONATHAN, 1635-1709. Constable, Huntington, L.I., 1670. Overseer, 1679.

ROGERS, LIEUT. JOSEPH, 1608-1678. Passenger on the "Mayflower," 1620. Constable, 1640. Lieutenant, 1647. Council of War, 1658.

ROGERS, REV. NATHANIEL, circa 1598-1655. Minister, Ipswich, Mass., 1638-1655.

ROGERS, REV. NATHANIEL, 1669-1723. Born in Ipswich, Mass. Graduated from Harvard, 1687. ordained minister of the First Church of Portsmouth, N.H., 1699.

ROGERS, SAMUEL, 1640-1713. Commissioner on fortifications in the North Parish of New London (Mohegan), 1675.

ROGERS, THOMAS, 1586-1621. Passenger on "Mayflower," 1620. Eighteenth signer of the Compact. One of the founders of Plymouth, Mass.
Bumpass, Mrs. Thomas Scott — Oklahoma
Pease, Miss Shirley Ann — Missouri

ROGERS, WILLIAM, —— 1664. "Clerk of the Band," Southampton, L.I., 1663.

ROLFE, JOHN, 1585-1622. Recorder General of Va., 1614. Member of Governor's Council, 1614, 1619.

ROLFE, LIEUT. THOMAS, 1616-1663/73. Lt. Col. in Va. militia, in command at Chickahominy Fort, 1646. Burgess from Jamestown, Va.

ROMBOUT, CAPT. FRANCIS,—— 1691. Mayor of New York City, 1679. Member of Governor's Council, 1691. Capt. of Provincial Troops, 1684.

ROOSA, CAPT. ALBERT HEYMANSE, —— 1679. Schepen, Wiltwick, 1661. Overseer, Hurley, N.Y., 1669. Sergt., Marbletown, 1670. Capt. of Militia, Hurley and Marbletown, 1673.
Burdick,, Mrs. Joanne Carney — Oklahoma
Foster, Mrs. William David — Ohio
Long, Mrs. Alfred T. — Founders
Seimes, Mrs. Erwin Frees — Pennsylvania

ROOSA, ARIEN ALBERTSON, —— after 1728. Served in Militia Marbletown, N.Y., 1670.
Long, Mrs. Alfred T.   Founders

ROOSEKRANS, HARMEN HENDRICKSEN, 1612-1703/26. Soldier at Kingston, 1659. Only captive to escape the Indians after their uprising.
Baxter, Mrs. Harry   Illinois

ROOT, JOHN, 1608-1684. One of the Founders of Farmington, Conn., 1640.
Cook, Mrs. Ralph William, Sr.   Michigan
Garrigus, Miss Alice June   Territorial
Grimes, Mrs. William Schuyler   Michigan

ROOT, THOMAS, 1605-1694. Born in England. An original proprietor of Hartford, Conn. Name on Founders' Monument. Served in Pequot War, 1637.

ROSE, ROBERT, circa 1594-1665. Soldier in Pequot War, 1637. Constable, 1639-1640. Deputy to Conn. Legislature, Wethersfield, 1641, 1642, 1643. One of the first settlers of Branford, Conn., 1644.
Armstrong, Mrs. Donald George   Illinois

ROSS, GEORGE, circa 1629-1702/5. Selectman, 1676. Lieut., 1683. First Presbyterian, Church, 1687.
Finfgeld, Mrs. Clifford   Illinois

ROSSITER, DR. BRYAN (BRAY), —— 1672. Ensign, Windsor Train Band, 1640. Deputy to Conn. Legislature, April, 1643, Sept. 1645. Surveyor, 1656. The first Physician of whom there is any notice in the records of Guilford.

ROSSITER, EDWARD, —— 1630. Born in England. Assistant to Governor, Colony, Mass. Bay, 1629-1630.

ROSSITER, ENS. JOSIAH, 1646-1716. Ensign, 1676. One of the Magistracy and Council, March, 1672. Deputy to General Court from Guilford, 1683, 1684, 1689, 1690, 1694-1699. Justice, 1698. Town Clerk, 1685.

ROYCE, ROBERT, —— ——. Deputy from New London, to Conn. Legislature, May, 1661.
Milburn, Mrs. John T.   Blue Grass

RUDD, LIEUT. JONATHAN, —— 1688. Assistant to Capt. Mason in defense of Saybrook, Conn., 1652.

RUDDOCK, HENRY, —— 1674. Of Providence, R.I., 1645. Deputy, 1654. Town Clerk, Warwick, 1657.

RUSSELL, JOHN, 1608-1694/5. Born in England. Constable, Marshfield, Mass., 1642. Representative from Dartmouth, 1665-1680, excepting 1666, 1673.

RUSSELL, JOSEPH, 1650-1739. Governor's Assistant, Mass., 1685.

RUST, HENRY, —— 1685. Selectman, Hingham, Mass., 1637. Town Clerk, 1645.

RUTSEN, COL. JACOB, 1650-1730. Ensign of Foot, Kingston and New Paltz, N.Y., 1685-1687. Became Capt., Major, Lieut. Col., and Col. Member of New York Assembly, 1693-1695, 1699.

RYNO, JOHN, JR., 1679/80-1750. Among the first settlers of Elizabethtown, NJ.
Finfgeld, Mrs. Clifford W.   Illinois

SABIN, WILLIAM, 1600-1687. Born in England. Deputy from Rehoboth, Mass., 1657.

SACKETT, JOHN, JR., circa 1628-1684. Born in England. Member of the New Haven Train Band, Conn., 1646.

SACKETT, LIEUT. JOSEPH, 1656-1719. Lieut. of Foot Company, Newtown, L.I., 1690.

SACKETT, RICHARD, 6 June 1655 ——. Captain of Seven Companies of New York City Regiments 1699-1704.
Fysh, Mrs. Walter   Michigan

SALMON, WILLIAM, 1610-1657. Co-Founder of Southold, L.I., 1636/7-1657.

SAMMIS, JOHN, 1st., 1648-1692. Deputy from Huntington, L.I., 1683, 1688. Selectman, 1692.

SAMPSON, HENRY, —— 1685. Passenger on the "Mayflower," 1620.

SANDS, CAPT. JAMES, 1622-1695. Commissioner to General Court of R.I., 1657. Deputy from Block Island, 1660.

SANDS, CAPT. JOHN, 1649/50-1712. Born in Rhode Island. Deputy to General Assembly from Block Island, 1678-1680. Capt. of New Shoreham Co., R.I., Troops.

SANFORD, LIEUT. JOHN, —— 1653. One of the Founders of Portsmouth, R.I., 1638. Lieutenant, 1644. Assistant to Governor 1647-1649. President of Portsmouth and Newport, 1653.

SANFORD, GOV. PELEG, 1639-1701. Governor's Assistant, R.I., 1667-1670, 1670-1679. Capt. of Troop of Horse, 1667. Deputy from Newport to General Assembly of R.I., 1670, 1677. Agent to England, 1677, 1683. General Treasurer of R.I. Colony, 1678-1681. Served in King Philips's War, 1676. Major, 1679. Lt. Col 1687. Governor of R.I., 1680-1683.

SANFORD, ROBERT, —— ——. Member of Ancient and Honorable Artillery Co. of Boston, 1661.

SANFORD, THOMAS, 1673 ——. Member of the Ancient and Honorable Artillery Co., 1696.

SANGER, NATHANIEL, 1652-1735. Soldier in King Philip's War, from Watertown, Mass., 1675.

SANGER, RICHARD, —— 1691. Soldier in King Philip's War, from Watertown, Mass., 1675.

SARES (SEARS), RICHARD, —— 1676. Settled in Yarmouth, Mass., 1639. Member of Militia, 1643. On Committee, 1658. Constable 1660. Representative to Court, Plymouth, 1662.
Smith, Miss Crista Linn   Jamestown Virginia
Wasilik, Mrs. John R.   Jamestown Virginia

SARGENT, JOHN, 1639-1716. Born in Charlestown, Mass. Selectman, Malden, 1669.

SARGENT, WILLIAM I, —— 1675. Born in England. One of Grantees at Agawam (Ipswich), Mass., on list in General Court Records of Mass., 1633. A First Settler of Wessacucon (Newbury), 1635.

SARGENT, WILLIAM, —— 1682. Born in England. Lay Preacher, Malden, Mass., 1648-1650.
Davis, Mrs. Frank V.   Illinois

SAUNDERS, TOBIAS, —— 1695. Deputy from Westerly, R.I., to General Assembly of R.I., 1669, 1671, 1672, 1680, 1681, 1683, 1690.
Erickson, Mrs. Melville A.   Florida

SAXTON, CAPT. JOSEPH, 1656-1715. Born in Boston, Mass. Capt. in King Philip's War, 1675-1676.

SAYRE, JOSEPH, —— 1695. Named in the original Associate Founders of Elizabethtown, N.J., 1665, 1666.

Long, Mrs. Alfred T.   Founders

SAYRE, THOMAS, 1597-1670. Born in England. One of eight men who settled Southampton, L.I., 1639. Townsman, 1654. Overseer, 1657, 1658.

Faw, Mrs. Wylie M., Jr.	Florida
Long, Mrs. Alfred T.	Founders
Morrison, Mrs. Richard W.	Florida

SCARBOROUGH, CAPT. EDMUND, 1584-1634. Born in England. Burgess for the Va. Assembly, 1629-1633.

DeVan, Mrs. William Todd	Pennsylvania
Stewart, Mrs. Frank C., Jr.	Florida
Stewart, Miss Stephanie	Florida
Winder, Mrs. William James	Pennsylvania

SCHENCK, JOHANNES, 1656-1748. Came from Holland to America, 1683. Town Clerk, Flatbush, L.I., 1691-1694.

SCHENCK, CAPT. ROELOF MARTENSE, 1619-1705. Came from Holland, 1656. Settled in Flatlands, L.I. Magistrate, 1662, 1663, 1664. Deputy, 1665. Sherifi, 1685. Justice of Peace, 1689-1692. Schepen, one term. Captain of Cavalry, 1690.

SCHERMERHORN, JACOB JANSE, 1622-1688. Acting Indian Commissioner under Dutch Rule and Magistrate of Fort Orange, 1656, 1657, 1664, 1674.

SCHOONMAKER, LIEUT. HENDRICK JOCHEMISE,——1683. Of Kingston, N.Y. Lieut. of Burgher Guard, Kingston, N.Y. Served at Esopus (Kingston) during Indian attack, 1659.

DuRocher, Mrs. Linus F.   Renss.

SCHUMAKER, PETER, 1622-1701. A Founder of Germantown, Philadelphia, Pa., 1685.

SCOTT, DANIEL, —— 1745. Of Baltimore, Md. Ensign, 1696. Signed military officer's oath of fidelity, Feb., 1696. Vestryman of St. John's, Baltimore, Md.

SCOTT, HUGH, 1630-1718. First settler and landowner Chester County, PA.

Williams, Mrs. Si J.   Ohio

SCOTT, THOMAS, 1603-1643. Original Proprietor of Hartford, Conn., 1636. A Founder and Settler with Rev. Hooker's party.

SCRUGGS, RICHARD, ————. James City Co., VA. Vestryman St. Peter's Parish, New Kent Co., VA.
Trollinger, Mrs. Donald C.   Oklahoma

SCUDDER, ENS. JONATHAN, 1657-1690/91. Born in Southold, L.I. Commissioned Ensign, for Huntington, L.I., 1685.

SCUDDER, THOMAS, —— 1690. Constable, Huntington, L.I., 1668.

SEAMAN, CAPT. JOHN, 1610-1695. Born in England. Settled in Hempstead, L.I. Magistrate, ten years, 1647-1673. Deputy, 1653. Captain, 1665. Moved to Jerusalem, 1665. Served in Indian Wars, 1668-1695. Justice of the Peace, 1685.
Long, Mrs. Alfred T.   Founders
Miller, Miss Florence Emeline   Illinois

SEAMER (See SEYMOUR).

SEAMAN, JONATHAN, ————. Patentee, Hempstead, L.I., 1660. Moved to Jerusalem, 1665.

SEARS, LIEUT. SILAS, 1637/8-1697/8. Ensign, East Precinct, Yarmouth, Mass., 1681. Lieut., 1682. Representative to General Court, Plymouth, 1685-1691. Selectman, 1680-1694. On Committee, 1694.

SEBRING, CORNELIS, 1662-circa 1723. Member of Assembly from Kings Co., N.Y., 1695.

SEELEY, CAPT. NATHANIEL, —— 1675. Born in England. Capt. in King Philip's War from Fairfield, Conn., 1675.
Greason, Mrs. James B., Jr.   Founders

SEELEY, LIEUT. NATHANIEL, —— 1688. Lieutenant of Militia at Fairfield, Conn., 1688.
Greason, Mrs. James B., Jr.   Founders

SEELEY, CAPT. ROBERT, 1601-1667/8. Born in England. Signed Fundamental Agreement, New Haven, 1639. Marshal of New Haven Colony, 1639-1642. Served in Pequot War, 1637. Lieutenant, 1646-1647. Captain of Artillery, 1648. Commissioner, Huutinton, L.I., 1663. Served with the Dutch against Indians, 1643.

Bohn, Mrs. Harold D.   Renss.
Eldrett, Mrs. H. Carleton   Renss.
Greason, Mrs. James B., Jr.   Founders
Long, Mrs. Alfred T.   Founders
Love, Mrs. Frank Campbell   Renss.

SEIMAN (SEIMENS, SIMONS), JAN, —— ——. Of Pennsylvania. One of Founders of Germantown, Philadelphia, Pa. 1685.
Balderston, Miss Bryn Elizabeth   Pennsylvania
Dutch, Miss Deborah   Pennsylvania
Finley, Mrs. John Kent   Pennsylvania
Hobin, Mrs. David Joseph   Pennsylvania
Hodge, Mrs. John Hires   Pennsylvania
Mayer, Mrs. Cyril   Pennsylvania

SELLEN, HENDRICK, 1670-1735. A Founder of Germantown, Pa, 1685.

SELOVER, ISAAC, —— after 1715. Schoolmaster and Assistant pastor, Flatlands, (New Amersfoort), before 1695 and later.

SEVERANS (SEVERANCE), JOHN, 1609-1682. Born in England. Resident of Ipswich, Mass., 1636. Freeman, Boston, 1637. Member Ancient and Honorable Artillery Co., 1638. Removed to Salisbury, Mass., 1640. As Prudential man issued order designating what arms and ammunition were to be carried to church, 1643. Commissioned officer, 1671.

SEWALL, HENRY, JR., 1614-1700. From England to Ipswich, Mass., 1634. One of early settlers of Newbury, 1635. Deputy from Newbury, 1661.

SEYMOUR (SEAMER), RICHARD, 1604/5-1655. Born in England. Served in Pequot War, 1637. One of original settlers of Norwalk, Conn., 1650. Selectman, Norwalk, Conn., 1655.
Cook, Mrs. Ralph W., Sr.   Michigan
Scheiner, Mrs. Carl J.   Renss.

SEYMOUR, THOMAS, 1632-1712. Born in England. Deputy from Norwalk, Conn., 1690. Selectman, 1689-1692.

SHARP, LIEUT. JOHN, —— 1675. Killed at Sudbury, Mass., during King Philip's War.

SHARPE, SERGT. SAMUEL, 1561-1625. From England to Va., 1609. Burgess, 1619-1625. Sergeant.

SHATTUCK, SERGT. JOHN, 1647-1675. Sergt. in Capt. Richard Beer's Co., King Philip's War, for relief of Northfield, 1675.

SHATTUCK, WILLIAM, 1621/2-1672. Born in England. Constable, Watertown, Mass. Surveyor of Highways, 1654.

SHAW, ABRAHAM, 1592-1638. Born in England. Constable, Dedham, Mass., 1638.

SHAW, ROGER, 1594-1661. Town Clerk, Cambridge, Mass., 1640. Selectman, 1641, 1643, 1645, 1649-1654. Representative to the General Court, 1651-1654.

SHEAFE, JACOB, 1616-1658. Member of Ancient and Honorable Artillery Co. of Boston, Mass., 1648. Clerk of Co., 1652. Constable, 1651. Selectman, 1657-1658.
Davis, Mrs. Frank V.	Illinois

SHEAFE, SAMPSON, 1650-1724. Assistant Secretary of Mass. Bay Colony, 1698.

SHED, DANIEL, baptized 1620-1708. Served in King Philip's War, Rev. Samuel Whiting's Garrison House, Billerica, Mass., 1675.

SHED, ZACHARIAH, 1656-1735. Served in King Philip's War, at Chelmsford, Mass., 1675.

SHEDD, JOHN, 1654/5-1736. Received Credits under Major Willard, King Philip's War, 19 Oct. 1675. Served in Garrison House, Billerica, Mass.

SHELDON, ISAAC, 1628-1708. Selectman, Northampton, Mass., 1656.

SHELTON, JAMES, —— 1668. VA. Member of the Courts from 1619-1624.
Moore, Miss Candace Nealie	Tejas

SHEPARD, EDWARD, —— circa 1680. Constable, Cambridge, Mass., 1656. Town Surveyor.

SHEPARD, REV. JEREMIAH, 1648-1720. Graduate of Harvard, 1669. Minister, Rowley, Mass., 1673-1676; of Lynn, Mass., 1679, where he served many years. Deputy to General Court, 1689.

SHEPARD, JOHN, circa 1627-1707. Constable, Cambridge, Mass., 1658.

SHEPARD, REV. THOMAS, 1605-1649. One of the founders of Harvard College. Preacher of Election Sermons, 1637-1638. Minister, Cambridge, Mass., 1635 until death.

SHEPPARD, ROBERT, 1604-1653. Lt., Capt. and Major in the Militia, Justice of Surry Co., Burgess in 1646, 1647, and 1648, VA.
Weaver, Mrs. James M., Sr.   Florida

SHERBURNE, HENRY, 1611-1680. Born in England. Judge to end small causes, 1644. Associate Judge, 1651. Selectman, Town Clerk, Treasurer, Deputy, Portsmouth, N.H., 1656-1660.
Lofguist, Mrs. Alden A.   Tennessee

SHERBURNE, CAPT. SAMUEL, 1638-1691. Born in Portsmouth, N.H. Selectman, Hampton, 1683, 1688. Deputy, 1689. Served in King William's War, 1689-1691. Commissioner, 1690.

SHERMAN, EDMUND, 1572-1641. Born in England. Selectman, Watertown, Mass., 1636.
Witting, Miss Victoria Leigh   Florida

SHERMAN, REV. JOHN, 1613-1685. Born in England. Magistrate, New Haven, Conn., several years. Minister, Watertown, Mass., 1644-1648.

SHERMAN, PHILIP, 1610-1687. One of the founders of Portsmouth, R.I., 1638. General Recorder, 1648-1651. Commissioner, 1656. Deputy, 1665, 1667.
Gardner, Miss Catherine   Rhode Island

SHERMAN, SAMUEL, 1618-1700. Deputy to General Court of Conn., 1637. On committee to defend the coast against the Dutch, 1665. Assistant to Governor of Conn., 1663-1668.

SHERWOOD, HUGH, 1632-1710. Member of Maryland Assembly, 1692.

SHERWOOD, THOMAS, 1586-1655. Born in England. Deputy to Hartford, Conn., from Stratford, 1645-1647; from Fairfield, 1653-1654.

SHINN, JOHN, 1632-1711. Leader in "Friends" Church called an "Overseer," Burlington Co., N.J.
Lucas, Mrs. J. Victor   Illinois

SHOTWELL, ABRAHAM, —— circa 1680/83. One of Associates of Elizabethtown, N.J. Took Oath of Allegiance, 1665.

SHURTLEFF, WILLIAM, 1624——. Born in England. Constable, Plymouth, Mass., 1659. Treasurer, 1665.
Fiesinger, Mrs. Charles H.   Renss.

SHURTLEFF, CAPT. WILLIAM, 1657-1729/30. Born in England. Selectman, Plymouth, Mass., 1692-1693. Capt. and Deputy, 1694.

SHUTE, RICHARD, —— 1704. Town Clerk, Eastchester, N.Y., 1673-1699.

SIBLEY, JOHN, 1600-1661. Selectman, Salem, Mass., 1636.

SILL, CAPT. JOSEPH, 1636-1696. Of Cambridge, Mass. Served in King Philip's War, 1675.

SIMONS, WILLIAM, circa 1630-circa 1677. Ensign in Surry Co., Va. Militia, 1687.
Maxwell, Mrs. Eugene K.   Quivira

SIMPKINS, NICHOLAS, —— ——. Of Boston, Mass. Member of Ancient and Honorable Artillery Co., 1650.

SINGLETARY, RICHARD, 1599-25 Oct 1687. Salem, Massachusetts Bay. Selectman, Salisbury, MA Bay 1650. Proprietor Haverbill 1653.
Boyd, Mrs. Thomas W.   Pennsylvania

SKELETON, REV. SAMUEL, 1584-1634. First Minister of Salem, Mass., 1629.

SKIDMORE, THOMAS, 1600-1683/4. Born in England. Settled at Cambridge, Mass., 1635. Town Clerk, Huntington, L.I., 1666. Member of General Assembly, 1673.
Thompson, Miss Jennifer Dawn   Tennessee

SKILLMAN, THOMAS, —— 1697. Soldier under Col. Nicoll who captured New Amsterdam from the Dutch, 1664. Served in Esopus War, 1690.

SKINNER, SERGT. THOMAS, 1617-1703/4, of Malden, Mass. Freeman, 1653. Selectman, Malden, 1680. Sergt. of Malden Co., 1680.

SKINNER, THOMAS, II, 1645-1722/32. Clerk of Company in King Philip's War, 1675/6.

SLAWSON, GEORGE, —— 1694. One of leading men in First Church of Sandwich, Mass., 1642. Deputy, 1670.

SLEGHT, CORNELIS BARENSTEN, —— ——. Original land patent holder, Esopus. Officer in the Militia, Esopus, 1660. Schepen (Magistrate), charter of Esopus, 1661.
Dietrich, Mrs. Ira J.   Oklahoma

SLOCUM, ANTHONY, —— 1689. One of the original settlers and purchasers of Taunton, Mass., 1638.

SLOCUM, EBENEZER, 1650-1715. Born in Portsmouth, R.I. Deputy from Jamestown, R.I., 1679, 1681-1685, 1696.

SMITH, ENS. CHILEAB, 1635-1731. Ensign, Hadley, Mass., 1692-1699.
Greason, Mrs. James B., Jr.   Founders

SMITH, DANIEL, —— 1692. Born in England. Deputy from Rehoboth, Mass. to Plymouth, 1672, 1674, 1678.

SMITH, EDWARD, —— 1675. Town Clerk, Rehoboth, Mass., 1645. Assistant, Newport, R.I., 1654, 1655, 1658, 1659, 1665, 1666. Commissioner, 1655, 1659. Deputy, 1665, 1666, 1669.

SMITH, GILES, 1603-1669. Member of Train Band, Fairfield, Conn., and freed from training in April, 1663.

SMITH, HENRY, —— 1649. Born in England. Deputy for Hingham, Mass., 1641.

SMITH, HENRY, 1619-1685. Commissioner from Wethersfield, Conn., 1632. Served in Pequot War, 1637.

SMITH, JAMES, —— 1676. Selectman, Weymouth, Mass., 1656, 1663.

SMITH, LIEUT. JAMES, 1645-1690. Born in Newbury, Mass. Lieut. in expedition to Canada, 1690, and lost at sea.

SMITH, JOHN, —— 1643. One of first settlers of Taunton, Mass., 1639. Removed to Newtown, L.I., before 1643, and killed in Indian War.
Corder, Miss Lois B.   Founders

SMITH, JOHN, 1595-circa 1648. One of first settlers with Roger Williams in Providence, R.I., 1636. Town Clerk, 1641. One of a committee of ten entrusted in organizing government for the Colony, 1647.

SMITH, JOHN, 1662-1698, of "Purton," Va. Captain in Colonial Militia. Trustee of College of William and Mary. Vestryman, Petsworth Parish. Burgess from Gloucester Co., Va.

SMITH, CAPT. JOHN, 1630-1669. Captain in Virginia militia.
Spain, Mrs. Frank Edward   Pennsylvania

SMITH, ENS. JOHN, JR., 1642-1687. Ensign, 1664. Deputy, 1666- 1672.
Town Clerk, R.I., 1672-1676.

SMITH, QUARTERMASTER JOHN, —— 1678. Born in England. Selectman,
Dorchester, Mass., 1650. Quartermaster, Sulfolk Co., Mass. Troops,
1652.

SMITH, LAWRENCE, —— 1665. Born in England. Member of Ancient and
Honorable Artillery Co. of Boston, Mass., 1642.

SMITH, LAWRENCE, —— 1700. Lieut. Col., Gloucester Co., Va. Militia,
1680. Surveyor, Gloucester Co. and York Co., Va., 1686. Burgess, 1688,
1691, 1692.
Collier, Mrs. H. Grady, Jr.   Louisiana
Hubbard, Mrs. Glenn W.   Illinois
Ross, Miss Dana   Illinois
Zatarain, Mrs. Charles C.   Louisiana

SMITH, NEHEMIAH, 1605-1684. Born in England. Served in King Philip's
War, from Norwich, Conn., 1675-1676.

SMITH, RICHARD, 1643-1696. From England to Boston, Mass., 1673. Town
Clerk and Tax Assessor, Bristol, R.I., 1682.
Bailey, Mrs. William   Member-at-Large

SMITH, LIEUT. SAMUEL, 1602-1680. Born in England. Sergeant and
Deputy, Wethersfield, Conn., 1640-1641. Lieutenant, Hadley, Mass.,
1663-1678. Deputy to Mass. Bay Colony, 1661-1678. Commissioner to
the Mohawks, 1667.
Greason, Mrs. James B., Jr.   Founders
Mullis, Mrs. David William   North Carolina

SMITON, WILLIAM, —— 1671. Troop of Horse, 1667. Deputy to General
Court in Portsmouth, Mass., 1671.

SMOCK (SMACK), HENDRICK MATTHYSE, , —— 1708. Came to America,
1654. Magistrate, New Utrecht, L.I., 1669, 1673, 1676, 1679, 1682, 1689.
Hillemeyer, Mrs. John Wright   Missouri

SNEDEKER, GERRET JANSE, 1660-1694. Magistrate, Brooklyn, N.Y.,
1679.

SNEDEKER, JAN, —— 1679. Magistrate, Flatbush, L.I., 1654-1674.

SNOW, ANTHONY, —— 1692. Surveyor, Marshfield, Mass., 1651. Constable, 1652. Deputy to Plymouth Colony, 1656-1676. Selectman, 1666 and other years. Member of War Council for Plymouth Colony, 1675.

SNOW, NICHOLAS, 1599-1676. Born in England. Landed at Plymouth, Mass. In Plymouth Militia, 1643. A First Settler of Eastham, Mass., 1645. Town Clerk, 1646. Deputy Sheriff, 1646. Selectman.
Duryea, Mrs. Harold B.						Quivira

SOULE, GEORGE, 1590-1680. Born in England. Settled at Duxbury, Mass. A signer of Mayflower Compact. Served in Pequot War, 1637.

SOUTHWORTH, GEN. CONSTANT, 1615-1678/9. Born in Holland. Deputy from Duxbury, Mass., 1647-1649, 1656-1669. Treasurer of Plymouth Colony, 1659-1678. Assistant, 1670-1678. Ensign, 1646. Member Council of War, 1658-1667. Commanding General in King Philip's War, 1675-1676.

SPALDING (SPAULDING), EDWARD, 1619-1670. Born in England. Selectman, Chelmsford, Mass., 1654, 1656, 1660, 1661.

SPALDING, JOHN, 1633-1721. Died at Chelmsford, Mass. Served in King Philip's War, 1675.

SPAULDING, DEA. ANDREW, 1653-1713. Deacon in Church, Chelmsford, Mass., many years.

SPENCER, GERRARD, 1614-1683. Born in England; died at Haddam, Conn. Ensign of the Train Band, 14 Sept. 1675. Deputy from Haddam, 1674-1675.

SPENCER, JOHN, —— 1684. Town Clerk, East Greenwich, R.I., 1677-1683. Deputy, 1680.

SPENCER, JOHN, JR., 1666-1743. Deputy from Greenwich, R.I., 1699.

SPENCER, SERGT. THOMAS, —— 1687. Born in England. Served in Pequot War, from Cambridge, Mass., 1637. Sergeant, Hartford, Conn., 1649. Constable, 1658.

SPENCER, WILLIAM, circa 1582 ——. Arrived Jamestown, Va., 1607. Member of House of Burgesses, 1624-1632. Member of Surry Co. militia.
Bond, Mrs. Harry						Michigan
Burrage, Mrs. Robert L., Jr.						North Carolina

Lafferty, Miss Amy   North Carolina
Lafferty, Mrs. Martin L.   North Carolina
Miner, Miss Sarah Avice   Illinois
Weaver, Miss Mary Alice   Florida

SPENCER, LIEUT. WILLIAM, 1601-1640. Charter Member of the Ancient and Honorable Artillery Co., 1637. Deputy from Cambridge, Mass., 1634-1638; from Hartford, Conn., 1639. Lieut. of Train Band, Newtown, Mass., 1636.
Aul, Mrs. Clyde   Florida
Papapetrou, Mrs. Dean   Florida

SPICER, THOMAS, 1591/2-1693. Signer of Newport Compact, 1638. Surveyor, Portsmouth, R.I., 1639. Treasurer, 1642.

SPRAGUE, CAPT. EDWARD, ca 1663-13/14 April 1713. Massachusetts Bay. Assessor 1695. Commissioner 1695/6. Town Treas. 1695-1697. Constable 1696, Selectman 1696 and 1699, Malden, MA.
Meadown, Miss Edna-Leone   Illinois

SPRAGUE, CAPT. JOHN, 1624-1692. King Philip's War, 1676. Selectman; Captain, 1685. Representative to General Court, 1689-1691.
Gleason, Mrs. Richard J.   Illinois
Meadown, Miss Edna-Leone   Illinois

SPRAGUE, LT. RALPH, 1603-1650 MA. Depute 1635-1641, 1643, 1645. Charlestown, MA Bay, Lt. Militia 1637-1646. Member A & HAC 1638. Slectman 1634.
Meadows, Miss Edna-Leone   Illinois

SPRAGUE, WILLIAM, 1609-1675. Born in England. One of the original settlers, Charlestown, Mass., 1636. Selectman, Hingham, 1645. Constable, 1662.

SPRIGG, THOMAS, 1630-1704. Born in England; arrived in Md., 1653. Commissioned High Sheriff, Calvert Co., Md., 1664. Justice of Quorum, Calvert Co., Md., 1658, 1661, 1667, 1670, 1674. Retired as presiding Justice, Prince Georges Co., Md., 1697.
Killpatrick, Mrs. Claude Paxton   Blue Grass
Ragsdale, Mrs. Charles E.   Missouri

SPRIGG, THOMAS, circa 1665-circa 1728. Justice of Peace, Prince Georges Co., Md., 1697.

SPRING, HENRY, SR., 1628-1697. Born in England. Resided Watertown, Mass. Member of Train Band, 1653. Served in King Philip's War, 1675; in French War, 1690.

SPRING, JOHN, 1589 ——. Born in England. Original Proprietor and settler, Watertown, Mass., 1636.

SPRINSTEEN, JOHANNES CASPERSEN, —— after 1676. On Muster Roll of Bushwick Long Island Militia, 1663.

STAATS, MAJ. ABRAHAM, —— 1694. Councillor, Rensselaerwyck, N.Y., 1643. President of the Board, 1644. Magistrate, Fort Orange, 1657, 1658, 1661, 1662. Capt. and Major of Troops, under Lovelace at Esopus, 1669. Surgeon.
Davis, Mrs. Frank V.   Illinois

STAATS, DR. JACOB, —— 1735. Deacon of Dutch Church, Albany, 1678. Justice of the Peace, Albany, 1690. Surgeon of Albany Garrison, 1698-1699.

STAATS, LIEUT. PIETER JANSE, —— after 1706. Lieut. of Troop of horse, Kings Co., N.Y., 1690.

STACY, MAHLON, 1638-1704. Commissioner, 1681, 1682. Member of General Assembly of New Jersey, 1682, 1684, 1685. Member of the Council, 1682, 1683. Justice 1685; on the Burlington Bench, 1695.

STAFFORD, THOMAS, 1605-1677. Born in England. Deputy from Warwick, R.I., 1673.

STALLYON, EDWARD, —— 1703. Early settler of New London, Conn.

STANDISH, MYLES, 1586-1656. Born in England. "Mayflower" passenger, a signer of the "Mayflower" Compact, 1620. Capt. during Indian and Dutch Wars. Member of Councils of War, 1642, 1643, 1646, 1653. Treasurer, 1644-1645.
Day, Mrs. John E.   Michigan
Korte, Mrs. Anthony S.   Michigan
Marquart, Mrs. Wayne William   Illinois

STANLEY, JOHN, 1624-1705/6. Born in England. Died in Farmington, Conn. Deputy to General Court, 1659-1696. Lieut. and Capt. in King Philip's War, 1675.
Armstrong, Mrs. Donald G.   Illinois

STANLEY, THOMAS, —— 1663. From England to Lynn, Mass., 1635. Freeman, 1635. Member Ancient and Honorable Artillery Co., Boston, Mass., 1640. Constable, Hartford, Conn., 1644, 1648, 1653. Townsman, Haldey, Mass., 1659.

STANSBOROUGH, JOSIAH, —— 1661. One of five men to order all affairs of Southampton, R.I., 7 Oct. 1650.

STANSBOROUGH, JOSIAH, JR., —— after 1695. Associate Judge, Elizabeth, N.J., 1695.

STANTON, JOHN, 1645-1728. Deputy from Newport, R.I., 1696.

STANTON, CAPT. JOHN, 1641-1713. Died at Stonington, Conn. Capt in King Philip's War, 1675.

STANTON, SERGT. ROBERT, 1599-1672. Sergeant Jr., 1642. Sergeant, 1644. Deputy, R.I., 1670.

STANTON, ROBERT, 1653-1724. Born in Stonington, Conn. Served in King Philip's War, 1675-1676.

STANTON, THOMAS, 1609/10-1677. Served Gov. Winthrop and Conn. Authorities as Interpreter from 1636. Name appears on Founders Monument in Hartford. Fought in Pequot War, 1637. Removed to Stonington, 1657. Magistrate, 1658. Selectman, 1662-1677. Deputy, 1666-1675.
Finch, Mrs. Stuart   Territorial
Trau, Mrs. Frank Garland   Pennsylvania

STAPLES, THOMAS, —— before 1688. Died in Va. One of first settlers, Fairfield, Conn.
Greason, Mrs. James B., Jr.   Founders

STARBUCK, EDWARD, 1604-1690. Representative from Dover, N.H., 1643-1646.

STARK, AARON, 1602-1685. Born in England. Died at New London, Conn. Served in Pequot War under Capt. Mason, 1637; also King Philip's War, 1675.

STARR, DR. COMFORT, 1589-1659. Born in England. resided Duxbury, Mass. Deputy to General Court, 1642. Non-commissioned officer in Duxbury Co., 1643.

STARR, DR. THOMAS, 1615-1658. From England to Boston, Mass., 1635. Appointed Chirurgeon to the forces sent against the Pequots, 1637. "Clerk of the Writs," Charlestown, Mass., 1654.
Greason, Mrs. James B., Jr.   Founders

STEARNS, CHARLES, —— ——. Selectman, Watertown, Mass., 1680.

STEARNS, ISAAC, before 1627-1671. Born in England. Arrived Salem, Mass., 1630. A first settler of Watertown, Mass. Selectman, 1659, 1670, 1671. One of Major Willard's troopers, Dedham, 1554.
Ellis, Miss Elizabeth   Member-at-Large
Gary, Mrs. Dan Carmack   Tennessee

STEBBINS, DEACON EDWARD, —— 1668. Constable Hartford, CT. Served on Legislature various times from 1639-1656. Deacon.
Armstrong, Mrs. Donald G.   Illinois
Lang, Mrs. Robert E.   California

STEELE, GEORGE, —— 1663. Served in Pequot War, 1637. One of original proprietors of Hartford, Conn.

STEELE, JAMES, 1622-1676. Served in Pequot War, from Hartford, Conn., 1637; in King Philip's War, 1675.

STEELE, JOHN, 1591-1665. Born in England. Died in Farmington, Conn. Appointed Commissioner of Conn., 1635. Deputy from Hartford, Conn., 1636-1645; from Farmington, Conn., 1646-1658.

STEERE, JOHN, 1634-1724. Town Sergeant, 1663.

STERLING, WILLIAM, 1637 ——. Selectman, Haverhill, Mass., 1684. Constable, 1694, 1695.

STETSON, ROBERT, 1613-1703, of Scituate, Mass. Cornet of first Horse Co., Plymouth, Mass., 1658-1659. Member of Council of War, 1661. Deputy to General Court, 1654 and intermittently until 1678.

STEVENS, CYPRAIN, —— ——. In Lancaster, Mass., 22 Jan. 1671/2. Town Clerk, Lancaster, Mass. Owned Garrison House, King Philip's War, Lancaster, Mass., 1675.

STEVENS, ENSIGN JOHN, 1637-1691. Ensign of Foot Company of Chelmsford, Mass., 1689. Indian Fighter.
Cook, Mrs. Ralph William, Sr.   Michigan

STEVENS, HENRY, 1611-1690. Born in England. Constable, Muddy River (now Brookline), Mass., 1655/6.
Cook, Mrs. Ralph William, Sr.   Michigan

STEVENSON (STIMPSON, STIMSON), ANDREW,—— 1681/3. Officer as prison keeper, Middlesex Co., Mass. 1656-1672. In King Philip's War, 1675/6.

STEVENSON, THOMAS, —— 1668. Served in Dutch and Indian Wars, under Capt. Underhill, Stamford, Conn., 1643.

STEVENSON, THOMAS, JR., 1648/1725. Overseer, Newton, L.I., 1676, 1678. Constable, 1678. Justice of the Peace, 1685.

STILES, ROBERT, —— 1690. Constable, Boxford, Mass., 1686.

STILLWELL, LIEUT. NICHOLAS, —— 1671. Came from Leyden, 1638. Organized Troop in Va., 1644. Early settler, Kings Co. Schepen, 1650, 1651, 1654-1657. Lieutenant, 1663. Served in Indian Wars. Captured King Opechancanough. Schout, Gravesend, L.I., 1664.

STILLWELL, CAPT. NICHOLAS, II, 1636-1715. Born in Holland. Settled in Gravesend, L.I. Justice of Peace, 1685 and after. Captain, 1689. Deputy, 1691-1694. In expedition against French and Indians, 1693.
Klausner, Mrs. Karl R.   Renss.

STITES, DR. JOHN, 1595-1717. Physician and surgeon, Plymouth, Mass., and Hempstead, L.I., 1653-1699.
Finfgeld, Mrs. Clifford   Illinois

ST. JOHN, MATTHIAS, 1603-circa 1669. Dorchester, Massachusetts Bay. Freeman 3 Sept 1634. Keeper of Cows 1636/7. Original Landowner, Juryman 1643, 1644, 1650, and 1651.
Warda, Mrs. C. Wernecke   Michigan

STOCKBRIDGE, JOHN, —— 1675. Died at Scituate, Mass. House used as garrison, King Philip's War, 1675.

STOCKETT, CAPT. THOMAS, 1625-1671. Settled in Baltimore, Md., 1658. Burgess for Baltimore Co., Md., 1661-1665. High Sheriff, Anne Arundel Co., 1666-1670. Deputy Surveyor General of Md., 1670-1671.

STOCKTON, LIEUT. RICHARD, 1626-1707. Born in England. Died in Burlington Co., N.J. Settled first at Flushing, L.I. Commissioned Lieut. of Horse Co. of Flushing L.I., 1665.

STODDARD, ANTHONY, —— 1687. Deputy from Boston, Mass., to Mass. Bay Colony, 1656-1660, 1665.

STODDARD, SERGT. SAMUEL, 1640-1731. Constable, Hingham, Mass., 1674, 1678. Sergt. in King Philip's War, 1675/6. Selectman, 1691.

STODDARD, REV. SOLOMON, 1643-1729. Minister, Northampton, Mass., before 1675.

STONE, DEA. GREGORY, 1592-1672. Born in England. Deputy from Cambridge, Mass., to Mass. Bay Colony, 1638. Deacon, Cambridge Church, 34 years.

STONE, JOHN, 1619-1683. Born in England. Town Clerk, Sudbury, Mass.

STONE, REV. SAMUEL, 1602-1663. Teacher in church, Cambridge, Mass., 1633. An Original Proprietor of Hartford, Conn. Chaplain, Pequot War, 1637. Pastor of First church after Rev. Hooker, Hartford.

STONE, DEA. SIMON, 1585/6-1665. Born in England. Deacon, Watertown, Mass. Selectman, 1637-1656.

STONE, WILLIAM, 1608-1683. Born in England. One of the signers of the Covenant, Guilford, Conn., 1639.

STONE, GOV. WILLIAM, 1603-1660. Commissioner of Accomac Co., Va., 1633. Vestryman of Hugar' Parish, 1635. Third Proprietary Governor of Md., 1648-1653. Justice of Accomac Co., 1653. Member of Council, Md. 1657.

STORM, DIRCK, circa 1636-after 1697. Secretary of Brooklyn, 1669. Clerk of Sessions, Orange Co., N.Y., 1691-1703. Clerk of Dutch Church, Tarrytown, N.Y., 1697.

STOTT, BRIAN (BRYAN), SR., 1627-4 Mar 1704/5. Justice of the Peace. Court member 1671. VA.
Harmonson, Mrs. Alva B.					Tejas
Neidemairer, Mrs. Edward John					Tejas

STOUGHTON, COL. ISRAEL, 1580-1645. Born in England. Served in Pequot War, 1637. Deputy to General Court, 1634-1637. Governor's Assistant, 1637-1644. Capt. Ancient and Honorable Artillery Co. of Boston.

STOUT, RICHARD, 1602-1705. Born in England. Member of Constables Court, Middletown, N.J., 1678. Overseer, 1669.

STOWE, JOHN, 1581/2-1643. Born in England. Member Ancient and Honorable Artillery Co., Boston, Mass., 1638.

STOWE, REV. SAMUEL, 1623/4/1704. Born in England. Minister, Middletown, Conn., 1653-1668.

STRATTON, JOHN, 1626-1685. Born in England. Overseer, Easthampton, L.I., 1665. Magistrate, 1673.

STRATTON, JOHN, 1635-1691. Selectman, Watertown, Mass., 1683.

STRICKLAND, SERGT. JOHN, —— 1691. One of the original settlers of Charlestown, Mass., 1630. Freeman, 1634. Moved to Watertown; then to Wethersfield, Conn. Served in Pequot War, 1637. Patentee of Hempstead, L.I., 1644. At Huntington, L.I., 1650. Magistrate, 1658-1660.

STRONG, ELDER JOHN, 1605-1699. Born in England. Deputy from Taunton, Mass., 1641-1643. Ordained the first Ruling Elder, Northampton, Mass., 1663.
Bachner, Mrs. Thomas Edgar					Tejas
Henke, Mrs. Orvis L.					Michigan

STRONG, LIEUT. RETURN, SR., circa 1641-1726. 2nd Lieut. of Cavalry Troop, Hartford Co., Conn., 1689. Lieut. 1692. Deputy from Windsor to General Court in Hartford, 1689, 1690.

STROTHER, WILLIAM V., 1653-1702. Born in Va.; died in King George Co., Va. Sheriff of King George Co., Va. Vestryman, Hanover, Va.
Albertson, Mrs. David W.					Oklahoma

STRYKER (STRYCKER), CAPT. JAN, circa 1615-circa 1697. Delegate from Midwout, L.I. to the Conventions under Dutch rule, 1653, 1663, 1664, 1674. Capt., 1673.

STRYKER, CAPT. PIETER, 1653-1741. Captain, Flatbush, L.I., 1689.

STURGES, JOHN, 1623-1697/8. Selectman, Fairfield, Conn., 1669.

Berry Mrs. James L.	Renss.
Fiesinger, Mrs. Edward H., Jr.	Renss.
Fiesinger, Miss Emma-Jane	Renss.

STURGESS, ANTHONY, —— ——. A Founder and first settler of Philadelphia, Pa., lot no. 49 on Holmes map, 1681. Grant from Wm. Penn, 1683.

STURGIS, EDWARD, SR., 1624-1695. Constable, Yarmouth, Mass., 1640, 1641, 1662. Deputy, 1664, 1666, 1667, 1672. Selectman, 1670, and many years.

STURTEVANT, SAMUEL, 1622-1669. Member, Plymouth Military Co., 1643.

SUMNER, WILLIAM, 1605-1688. Selectman, Dorchester, 1637, for more than 25 years. Commissioner, 1663-1671. Clerk of the Train Band, 1663.

SUNDERLAND, JOHN, 1618-1703. Member of Ancient and Honorable Artillery Co. of Boston, 1658.

SUTTON, ENS. JOHN, 1642 ——. Served in King Philip's War from Scituate, Mass., 1675.

SUTTON, JOSEPH, 1630-1695. Town Clerk, Hempstead, L.I., 1667, and many years after.

SUTTON, WILLIAM, 1641-1718. Constable, Piscataway, N.J., 1693.

SWAIN, JEREMIAH, 1643 ——. Born in Mass. Physician. Selectman. Justice of Peace. Representative, 1689. Major in command of regiment sent against Indians, 1689. Assistant to Governor, 1690.

SWAINE (SWAYNE), CAPT. SAMUEL, 1610-1682. Lieut. of Colonial Conn. forces, 1663; of Newark, N.J. soldiers, 1667-1673. Capt. East Jersey Provincial forces. Deputy to General Court in Conn., 1663. Deputy and "Third Man" to Provincial Assembly of East Jersey during Indian hostilities, 1673-1676.

SWAINE (SWAYNE), WILLIAM, 1585-1664. Deputy to Mass. Bay Colony, 1636. Commissioner to establish the New Colony of Conn., 1636. Assistant, 1637. Deputy, New Haven Colony, 1653-1657.

SWAN, RICHARD, 1604-1678. Born in England. Deputy from Rowley, Mass., 1666-1667. Served in King Philip's War, 1675.

SWART, JACOB, ———— ————. Magistrate, New Utrecht, 1661, 1664.

SWARTHWOUT, ROELOFF, 1634-1715. Born in Holland, died in Ulster Co., N.Y. One of the First Schepens of Wyltwick at Esopus, 1661. Justice, Ulster Co., N.Y., 1689-1690. Member of Governor's Council, 1689. Long, Mrs. Alfred T.   Founders

SWASEY (SWAZEY), JOHN, circa 1585-after 1675. Born in England. Member of Assembly at New Haven, Conn., from Southold, L.I., 1655.

SWEET, JAMES, 1622-1693. Born in England. Commissioner from Warwick, R.I., 1653, 1658-1659.

SWETT, CAPT. BENJAMIN, 1626-1677. Ensign, Newbury, Mass., 1651. Lieutenant, 1675. Captain, 1677.

SWIFT, THOMAS, —— 1675. Born in England Supt. of Highways, 1658. Fence Viewer, 1659-1662. Quartermaster of Troop of Horse, Dorchester, Mass.

SWIFT, WILLIAM, —— 1644. Born in England. In Lieut. John Blackmer's Co., Sandwich, Mass., 1643.

SWIFT, WILLIAM, JR., —— 1705. Deputy from Sandwich, Mass., 1673-1678.

SYLVESTER, RICHARD, —— 1663. Constable, Marshfield, Mass., 1655. Surveyor of Highways.

SYMONDS, MARK, 1584-1659. Constable, Ipswich, Mass., 1639. One of eleven men to govern town affairs, 1640-1641.

SYMONDS, DEP. GOV. SAMUEL, 1595-1678. Born in England. Deputy from Ipswich, Mass., 1638-1642. Governor's Assistant, 1643-1673. Deputy Governor, 1673-1678.

SYMONDS, WILLIAM, ———— ————. Constable, Concord, Mass., 1645.

TABOR, PHILIP, 1602-1672. Born in England. One of first settlers of Yarmouth, Mass. Deputy, 1639-1640. Deputy from Portsmouth, R.I., 1660-1661, 1663.

TABOR, WILLIAM, 1630-1691. Deputy to Portsmouth, R.I., 1678.

TAINTOR, CHARLES, —— 1658. Born in England. Deputy from Wethersfield, Conn., 1643-1646.

TAINTOR, CAIII'. MICHAEL —— 1673. Captain of sailing vessel bound to Va. Town Clerk, Branford, Conn., 1667. Judge, 1669. Representative, 1670-1672.

TALIAFERRO, LIEUT. COL. JOHN, circa 1660-1720. Lt. Commander of Rangers against Indians, 1692. Member of House of Burgesses, 1699. Sheriff, 1699. Justice, Essex Co., Va.
Hubbard, Mrs. Glenn W.   Territorial

TALLMAN, PETER 1623-1708. 1661-2 Commissioner for the Colony of Rhode Island. 1662-1665 Deputy for the Colony. Interpreter between English and Dutch.
Riddle, Mrs. William McKinley   Oklahoma

TALMAGE, LIEUT. ENOS, 1656-1690. Went from New Haven, Conn., to defense of Schenectady, N.Y., 1690.

TALMAGE, NATHANIEL, 1643-1716. Constable, Easthampton, L.I., 1687. Trustee, 1687, 1692.

TALMAGE, THOMAS, —— 1653. Born in England. Selectman, Easthampton, L.I., 1651.

TALMAGE, LIEUT. THOMAS, —— 1653. Born in England. Selectman, Easthampton, L.I., 1651.

TALMAGE, LIEUT. THOMAS, —— 1690. Lieut., Easthampton, L.I., 1665. Recorder for twenty years.

TANDY, HENRY, JR., 1660-circa 1703. Served against the Indians from Rappahannock Co., Va., 1684.

TAPP, EDMUND, —— 1653. Born in England. Judge of Civil and Criminal Court, 1639. One of the first two Magistrates under the union of Milford, New Haven, Stamford, Guilford, Conn., and Southold, L.I., 1644.
La Tarte, Mrs. Robert L.   Michigan

TAYLOR, ANTHONY, 1607/11-1687. New Hampshire. Selectman of Hampton 1668, 1672, 1673, 1674. Constable. Keeper of County Prison.
Hardy, Mrs. George A.   Territorial

TAYLOR, DR. HENRY, —— 1719. Physician and Surgeon in Boston, 1666; in New York City, 1674.

TAYLOR, JAMES, I, 1615-1698. Born in England. Emigrated to Va., 1635.
Sheriff, New Kent Co., Va., 1690.
Davis, Mrs. Frank V.   Illinois
Metsopulos, Mrs. Peter J.   CT Farms
Robinson, Mrs. Mary Davidson   Oklahoma

TAYLOR, JONATHAN, ——1683. Constable, Springfield, Mass., 1668. Ser–
ved in King Philip's War, in Falls Fight, under Capt. Turner, 1675/6.

TAYLOR, RICHARD I., 1572-1638. 1627-1628 Member of house of Bur-
gesses. VA.
Burns, Mrs. Marie Jones   Blue Grass
Jones, Mrs. William M.   Blue Grass
Thompson, Mrs. James William F., Jr.   Blue Grass

TAYLOR, CAPT. THOMAS, 1600-1657. Born in England. Member of Va.
House of Burgesses, from Warwick Co., 1646.

TAYLOR, WILLIAM, —— 1706. Served in King Philip's War from
Marlborough, Mass., 1675. Name on list of defenders in Dea. Ward's
house.

TELLER, LIEUT. WILLIAM, 1620-1701. Born in Holland. Corporal, Fort
Orange, 1639. Lieutenant, 1669.

TEN EYCK, CORP. CONRAEDT, —— 1687. Born in Holland. Lance
Corporal, 3rd Co., Burgher Corps., New Amsterdam, 1653. Shepen, 1657.
Long, Mrs. Alfred T.   Founders

TENNEY, THOMAS, 1616-1699. Emigrated from Yorkshire, England to
Mass., 1638. A first settler of Rowley, Mass., 1639. Selectman. Constable, 1665-1666.

TERHUNE, LIEUT. JAN ALBERTSE, —— 1696/7. Born in Holland. Lieut.
of Militia, Flatlands, L.I., 1691.

TERRY, RICHARD, 1618-1676. Recorder and Clerk of the Court at Southold,
L.I., 1664-1673. Overseer, 1666.

TERRY, SERGT. SAMUEL, —— ——. Constable, Springfield, Mass., 1669.
Sergeant before 1635.

TERRY, THOMAS, —— 1672. Overseer, Southhold, L.I., 1666.

TERRY, LIEUT. THOMAS, —— 1702. Selectman, Freetown, Mass., 1685,
1686-1690. Lieutenant, 1686. Deputy, 1665, 1689.

TEW, MAJ. HENRY, 1654-1718. Deputy from Newport, R.I., 1680-1696. Captain, 1698.Major, 1699.

TEW, RICHARD, —— 1673. Born in England. Commissioner from Newport, R.I., 1654-1658, 1660, 1663. Assistant, 1657, 1662, 1663,1666,1667.

THACHER, ANTHONY, 1588/9-1667. Born in England. Town Clerk and Treasurer, Weymouth, Mass., 1639-1667. Deputy to Plymouth, 1643-1647, 1651-1654, 1659, 1663, 1665. Member of Council of War, 1658, 1667.

THACHER, COL. JOHN, 1638/9-1713. Born in Marblehead, Mass. Deputy from Yarmouth, 1668-1672, 1674-1681. Member of Council of War, 1681. Assistant to the Governor, 1682-1692. Ensign, 1676. Lieut., 1681. Capt., 1685. Col. after 1693.

THACKER, HENRY, 1632-after 1673. Born in Va. Sheriff, Middlesex Co., Va., 1672.

THATCHER, REV. PETER, 1651-1727. Fellow at Harvard College, 1674-1676. Minister, First Church, Boston, Mass.

THATCHER, REV. THOMAS, 1620-1678. Born in Salisbury, England. Minister, Weymouth, Mass., 1645-1667. First Minister, Old South Church, Boston, Mass.

THAYER, FERDINANDO, 1625-1713. Born in England. Selectman, Mendon, Mass., 1667. Member of Mendon militia, King Philip's War, 1675.

THAYER, RICHARD, 1601-1627 Aug 1695. Braintree, Massachusetts Bay. Soldier in King Philip's War 1675.

THOMAS, CHRISTOPHER, 1600-1670. Born in England. Emigrated to Md. Member of Md. House of Burgesses, 1637-1638.

THOMAS, CAPT. NATHANIEL, SR., 1606-1674. Born in England. Captain, Marshfield, Mass., 1643. Lieutenant, 1643. Ensign, 1640.

THOMAS, CAPT. NATHANIEL, JR., 1643-1718. Born in Marshfield, Mass. Representative, 1672. Captain, King Philip's War, 1675.

THOMAS, THOMAS, 1618-1671. Born in England. Settled in Maryland. Parliamentary Commissioner, 1654, 1657. High Commissioner, Provincial Court, 1656.

THOMAS, WILLIAM, 1574-1651. Born in Wales. One of the founders of Marshfield, Mass. Moderator Town Meeting, 1643. Assistant to Governor, 1642-1651, excepting 1645-1646.

THOMPSON, AMBROSE, 1651-1742. Deputy from Stratford, Conn., 1697.

THOMPSON, JAMES —— ——. A signer of Town Orders of Woburn, Mass. Selectman, Woburn, 1642.

THOMPSON, JOHN, —— 1678. Born in England. Constable, New Haven, Conn., 1673.

THORNDIKE, JOHN, 1603-1668. One of twelve men who settled Ipswich, Mass., 1633. Deputy Sheriff, Essex Co. Delegate, Court of Boston, 1633. Assessor, 1665, 1667.

THORNE, WILLIAM, —— 1688. Born in England. One of the first settlers of Flushing, L.I. Named in the Patent of 1645.

THORNTON, WILLIAM, —— -after 1708. 1677 Vestryman, Petsworth Parish, Goucester, Co., VA.
Pittman, Mrs. Wilmer T.　　　　　　　　　　　　　　　　　　Florida

THOROUGHGOOD, CAPT. ADAM, 1603-1640. Born in Norfblk, England. Emigrated to Va., 1621. Member of Va. House of Burgesses, 1629-1630, 1632. Member of King's Council, 1637. Commissioner, Elizabeth City, 1628.

THORPE, WILLIAM, 1605-1684. Born in England. One of the first settlers of New Haven, Conn., and signed Fundamental Agreement, 1639.
Greason, Mrs. James B., Jr.　　　　　　　　　　　　　　　　Founders

THRALL, WILLIAM, 1606-1679. Soldier in Pequot War from Windsor, Conn., 1637.

THROCKMORTON, JOHN, —— 1687. Of Providence, R.I. Moderator, 1652.
Deputy, 1664, 1674. Treasurer, 1677.
Giulvezan, Mrs. Isabel Stebbins   Missouri

THURSTON, DANIEL, —— 1693. Served in King Philip's War, from
Newbury, Mass., 1675/6.

THURSTON, EDWARD, 1617-1707. Commissioner, Newport, R.I., 1663.
Deputy, 1667, 1671-1674. 1680-1686. Assistant to Governor, 1675, 1686,
1690, 1691.

TIBBALS, SERGT. THOMAS, 1615-1703. Served in Pequot War, 1637.
Sergt., Milford, Conn. Train Band, 1665.

TICKNOR, SERGT. WILLIAM, ————. Served in King Philip's War, Mass.,
1675/6.

TILDEN, ELDER NATHANIEL, 1583-1641. Born in England. Ruling Elder,
First Church, Scituate, Mass., 1634.

TILLEY, ELIZABETH, 1607-1687. Passenger on "Mayflower," 1620.
Lyon, Mrs. William L.   California

TILLEY, JOHN, —— 1621. Born in England. Passenger on the "Mayflower,"
1620.

TILLEY, MRS. JOHN, —— 1621. Passenger on the "Mayflower," 1620.

TILLINGHAST, ELDER PARDON, 1622-1718. Born in England, died in R.I.
Deputy, six times, from 1672. Town Council, R.I., many years from
1688.

TINDALL, THOMAS, circa 1663-1713. 1692 Constable Nottingham
Township, West Jersey. Overseer 1699 Notthingham Township.
Riddle, Mrs. William McKinley   Oklahoma

TINGLE (TINGLEY), PALMER, 1614 ——. Served in Pequot War, 1637.
Received a grant of land for services, 1639.
Adams, Mrs. Paul Augustus   Prairie State

TINKER, JOHN, —— 1662. New London, CT. Deputy to CT Legislature
1660. Judge 1660-1661.
Allie, Mrs. Richard J.   Tejas

TIPLADY, CAPT. JOHN, —— 1689. Of Virginia, Church Warden, 1661.
Justice, York Co., Va., 1677.
Crowder, Mrs. Roy Hester   North Carolina

TISDALE, JOHN, —— 1675. Deputy from Taunton, 1674. Constable, 1659.
Killed in King Philip's War.

TISDALE, CORP. JOSEPH, 1656-1721/2. Served in King William's War,
Taunton, Mass., 1690.

TITUS, CAPT. CONTENT, 1643-1730. Captain of Foot, Newtowne, Queens
Co., N.Y., 1689. Commissioner of Town Court, 1686, 1690. Overseer,
1679-1681. Supervisor, 1686.

TITUS, ROBERT, 1600——. Born in England. Commissioner from Rehoboth,
Mass., 1648/9, 1650, 1654.
Walter, Mrs. Charles F., IV   CT Farms

TODD, JOHN, —— 1689/90. Representative to General Court from Rowley,
Mass., 1664, 1686. Town officer.

TODD, CAPT. THOMAS, SR., 1619-1677. Born in England. Emigrated to Va.,
circa 1631. Resided Gloucester Co., Va. and Baltimore Co., Md. Burgess
for Baltimore Co., Md., 1674-1675.
Buck, Mrs. James Marshall   Blue Grass
Kincaid, Mrs. Dennis Gill   Blue Grass
Roberts, Mrs. Richard Lindsay   Blue Grass

TOLLE, ROGER, circa 1643-1709. Born in England. Constable, St. Mary's
Co., Md., 1693.

TOLMAN, JOHN, 1632-1725. Selectman, Dorchester, Mass., 1683, 1694, 1695.

TOMASSEN, JUREAEN, —— 1695. Arrived Bergen, N.J., 1664. Member of
Acquackanock Patent syndicate (in present Passaic Co., N.J.), 1684/5.

TOMPSON, REV. WILLIAM, 1598-1666. Ordained, Braintree, Mass., 1639.

TOOGOOD, NATHANIEL, —— 1703. A first settler of Swansea, Mass., 1669.

TOOL (TOLL), JOHN, —— 1690. Born in England. Original grantee and a
First Settler, of Sudbury Plantation, 1638.

TOPPAN, ABRAHAM, 1606-1672. Born in England. Selectman, Newbury,
Mass., 1638, 1647, 1666, 1667.

TOPPAN, LIEUT. JACOB, 1645-1717. Ensign of Militia, (later Lieut.), Newbury, Mass., 1690.

TOPPING, CAPT. ELNATHAN, 1640-1705. Captain, Southampton, L.I., 23 June 1691.

TORREY, CAPT. WILLIAM, 1608-1691. Member of Ancient and Honorable Artillery Co., 1641. Court Clerk, Weymouth, Mass., 1650. Selectman, Capt. of Weymouth Train Band, 1655. Clerk of Deputies, 1648-1658, 1661-1666. Representative, 1642.
Barber, Mrs. Robert C.   Prairie State
McShane, Mrs. Raymond   Prairie State

TOURNEUR, CORP. DANIEL, 1626-1673. Corporal of Militia, Flatlands, L.I., 1654. Schepen, Harlem, N.Y., 1660, 1661, 1663. Magistrate, 1660-1673. Deacon, First Church, Harlem, 1661-1673. Delegate to General Assembly, in New Amsterdam, 1664. Deputy Sheriff, 1665-1670. Overseer, 1666, 1671.

TOWER, JEREMIAH, SR., 1645/6-1676. One of four brothers, who, with their father, defended his Garrison House on outskirts of Hingham, MA.
Weisgerber, Miss Virginia Edna   Quivira

TOWER, JOHN, 17 May 1608-13 Feb 1701/2. Hingham, MA. 1638 Hingham Military. 1675/6 Owner and defender of a Garrison House.
Christie, Mrs. Bruce A.   Michigan
Doud, Mrs. Howard R.   Michigan

TOWNE, JACOB, 11 Mar 1632-27 Nov 1657. Selectman Topsfield, Massachusetts Bay ca. 1678-79, 1682-1684.
Dietze, Miss Mary Fitzsimons   Louisiana

TOWNSEND, RICHARD, —— 1670. Born in England. Commissioner, Warwick, R.I., 1652-1659. From Oyster Bay, L.I., 1661.

TRACY, LIEUT. THOMAS, —— 1685. Lieut. of New London Co., Conn. Dragoons, 1673. Deputy, 1662.

TRACY, STEPHEN, —— 1654. Constable, Duxbury, Mass., 1639.
Weaver, Mrs. John F., Sr.   Michigan

TRAPHAGEN, WILLEM JANZEN, ————. Born in Holland. A First Settler of Bushwick, L.I., 1661.

TREADWAY, NATHANIEL, —— 1689. Born in England. Selectman, Watertown, Mass., 1653.

TREADWELL, NATHANIEL, 1637-1726/7. Selectman, Ipswich, Mass., 1687.

TREAT, RICHARD, 1584-1669. Born in England. Deputy from Wethersfield, Conn., 1644-1657. Assistant Magistrate, 1658-1664. Member Governor Winthrop's Council, 1663-1664. One of Patentees named in royal charter for Conn., 1662.

Blakely, Mrs. Jonathan   CT Farms
Greason, Mrs. James B., Jr.   Founders
La Tarte, Mrs. Robert L.   Michigan

TREAT, GOV. ROBERT, 1624-1710. Born in England. Deputy from Milford, Conn., 1653-1656, 1658. Magistrate, New Haven Colony, 1659-1663. Major, commanding at battles Hadley and Springfield, Commander-in-Chief of Conn. Troops, 1675. Commissioner for United Colonies, 1681, 1682, 1684. Deputy to Governor, 1676-1682, 1698-1699. Governor, 1683-1687, 1689-1698.

La Tarte, Mrs. Robert L.   Michigan

TRIPP, JOHN, 1610-1678. Born in England. Assistant to Governor of R.I., 1670, 1673-1675. Deputy from Portsmouth, R.I., 1648-1654, 1655, 1658, 1666-1672.

TRIPP, JOSEPH, 1644-1718. Deputy from Dartmouth, Mass. to General Court, 1685.

TRIPP, PELEG, 1641-1714. Town Council, Portsmouth, R.I., 1677- 1679, 1683. Deputy, 1680-1681, 1686.

TROWBRIDGE, JAMES 1636-22 May 1717. Dorchester, Massachusetts Bay. Soldier in King Philip's War. Selectman 1679.

Finenco, Mrs. John, Jr.   Florida
Nichols, Miss Rebecca Ann   Tennessee

TUBBS, WILLIAM, circa 1617-1688. Member of Myles Standish's Military Co., 1637. Surveyor of Highways, 1678.

TUCKER, HENRY, 1619-1694. Born in England. One of first settlers of Dartmouth, Mass.

TUCKER, ROBERT, 1604-1682. Born in England. Deputy from Gloucester, Mass., 1652; from Milton, 1669, 1680, 1681.

TURNER, CAPT. NATHANIEL, —— 1647. Born in England. Captain, Salem, Mass., 1634. In Pequot War, Block Island, 1636. Magistrate, New Haven, Conn., 1639-1643. Governor's Assistant, 1639. Deputy from Saugus, 1634-1636. Deputy to New Haven Colony, 1643-1645, Commissioner for United Colonies, 1643. Captain and Chief Military Officer, New Haven Colony, 1640.
Nelson, Mrs. Lawrence T.   Tejas

TURNER, ROBERT, 1635-1700. Commissioner, Pa., 1688. Registrar General, 1690. Receiver General, 1693. Councillor, 1686-1693.

TUTHILL, HENRY, 1612-1650. Born in England. Constable, Hingham, Mass., 1640.

TUTHILL, JOHN, 1635-1717. Commissioner, Southold, L.I., 1686, 1691.

TUTHILL, JOHN, 1658-1754. Member Assembly, Southold, L.I., 1693-1698.

TUTTLE, JOHN, 1596-1656. Deputy to General Assembly, 1644. Member of Ancient and Honorable Artillery Co., Mass., 1644.

TUTTLE, WILLIAM, 1609-1673. Born in England. Constable, New Haven, Conn., 1666-1667.

TYSON, CORNELIUS, 1652-1716. A Founder of Germantown, Province of Pa., 1684.
Watson, Mrs. Joseph A., Jr.   Michigan

TYSON, REGNIER, 1659-1745. Born in Rhineland, died at Abington, Pa. A Founder of Germantown, Pa., 1683. Burgess of Germantown, 1692.

UMSTAT, HANS PETER, 1655-1694. A Founder of Germantown, Province of Pa., 1685.

UNDERHILL, CAPT. JOHN, 1597-1672. Deputy to General Court, Boston, 1634. Served in Pequot War, 1636/7. Capt. of Mass. Troops. Member of Ancient and Honorable Artillery Co., 1637. Governor of Dover and Exeter, N.H., 1641. One of eight men to govern at New Amsterdam, 1645. Commander-in-Chief of Land Forces, Providence Plantations, 1653. Delegate to Hempstead, L.I., 1665.

UNDERWOOD, WILLIAM, —— 1697. Chosen to order the affairs of Chelmsford, Mass., 1654.

UNDERWOOD, COL. WILLIAM, —— 1662. Born in Isle of Wight Co., Va. Died in Rappahannock Co., Va. Burgess for Lancaster Co. Va., 1652. Justice for Rappahannock Co., 1656.

UPDIKE, GILBERT, baptized 1605 ——. Commissary at Fort Good Hope, 1638-1639, 1640. Commander of Fort Good Hope, 1647.
Dawson, Mrs. W. N.   Tejas

UPHAM, DEA. JOHN, —— ——. Emigrated from England to Plymouth, Mass. Representative, for six sessions. Moved to Malden, Mass. Deacon, First Church, 1659-1681. Moderator, Malden, 1680.

USHER, HEZEKIAH, 1615-1676. Member of Ancient and Honorable Artillery Co., 1638. Ensign, 1664. Constable, 1651. Selectman, Boston, 1659-1676. Deputy to General Court from Billerica, 1671, 1672, 1673.

VALENTINE, RICHARD, 1620-1684. Born in England. Selectman, Hempstead, L.I., 1659. Constable, 1679.
Eberlin, Mrs. Harry W.   Founders
Starkie, Mrs. Robert A.   Founders

VAN ARSDALEN, ELDER SYMOND JANSE, 1629-1710. Magistrate, Flatlands, L.I., 1661, 1686. Elder in Dutch Church, 1693.

VAN BREVOORT, JAN HENDRICKSZEN, —— 1714. Overseer, Harlem, 1678, 1679.

VAN BRUGH, CAPT. JOHANNES PIETERSE, 1624-1697. Born in Holland. Settled in New Amsterdam. Corporal, Blue Flag Co., 1652-1653. Member Board of Schepens, 1655-1656, 1659, 1661- 1662. Burgomaster, 1656, 1673-1674. Provincial Agent to Holland, 1663. Captain, New Amsterdam, 1668; at New Orange, 1673-1674. Commissioner to the Dutch, 1673.
Davis, Mrs. Frank V.   Illinois

VAN BRUNT, CORNELIS RUTGERSZ, —— 1748. Member, N.Y. Assembly, 1698 and later.

VAN BRUNT, RUTGER, JOOSTEN, 1618-1688. Emigrated from Netherlands, 1653. Settled in New Utrecht, L.I., 1657. Member of Court of Schepens, 1661-1665. After English Conquest, became principal Magistrate, 1678-1681, 1685.

VAN CLEEF, JAN, 1628——. Came from Holland to New Utrecht, L.I., 1653. Constable, 1678.

VAN CORTLANDT, COL. OLOFF STEVENSEN, circa 1600-1686. Col. of Burger Corps, New Amsterdam, 1649. Special Commander of Indian affairs under Dutch Rule, 1645. Commander to treat with English Forces, 1664. Member of Governor's Council, 1674.

VAN COWENHOVEN, GERRIT WOLFERTSE, 1610-1645. Came from Holland, 1630, and settled in Flatlands, L.I. One of eight men representing the people, 1643. Magistrate, 1644.

VAN COUVENHOVEN, WOLFERTE GERRITSE, 1588-1661. Born in Holland. Died in New Amsterdam, N.Y. Commissioner to Holland, 1653. Burgher of New Amsterdam.
Wallen, Mrs. Lloyd Farwell   Prairie State

VANDER BECK, PAULUS, circa 1623-1680. Surgeon in the employ of the Dutch West India Co., when he came to New Amsterdam, circa 1643. Member Convention, 1653. Great Burgher, 1657. Patentee of the Brooklyn Patent, 1677.
Andersen, Mrs. Thor Bjorn   CT Farms
Hardwick, Mrs. Robert Duncan   CT Farms

VANDERBEECK, REM JANSEN, —— 1681. Magistrate, Brooklyn, N.Y., 1673.

VANDERBILT, JANS AERTSZEN, —— ——. Overseer, Flatbush, L.I., 1683.

VAN DER BOGART, DR. HARMEN MYNDERTSE, 1612-1647/8. Appointed Commissary, Fort Orange, 1637.
Ager, Mrs. Snowden   Florida

VAN DER GRIFT, JACOB LEENDERTSEN, —— before 1697. Born in Holland. Elected Schepen, Kings Co., N.Y., 1673.

VANDER HEYDEN, JACOB, —— ——. Of Tyssen, New Amsterdam. New Amsterdam Burgher Corps., 1653.

VANDERMARK, THOMAS, 1643-1724. Took part in Mutiny of Esopus, 1667. Served in Foot Co., Ulster Co., N.Y., 1687.

VANDERVEER, CORNELIS JANSE, —— ——. Emigrated from Holland, 1659. Settled in Flatbush, L.I. Magistrate, 1678, 1680.

VANDER VLEIT, DIRCK JANSEN, —— 1680. Magistrate, Flatbush, L.I., 1679, 1680.

VANDERVOORT, MICHAEL PAULUS, circa 1610/19-1692. "Chirur" or Surgeon, New Amsterdam (Brooklyn), N.Y., 1645.
Russ, Mrs. Roland G., Jr.   Tejas

VAN DEVER, JACOB, —— ——. Sergt. in garrison at Ft. Wilmington, Del., 1660.
Finley, Mrs. John Kent   Pennsylvania
Roebling, Mrs. Seigfried   Pennsylvania

VAN DITMARSEN, JAN JANSEN, 1643 ——. Of Flatbush, L.I., 1681. Constable, 1687-1688.

VAN DUYN, CORNELIS GERRETSE, 1644-1752. Justice of the Peace, Kings Co., 1689.

VAN DUYN, GERRET CORNELISE, —— 1706. Magistrate, New Utrecht, 1687, 1688. Justice of the Peace, 1689, 1690.

VAN DYCK, FRANZ CLAESEN, —— 1658. School Teacher, New Amsterdam, before 1655.

VAN DYCK, ENS. HENDRICK, —— 1687/8. Born in Holland. Ensign, 1642. Schoutfiscal, New Amsterdam, 1647-1652. Member of Stuyvesant's Council, 1646-1652.

VAN DYCK, CAPT. JAN JANZE, circa 1652-1736. Came from Holland, 1652. Settled in New Utrecht, L.I. Magistrate, 1679. Took oath of allegiance, 1687. Lieutenant, 1689. Captain.

VAN DYCK, JAN THOMASSE, —— before 1678. Came from Holland, 1652. Settled in New Utrecht, L.I. Magistrate, 1651661. Appointed Schepen by Governor Colve, 1673.

VAN EPS, LIEUT. JOHANNES, —— 1690. Magistrate, Schenectady, N.Y., 1672, 1676. Lieutenant, 1685.

VAN HORN, CHRISTIAN, 1651-1726. Of New York. Building Inspector and Referee, 1653. Fire Warden, 1656. Arbitrator for courts of New Amsterdam and Burghomaster.

VAN HORN, JAN CORNELIS, —— ——. Teacher, New Amsterdam, 1648-1650.
Fenlon, Mrs. Edward H.   Michigan

VAN HOUTEN, ROELOF CORNELISSEN, 1628-1672. Served as Soldier, Amersfoort, L.I., 1648.

O'Daniel, Miss Meghan Allen	Illinois
Saville, Mrs. Edgar S.	Illinois

VAN KEUREN, CAPT. MATHYS MATTHYSEN, —— ——. Of New York. Ensign, New Paltz, 1670. Captain, Foot Company, Kingston, and New Paltz, 1685-1689.

Collins, Mrs. John A.	Michigan
Long, Mrs. Alfred T.	Founders
Long-Reed, Mrs. Suzanne	Founders

VAN KOUWENHOVEN, WILLEM GERRETSE, 1636-circa 1728. Magistrate, Brooklyn, N.Y., 1661, 1662, 1664. Schepen, Brooklyn, 1662. Deacon, Dutch Reformed Church, Brooklyn, N.Y., 1663.

Barnett, Mrs. Charles Crippen, Jr.	Missouri

VAN METEREN, DEA. KRYN JANSEN, —— 1719. Born in Holland. Deacon, Dutch Church, New Utrecht, L.I., 1699.

VAN METEREN, JAN JOOSTEN, —— ——. New York. Oath of Allegiance 26 Oct 1664. Magistrate 6 June 1673.

Frantz, Mrs. Leonard Edwin	Florida

VAN NESS, CAPT. CORNELIUS, —— ——. Captain, 1663. Councillor, 1658, 1660, 1661, 1663, 1664. Acting Indian Commissioner under Dutch Rule, as Magistrate, Fort Orange, 1665, 1666.

VAN NUYSE, AUCKE JANSEN, —— 1694. Came from Holland to Flatbush, L.I., 1651. Magistrate, 1673. Deputy, 1674.

VAN RENSSELAER, CAPT. JEREMIAS, 1630-1674. Director of Colony of Rensselaerwyck, 1658. Chief of the Delegates to the Mohawks, 1659. Magistrate, Fort Orange, 1659, 1660, 1663, 1665. Commissioner of Indian Affairs under Dutch rule, 1659, 1663, 1665, 1666. Captain of Troop of Horse, 1670.

VAN SCHAICK, CAPT. ADRIAEN CORNELISZEN, 1642-1700. Common Councilman of New York, 1684. Assistant Alderman, 1687. Captain of Foot, 1689.

VAN SCHOENDERWOERT, RUTGER JACOBSEN, —— 1711. Acting Indian Commissioner as Magistrate at Fort Orange, 1655, 1656, 1660, 1661.

VAN SLICHTENHORST, BRANT ARENTSE, —— 1668. Chief Magistrate, Rensselaerwyck, N.Y., 1648-1652.

VAN STELTYN, EVERT PELS, —— after 1688. One of the first Schepens of Wyltwick, 1661. Overseer, Esopus, 1667.
Long, Mrs. Alfred T.   Founders

VAN SWEARINGEN, GERRETT, 1636-1698. Emigrated from Holland to Del., thence to Md. Councillor at Amstel on Delaware, 1659. Commissioner to Holland, 1651-1652, Council Member, 1694. Sheriff, St. Mary's Co., Md., 1696-1697.

VAN TEXEL (TASSEL), ELDER CORNELISE, —— after 1720. Deacon and Elder in Dutch Church, Tarrytown, N.Y., 1697

VAN TEXEL (TASSEL), DEA. JACOB, 1676-after 1720. Deacon, Dutch Church, Tarrytown, N.Y., 1697.

VAN TEXEL (TASSEL), ELDER JAN CORNELISE, circa 1625-1704. Deacon and Elder in Dutch Church, Tarrytown, N.Y., 1697.

VAN VECHTEN, CAPT. DIRCK TEUNISE, 1634-1702. Capt. of Militia, Albany, N.Y., 1686-1689. Justice of the Peace, 1691, 1693, 1699.

VAN VLECK (VLEECK), CAPT. ISAAC, 1645-before 1695. Granted Commission as Captain, 1684. Alderman, City of New York, 1684, 1686, 1693, 1694.

VAN VOORHEES, ENS. ALBERT COERTE, —— circa 1748. Appointed Ensign of Foot Co., Gravesend, 2 Jan. 1691.

VAN VOORHEES, ELDER ALBERT STEVENSE, 1654-after 1695. Elder in the Reformed Dutch Church, Hackensack, N.J., 1686. Elder in 16 Apr. 1695.

VAN VOORHEES, CAPT. COERTE STEVENSE, 1637-1702. Came from Holland, 1660. Settled in Flatlands, L.I., 1664. Magistrate, 1664-1673. Deputy, 1664, 1674. Captain, 1689.

VAN VOORHEES, LUCAS STEVENSE, 1650-1713. Magistrate, Flatlands, L.I., 1680.

VAN VOORHEES, ELDER STEVEN COERTE, 1600-1684. Elder of Flatlands Dutch Church. Magistrate, Amersfoort, L.I., 1664.

VAN WIE, HENDRICK GERRITSEE, —— circa 1691. Born in Holland, died in Albany Co., N.Y. Volunteer in Expedition to Canada under Peter Schuyler, 1690.

VAN WINKELEN, JACOB WALING, —— 1657. Member of Representative body of New Netherlands known as the Twelve Men, 1641.

VAN WOERT, ELDER JOCHEM WOUTERSE, 1637-1699. Elder in Tarrytown, N.Y., Dutch Church, 1699.

VAN WYCK, CORNELIUS BAREND, circa 1630-1713. Constable, Flatbush, L.I., 1675.
Corder, Miss Lois B.   Founders

VASSALL, WILLIAM, 1592/3-1655. Came from England to assist Governor, Mass. Bay Co., 1629-1630. Settled in Roxbury, 1636. Scituate, 1642. Member Council War, 1642.

VAUGHAN, GEORGE, 1650-1704. Born in Newport, R.I. Deputy from East Greenwich, R.I., 1684, 1698, 1699.

VEEDER, SIMON VOLKERTSE, 1624-after 1696/7. Born in Holland. A Founder and first settler of Schenectady, N.Y., 1662.

VEGHTE, GERRIT CLAESEN, 1656-1732/3. Member of Colonial Assembly, Richmond Co., N.Y., 1699.

VEGHTE, HENDRICK CLAESEN, —— 1716. Commissioner, Brooklyn, 1690-1699.

VEITCH (VIETCH), JAMES, 1628-1685. Born in Scotland; settled in Md., 1651. Sheriff of Patuxent, St. Marie's and Potomac, Md., 1652-1657.
Alvey, Mrs. Homer Watson   Prairie State
Bonifacius, Mrs. Arthus W.   Illinois
Morganthaler, Mrs. Michael L.   Illinois
Wood, Mrs. Neil V.   Illinois

VER KERK, JAN JANSE, —— 1688. Came from Holland To New Utrecht, L.I., 1663. Magistrate, 1679, 1684.

VERMILYE, ISAAC, 1601-1676. Born in England. Settled in New Amsterdam, 1663. Commanded Harlaem Volunteers, Esopus, 1663. Magistrate, Harlaem, N.Y., 1666.

VERMILYE, JOHANNES, 1632-1696. Born in Holland. Settled in New Amsterdam, 1663. Court messenger, 1655. Constable, 1667. Magistrate, 1670. Member of Governor's Council, 1690.

VERNON, RANDALL, 1640-1725. Member of the Assembly, Chester Co., Pa., 1687. Justice of Peace, Chester Co., Pa., 1692.

VINCENT, JOHN, —— ——. Deputy from Sandwich, Mass., 1639-1645.

VIVION, JOHN, 1655-1705. Constable, Middlesex Co., Va., 1681.

VOLKERTSE, DIRK, 1667-1754. Born at Bostwyck, L.I., N.Y.; died in Somerset Co., N.J. Ensign of Foot, Bushwick, Kings Co., N.Y., 1689.

VOSE, ROBERT, circa 1599-1683. Selectman, Milton, Mass., 1669, 1677. Supervisor of Highways, 1657.
Plett, Miss Norma Vose   Founders

VOWLES, RICHARD, —— ——. Of Hastings, Conn. Deputy for Hastings to Conn. Legislature, 1655. Deputy for Rye, 1668.

VREELAND, CORNELIS, 1660-1727. One of the Patentees of Acquackanock, N.J., 1684.

VREELAND, MICHAEL JANSEN, —— 1663. Fought in Indian uprising, Sept. 1655. One of the Incorporators, Bergen, N.J., 1661, and First Magistrate of the First Court of Justice erected within the limits of the present State of N.J. Represented Pavonia, N.J. in the Council of Nine, New Amsterdam, 1647, 1649, 1650.

VROOMAN, HENDRICK MESSE, —— 1690. Killed in defense of Schenectady, N.Y.

WADE, CAPT. JONATHAN, 1614-1683. Selectman, 1662. Capt. of the Three County Troop (Cavalry), Mass., 1677. Deputy, Poswich, 1681.

WAINRIGHT, CORP. FRANCIS,—— 1692. Born in England, died at Salem, Mass. Served in Pequot War, 1637; King Philip's War, 1675. Corporal, 1664.

WAITE, JOHN, 1618-1693. Town Clerk, Malden, Mass., 1662. Deputy to General Court, 1666-1684. Member of Ancient and Honorable Artillery Co., 1673-1674.
Davis, Mrs. Frank V.   Illinois
Randazzo, Mrs. Marco Antonio   Illinois

WAITE, SAMUEL, —— 1676/7. Interpreter, Narragansett, 1656.

WAITE, THOMAS, 1615-1669. Born in England. Constable at Portsmouth, R.I., 1658, 1663.

WAKEMAN, JOHN, —— 1661. Born in England. Settled in New Haven Colony, Conn. Treasurer, 1600-1665. Deputy, 1641-1647, 1655-1660. Signed New Haven Compact, 1639.

WALCOTT, CAPT. JONATHAN, 1639-1699. Commander-Captain, Salem, Mass., 1689.

WALDO, DEA. CORNELIUS, 1625-1700. Born in Ipswich, Mass. Served in King Philip's War, Chelmsford, Mass., 1675. Selectman, 1676. Deacon. Representative to General Court, 1673, 1674.
Ploog, Mrs. Larry   Prairie State
Weaver, Mrs. John F., Sr.   Michigan

WALDO, JOHN, 1659-1700. Served in King Philip's War, 1675/6. Representative, Dunstable, Mass., 1689.
Weaver, Mrs. John F., Sr.   Michigan

WALDRON, CORP. BARENT, 1655-1740. Born in New Amsterdam, Corporal, Harlem, 1673.

WALDRON, DANIEL, 1650 ——. Born in Holland. Member of City Guards against Leister, Amsterdam, N.Y.

WALDRON, JOSEPH, —— 1663. Born in Holland. Butler for the Garrison and had charge of magazine of the West India Co., New Amsterdam, N.Y.

WALDRON, RESOLVED, 1610-1690. Born in Holland. Deputy Sheriff, New Amsterdam, 1658. Constable, Harlem, 1665.

WALKER, EDWARD, 1663-1735. Born in Charlestown, Mass. Served in King Philip's War, 1675/6.

WALKER, JOHN, —— 1671. One of the Founders of the Historic Charter Colony, Portsmouth, R.I., 1638.

WALKER, LIEUT. COL. JOHN, —— 1671. Burgess, Warwick, Co., Va., 1644, 1646, 1649. Lieut. Col. and Councillor, Gloucester Co., Va., 1657-1658.

WALKER, DEA. PHILIP, —— 1679. Deputy from Rehoboth, Mass., 1669.

WALKER, COL. SAMUEL, 1653-1712. In King Philip's War, 1675. Lieutenant, Captain and Colonel in the Militia.

WALKER, WIDOW, —— 1646. A Founder of Rehoboth, Mass., 1643.

WALL, JARRETT, —— ——. Of Monmouth, N.J. Treasurer of Town, 1697. Deacon Baptist Church, Middleton, N.J.

WALL, WALTER, —— ——. Of New Jersey. Arrived in Colonies, 1640. Associate member of Monmouth, Pat., 1670. A Founder of Old Middletown, N.J., 1670.

WALLACE, REV. JAMES —— ——. Born in Scotland; died in Elizabeth City Co., Va. Minister and Physician, 1692-1699.

WALLACE (WALLIS), MATTHEW, —— ——. Maryland. 22 Nov 1692 Member of Council
Whitten, Mrs. James Malcolm   Florida

WALLER, COL. JOHN, 1670/3-1753/4. Born in England, settled in Spotsylvania Co., Va., circa 1689. Sheriff, King and Queen Co., Va., 1699. Justice of Peace, 1698, 1699.
Davis, Mrs. Betty Lee Manley   Illinois
Johnson, Mrs. Hellen M. Manley   Illinois
Korkosz, Mrs. Elizabeth A. Johnson   Illinois
Sherman, Mrs. Winthrop C.   Tejas
Wollesen, Mrs. James B.   Illinois

WALLING, THOMAS, —— 1674. Of Rhode Island. Townsman, Narragansett, R.I., 1655. Land Commissioner, 1657.
Herod, Miss Kelly Lyn   Tejas

WALLIS, NICHOLAS, 1632-1710/11. Representative to General Court, from Ipswich, Mass., 1691.

WALTON, SHADRACK, 1658-1741. Ensign, New Castle, N.H.: Capt., Fort William and Mary, before 1694. Judge of Court of Common Pleas, 1695-1698. Judge of Supreme Court, 1698-1699. Selectman, Portsmouth, 1688-1692.
Davis, Mrs. Frank V.   Illinois

WARD, ANDREW, 1597-1659. Born in England. Governing Magistrate, New Haven Colony, 1646. Deputy from Wethersfield, Conn., 1636-1639, 1648-1656; from Stamford, Conn., 1643-1644.
Hofmeister, Mrs. George Carl   Louisana

WARD, ENS. JOHN, 1626-1708. Born in England. Deputy from Newton, Mass., 1692-1694, 1696, 1698. Ensign, Newton Co., 1689.

WARD, LIEUT. JOHN, SR., 1625-1694. Signed the Fundamental Agreement, Newark, N.J., 1666. Sergeant, before 1673. Lieutenant, 1673. Deputy to New Jersey Assembly, 1680.

WARD, DR. WILLIAM, 1630-1675. Of Fairfield, Conn. Surgeon in King Philip's War, 1675, and was killed in service.

WARD, DEA. WILLIAM, 1597-1687. Chairman of Selectmen, Sudbury, Mass., 1661-1665. Deputy, 1643, 1644; from Marlborough, 1666. Deacon, 1666. Served in King Philip's War, 1675. Magistrate, Sudbury, 1645, 1646.

WARDE, ANDREW, 1645/7-1690. Watertown, MA. Commissioner "to govern" Wethersfield, CT.
Brady, Mrs. Joseph L.   California

WARDELL, UZALL, 1639-1732. Served in King Philip's War, 1675-1676. First settler, Bristol, R.I., 1681.

WARDELL, WILLIAM, 1604-1693. One of first settlers, Shawmut, R.I., 1642. Deputy, 1664, 1666.

WARHAM, REV. JOHN, —— 1670. Minister at Dorchester, Mass., 1630; at Windsor, Conn., 1636-1670.

WARNER, ANDREW, —— 1684. Born in England. Sent by Governor Winthrop to regulate affairs in Conn., 1635-1636. Active in Indian uprising, 1658.

WARNER, COL. AUGUSTINE, I, 1610-1674. Burgess, from York Co., Va., 1652; from Gloucester Co., 1658. Member of the Council, 1659-1674.
Rauch, Mrs. Bernard E., Jr.   Missouri

WARNER, COL. AUGUSTINE, II, 1642-1681. Born in Va. Speaker of the House of Burgesses, 1675-1677.

WARNER, WILLIAM, —— before 1648. One of the first settlers of Ipswich, Mass., 1636.

WARREN, JACOB, 1642-1722. Selectman, Chelmsford, Mass., 1683. Surveyor, 1686. Member of Garrison, West Regiment in Middlesex, at Chelmsford, Mass., 16 Mar. 1692.
Browder, Mrs. E. Jefferson   CT Farms

WARREN, JOHN, 1585-1667. On committee to lay out highways, 1635.
Selectman, 1636-1640.
Gary, Mrs. Dan Carmack   Tennessee

WARREN, JOHN, —— 1732. Constable, Burlington County, N.J., 1696.

WARREN, RICHARD, 1590-1628. Came from England to Plymouth, Mass.,
in the "Mayflower," 1620. Twelfth signer of the Compact.
Amos, Mrs. Frederick C.   Quivira
Bush, Mrs. Ralph Royal   CT Farms
Donchian, Mrs. Richard D.   Florida
Miner, Mrs. Ross H.   Founders
O'Kneel, Mrs. George Wellington   Rhode Island

WARREN, THOMAS, 1624-1670. Emigrated from Kent Co., England to
Surry Co., Va. Member, House of Burgesses, James City Co., Va., 1644;
Surry Co., Va., 1658, 1666.
Bourne, Mrs. Robert Gordon   North Carolina
Davis, Mrs. David   North Carolina
Guzak, Mrs. Joseph Paul   Michigan

WARRINER, CORP. JOSEPH, 1644/5-1697. Corporal, King Philip's War,
Enfield, Conn., 1675.

WARRINER, WILLIAM, —— 1676. Selectman, Springfield, Mass., 1658-
1659. Surveyor, 1646, 1660, 1670. Constable, 1656, 1665, 1672,1673.

WASHBURN, JOHN, 1585-1676. Born in England. First Secretary of Mass.
Bay Colony, Duxbury. Member of Capt. Myles Standish Military Co.,
1643. Served in Expedition against the Indians, 1645.

WASHBURN (WASHBURNE), WILLIAM, —— 1659. Born in England.
Deputy from Hempstead, L.I., to Convention in New Amsterdam, 1653,
to New Haven, 1654.
Long, Mrs. Alfred T.   Founders

WASHINGTON, COL. JOHN, 1636-1677. Member of House of Burgesses,
Westmoreland Co., Va., 1666-1672, 1675-1677. Commander of Va.
Troops against the Susquehannahs, 1675.
Alexander, Mrs. James Atwell   North Carolina
Gibson, Mrs. Hubert Lynn   Tejas
Leach, Mrs. Hal Thomas   North Carolina
Linney, Mrs. Chauncey Depew   North Carolina
McLain, Mrs. Harry Phillip   North Carolina
Sparks, Mrs. Laurence   Tejas
St. Clair, Mrs. Holland   North Carolina

WATERBURY, JOHN, 1615-1658. Deputy from Stamford, Conn., 1657.

WATERMAN, JOSEPH, 1643-1712. Constable, Marshfield, Mass., 1681.

WATERMAN, RICHARD, —— 1673. Born in England. Commissioner, Providence, R.I., 1655, 1656, 1658.

WATERMAN, ROBERT, —— 1652. Representative, Marshfield, Mass., 1644-1649.

WATERMAN, SERGT. THOMAS, 1668-1708. Deputy to General Court for Norwich, Conn., 1685.

WATSON, CAPT. GEORGE, 1602/3-1689. Member of Plymouth Militia. Capt. of a ship in expedition against the Dutch, 1653.

WATSON, JOHN, —— 1650. Surveyor of Highways, Hartford, Conn., 1647.

WATSON, MATTHEW, —— 1703. Constable, Chesterfield, N.J., 1693, 1695, 1697.

WEAVER, CLEMENT, SR., 1590-1683. Born in England. Representative to General court from Newport, R.I., 1678.

WEBSTER, GOV. JOHN, 1590-1661. Born in England. Resided in the Colonies of Mass. and Conn. 1635-1661. One of the Committee who sat with Court of Magistrates. Magistrate, 1637. Assistant, 1639-1659. Commissioner of the United Colonies, 1654. Dep. Governor, 1655. Governor of Conn., 1656.

Barrick, Mrs. William H.	Florida
Bland, Mrs. Elmer F., Jr.	Illinois
Hamm, Mrs. James J.	Illinois
Johnson, Mrs. David Scott	Ohio
Macey, Mrs. J. Hugh	Ohio
Morse, Mrs. Frederick Tracy	Jamestown Virginia

WEBSTER, JOHN, —— 1646. Born in England. Clerk of Bonds, Ipswich, Mass., 1642.

WEED, LIEUT. JOHN, 1627-1689. One of the original settlers of Amesbury, Mass., 1654. Trustee for the town 1683, 1684. Lieutenant, King Philip's War, 1676.

WEEKES (WICKES), FRANCIS, 1616-1687. Born in England. One of the thirteen original proprietors and settlers of Providence Plantation, 1639.

WELD, JOHN, 1623-1691. Born in England, died at Roxbury, Mass. Served in King Philip's War, at Brookfield and Mendon, Mass., 1675/6.

WELD, CAP'T. JOSEPH, 1595-1646. Born in England. Settled in Roxbury, Mass., 1635. One of the founders, Ancient and Honorable Artillery Co., 1637. Ensign, 1638. Captain, Deputy, 1636-1638,1641,1643.
Greason, Mrs. James B., Jr.   Founders

WELD, REV. THOMAS, 1595-1661. Born in England; died in Roxbury, Mass. Arrived in Mass., 1632 and became pastor of Roxbury Church and joint author of the Bay Psalm Book.

WELLES, JOHN, SR., 1621-1659. Born in England. Deputy from Stratford, Conn., 1656-1657, 1659. Assistant to Governor, 1658.
Greason, Mrs. James B., Jr.   Founders

WELLES, JOHN, JR., 1648-1713/14. Born in Wethersfield, Conn. Deputy from Stratford, Conn., 1689-1693.
Greason, Mrs. James B., Jr.   Founders

WELLES, CAPT. ROBERT, 1651-1714. Deputy from Wethersfield, Conn., 1690-1694, 1697-1699. Member of Governor's Council 1697-1698. Captain, Train Band, 1689.

WELLES, SAMUEL, 1656-1729. Sergt. of Train Band, Stratford, Conn.

WELLES, QUARTERMASTER THOMAS, 1627-1668. Quartermaster, 1658. Deputy from Wethersfield, Conn., 1662. Assistant to Governor, 1668.
Greason, Mrs. James B., Jr.   Founders

WELLES, GOV. THOMAS, 1598-1660. Came from England to Conn., 1636. Magistrate, 1637. Second Treasurer, 1639-1657. Secretary, 1640-1648. Commissioner, United Colonies, 1649. Governor pro-tem, 1651. Dep. Governor, 1654. Governor, 1655-1660.
Bienlien, Mrs. William Walter   Michigan
Buenker, Mrs. Robert   Illinois
Bland, Mrs. Elmer Francis, Jr.   Illinois
Crull, Mrs. Ralph L.   Territorial
Domson, Mrs. Andrew, Jr.   Michigan
Francis, Miss Bernice M.   Michigan
Greason, Mrs. James B., Jr.   Founders
Lee, Mrs. Rolland Porter   Michigan
Lyons, Miss Rebekah Ellyn   Illinois

WELLS, ENS. HUGH, 1625-1678. Born in England. Ensign, Wethersfield, Conn., 1645.

WELLS, JOSHUA, 1663-1744. Selectman, Southold, L.I., 1697, 1698.

WELLS, NATHANIEL, 1636-1681. Selectman, Ipswich, Mass., 1675.

WELLS, RICHARD, circa 1605-1667. Member House of Burgesses, Md., 1645, 1647. Appointed Parliamentary Committee, 1654. Member 7th Provincial Council, 1655. Commissioner, 1657-1661. Justice of Peace, 1658. On Puritan Council, 1658. Justice/Court, 1661. Chirugeon (surgeon).

WELLS, THOMAS, 1620-1676. Died in King Philip's War, Hadley, Mass., 1676.

WELLS, DEA. THOMAS, 1605-1666. Ensign, Ancient and Honorable Artillery Co., 1644. Deacon, Ipswich, Mass., 1646.

WELLS, WILLIAM, 1608-1671. Deputy from Southold to New Haven, 1653, 1657. Constable, 1657, 1659. Town Clerk, 1660. Magistrate, 1661. Member of Governor's Council, 1664. Deputy to N.Y. Colonial Assembly at Hempstead, 1665. High Sheriff, 1665, 1669.

WELSH, MAJOR JOHN, 1622-1683/4. Justice of Peace Anne Arundel Co. MD 1668. Justice of the Court 1676. Commissioner 1683.
Pamplin, Mrs. Jack C.   Quivira

WENDELL, EVERT JANSE, 1615-1709. Born in Holland. Settled in Beverwyck (Albany), N.Y. Magistrate, 1660-1661.

WENDELL, CAPT. JOHANNES, 1649-1692. Born in Fort Orange (New Amsterdam), N.Y. Captain, 1684. Magistrate, 1684-1685. Commissioner Indian Affairs, 1685. Alderman, 1686-1690. Mayor, 1690.
Davis, Miss Felicia Louisa Budreck   Illinois
Davis, Mrs. Frank V.   Illinois
Fitzmorris, Mrs. Stanley R.   Renss.

WENSLEY, SAMUEL, —— 1663. Born in England. Representative from Salisbury, Mass., 1642, 1645, 1653.

WENTWORTH, ELDER WILLIAM, 1616-1696. Born in England. Constable, Wells, Me., 1648. Ruling Elder, 1650. Selectman, Dover, N.H., 1651, 1657, 1660, 1664, 1665, 1670.

WEST, GOV. JOHN, 1590-1659. Born in England. Member Va. House of Burgesses, 1629-1630. Member of the Council, 1634-1659. Governor of Va., 1635-1637, 1656-1658.

WEST, SAMUEL, 1640/45-1701. 1670-1677 Member of Council Charlestown/
　　Charleston, S.C. as of 1671.
　　Birmingham, Miss Georgia Atchison　　　　　　　　　　Illinois
　　Birmingham, Mrs. John M.　　　　　　　　　　　　　　Illinois

WESTBROECK (WESTBROOK), ANTHONY JANSEN, —— after 1682.
　　Court Messenger for Rensselaerwyck, 1662.
　　Long, Mrs. Alfred T.　　　　　　　　　　　　　　　　Founders

WESTBROOK, JOHANNES, 1665-1727. Member of Foot Co., Kingston,
　　N.Y., 1686/7. Trustee, Kingston, 1694.
　　Long, Mrs. Alfred T.　　　　　　　　　　　　　　　　Founders

WESTCOTT, STUKELEY, 1592-1677. One of the Founders of the Colony of
　　Providence; one of the thirteen original proprietors. Commissioner
　　from Warwick, R.I., 1651, 1652, 1653, 1655, 1660. Governor's Assistant,
　　1653. Deputy, 1671.

WESTERVELT, DEA. JURRIEN, after 1662-after 1738. Deacon, Hackensack,
　　N.J., Dutch Church, 1694 and later.

WESTWOOD, WILLIAM, 1606-1669. Came from England, 1634. Settled in
　　Cambridge, Mass. Freeman, 1634. One of eight Commissioners ap-
　　pointed by General Court of Mass. to govern the people of Conn., 1635.
　　"Constable of the Plantation of Conn., 1635. Deputy for twenty-one
　　sessions. Removed to Haldey, Mass.

WHEELER, SERGT. EPIIRIAM, —— 1670. Born in England. Sergt. of Train
　　Band, Fairfield, Conn.

WHEELER, GEORGE, —— 1687. Held many positions of trust, Concord,
　　Mass. Selectman, 1660.

WHEELER, ISAAC, 1646-1712. Born in Lynn, Mass. Served in King Philip's
　　War, from Stonington, Conn., 1675, 1676. Deputy, 1692. Selectman,
　　1694, 1695.
　　Parenteau, Mrs. Jerome Francis　　　　　　　　　　　Quivira

WHEELER, CAPT. THOMAS, 1602-1686. Born in England. Constable,
　　Lynn, Mass., 1635. Deputy from Stonington, Conn., 1673. Capt. of
　　Horse, 1669. In King Philip's War, 1675/6.

WHEELER, LIEUT. THOMAS, —— 1659. As Lieut. of Fairfield, Conn.,
　　ordered to serve as Ensign of a Military Company, under Lieut. Cook,
　　21 May 1653.
　　Parenteau, Mrs. Jerome Francis　　　　　　　　　　　Quivira

WHEELER, SERGT. THOMAS, 1620-1704. Born in England. Sergt. at Concord, Mass., 1642.

WHEELOCK, RALPH, 1600-1683. Left England, 1637. Settled in Watertown, Mass. Later, to Dedham, where he signed the Covenant. Clerk of the Writs, 1642. One of the Founders of Medfield, 1651. Selectman, first four years. Magistrate, 1656. Deputy, 1663-1667.
Pollard, Mrs. Earsel W.   Missouri

WHEELWRIGHT, REV. JOHN, 1592-1679. Born in England, died in Salisbury, Mass. Arrived at Boston, 1636. Minister at Braintree, Exeter, and Wells, Mass., 1636-1679.

WHEELWRIGHT, JOHN, 1664-1745. Of Wells, Me. Deputy, 1692 and later. Lieut., 1693.

WHEELWRIGHT, COL. SAMUEL, 1635-1700. Of Wells, Me. Lieutenant, 1665. Deputy, 1671, 1677, 1684, 1693. Commissioner and Judge Common Pleas, 1692. Probate Judge, 1694. Member Council, 1694-1699. Colonel Assistant to Governor, 1695-1699.

WHIPPLE, CAPT. JOHN, 1617-1685. Born in England. Settled in Dorchester, Mass.; and moved to Providence, R.I., 1659. Took Oath of Allegiance, 1666. Deputy, 1666-1667. Served in King Philip's War, 1675-1676.

WHIPPLE, ELDER JOHN, —— 1669. Deacon and Ruling Elder of the church, Ipswich, Mass. Deputy, eight years, between 1640 and 1653.

WHIPPLE, SAMUEL, 1644-1710/11. Born in Dorchester, Mass. Constable, Providence, R.I., 1688. Deputy, 1691.

WHITAKER, JABEZ, 1596-1626. Member House of Burgesses 1623-1624. Member of Council 1626.
Wheeler, Mrs. H. Lindsay, Jr.   Florida

WHITAKER, RICHARD, —— ——. One of the founders of Attleborough, Mass., 1668.

WHITE, REV. EBENEZER, 1672-1756. Ordained 9 Oct. 1695. First Pastor of the Church, Bridgehampton, L.I.

WHITE, CAPT. JOHN, 1602-1673. Soldier in Lancaster, Mass. Company.

WHITE, ELDER JOHN, 1596-1683. Arrived at Boston, Mass., from England,

1632. Settled in Cambridge. Freeman, 1633. Townsman, 1635. Removed to Hartford, Conn., 1636. Townsman, 1642, 1646, 1651, 1656. Fifth on list of signers of the Agreement to move to Hadley, Mass. Townsman, 1660, 1662, 1665. Representative, 1664, 1669. Ordained Ruling Elder, 1677.

Busch, Mrs. Edwin L.	Prairie State
Busch, Olivia Nicole Maedgen	Prairie State

WHITE, CAPT. JOSEPH, 1639-1706. Born in England. One of founders of Mendon, Mass., 1662. Selectman, 1670, 1673, 1680, 1681, 1685-1686. Captain, 1689. Sergt. in King Philip's War, 1675, 1676.

WHITE, ENS. NICHOLAS, —— 1727-8. Member of Taunton Militia, 1682. Ensign, 1698.

WHITE, RESOLVED, 1614-1690. Passenger on the "Mayflower," 1620.

WHITE, SUSANNA (FULLER),—— 1680. Passenger on the "Mayflower," 1620.

WHITE, WILLIAM, —— 1621. Passenger on the "Mayflower," 1620.

WHITEHEAD, DANIEL, 1603-1668. Overseer, Newtown, L.I., April, 1666; Nov., 1666; April, 1668.

WHITEHEAD, CAPT. DANIEL, 1646-1704. Ranger General of L.I., 1685. Member of N.Y. Assembly, 1691, and later. Capt., Queens Co. Troops, N.Y., 1692.

WHITING, MAJOR (DR.) HENRY, —— 1693. Born in Va. Settled in Gloucester Co., Va., 1674. Vestryman and Church Warden, Ware Parish, 1674. Justice of Peace, Major of Horse, 1680. Burgess for Gloucester Co., 1680-1682. Member of Council, 1691-1693. Treasurer of Va., 1692-1693.

WHITING, REV. JOHN, 1635-1689. Born in England. Minister, Hartford, Conn., 1670-1689. Chaplain of Conn. Troops in King Philip's War, 1675.

Greason, Mrs. James B., Jr.	Founders

WHITING, JOSEPH, 1645-1717. Treasurer of Conn., 1678-1699. Captain of Hartford Co. Conn. troops, 1692.

Mielke, Mrs. Gary Theo.	Prairie State
Mielke, Katherine	Prairie State
Woods, Miss Laura	Prairie State

WHITING, REV. SAMUEL, 1597-1679. Arrived at Boston, Mass. Settled at Lynn, Mass., as pastor of First church, 1636-1676.

WHITING, REV. SAMUEL, 1670-1725. Born in Hartford, Conn. Minister, Windham, Conn., 1692-1699.
Greason, Mrs. James B., Jr.   Founders

WHITING, WILLIAM, —— 1647. Treasurer, 1641-1647. Magistrate, 1642-1647. Major, Colony of Conn., 1647.

WHITMAN, VALENTINE, —— 1701. Surveyor, Providence, R.I., 1656. Commissioner, 1658. Deputy, 1675, 1679, 1682, 1685, 1686.

WHITMORE, THOMAS, 1615-1681. At Boston Mass., 1635; Wethersfield, Conn., 1639-1640. A first settler at Middletown, Conn., 1649.

WHITNEY, HENRY, 1620-1673. A Founder of Norwalk, Conn. Chosen Townsman at Jamaica, L.I., N.Y., 1664.
White, Mrs. Robert Sunderland   Rhode Island

WHITNEY, JOHN, 1599/1600-1673. Came from England to Boston, Mass., 1635. Constable, Watertown, Mass., 1641. Selectman 1638-1656. Town Clerk, 1655.
Cook, Mrs. Ralph William, Sr.   Michigan
Zimmerman, Mrs. Donald D.   Illinois

WHITNEY, JOHN, JR., 1624-1692. Born in England. Selectman, Watertown, Mass., 1673-1680. Served in King Philip's War, 1675-1676.
Cook, Mrs. Ralph William, Sr.   Michigan
Zimmerman, Mrs. Donald D.   Illinois

WHITNEY, DEA. JOSHUA, 1635-1719. Born in Watertown, Mass. Deacon and Original Proprietor of Groton, Mass. Selectman 1681, 1683, 1687. Constable, 1684. In garrison, Groton, during King William's War, 1691/2. Overseer of Highways, Groton, Mass., 1693.
Cook, Mrs. Ralph William, Sr.   Michigan

WHITTIER, THOMAS, circa 1620-1696. Appointed Surveyor by General Court of Mass., 30 May 1651. Constable, 1669. Surveyor, 1680.

WHITTLESEY, JOHN, 1623-1704. Representative from Saybrook, Conn., between 1644 and 1685. Collector of Minister's Rates, 1681-1682. Attorney, 1684. Representative, 1697-1699. Townsman, 1697.

WICKENDEN, WILLIAM, 1614-1670. A signer of the Compact of Providence, R.I., 1637. Deputy, Commissioner, Pastor of First Baptist Church, 1647.

WICKES, THOMAS, 1612-1671. Constable, Huntington, L.I., 1663.

WICKES, CAPT. THOMAS, JR., 1650-after 1725. Born at Oyster Bay, L.I., N.Y. Commissioned Captain, 1690.

WICKLIFFE, DAVID, SR., —— 1642. Born in England; died in Md. Member of Md. House of Burgesses from St. George's Hundred, 1637-1638, 1641-1642.
Privett, Mrs. John Blevines   BlueGrass

WILBUR, CAPT. SAMUEL, JR., 1614 ——. Of Portsmouth, R.I. Member Military, 1653. Commissioner, 1655-1657, 1659-1663. Lieutenant, 1656. Deputy, 1664, 1669, 1670, 1675, 1676. Assistant, 1665, 1666, 1669, 1677, 1678. Captain, 1670.

WILBUR (WILBORE), SERGT. SAMUEL, SR., —— 1656. Born in England. Clerk of Train Band, Portsmouth, R.I., 1638. Constable, 1639. Sergeant, 1644.

WILBUR, WILLIAM, 1630-1710. Deputy, Portsmouth, R.I., 1678.

WILCOX, STEPHEN, 1633-1690. Deputy, Westerly, R.I., 1670-1672.

WILCOXSON, WILLIAM, 1601-1652. Born in England. One of the first settlers of Stratford, Conn., 1639. Deputy, 1647.

WILKINS, JOHN, 1596-1650. Member of House of Burgesses from Northampton Co., Va., 1641.

WILKINSON, LAWRENCE, —— 1692. Deputy to General Court, from Providence, R.I., 1658, 1667-1673. Commissioner, 1659-1667.
Moore, Mrs. Gedie Clarence   Tennessee
Newby, Mrs. George   Tennessee
Page, Mrs. Lee R.   Tennessee

WILLARD, HENRY, 1655-1701. Born in Concord, Mass. Commander of garrison, Lancaster, 1692.

WILLARD, JOSIAH, circa 1635-1674. School Teacher, Wethersfield, Conn.,1665.

WILLARD, MAJ. SIMON, 1605-1676. Born in England; died in Charlestown. Founder of Concord, Mass., 1635. Deputy, 1636-1654. Lieutenant, 1637. Captain, 1646. Assistant, 1654-1676. Commander-in-Chief of the expedition of the United Colonies against the Nyantics, 1655. Commanded Middlesex Regiment of Mass. Troops in King Philip's War, 1675.

Pearsall, Mrs. Willard H.   Founders

WILLETT, CAPT. ANDREW, 1655-1712. Born in Plymouth, Mass. Deputy from Kingston, R.I., 1696, 1698. Captain, 1696.

WILLETT, CAPT. THOMAS, 1610-1674. Came from Leyden to Plymouth, Mass., 1632. In command Militia, 1637. Captain, Plymouth Colony Train Band, 1647. Member Council of War. Magistrate and Assistant to Governor, 1651-1664. Served in expedition which captured New Amsterdam from the Dutch, 1664. First English Mayor, 1665-1666, 1668. Alderman, 1666-1667. Returned to Plymouth, 1672.

Davis, Mrs. Frank V.   Illinois
Lo Presti, Mrs. Basil G.   CT Farms

WILLETT'S, RICHARD, SR.,—— 1664. Of Jericho and Hempstead, L.I. Assistant Magistrate, 1658. Surveyor, 1659. Townsman, 1661-1662.

WILLETTS, RICHARD, JR., 1660-1703. Born in Jericho, L.I. Patentee, Oyster Bay and Islip.

WILLIAMS, CAPT. ISAAC, 1638-1707. Born in Roxbury, Mass. Surveyor, 1663. Constable, 1664. Lieutenant, King Philip's War, 1675. Select-man, 1691. Representative from Newton, 1692, 1695, 1697, 1699. Deacon First Church.

WILLIAMS, JOHN, —— ——. Born in Hempstead, L.I. Overseer, 1666. Deputy, 1676. Townsman, 1695. In charge Public Loan, 1697.

WILLIAMS, ROBERT, —— ——. Signed Compact, Providence, R.I., 1637. Member Assembly, 1643. On committee to form Government, 1647. Commissioner, 1648, 1651, 1652. Deputy, 1651, 1652. Magistrate, 1664. Patentee, Huntington, Hempstead, Jericho, L.I. General Solicitor to Assembly, 1673-1680.

WILLIAMS, ROBERT, baptized 1608-1693. From England to Boston, Mass., 1637. Settled in Roxbury. Freeman, 1638. Town Clerk. Member of Ancient and Honorable Artillery Co., Mass., 1644; and Roxbury Militia Co., 1644.

Dunn, Mrs. Mathon Baldwin   Florida
Parenteau, Mrs. Jerome Francis   Quivira

WILLIAMS, ROGER, 1599-1683. Born in England. Founder of R.I. and Providence Plantations, 1636. Agent to England to secure charter,

1642. Governor's Assistant, 1647, 1648, 1664, 1665, 1670-1672. Deputy President of the Colony, 1649. President, 1654-1657. Commissioner from Providence, 1655, 1656, 1658, 1659, 1661. Captain of the Train Band in King Philip's War, 1676.

Brown, Mrs. Clifford	Rhode Island
Colwell, Mrs. E. Warren	Rhode Island
Greenhalgh, Mrs. John, Jr.	Rhode Island
Hall, Mrs. Stuart	Renss.
Hargraves, Mrs. Jeffrey H.	Rhode Island
Havens, Mrs. Irving Hudson	Rhode Island
Steere, Mrs. Everett M.	Rhode Island
Steere, Mrs. Robert E.	Rhode Island
Van Bever, Mrs. Gerald E.	Rhode Island
Wilson, Mrs. Richard A.	Rhode Island

WILLIAMS, DEA. SAMUEL, 1632-1698. Came to Mass., 1637. Deacon and Ruling Elder of Church, Roxbury, Mass., 1674.

Parenteau, Mrs. Jerome Francis   Quivira

WILLIAMS, THOMAS, —— 1682. 1653 Selectman; 1655, 1656, 1664, and 1665, Commissioner for Saco. 1656 Town Treasurer. 1657 Constable. (NH, now ME).

Zimmerman, Mrs. Donald D.   Illinois

WILLIAMS, REV. WILLIAM, —— 1712. Born in Wales; died in Albermarle Co., N.C. Pastor of St. Stephen's Parish, Va., 1680.

Poe, Mrs. John Hunter   Oklahoma
Poe, Miss Suzanne Lee   Oklahoma

WILLIAMSON, DR. JAMES, —— ——. Justice, Isle of Wight Co., Va., 1646. Justice, Lancaster Co., Va., 1652-1656.

WILLIS, DEA. JOHN, —— circa 1692. Born in England. Settled in Duxbury, Mass., by 1637. A first settler of Bridgewater, Mass., and first Deacon there. Representative to Plymouth General Court, 1657-1661, 1667-1676, 1677-1681.

WILLIS, HENRY, 1628-1714. Born in England commissioner from Huntington, L.I., 1688.

WILLIS, CAPT. HENRY, —— ——. In Va. as land owner by 1638. First Justice of Peace for Gloucester Co., Va.

WILLOUGHBY, FRANCIS, —— 1671. Born in England. Arrived Charlestown, Mass., 1638. Ensign of Artillery Co., 1643. Selectman, Deputy, Magistrate, 1654-1660. Deputy Governor, Mass., 1665-1667, 1668-1670.

Glover, Mrs. Hugh Wallace   Michigan

WILLOUGHBY, THOMAS, 25 Dec 1632-1672. Captina, VA. Presiding
Justice Lower Norfolk 1639.
Edwards, Lt. Col. Frances   Tejas
Vowell, Mrs. Morris A.   Tennessee

WILLS, DR. DANIEL, 1633-1698. Born in England. Died, Barbadoes, Br.
West Indies. A signer of "Concessions and Agreements" for West Jersey,
1676. Commissioner for Province of West Jersey, 1677. Member of
Governor's Council and of Assembly. Justice of Peace, 1684, 1685, 1696,
1697.

WILSON, STEPHEN, circa 1668-1707. Constable, Hopewell, N.J., 1699.

WILSON, THEOPHILUS, —— 1690. Constable, Ipswich, Mass., 1647, 1649,
1654.

WILSON, THOMAS, —— ——. Served in King Philip's War, Brookfield,
Mass., 1675.

WILSON, WILLIAM II, —— circa 1646. Born in England; died in Boston,
Mass. Deputy Marshal, Boston, Mass.

WILSON, COL. WILLIAM, 1646-1713. Member of Va. House of Burgesses,
1685-1688. Magistrate and County Lieutenant, 1699. Naval officer in
the Lower James River District, 1699.

WILTSEE, HENDRICK MARTENSEN, 1623-1712. Born in Copenhagen,
Den. Served in Esopus War, N.Y., 1663.
Corder, Miss Lois B.   Founders

WILTZE, PHILIPPE MATON, 1570-1632. In Military service of Holland
West India Co., Fort Orange, N.Y., 1624-1632.

WINCHESTER, JOHN, SR., before 1616-1694. Member of the Ancient and
Honorable Artillery Co., Boston, 1638.

WINES, CORP. BARNABAS, —— 1679. Corporal of Militia, South old, L.I.,
before 1654. Deputy to New Haven from Southold 1661. Overseer
Southold, 1661.

WING, ANANIAS, 1651-1718. Born at Sandwich, Mass., settled at Yarmouth,
Mass., 1659. Served in King Philip's War, Narragansett Campaign,
1676.

WINN, EDWARD, —— 1682. Selectman, Woburn, Mass., 1669.

WINNE, MAJ. PIETER, ―― 1693. Born in Holland. Settled in Albany, N.Y. Magistrate, 1650, 1674. Major, 1689. Commissioner to treat with the Indians, 1690.

WINSLEY, SAMUEL, ―― 1663. Representative, Salisbury, Mass., 1642, 1645, 1653.

WINSLOW, LIEUT. JOB, 1641-1720. Selectman, Freetown, Mass., 1686, 1689, 1692. Representative, 1686, 1692.

WINSLOW, JOHN, 1597-1674. Born in England. Deputy from Plymouth to the General Court, 1652, 1654.
Powell, Mrs. Harold F.　　　　　　　　　　　　　　　　　　Michigan

WINSLOW, KENELM, 1599-1672. Came to Plymouth, Mass., from England, circa 1629. Freeman, 1632. Surveyor, 1640. Deputy, 1642-1644, 1649-1653. One of the proprietors of Assouit (Free- town), 1659.

WINSTEAD, SAMUEL, ―― ――. Living in St. Stephen's Parish, Northumberland Co., Va., by 1666. Line closed pending correction of service.

WINSTON, SERGT. JOHN, circa 1621-1696/7. Corporal of New Haven Train Band, 1661. Sergeant, 1665.

WINTHROP, GOV. JOHN, 1588-1649. First Governor of Colony of Mass. Bay, 1629, 1631-1633, 1637-1639, 1642, 1643, 1646-1648. Colonel of Suffolk Co. (Mass.) Regiment, 1646. One of the founders of Harvard College.

WISE, JOHN I, 1617-1695. Born in Devonshire, England; died, Accomac Co., Va. Justice of Accomac Court, 1663. Warden of Hungor's Parish, 1665.

WITHUNGTON/WITHINGTON, HENRY, 1589-1666. Selectman 1636 MA. Ruling Elder 1637 to 1666.
Warder, Mrs. William O.　　　　　　　　　　　　　　　　　　Renss.

WOERTMAN, DIRCK JANSE, ―― 1694. Came from Amsterdam to Brooklyn, N.Y., 1647. Town Officer, 1673.

WOLCOTT, HENRY, 1578-1655. Constable, 1636. Member of the First General Assembly of Conn., 1637. Magistrate, Conn., 1643 and served until death.

WOMACK, ABRAHAM, 1645-1733. Constable 1685. Attorney 1690. Surveyor 1696 Henrico Co., VA.
Layson, Mrs. J. Vimont   Blue Grass

WOOD, DEA. DANIEL, —— ——. Selectman and Deacon, Boxford, Mass., 1688, 1689.

WOOD, JOHN, —— ——. Deputy, Newport, R.I., 1673, 1674, 1675.

WOOD, THOMAS, 1635-1687. Of Mass. Soldier in King Philip's War, 1675/6.

WOODBURY, JOHN, 1579-1641. Constable, Salem, Mass., 1630. Deputy, 1635-1639. Selectman, 1636-1641. Town Treasurer, 1640-1641. Surveyor.

WOODHULL, RICHARD, 1620-1691. Born in England. Magistrate, Setauket, L.I., 1661, 1673. Representative, 1663. Justice, 1666, 1673-1690.
Denton, Mrs. E. Brady   Michigan
Hoopes, Mrs. Rae Stevens   Michigan

WOODIS, HENRY, —— 1700. Representative, Concord, Mass., 1685, 1690-1692. Quartermaster of Concord Co, 1671.

WOODMAN, LIEUT. EDWARD, baptized 1606-1694. Born in England; settled in Newbury, Mass. Lieut. of Newbury Co., Pequot War, 1637. Deputy to General Court, 1636, 1637, 1638, 1639, 1643.
Weaver, Mrs. John F., Sr.   Michigan

WOODMAN, EDWARD, 1628-1694. Deputy to General Court, Newbury, Mass., 1664, 1670.
Weaver, Mrs. John F., Sr.   Michigan

WOODRUFF, JOHN, 1604-1670. One of the first settlers of Southampton, L.I., 1640.

WOODRUFF, JOHN, 1637-1691. A Founder of Elizabethtown, N.J. and commissioned Ensign of Co. militia, 1670. High Sheriff, 1684.
Denny, Miss Josephine   Pennsylvania

WOODS, SERGT. JOHN, 1619-1678. Born in England. Selectman, Marlborough, Mass., 1664, 1665.. Served in King Philip's War, 1675,1676.

WOODSON, DR. JOHN, 1586-1644. Born in England. Settled at Jamestown, Va., 1619. Physician and Surgeon for Company of Soldiers sent to Jamestown, Va., to protect Colonists, 1619.
Macey, Miss Catherine Elizabeth   Ohio

WOODWARD, QUARTERMASTER HENRY, 1607-1685. Quartermaster of the Hampshire Troop, 1663/4. Surveyor of Highways, 1664. Commissioner, 1667. Member of First Board of Tithingmen, Northampton, Mass., 1678. Constable, 1681.
Cook, Mrs. Ralph William, Sr.   Michigan

WOODWARD, DR. HENRY, circa 1646-1686/90. Deputy to Lord Shatesbury, Lords Proprietors, S.C., 1673-1685. Surgeon.

WOODWARD, JOHN, —— 1688. Born in Taunton, Mass. Served, King Philip's War, 1675/6.

WOODWARD, NATHANIEL SR., —— after 1661. Surveyor to run the line between Plymouth and Mass. Bay Colonies and between Mass. and Conn., 1638.

WOODWARD, PETER, —— 1685. Selectman, Dedham, Mass., 1651- 1658, 1659, 1661-1668. Member Mass. General Assembly, 1665, 1669, 1670.

WOODWORTH, WALTER, circa 1610-1685/6. Surveyor of Highways, Scituate, Mass., 1645, 1646, 1656.
de Zeeuw, Mrs. Donald John   Michigan

WOOLSEY, GEORGE, 1610-1698. From England, 1623. Purchased plantation, Flushing, L.I., 1647. Cadet in Burgher Corps. Overseer, 1665-1666, and original Patentee, Jamaica. Town Clerk, 1667-1673.

WOOLSEY, CAPT. GEORGE, 1652-1740. Baptized, New Amsterdam. Captain of Militia, Jamaica, L.I., 1698.

WOOLSON, THOMAS, 1626/7-1713. Born in England; died in Mass. Selectman, Weston, Mass., 1699. Served in King Philip's War, 1675-1676.

WOOSTER, EDWARD, 1622-1689. Came from England before 1652. Settled in Derby, Conn. Constable, 1669. Commissioner to establish boundaries, 1675.
Bergelt, Mrs. Edward C.   Founders

WORDEN, PETER, 1609-1681. Born in England. Member Militia, Yarmouth, Mass., 1643.

WORTH, WILLIAM, —— 1724. Town Clerk, 1676. Assistant to Governor, 1679. Justice of the Peace, Nantucket, 1692. Member Court of Common Pleas, 1696.

WRIGHT, ABEL, 1631-1725. Selectman, 1689, 1698. Deputy to Mass. General Court, 1695.

WRIGHT, FRANCIS, 1660-1713. Surveyor, Captain, Attorney. Special Justice of Superior Court, Westmoreland Co., Va., 1682.
Palmer, Mrs. Thomas W.   North Carolina

WRIGHT, HENRY, —— 1676. A first settler of Dorchester, Mass., 1634. Served in King Philip's War, 1675.

WRIGHT, DEA. JOHN, 1601-1688. Born in England. Selectman, Woburn, Mass., 1645, 1649, 1658, 1660-1664, 1670, 1680, 1683. Deputy, 1646-1683. Deacon, 1664-1688.

WRIGHT, JOHN, JR., 1630/1-1714. Selectman, Woburn, Mass., 1690.

WRIGHT, JOHN, 1662-1730. Born in Chelmsford, Mass. Selectman, Chelmsford 1683. Member of the First Garrison, 1691/92.

WRIGHT, JOSHUA, —— 1695. Member of the General Assembly of West Jersey, 1682-1683. Commissioner of Highways, 1684-1685.

WRIGHT, NICHOLAS, 1609/10-1682. Surveyor, Sandwich, Mass., 1651. One of the first settlers of Oyster Bay, L.I., 1653.

WRIGHT, PETER, circa 1595-1663. Born in England. Sergeant of the Train Band, 1652. A first settler of Oyster Bay, L.I., N.Y., 1653.
Evans, Mrs. George Webster   Pennsylvania

WRIGHT, DEA. SAMUEL, 1614-1665. Appointed Deacon by Town of Springfield, Mass., 1655. Deputy to General Court, 1656.
von Kempf, Mrs. Paul   California

WRIGHT, THOMAS, SR., 1610 ——. Of Wethersfield, Conn. Deputy to General Court of Conn., 1643. Selectman, 1658. Constable, 1668/9.

WRIGHT, THOMAS, JR., —— 1683. Constable, Wethersfield, Conn., 1662.

WRIGHT, THOMAS, —— 1705/6. Signer of "The Concessions and Agreement," 3 Mar. 1676. Member of the General Assembly of West Jersey, 1682.

WYATT, ANTHONY, circa 1605-circa 1686. Burgess, Charles City Co., Va., 1653-1656. Sheriff and Justice, 1655-1657.

WYATT, REV. HAWTE, 1594-1638. Born in England. Arrived at Jamestown, Va., 1621. Minister, Jamestown Church, 1621-1625.

WYCKOFF, PIETER CLAESEN, 1625-1694. Came from Netherlands, 1636. Settled in Flatlands, L.I. Land owner, 1653. Magistrate, 1655, 1662, 1663. Delegate, 1664.
Arnold, Mrs. Leavitt G.   Illinois

WYETH, JOHN, 16 July 1655-13 Dec 1706. Constable, Cambridge MA Bay 1687-1688.
Grousset, Mrs. Richard J.   Renss.

WYNKOOP, CORNELIUS, —— ——. Left Albany, N.Y., 1644. Elder of Reformed Dutch Church, Kingston, N.Y., 1671. Commissary of Kingston, 1671-1674.

WYNN, ROBERT, 1622-1675. Member House of Burgesses. VA.
Dean, Mrs. Robert S., Sr.   Florida

WYNNE, DR. THOMAS, 1669-1721. Emigrated from Wales, settled at Philadelphia. Speaker at first Assembly of Colonies, representing Philadelphia Co., 1683.
Brooks, Mrs. Clifford R.   Pennsylvania

YALE, THOMAS, 1616-1683. Born in England. Signed Fundamental Agreement at New Haven, Conn., 1639.

YEARDLEY, SIR GEORGE, —— ——. Born in England; arrived in Jamestown, Va., 1610. Deputy Governor of Va., 1616. Governor, 1619,1621,1626.

YOUNG, DEA. ROWLAND, 1648-1721/2. Born and died in York, Me. Selectman, York, Me., 1695. Deacon, 1696.

YOUNGS, CAPT. BENJAMIN, 1668-1742. Town Clerk and Recorder, Southold, L.I., 1697 and later.

YOUNGS, GIDEON, 1638-1699. Overseer, Southold, L.I., 1693.

YOUNGS, COL. JOHN, 1623-1698. Commissioner of United Colonies, 1654. Captain, Suffolk Co., N.Y., Militia, 1664. In command when the Dutch landed in Southold, 1673. Member of Governor's Council, 1686, 1688, 1692, 1697. Colonel, 1693.

YOUNGS, LIEUT. JOHN, 1654 ——. Ensign of Troop of Horse, Southold, L.I., 1683. Commissioned Lieut., 1685.

YOUNGS, REV. JOHN, 1598-1672. Born in England. Settled in Southold, L.I. Organized first church, 1640.
Chumasero, Mrs. Robert E., Jr.   Founders

ZABRISKIE, ALBERT, circa 1638-1711. First Justice of the Peace, Upper Bergen, N.J., 1682.

ZANE, ROBERT, 1642-1695. Signer of Concessions and Agreements for West Jersey 1676. Constable 1683-1684. One of founders of First Friends at Salem, NJ 1675.
Canfield, Mrs. Leo, Jr.   Prairie State

www.ingramcontent.com/pod-product-compliance
Lightning Source LLC
Chambersburg PA
CBHW071847270326

41929CB00013B/2133